Soraya Soobnany-Chehou

May 2020

Your Story with Musart

by

Musart Ellaahi & Adielah Armien

Your Story with Musart

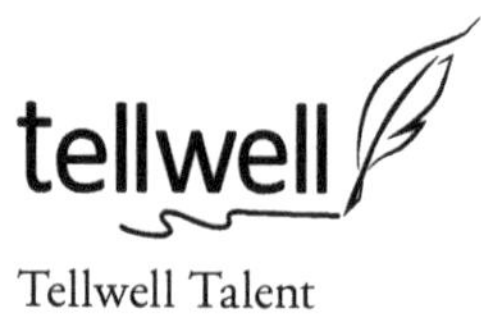

Tellwell Talent
www.tellwell.ca

ISBN
978-0-2288-2909-6 (Hardcover)
978-0-2288-2908-9 (Paperback)
978-0-2288-2910-2 (eBook)

Table of Contents

I dedicate this book to my dear uncle Noor Ellahi, My Parents, especially my Father who is the anchor of my success, My supportive daughter Anabah, My Amazing Husband Naseer, and to each and every soul who picks up this book, this is for you…

- Musart Ellaahi -

I dedicate this book to my loving mother Armina Abraham, my incredibly supportive & hardworking husband Nadeem, our three beautiful children who are always patient; Bilqees, Ammarah & Fawwaz. All this would not have been possible without our guardian angel Musart Ellaahi, who has always been my rock in times when I wanted to give up. May this book give everyone who reads it, the courage to believe in miracles.

- Adielah Armien -

Introduction

In my life I have always learned from others. Whilst growing up and the things that we go through as human beings which come under the name of *life,* has been the biggest teacher to me. Being the youngest of seven, I have always had the benefit of learning from others. I loved observing others, (I still do!) and seeing what I could learn from them. I could always identify what was the cause of the problem or what caused an argument as well as even suggest a suitable solution from a young age. This highly educated me into having an emotional intelligence and feeling great empathy for others. This guided me towards becoming an Empowering Mindset Coach, Author, and a TV Host. As part of my show series I wanted to gather a book full of inspirational stories and some amazing hidden souls out of the 7.2 billion human race who are ALL as amazing as each other. But what we never get to understand or feel is what made them into who they are or what they are today. We only look on the exterior of these successful souls and not knowing the hidden hardships or their hidden powers of the mind that made them see through those struggles. When I first decided to put this book together I wasn't sure if it would benefit the mankind as I had intended. But the people that came forward to contribute are completely apart from each other and from all walks of life that you could ever imagine! I went away a with a renewed mindset being awed at what many have gone through and are still standing, not just standing, but standing with dignity. Their strengths will give you strength, and make you realise wow if they can do this, SO CAN I!!! - Musart Ellaahi

When I read the many adversities & hurdles that so many have faced and conquered, I realised that there is always hope if you believe. The contributors of these short stories, transformed from victims to phenomenal role models. I feel privileged to be part of this motivational compilation of a journey from despair to self confidence & positive change. Which can only happen when a human being takes the first step to empower themselves to heal. - Adielah Armien

Life of a Butterfly Queen

In August 1987 I was born with a very rare skin condition called Epidermolysis Bullosa (EB); a rare genetic condition in which my skin blisters or easily grazes with the slightest friction. I get blisters internally and externally from head to toe. There isn't a millimetre on my body where I've not blistered. Subhan'Allah. I get blisters in my mouth, eyes, ears and on internal organs like my heart muscles.

Throughout my childhood I was treated like a freak, as though I came from another planet of some sort. I was like an outcast at school. I had a small group of friends, mainly boys. Girls wouldn't be my friend because I looked different to every other girl. I had a short boy cut for a hair style which was cut by my mum. I was covered in dressings as if I was a mummy. I had special hospital shoes, my dress sense wasn't like a typical girl.

You'd think that being in a 'special needs' school I'd be treated equally but that wasn't the case. I still got bullied because I looked different, I walked differently due to blistered feet. Sometimes I'd be in a wheelchair and other times I'd try to walk.

When I went to college I struggled so badly as it was a mainstream college, no extra help. I had everyone staring at me because I was going bald, I wasn't very girly, so I dressed like a tomboy. Due to my skin complexion, change in pigmentation majority of the college students thought I was mixed race so they'd talk about me in punjabi or Mirpuri, thinking I wouldn't understand.

The first week of my sixth form, I remember a family friend whose daughter was one of those who talked about me to others. Well I remember going to her house and realising she was the girl and my mum told her mum and I got a full apology in the end then her mum was like "how could you? she's family, you don't do that to anyone especially your family."

I bet you're wondering why a boy cut? Well that was so my hair wouldn't get stuck to any of my wounds around my ears, neck or forehead.

Throughout school and college I was bullied because I looked different to everyone else. Ironically most of the time the bullies were ALWAYS girls. In a time where we talk about women empowerment and girls supporting girls I didn't have that, I had girls hating me.

I remember one time in college a girl was complaining about her teenage spots/acne to her friends and they indirectly said "well look at her, imagine if you was like that omg I would rather die then look that ugly" I felt so disgusted with myself that I couldn't stop the tears from rolling down my face so I walked out the bathrooms and told my mentor that I wanted to go home.

I thought all that bullying and feeling like an outsider would end when I finished college, but it didn't. It continued from one college to another, then at university and even when I started to work.

When I got my first job, I was so overwhelmed with the fact I had a job, I was doing the "normal" life thing that any healthier person would be doing. But in reality yes I was working but I still got treated differently.

At my first work place I was sent to an occupational work assessment after 18 months of working there. When I went for the assessment, the assessor looked at me and questioned how long I was working there, when I told him it's been 18 months he just looked at me baffled to why after so long they sent me. When it was pretty obvious that I have a "disability" when you first look at me, so why now after 18 months.

When the final assessment results came back, my manager's attitude and behaviour towards me had changed in the most weirdest way. He was extra nice to me and I was beginning to think wait he's going to get rid of me. But in actual fact it was the opposite. In the report the assessor stated that he showed discrimination towards me as I have a disability and it was obvious. I didn't need to be assessed. I was shocked and I made sure my manager knew that. Yes I was unhappy but I wasn't going to take action because I've not been brought up to be ungrateful.

Every job opportunity that I came across and it's time limit was perfect. Alhamdulillah for every job that I've had.

Yes at times I was upset especially when I left Virgin Media. That was my favourite workplace. However it didn't last long as I had injured my knee and was on crutches. I was told to go home due to health and safety reasons as I worked on the 2nd floor. But I was given a written warning for not turning up to work when in fact they told me to go home. That wasn't the only reason I was upset, it was because my "team" that were nice to my face told ignorant jealous people who spoke about me to everyone about my skin flaking and how I smelt. In the end when I spoke up about my warning I was told by my agency that I was told my 3 months contract was not going to be extended.

Do you know how hard it is to explain to employers about my skin and how unpredictable it is and also explain why I've only ever worked temporary and for only short contracts. I have loved every job that I got to experience, even if it wasn't for a long time.

I understand that my skin condition does look extreme but that doesn't mean that I cannot do the things a healthier person can do. I know my ability and I also know what I can do without hurting myself and what I cannot do. When my EB flares up, I try my upmost to continue to work through the pain and just carry on but I also need to understand that for me to work, I need to rest my body and allow it to heal because without the healing process and being healthy enough to function I cannot do anything.

The saying 'Your Health is Your Wealth' is 100% true!! If you cannot physically, mentally or even emotionally function then how are you meant to do anything at all?!

We as humans try to fight ourselves and we're just hurting ourselves. We plan and plan but it never goes smoothly, but when Allah swt plans, His plans are so much better. We just need to understand and be patient.

When He plans, His plans are way better than ours, who are we to disagree. Yes, in that moment we moan and complain. But in the long run it works out in our favour. Alhamdulillah (Praise the Lord).

Everyday, everyone and everything that has happened to me until today has been a blessing or a lesson. Each one has been a learning curve for me. We learn a new thing every day. Alhamdulillah. Whether we see it or not, whether we understand it or not it has taught us something, that we later realise.

My life like most humans has been testing. We all get tested some more than others. When I was a kid I used to question why me, why is it always me. But as I grew older especially in the last 10 years I began to be more understanding and appreciative of what I've been through.

I have learnt so much about myself. The most important lesson was to **love** myself more than ever. To accept that just because I have EB doesn't make me any different to any other human, other than I look completely unique to everyone else. But that's why God created us all uniquely, I have different qualities, attributes and levels of patience, tolerance and understanding to someone else.

I learned to **forgive** my dad who in a way was unfortunate to understand the blessing that he had been blessed with (me) as he struggled to come to terms with having a child with special needs. It took me over 25 years to understand that he, my mum and all parents who are expecting want a healthy child. But when one is blessed with a child who is loved by God, some people cannot understand that blessing and unfortunately do and say things that maybe they didn't know or mean but actions speak louder.

I learned to **stop using EB as an excuse** to stop myself from doing things I was scared to do because it would make my EB worse when in fact it didn't. I restricted myself from living my life to the fullest as Allah had planned.

I learned to **appreciate** my family, my real friends who have loved me for me and to appreciate the life I have been blessed with without feeling guilty. The guilt was more of the fact that most people with EB die at such a young age and I was still alive. Alhamdulillah.

I have now turned that guilt into a passion. I want to show others who have EB, or to those first time parents who have a child with EB or anyone else who has a special needs child. That life doesn't have to be depressing, stressful or sad. Life is what you make it to be.

Continue to do what the medical professionals say and do, but also place your trust in God. He is the Healer of all Mankind. He the Most Merciful, All Forgiving. If you place your Trust and Faith in Him, everything will fall into place.

Sometimes when we lose a loved one we don't understand why they left us, we're hurt and upset. But the way I see it is, that their life was fulfilled in this world. That was their time to leave this materialistic life and enjoy the Aakhirat (Afterlife). Where there is no test, no hardships, no pain, everything and everyone is the most beautiful. Everything you wished of was perfect. So why would I want to stop that soul from enjoying that life, when Allah has written our life's destiny the moment we are in the womb of our mother.

I have so many things to be **grateful** for, Alhamdulillah. I have a loving, caring and strong supportive family who are my rock, my backbone. I am forever grateful for them all. I love you mum, bhaijaan, Atiya. Especially my babies Aminah-Batool, Momina-Batool, Zakariyya Ahmad and Hasnaat Sultan.

I have a very small circle of friends who I call my souls sisters. My sisters love me for me, support me without even saying and are always there when I need them, even though they have their own lives and children. They always make time for me. I love you girls so much!!

I am so lucky to have been around people who have helped me to stay grounded, to be appreciative and thankful for life. My whole life I've been in and out of hospitals, which like anyone to be honest wouldn't like.

However in the best parts of my childhood, teenage and early adulthood I spent a lot of time at Acorns Children's Hospice.

Acorns children's hospice is a place for children from 0-16 years old; who have a terminally ill and/or need end of life care. Acorns was my second home and the staff were my second family. I absolutely loved going to Acorns, the night before my stay I'd pack my stuff and wouldn't sleep with excitement. However when I was meant to come home sometimes I wished I could stay there long.

After leaving Acorns children's hospice as a client I was honoured to be asked to become an ambassador for them. It's the best role EVER!! The fact I get to give back to them by helping raising awareness and funds makes me happy. Acorns has helped me become the person I am today.

I have been so blessed to have achieved so many milestones that I never thought I'd do because of EB. However I have exceeded limits that I thought were impossible for me, accomplished my ambitions and goals that I had set for myself.

I passed my driving (3rd time lucky) but at least I did it! A lot of people thought I'd never drive but I proved them wrong. I was so proud of myself, as I had started driving at 17 but kept stopping my lessons due to health, however I finally passed at 25 years old.

I went to university, completed my foundation degree in Business Marketing and Sales. Unfortunately due to unforeseen circumstances I couldn't continue.

My biggest and proudest accomplishment was performing Umrah at the age of 17 in 2004.

I faced my biggest fear of heights head on and decided to do a sky dive for charity, Acorns Children's Hospice and Debra back in April 2017. It was the best experience ever, the adrenaline rush and the fact everyone doubting that I wouldn't go through with it, pushed me to do it.

Throughout my lifetime I have been so blessed to meet so many beautiful souls, including a few famous celebrities and some of the Royal Family.

As a child when I used to go to Acorns children's hospice as a client I was blessed to have met the stars of The Gladiators, Earl Spencer (late Princess Diana brother). Noel Edmunds and Mr Blobby. The 2004/2005 squad of Manchester United. I have a faint memory of meeting the Late Princess Diana at Great Ormond Street.

In 2003 I also got the chance to meet Prince Charles and Camilla. Along with Lenox Lewis and Tanni Grey-Thompson at Stoke Mandeville Stadium when it was opened as my school was chosen to represent able bodied and disabled students.

Most recently in 2018 I had the honour of meeting HRH Prince William at Acorns Children's Hospice. I was so honoured to give Prince William a tour of Acorns children's hospice Birmingham 30 years after his late mother Princess Diana opened the Hospice back in 1988. I got to share some memories with him and got to share interests with him too.

I was on BBC Inside Out which aired in November 2017. In the programme they covered my 30th Birthday as well as talking about my skin condition and how my dermatology team help with my skin care.

I was interviewed by Musart Ellaahi in her shows The Life Show with Musart and Umeed e Sehar on Islam Channel Urdu in April 2017. I was honoured to be asked to be on the show to talk about having a disability in today's society and in our Asian community.

I'm **mostly proud** of being a phupo (aunty from dads side) to 4 beautiful, loving, caring, sassy and cheeky souls. My babies are my biggest and most proudest accomplishments on this earth. I Thank God daily for them. They have helped me smile when I thought all I wanted to do was cry. They hug me when I need it the most, hold my hand when I'm in pain and kiss me when it hurts too.

A few years ago I was sent the Hadith of Prophet Ayub A.S and how he was tested with such a rare condition in which he had wounds bone deep and had maggots eating away at his skin and he'd place them back on his wounds if they fell off as he wanted them to be fed even if he was in excruciating pain. Allah had blessed him with such patience that he was later rewarded with such a reward where he was the most handsome man around. Subhan'Allah.

Ever since I heard the Hadith, I have always prayed for patience. I began to see my life as a blessing within itself. I started to become more appreciative, understanding and thankful for every pain, ache and hardship that Allah had and still has for me. I pray Allah showers His endless Mercy, patience and good health along with the understanding in his plans.

Just wish everyone understood that this life is merely a test, whatever we go through is to show Him that we are worthy of His love, protection and Mercy. May Allah be pleased with us all. Aameen ya Rab ul Alameen.

Assya Shabbir - Butterfly Queen - Accorn Brand Ambassador

Instagram on @ebqueen87

17

Our Miracle From God

Many of you may know me from rapping, producing music or even Instagram, but today the topic I want to talk about is much more important than anything, which is after four years of struggle and a test of time me and my wife Saima were blessed with a beautiful daughter, Inaya.

The reason we are sharing our story is because I had posted something on Instagram and the reaction I got out of that post was incredible, it's not the reaction or the post where everyone was commenting or congratulating, it was more of the personal messages that I had received of married couples who are finding it difficult to conceive. And what that made me realise was that how many people are suffering in silence, what I want to remind you is that if you can't for what ever reason can't conceive or have a baby, it's not a bad thing, its absolutely *normal.* We have been through it and we are going to tell you *our* miracle story. Because that's exactly what it is and I just want everyone who is reading this to know it's absolutely normal, if you are going through struggles of having a baby you have to trust Allah and you have to trust in his timing. Just like we did and after four years Alhamdulilah we have been blessed.

Into one year of our marriage we were not conceiving. Whenever Saima used to go out with my mother, aunties would always ask her "when are you going to give us the good news?" This would disappoint her and she would come home and cry. She would break down and cry to me. In the end we decided to get a check up to see what was going on, the Dr reassured us to not to worry, a year isn't a long time, also you are very young and lots of couples take time to conceive in the first year. She just told us to go home and relax, and God willing you will conceive. She reminded us to enjoy life and just not to worry.

When we came back home however Saima's mind was still stuck as to why is she not pregnant yet. Nothing happened for the next five months, so we went back to the Dr and then the Dr sent us for a check up. They did ultrasounds, we both went through many tests. The Dr called us to discuss our reports. When we got there the Dr said "Your husband's reports are fine but your uterus is a little bit abnormal, so even if you have a chance to get pregnant you might miscarry." Saima had a 15% chance to miscarry.

What they diagnosed was that Saima has a bicornuate uterus, what it means basically is that its got an abnormal shape, but that doesn't mean you can't conceive, that just means theres a 15% chance of miscarriage into 7 months of a pregnancy. But that wasn't the reason why we weren't conceiving, or that my wife was unable to get pregnant. They just did a test to check everything and this is what they found.

When we got back home Saima was just continuously getting upset. I tried to reassure her to not to worry, if Allah wishes to give us a child he will one day God willing. But that wasn't suffice for her she was still upset and continually worried. I even said to her I still love you even if we don't have a baby, that doesn't change anything. But it wasn't enough for her.

What used to happen was this is the first hospital we went to and you have to understand from a woman's point of view, they get very lonely and theres no one they can discuss this with other than their partner. Someone like me was chilled out and thought oh it will happen one day why worry about it. I had the whole positive outlook. Don't get me wrong, so did my wife, she also believed. But when the results came it just added even more worry to her. She was on google all day long, understanding a bicornuate uterus and then said to me, let's get another check up.

We got to Homerton and all of our tests started again and with every appointment we would go with a new hope or solution of some kind. But every time we went they just kept on telling us to take more and more tests. We spent two years doing just this.

Literally two years we just kept going to appointment after appointment, our dressing table was full of testing pockets and letters of different appointments. Our life just became revolved around that. Our marriage was just about appointments, thats ALL we spoke about. Whether we were eating or doing something our conversations would be like "Oh you know 18th September, 19th October we have to go to this appointment" etc. Even if we went out thats all we spoke about. The second hospital that we went to was a fertility centre, I had to go and give my tests, they needed to check the volume of my sperm samples. I had to go 5am in the morning for 3 weeks in a row. It's actually difficult, each time you go and give tests you feel like something is wrong with you. But you have to just believe and go with faith. My wife became depressed, our relationship suffered badly and our marriage was being affected. Once we got our tests back from Miss Sharma, the Dr who was looking after our case, she kept giving us hope so we continued doing numerous blood tests and what not.

On Eid day in 2016, after Eid Salat, we went to the hospital to collect all of our reports and our specialist was busy, so another Dr said she will give us our reports and discuss them with us. We insisted to meet Miss Sharma, and said look if she's busy we will wait for her.

We had been dealing with Miss Sharma since day one, she was dealing with our case and when we had to have our final results we wanted her to discuss them with us and not anyone else. Saima saw her in another room and said look we know she's here we insist to speak to her only. So after perseverance Miss Sharma saw us within 30 mins of waiting and broke it down to us that we don't understand why you aren't conceiving. She said it in the most politest way that we cant actually get pregnant and didn't know why. Like a unexplained infertility. I felt like a school child being told after working for 2 years that you have failed your exam results. It was tough, when I think of it now.... I didn't know how to control Saima, she started crying.

Into almost 3 and half years we weren't conceiving. We sat in the Uber and Saima kept crying "why me", I kept trying to comfort her, telling her its ok don't worry we will have a baby one day. I reassured her even if we don't have children I will love you the same I won't ever change or leave you. Saima thought otherwise. It's hard as a guy to understand what a woman is going through. Internally I was wishing I was the problem and not her. After the results I tried to get back to normality, I released an album, I continued working on my music. But every time I came home, Saima would hit me with one word and that was to give her a divorce and to remarry. The first time she said it I didn't take it to heart. I thought maybe she's upset let her take it out. But when she began to say it everyday it would hurt. We would fight continuously and not talk for many days. We were so close to breaking our marriage. During that time I made some mistakes that I regret but she wouldn't just stop. I would come home wanting to hug my wife and all she would say is "go live your life and divorce me." For three months this divorce thing would continue. We were fighting so badly that one day in the studio, I threw a Lucozade bottle at her trying to tell her to stop. She fell on her knees and started screaming "Ya Allah why me?!" I looked at her in amazement and realised oh my God that is suffering she is in so much pain. It moved me, I hugged her and said look we will pray and find a solution.

We went to the Dr again and they suggested IVF. But Saima wasn't too keen. So we went to a private clinic in London which would cost us £6000. Saima agreed and said lets try this. I was in the mosque and deeply prayed to God saying "God you know what I am going through, Ya Allah please support me and please guide me, and help me finance this." I had savings but not the full amount, I sold so many musical instruments that I had in my studio, I sold productions near enough just to get the money together. Saima had some money we put it together and then we went to St Pauls, October 2017 to book ourselves for IVF. We began filling all of the forms and they took the payment in advance. The service was amazing, they took many tests to make sure we were fit enough.

We paid and left, they told us to come back in January and the treatment will begin. We left and decided we will not talk about this and we will live happily and if Allah wants to bless us with a child he will bless us. We focused on being with each other. November 17th Saima started to have back pain and I told her to just take paracetamol. The pain wouldn't go so she went to the Drs. The Dr said maybe we should do a pregnancy test. Saima was shocked and thought but we have been trying for 4 years how can this be possible. So Saima came home with the pregnancy test and told me. I thought ok maybe its just a false alarm. Saima went into the bathroom to do the test, I knew she got a positive with the way she slammed the door open, I was sitting hunching in my seat and was pushed up abruptly with the way Saima opened the door. Saima just smiled, I just said to her wait hold that thought! I ran to the chemist and bought another test. Again it was positive. I grabbed Saima and rushed to the Drs taking the pregnancy tests to show the doctors like a trophy. The Dr sent us to the early gynaecology unit to see if they can check if Saima is pregnant with other tests. We rushed to the hospital for a check up and after the ultrasound checks they said its too early for them to check and we were brought back to reality.

However they said we will do a blood test and come back within 4 to 5 days later we will let you know. We came back home disappointed, a part of us wanted to be happy but we controlled our emotions. Saima was on the prayer mat 24/7 praying for a positive result. After four days of waiting, 9.30am was our appointment, you know how they say

Asians are always late, we got there 8.30am. We walked in and were told to wait. Saima was so nervous, the doctor called us in, she walked in with a piece of paper and goes "Where are you taking your wife out to dinner tonight?" she didn't confirm the results but I knew what she meant. Saima started crying and jumped onto the doctor like king kong giving her a big hug and then she jumped on me. She then said "Congratulations you are pregnant." I remember I hugged my wife and we were crying, you know in a bathroom that has a cupboard that had mirrors, I see a mirror behind Saima, I'm hugging her and crying but these are tears of happiness. That was the day I realised what tears of joy meant. We got our IVF money back and most importantly we got our marriage back.

We came out of the hospital and looked at the sky and said "Thank you Allah." She was three weeks pregnant. We were still afraid, I didn't want anything to disappoint her. I kept telling her to keep it quiet, however within 2 months we told our immediate family. They all were crying out of joy for us. Then 6 months went by, 7 and then 9. We gave birth to a beautiful daughter, we named her Inaya. Inaya means 'Allah's Gift, (God's Gift)' And thats exactly what she is to us. Saima had an amazing pregnancy, she was eating well and looking well, the due date was the 31st of July 2018, trust me the first born never goes by the due date! Then on the 10th of August 2018 and weirdly at 10.08pm Inaya was born. The day that changed our life. I held her for the first time and started crying, I cried so much I couldn't see her. My eyes were blurry with the tears. Nothing else mattered, the 4 years of pain was gone. We know what we went through, maybe we wouldn't still be together. Soon as I put my story out it went viral on Instagram. We did this because so many were suffering like we did and we wanted to give them hope. And today we continue giving them hope through this book.

I want to tell all the couples out there anything is possible, if you aren't conceiving trust me anything can happen and all you have to do is believe in Allah. Men, you have to support your wives and stay united.

Like Saima says she's learned to not get down and lose hope, anything is possible. Saima also made a pledge to build a madrasah for orphans to thank Allah for Inaya, and today we are making that dream come true.

TaZzZ & Saima - Music Artist - Youtuber - Song Writer

Instagram - https://www.instagram.com/tazzzartist
Facebook - https://www.facebook.com/TaZzZMusic/
Youtube - https://www.youtube.com/user/officialTaZzZ
www.youtube.com/MadeBySaima
Website - http://www.tazzzmusic.com
Email - tazzzmusic1@gmail.com

17

Sindh Jii Hawwa (The Eve of Sindh)

In Sindh, patriarchal customs of control over women include the institutionalisation of extremely restrictive codes of behaviour for women, a practice of rigid gender segregation, specific forms of family and kinship, and a powerful ideology linking family honour to female virtue. Women in Sindh are particularly handicapped by the entrenched feudal system in rural Sindhi society. There are several factors that impede the development of women in Sindh, including a very low legal status women hold, as well as the lack of political power and will to change the gender disparity.

I was only 18 years old when i was married to a man who belonged to an affluent family in interior of Sindh, Pakistan. Life went on and the divinity blessed me with two healthy sons and a beautiful daughter. However, I never had a comfortable relationship with my ex-husband where i was always treated as a subject, and my views and outlook towards life were neither appreciated nor given any importance. In due course, tales of my ex-husband's romantic excursions started reaching me. I protested in the beginning and tried to convince my ex-husband to refrain from immoral activities but all my efforts were in vain. I soon realised that in the male chauvinistic society I was living in, social ailments like womanising, mistrust and polygamy instead of being reviled, are rather considered a feather in the cap. Then, one day, the shocking news of my ex-husband's second marriage reached me. This was not however, the end of the series of bad news for me as a few days later, on the insistence of his second wife, my ex-husband divorced me. It was a great setback for me, despite my husband's philandering ways, I was striving to make my marriage successful with a hope that one day my children, especially sons would help me achieve my due status; something that I, myself had been unable to accomplish during my married life.

Left at the mercy of circumstances, I had no choice but to find alternate means to support myself and my children. To this end, I joined a local school as a Headmistress enabling myself to bring some measure of stability in the lives of my children however, my struggle was not yet over. In my absence whilst at work, my ex-husband came to my house and took my children away. Left with no amicable recourse, I approached the law enforcement agencies but in countries like Pakistan, even such legal channels are unavailable to women. However, having a legal background myself, I decided to fight the battle of custody for my children and won but all the efforts went in vain as my ex- husband left the jurisdiction and fled somewhere with the little ones leaving me deprived of their love and presence for 7 long years.

Facing such unbearable loss at such a young age made me empathetic to the plight of other children suffering from similar circumstances, which ultimately motivated me to relocate to the UK and invest in educating myself further so I could work for the cause of women & children welfare around the world and someday be able to provide a safe and prospective future for my own children.

In 2015, 7 years down the journey I have been successful in getting my kids on board and Allah has blessed me with 3 more children from my current marriage.

I am continuously setting examples in breaking the cultural taboos of being a 'divorcee' and a 'victim of my circumstances' for women coming from similar backgrounds and I am actively combating the abuse of 'Domestic Violence' by supporting others through my TV program

'Saheli' & my Holistic Healing Therapy services. Alhamdulillah, the 12 long years of pain have made me gain a lot and I have been successful in building a steady and stronger relationship with my new hubby and his family. My husband reverted to Islam in 2009, exactly the time when I was going through a life changing event-divorce. At the time my perspective towards life was, why did Allah take this man away from me leaving my life empty? Little had I known that Allah up there was smiling down upon my silliness as he was preparing for a beautiful replacement for me.

Alhamdulillah, a reward for my patience and constant service to sustain my previous relationship. Allah not only gifted me with a believing and practising Muslim who understands his role as a husband but an affectionate father to our children. I now share 3 beautiful kids between us and 3 from my previous marriage so we have a house full where we live a life full of love, passion & challenges together. Having 3 under five year olds life seems quite interesting but if it wasn't for this hustle our lives would seem meaningless and boring. Me and my husband are struggling to get our me time alone but Alhamdulilah we go to perform Umrah every year with family where we recharge our batteries spiritually and bring back more strength to cope with any odds. Allah always provides us with opportunities to taste true love by drawing us closer to Him, obeying him and fulfilling his rights. May Allah gives us the strength to do justice to his commands, Ameen!

As an unconventional Management Consultant I have done commendable work in transforming Behavioural Patterns of many Senior Executives through programs like Strengths Discovery through NLP and Relationship Coaching. My aim through this initiative was to make people realise how important it is to build healthy relationships with family members especially your spouse since it has a direct impact on productivity and performance within workplaces and of course at home. I've been coaching women executives since 2005 and I'm currently focusing on one-to-one coaching for women and couples to build a healthier relationship, deal with the trauma from a previous bitter relationship or tackle the challenges of having step children at home.

I am an ENFJ personality type according to (MBTI) and an Influencer according to Disc which means I am a person who *places emphasis on openness, influencing or persuading others to build stronger relationships.*

I love connecting with mother Nature and produce immaculate results in clean, organised & a romantic environment. The Activator in me keeps encouraging me to do variety of projects at the same time and I have to calm it down by saying "I have been a Jack of all for long, now it's time to be the King of one – Relationship and Growth Coaching"

I love to serve my clients and watch them experience heightened bliss as they get closer to Allah- Indeed HE is the one who puts barakah in all relationships.

> *"Life is not easy, so we are in need of someone to find tranquillity with. That's why Allah put between the husband and wife Muwadda (permanent love)"*
>
> *Shaykh Muhammad Al Yaqoubi*

A very famous painter Picasso once said *"Men take women as Goddesses or as Door mats"* and what I took from that was I had stopped respecting myself, I was considering myself a slave to my man's needs, I gave him so much power and authority that he started owning and manipulating me based on his convenience. I could absolutely resonate to that in my previous relationship.

However, I took that learning on board and tried to understand my role from an Islamic perspective where a woman enjoys equal status to her man and marriage is not about 'him' or 'her' but about complimenting each other, feel mentally, emotionally and physically fulfilled while raising a pious family to please Allah.

That is where my self-development journey started as I felt the need of companionship and I wanted to give it my best in the light of Islam and lead by example like Hazrat Khadija pbuh.

That's the story of a simple & now empowered girl from Sindh, Pakistan, Sindh Jii Hawwa.

Hina Junejo - Relationship & Empowerment Coach, Soft Skills Trainer, CIPD HR Lecturer, Presenter on Takbeer TV - Saheli With Hina, Domestic Violence & Abuse Activist.

Facebook - www.facebook.com/hina.junejo
Instagram - @Hinajunejo
Youtube - https://www.youtube.com/user/hinajunejo
www.hinajunejo.com

The Walk To Freedom

Today I would like to share my story which is going to be coming from my book: "You Are Possible; How To Create Doable Success". The reason why I'm creating this book is because lots of people tell me that with the work I do by helping people to transform their lives, they want to know how they can actually do it themselves.

It would be a lot easier for me to tell you why I do it. I do it because for many years of my life I struggled with challenges going back to growing up as a child. I was the youngest of five children where in my household, if you can just picture it... there was a mother who loved her sons but a father who disciplined his children in a really tough way. It was not really anything for my dad to want to beat us to be honest and sometimes he would even beat my mom. This got very confusing for me. This lead me to be a very troubled child.

I would be running around in my little shorts and being a loveable rogue. I found that the only way I could get attention at school was to misbehave. I remember misbehaving so much at one stage that my teacher actually stuffed me in the bin and she has told me that I would be nothing but rubbish in my life. To be quite honest, for a lot of my choices later on... she was not wrong.

I had a bit of an entrepreneurial skill, I used to make those little chocolate rice crispy cakes. I tried to make them for myself and I used to sell them to the kids at school but eventually that was my first ever business that my father liquidated because he was getting so fed up with all the mess that I would leave in the the kitchen.

Going through school as I said I was a loveable rogue and I never really sat down and did any education or passed any exams, I just basically drifted through school. By the time I left school with no qualifications or anything I decided to make my own decisions in life, growing up I had decided something. I had decided that nobody would ever tell me what to do again because if the people who loved me were not looking after me, why should anyone else?

After leaving school I tried to get work. I got fired from a number of jobs for a number of reasons and with a laugh I can say some were not actually my own. I did not even try to progress in my life because I thought that life owed me a living and if I tried why wasn't anything happening...

I used to hang around guys that used to sell drugs, commit crimes... in actual fact my first motivational talk was from a gangster. He said to me: "In this country you get paid 12 or 52 times out of 300 and odd days a year" and out of his back pocket he pulled out a big bunch of money and said: "Well in this country because you get paid that way, I get paid my way and I get my money everyday". At that time it was very motivational to me.

I started a life of crime where I was the guy who could get you drugs from each part of the country, get stolen cars or jewellery etc. I was a bit of a "wheeler dealer".

It wasn't until the late 80s that I was smoking canabis. By that time I was in and out of prison where I saw the drug scene in the UK getting big especially in crack-cocaine. At the time I was a bit of a drug-user. I was taking cocaine, party drugs such as ecstacy, trips/drips, acids and more.

Later on I saw that crack-cocaine was making a lot of money for people and I got interested in that. It really drew me, the quickness of the money and what it bought.

They say money is the root of all evil and it truly was. It was the root to my evil where I became very selfish, where I became someone that didn't care and was just all about money, women and everything that came with it.

It was on one fateful day in a situation that has long since passed my mind that I'll never forget. What I often refer to as the "Beginning Of The End". You know there's a saying:"Never get high on your own supply" and that day I did...

That one moment, that one bad choice... Led me to twenty years of consequences. Where by taking crack-cocaine, I lost everybody. In the blink of an eye I lost all my respect, my morals, my codes and as an occupational hazard I started getting involved in prolific police offending just to feed my habit.

My mom lost a son... She lived my life of addiction with me. Up to this day her words haunt me, she said:"Mark I live the consequences of your life but don't even get the benefits of the high".

My addiction would rage further than that because from taking crack-cocaine I would escalate into taking heroin. Me being an "all or nothing" type of guy... I went straight to the needle. To be quite honest with you I found heaven in a high, it was the most comforting, most euphoric feeling ever.

I began to chase the life of being a heroin and crack-cocaine addict but from there my life took an even more dangerous toll. A toll so severe that I would literally lose my leg due to an infection, I would suffer from ulcers and all kinds of medical injuries because of injecting. Today I don't even have any veins.

At my worst I was seven and a half stone, eating off of the streets. Institutions and prisons became a norm for me, I suffered two heart attacks, died once and I even at one point tried suicide.

People used to ask me about heaven and hell but it didn't really matter to me because I was living in hell so I might as well just sell my soul. The one thing that used to get me wasn't the taking of the drugs, it was the fact that I couldn't understand why I use when I don't want to use and when I shouldn't use I still do.

I needed answers because I did treatment, I did rehabs, I did AA, I did NA and all the different programs yet nobody could answer me.

My family was lost... I was lost but in one last attempt I said to myself, I was giving it one final shot and its too long to tell the whole story of how I got into treatment but it was miraculous.

I always believe there is a higher power looking out for us so I entered into a treatment facility in New South Wales, where I gave myself my one chance to believe that it is possible for me to break free from addiction or else I would just go and get a gun and blow my brains out because I was fed up.

The treatment centre I entered was called Team Challenge and boy it really challenged me. It challenged my thinking, my thoughts and everything about myself. I was really blessed to have some real men of faith who really supported me and I was surrounded by good people who were there for me as well.

My biggest enemy though was me... because I didn't think I would be free. In my mind I really thought that I couldn't get away from addiction but then I actually discovered that I could. Each day I had to change the story of what I thought about myself. I remember putting up on my ceiling: "Today I choose not to use, today I choose not to leave the rehab" and boy that rehab was worth leaving because it was so disciplined. It was so disciplined that you would get "wash ups" for minor things, I once got a wash up for an eyelash in my sink.

I had been leading an undisciplined life so the sense of discipline was needed. I believe without discipline you don't have purpose or direction. As I went through this program which was supposed to be nine months, I stayed there for sixteen.

Once I completed the program people wanted to know who I was now that I was clean and I did not know who I was. I was either the mask of the loveable rogue I put on at school who tried to hide the fact that he was in a dysfunctional family that had emotional and behavioural problems, then I was the criminal putting on that mask to actually stay alive because in that time I was shot, stabbed and gutted like a fish so I had to put on a mask to survive in prison and then the biggest mask of all was the drug addict.

Over the five years I remained at the centre where I became a support worker, a volunteer doing outreaches by talking to other addicts... I actually began to learn a lot about myself because I attended a school of further learning where we learned counselling, human condition and mannerisms of people, psychosocial disorders etc.

From there I actually found my purpose because every single addict I spoke to, I made a point of asking the same question I asked myself:" Why do you use when you don't want to use and when you shouldn't use you do?". Is it so predictable that the minute you try to do good, your user side takes charge? Who could be guaranteed that every single person said that it was so.

With all my teachings I developed a program because I believe that sometimes things don't have to look like they are coming together for them to come together and I also believe that you can be transformed by the renewing of your mind. I also believe that dependencies and some mental illnesses are based on thought. I took a risk and challenged drug and alcohol dependancy.

With tears running a marathon down my cheeks I remember that during that time I had to suffer a great loss, my mom who saw me get clean... I think my addiction aided her illness and she passed away in August of 2011. This still hurts deeply today but I know she is watching over me because everything she left behind I took and started the charity we have today called THE WALK TO FREEDOM, where from her inheritance I started a charity for people who were like me and I do it in her honour.

I also realised there were families who were suffering the way my mom did so I developed a drug and alcohol course for people with a user in the home, who gave never been a user themselves and for professionals because I don't believe you need to have a broken lip in order to know how to fix one. We have managed to tutor and mentor over a hundred people with these courses and we are seeing lives change.

As I said earlier in the human condition there is nothing different that it takes for an addict to want to change their life around than what it takes for anybody else to want to change their life around. Whether you want to change your life to live better or whether you want to start a business, go on an adventure because I believe as Les Brown said: "We all have greatness within". I believe that we all are possible but life can hit us so many times that it makes it seem impossible but that doesn't mean that doesn't mean that it's not possible.

I have decided to take everything I've learned with the brilliant people I've worked with, who have transformed their lives and it's not just people who are addicts, I'm talking about young people who were getting into gangs and I used the very same principles and I've seen them all become free.

I want to give that opportunity to the world through listening to my story. I want to tell them that they have no excuse because if this seven and a half stone drug addict could make his life possible, so can you. Through my book, my workshops, my training... I want to tell the world that they are possible, no matter what they are going through.

People say:"Bad times may be here but don't worry they don't last long, the good times are around the corner and don't worry the bad times don't last long neither do the good " but it's the story that we tell ourselves that makes the difference.

It is possible to be free. The word freedom... there's nothing greater. For me when I close my eyes and picture freedom(you are welcome to do it with me and picture what freedom means to you) mine is a big stallion getting set free and running across a field where it can do whatever it likes.

I want to help and support other people to the success they want to see and when my book is published... You are possible and I want to take you on a journey and hold your hand while I show you how to create doable success through what I'm going to call the Belief System. On that journey I want to hold your hand as my hand was held through mine and help you to become the success you want to see.

I hope that one day when you pick up my book or see me doing a talk that you would want to do the same too.

I want to be the biggest infection to mankind, that cause people to affect other's lives for change. I just want to leave everyone with this last message by Henry Ford: "*The person who said I can and the person who said I can't are both right*" so I want to ask you which of the two you are because if you are the person who says "I can" then anything is possible and just remember you are a passionate, possible person.

Mark Anthony Clarke - CEO of Walk to Freedom

To donate to Marks Amazing Cause please go to
website - www.walktofreedom.co.uk - Instagram - @Iampossibleclarke

17

Noor - The Light that shines after the darkest nights

You live and you learn. There will come a time in your life when you will finally come to the realisation that not every hardship is a problem and not every loss is actually a loss. You will learn that every hardship brings opportunities and lessons. Another thing that I have learnt is that time isn't a healer unless you intentionally go on a journey of healing and transformation. Since I began self development I have uncovered layers of myself I wasn't aware of. It has been the difference from dark to light. I have uncovered my strengths and embraced my true power.

I am going to share with you some advice I would like to give to my younger self. I'm sure you will benefit from knowing the breakdown of my path first.

My major down falls in life were mainly after the age of 20 onwards. I am now 30 years of age and have been on my self development path for around 2 and a half years so there was 8 years of confusion and a sense of emptiness. So many good and not so good things happened in that time yet what I discovered about myself is that I had no control over my emotions, I was craving closeness to my creator but was lacking the tools to really develop myself mentally a spiritually.

There is one incident that I will share to inspire you to stand your ground and value your self worth. Unfortunately I learnt this the less easy and long way. I had given birth to my first child when I was thrown into a corrupt and unethical mess. I was emotionally blackmailed to lie about something to cover someone else's back! The police was involved and it eventually went to a huge trial. I will never forget the day, the police thumped on my door and came to arrest me for perverting the course of justice. I clearly remember the day I spent in a prison cell, I remember questioning myself "how the hell did I get into this mess, this is not what my life is about" it was so daunting and emotionally straining! I had so many thoughts and so many regrets.

Through a year of questions and the trial, I became anxious and depressed. It did not make sense why I had to suffer because of someone else's actions yet I never told the truth as much as I wanted to. It would haunt me, every single day. I found out I was pregnant with my second child. The parties involved cared about themselves whilst I wasn't allowed to! The truth is... I didn't value myself enough to speak up and protect myself. I didn't love myself enough to put me first. Alhamdulillah I was saved from serving a prison sentence yet the after math of my mental health was crazy! The lesson here is to never ever sacrifice your well being happiness and sanity for ANYONE!

As the days, weeks and months went by I just wasn't myself anymore. I stopped going out of the house and allowed myself to be isolated. Every time someone knocked on the door it would trigger fear inside me which would take over! Sounds petty right? It wasn't for me.

I often used to sit alone and really wander if I could just leave this world and avoid everything around me. One day I sat in my dark room and say 'Oh Allah, show me some light, send me some guidance, I don't want to live the rest of my life like this.' I receive a notification of a WhatsApp message on my phone, here's what it said "Allah does not change the situation of a believer until he changes it himself" SubhanAllah, what perfect timing!

The next part is where it all happened;

A short time after that message, I received a friend request from a coach. I had no idea what a coach was! I started following her and watching all her videos, in fact I was stalking two coaches thinking how can they help me? So I reached out to them and we spoke and I signed up for coaching with both of them. At that moment I was ready to heal, to unravel all the pain and negative thoughts and mostly I was ready to find the real me again! I had continuous sessions and worked on myself religiously, my mindset and my energy. The biggest thing that bought me change was having emotional breakthrough coaching. It was just WOW! You've got to go through the process to know what I mean. As I continued my journey of self development I kept getting insights and visions that I should share my stories and help other women see the light. As time went on I began to learn and train how to become a coach. All of my hard work and commitment to working on myself paid off; 2015 is the year that broke me, 2016 I was lost, 2017 I started to see the light, 2018 I found myself and 2019 was MY YEAR! I certified as and NLP practitioner and then 2 months later as a Master practitioner of NLP and as an emotional mastery coach. I appeared on takbeer tv and Islam channel, I co-authored a book called 'courage is my crown' and was nominated for two awards! It goes to show that when you take one step, Allah makes things easy for you. The journey of healing is an be painful yet so beautiful. I remember the day I looked in the mirror and said welcome home. I have had the honour to coach many women, helping them to master their emotions and become confident. I have huge goals for the future and know that I am living my true purpose through coaching women who move from darkness to light which is why my coaching business is called Noshiela NOOR coaching.

What did I learn from all of this?

To always put myself first, to value myself. No one will value you if you don't value yourself. Everyone has reasons as to why they behave the way they do. We all behave according to our values and our model of the world.

To work on my mental health and spiritually as a priority in my life. To step into my true power and share my gifts with the world. There is so much to life than this! Mindset is a priority and you must do what it takes to make sure your mental space is filled with positivity. Live in Love – nothing is worth it if love isn't there

If I could write a letter to my younger self it would be like this…

Dear Noshiela, I just want you to know that you are an amazing, powerful and intellectual young woman. Never let anyone ruin that. You are in control of your life's choices, make choices that empower you and allow you to spread your love far and wide. I want you to always remember life is happening for you and not to you. Be responsible for the energy you allow yourself to be surrounded by and be picky about who you share your energy and time with. Life will take you on some Rolla coasters, hold on tight and keep your eyes open for opportunities. Your mental health is your best asset, protect it and always work on strengthening it. Positivity changes lives so always stay positive and just remember you were not created to play small. Your journey of life is about understanding and knowing yourself, not others.

You are loving and loved.

You are beautiful, amazing and powerful. Live your dreams.

Love from Me. I am you.

I will now share some amazing tools that you can use daily to train your mind to see the best in every thing.

Here are some ways in which you can instantly change your state and work towards a positive mindset:

- Wake up early - stay awake after morning prayers and have some time alone
- Journaling - I use it as a form of contemplating the good I have done and where I need to improve. Hold yourself accountable
- Gratitude - Gratitude is the best attitude! Allah tells us in the Quran in Surah Ibrahim 'When you are grateful, I will give you more...'
- I want you to write at least ten things daily that you are grateful for. Focus on the feelings and not just the words. When a person is in the state of gratitude, it is impossible for them to feel any negative emotion! Try it!
- Meditation - Take a few minutes out of your schedule to sit and focus on yourself.
- Take a few deep breaths in and release. As you do this, let any negative thoughts pass you by and replace them with positive and loving thoughts!
- If you make these things part of your daily routine, you will feel a shift in your emotional state and in your mindset too.

Since then I have transformed my mindset and went on to achieve many of my goals. I have been working with women to remove their limiting beliefs, remove deep rooted negative emotions and to create a positive mindset so they can find their true purpose in life.

Here are some amazing facts about the unconscious mind so you can understand how powerful it really is:

- The unconscious mind stores memories and organises them it even represses memories with unresolved negative emotion for protection
- The unconscious mind preserves and runs the body
- Is a highly moral being
- Take everything personally - you will become whatever you tell yourself. Feed your mind with positive words. Positive affirmations are a great thing to practise every morning
- It presents repressed memories for solution - this is when you know it's time to heal and move on
- It's the domain of the emotions - to master your emotions you need to work on your mindset until the unconscious and the conscious mind merge to give you a powerful mind.
- Maintains instincts - have you ever ignored that gut feeling and then regretted it later, yes so have I! Always listen to your instincts!

How to find your true purpose

I want to share some tips with you on how to find your true purpose:

Write down all of your limiting beliefs - become aware of them and work on replacing them with beliefs that will serve you

- Work on shifting your mindset - daily gratitude, affirmations and journaling will give you a great head start
- Invest in yourself - Get yourself a coach! A coach will help you turn your doubts into strengths and will guide you on your new path

- Be open minded - know that nothing is impossible. Aim high!
- Write a list of things that you've always wanted to achieve and see what those things have in common
- Ask yourself - What can I offer to the world?

If you are easily affected by other people's energy, it is so important to protect your personal space. Your mind and your energy. I am going to share some ways in which you can protect your energetic space:

- Avoid negative people - these are the people who love engaging in gossip and find problems to every solution!
- Be mindful of what you watch on the t.v/media
- Practise meditation regularly
- Connect with nature and release negative energies
- Spend time with people who are positive and open minded
- Speak with those who want to see you grow - you will be like those who you choose as your company
- Understand other people before reacting. When we understand why a person behaves the way they do based on their programming and resources it's easier to forgive and move on

Always be you

Remember that being you is the best that you can do. No one can be like you so don't try and fit in or go out of your way to be like others. You have your very own qualities and your own personality that no one can take away from you. Live your life using your qualities to make a difference to those around you. Always remember that you were not created to be miserable or sad. Let go of the victim mentality and up your game!

Perception is projection

You will always see in others what you are feeling yourself. If you do not heal from the past and let go of what doesn't help you become a better person you will always project it onto others. The same goes for what people say about you, they will only see in you a reality of themselves. This is something important to think about!

Be at cause not effect

Being at cause is taking responsibility for everything that happens in your life. Even if there are things that happened in your life that were not pleasant, think about what could have been done to avoid it? And what can you learn from those situations, take those learnings and remember them for the future!

Being at effect is blaming everything and everyone for the things that happened in your life. It is the victim mindset that does not help you grow as a person. Life is full of lessons and tests, choose to see the good in them all and move on! I pray that you find peace and healing in your life and live your true purpose.

Noshiela Noor - Emotional Mastery Coach for Muslim women. Founder of Developing young minds – Teaching children about having a growth mindset and controlling their emotions & Motivational speaker.

Website - www.noshielanoorcoaching.co.uk
Instagram - @Noshiela.noor
Facebook group - https://www.facebook.com/groups/102911091 0583276/
Facebook - www.facebook.com/Noshielanoor

17

Lost and Found

My life has taught me many lessons, but most of all, it has taught me that struggles are only given to those that are also equipped with the strength and patience to cope with them. This may not be felt or acknowledged at the time of the event in question, but looking back at what life has thrown at me and how I have overcome it, it definitely is my motto for life!

> *'Great works are performed not by force, but by belief and perseverance'*
> *(Samuel Johnson).*

Being born in a British Muslim family may be a dream for many, but for it to be an orthodox, culture led family living in Britain can be a turn for the worst – especially for the women. It was by choice that I took on the Jilbab and Shiela (Islamic clothing) as well as the daily prayers. Upon seeing this, my father offered me the opportunity to perform Umrah (like a mini-Hajj). This was at the age of 14.

As I was coming to the end of my Secondary years, being a studious and – if I say so myself – a bright student, I wanted to study further. This was not as easy as it sounds. The traditional beliefs of the family showed their colours here when I was not allowed to enrol into further studies and it was much preferred for me to be domesticated and ready for marriage before the age of 20. This could be a breaking point for many. Not being able to study further would have life-changing effects.

Thankfully, having uncles of a more modern approach to life allowed for their involvement and with a bit of help, I was able to study further within the same school. These values were again tested when I wanted to head to University. However, this time, I was able to 'play my cards right' and live away from home too. Again, the perseverance, the patience and the determination helped. Knowing that I was a studius individual and wanted to secure my future wasn't enough for my father, but the opinions of outsiders from our immediate family was what influenced his decision to allow me.

As my family had entrusted me with such a big responsibility, I subconsciously obliged to their expectations. Ringing home daily and staying in touch with them as well as staying in touch with my religious roots and beliefs. This helped tremendously in keeping the trust and support of my folks as I completed that degree and enrolled onto a second Bachelors at the local University without too much drama. However, this time, I got myself a job while I studied. Not only was I able to pay for my fees, but the experience was invaluable towards my future teaching career. By this point, both my persona and society opinions had really helped turn my parents' views around. Now, they were forever supportive of my studies and career. Any marriage proposal that came now, would hear the same dialogue: '*my daughter is currently studying, wait if you wish or best of luck*'. It was the end of an era in my household, all because I was able to prove to my folks that not all stereotypes are true and one should not brush everyone with the same brush.

Having received so much support and backing from them, I felt the least I could give back to them was the decision that changes one's life – marriage. We all know that parent's only ever want what is best for their children, so I let them pick my groom while I focussed on my career. After a few proposals, both folks and my grandma agreed on a distant relative.

Claiming it is a lovely family and he is a simple, religious and straightforward individual – I was sold to the concept. The engagement and marriage had an 8 month gap, during which we (my fiancé and I) exchanged no more than 20 text messages at most. I didn't think of it too much as I was busy preparing for what is the biggest day of a woman's life.

To add to the dream, I was offered a teaching opportunity abroad. Consulting this with my uncle, he agreed that this opportunity would be great for us as a newly married couple as it will give us the space and privacy needed in getting to know one another. However, the fiancé was not too keen as he didn't want to move away from home. This was my first sacrifice towards my marriage, even before we were married. I ignored this and focussed on the wedding and the marriage. It really was a typical, week-long, Asian wedding full of colours, events and food!

After marriage, I couldn't have been happier with my in-laws. Honestly – it was like a dream come true. A cool friend in a father in law only happens in books and dreams, but was reality for me. I even remember saying to my dad that my father in law treats me better than he ever did. This is always a proud and happy moment for parents – to know their daughter has found a loving family in her in-laws. This happiness was a sugar coat to the truth, as the relationship between my husband and I was none-existent.

Not by choice, but after having no communication and lack of expression led to a deteriorated attitude to life in myself. Only six months into the marriage, and I had started to forget how to smile or be positive. Living in the same room as someone who isn't able to even acknowledge your presence was heart breaking. I understand that wasn't intentional on his behalf – but a little bit of casual communication and care isn't too much to ask from a marriage, is it? Being the only daughter and divorced have such a stigma in our society; I did everything I could to save my marriage. Including what is referred to as a 'honeymoon', we went on 3 holidays in 6 months, but no form of communication was formed, let alone anything else! I was convinced there were more problems than what meets the eye, but wasn't able to express this well enough for the in-laws to help me get somewhere in my relationship.

So after an excruciating battle with myself, I finally opened up to my mother and within 6 weeks (8 months of a marriage), I was bought back to my folks' home. Divorce papers were filed and I tried to gather myself back together again. This battle within not only took me deep down into depression, but also opened windows to suicidal thoughts. Someone as extrovert as me found comfort in the darkness of my bedroom. This could be another breaking point for many.

However, having the education and career behind me, I was able to stand up again and without wasting any time, was back into work. Keeping myself busy, I fully immersed myself in my job and very quickly was offered a permanent position at the school I was doing supply in. Having been honest with them from the start with regards to my condition, the SLT were ever so supportive, which really was a blessing!

Additionally, family and relatives can also cause detrimental, long lasting damage at such points through their opinions and advice. Again, knowing me for what I was, everyone (including my ex in-laws) knew that I would not have given up on a relationship without there being a solid reason. Having seen how happy I was living the domestic, housewife life, is came as a shock to them all, but their support was no less than a magical ointment on my mental health. Just the simple words like 'it was not your fault' were enough. Being in such a vulnerable position, it is painful to know that someone else's words and opinions matter so much, but they really did do their magic in my life.

Having stood on my feet again after such downfalls, my parents had also left that orthodox mentality behind and were able to see how strong their daughter had become. It became a blessing to have their support and backing – even if it wasn't always so easy to get.

Today, 4 years after my divorce, I am working abroad as a teacher, visiting home during the holidays and able to have my family visit me whenever is convenient for them. A life of so many ups and downs truly has made me the strong and determined woman I am today and I can confidently say *"what doesn't break you, only makes you stronger'* (Friedrich Nietzsche).

Nosheen Hanif

17

Marriage, motherhood, career & I

FACT: There are an estimated 700,000 young carers in the UK. Caring for someone may involve looking after an elderly or/and an ill family member. In my case, my parents.

As a young carer, it is very easy to become isolated. Most of your friends can't relate to your circumstances, nor do they share the same level of responsibilities as you do. Teachers and career advisors are not adequately trained to support young carers. With such lack of support from those we look up to as children, it becomes very easy to loose your own sense of purpose, your ambitions, your own sense of being. Not being able to focus on your homework due to the stress at home. Not getting enough rest. Not having anyone to guide you through your own challenges. Especially challenges that come with being a teenager. These are just some of the obstacles young carers face in their day to day lives.

I was just 10 years of age when my father was diagnosed with Parkinson's and alzheimer's disease. My mother had been diabetic since I was born and had her own challenges to deal with in terms of her health. Both of my parents health was deteriorating fast. Mum became partially blind and needed dialysis 3 times a week. Dad was becoming more and more forgetful and unable to do basic things like have a wash or go to the toilet.

Being the youngest of 7 and the only one living at home with my parents. I became a full time carer for both of them. Leaving the house to spend a couple of hours with friends was usually filled with guilt. I remember struggling to carry my father's weight when ever I helped him walk from one place to another, placing his arm around my shoulders, praying I would have enough strength to keep him from falling if he lost his balance. I remember one night very clearly. I had a couple of friends stay the night. They knew I had to stay at home due to my commitments and so couldn't stay away at their's. We talked, watched a movie and went to sleep. It was nice to have company over for a change. A few hrs later I heard my mum screaming and woke up to our house filled with smoke. We quickly evacuated the house and called the fire services. I realised that everyone was out, except my father. I panicked and rushed back into the blazing house to find him. The smoke was so thick I couldn't see anything. Somehow I ended up by the back door of the house. My instinct told me to open the door. I did, and to my relief I saw my father stood outside in the garden. Confused but safe. I grabbed him my the hand and took him round to the front of the house where everyone else was. My mother was distraught, father confused. I ended up with carbon dioxide poisoning and had to go hospital for treatment. My father not realising what he was doing, and many alzheimer patients suffer from this, had turned on the gas heater on and inserted some magazines into it. Which caused the fire. That day I told myself I couldn't leave my parents, there was no point in me working hard to get good grades. I wouldn't be able to go away for further education anyway. There was no point in me exploring what career I want to pursue. I wouldn't be able to pursue it anyway. There wasn't even any point in me finding the right man who I could marry one day. Because no man would be prepared to live with my parents anyway.

I began to give up on my vision, my ambitions - my own identity. My wants, my desires, my dreams. My purpose became caring for my parents. I was just a carer and believing that I could be anything more was unrealistic.

December 2007, at the age of 24, I lost my mother. My father was put into care, and I became homeless. With that my role as a carer had also ended. I felt lost without my purpose. I had no one to care for anymore. Those that I gave up my own identity for, were no longer with me. I needed someone else to care for. I accepted the first marriage proposal that came my way. He was a good guy and came from a culture that typically believed that a wife should care for her husband and in laws. Perfect! I could continue being the only thing I knew how to. I could care for my husband and I can care for his parents. I'll have children that | can care for too! What more could I ask for. Little did I know that in order to care for others, I needed to care for myself first. I needed to heal myself first. Of course when you enter any relationship unhealed, the chances of success are quite slim. Your inner wounds eventually catch up with you.

2017, age 34. After 9 years of marriage, divorce happened. I was now a single mum to 4 amazing boys. This was the turning point of my life. For the first time, I realised that I had to put myself first. Discovering myself after all these years and healing from past wounds was far from easy. Not in the least bit comfortable. But I understood this was something I needed to go through in order to come out stronger. I had a responsibility to demonstrate strength to my children.

In the past year, I've discovered myself, I've evolved, I've studied and worked towards a career I am passionate about, and i feel incredibly empowered by what i have achieved. I am still a carer, I care for my 4 beautiful boys. But not at the expense for caring for myself. The days they spend with their father I focus on me, and only me. My goals, my ambitions, my evolution. I have learnt that you can only give to others when your own cup is full. You cannot pour from an empty cup.

Our young carers need our love and support. They need more of us to understand their struggle. We need to provide opportunities for them.

Caring for someone you love is so rewarding. But even carers need to he cared for. Give them extra support during exams, train teachers and other professionals on how to effectively support young care givers. Set up support systems within communities. Most of all, teach these children, not to lose themselves or their ambitions, whilst caring for others.

Celina Hanif - Owner of 'In Harmony by Celina' Holistic therapist. Producer of In Harmony magnesium oils.

Master Practitioner of NLP, Hypnosis and NLP Coach, Practioner of energy healing.

Website - www.inharmonybycelina.com
Facebook - 'In Harmony by Celina'
Instagram: @in_harmony_by_celina_

17

Make The Shift

It is the mindset shift you make about an event that once made you feel victimised or disempowered, to making you feel empowered and nothing changed other than your perception about that event.

All my life, from about the age of 10 years, as I was becoming more conscious of problems around me, I started to feel really negative about life, and because I felt that way, more events happened that were making me feel more and more negative about life. Before that, I relied on my older sister to make me happy. She was my shield until she obviously had to move out.

A few events that happened... Not accepted by some people at school. Bullied for being brown in the neighbourhood. My Father getting ill and mum then becoming a full time carer while I had to take upon some household responsibilities, Dad passing away. Mum getting a heart attack and then me constantly being worried for her. To the point I would sleep in her room to watch her for some time.

This all happened before I was 15 years of age. During this time, I had a mentor whom I'm ever so grateful for during my secondary school. I thank Lisa for always being there for me and giving me the advice that I needed to get me through those difficult years. It was she who inspired me to become a nurse from one of our conversations.

As I got older, my resentment of life continued to grow, life was so hard by now! Thoughts like

"I wish I wasn't born" or "I wish I was 5 again!" used to be dominant. I remember life whenI was 5, life was good then, all of 7 of us siblings used to have laughs and now I rarely saw the elder ones and when I did, they were all so stressed and unhappy too.

By the time I was 18 years of age, my built up resentment was at it's peak, I was always stressed and looking back, living in anxiety. I was not fit for what was coming up next…Marriage!

I had to bring our marriage date earlier, I was about to start University that year, and so had to defer it. Marriage was to happen in Pakistan, my origin.

Mum's reason behind it was her poor health and she wanted all her children married and settled before her health took worse. After I got married, having never studied the rights of a husband and how to have a successful marriage, we had a love hate relationship which I will tell you more about.

I became so bitter, I remember thinking back, I was always unhappy by default, conversations I used to have with friends were dominating about everything that is wrong in my life that I never saw the blessings. My family loaned us a deposit and my brother helped us buy our first flat 3 months after I got married, me and Zaf (my husband) moved in October, the same year we got married. I was 19 years old and I had my own flat! Not many can say that at that age. I was in the first trimester in University doing my nurse training in learning disabilities/mental health.

And then... I was pregnant! Didn't plan this, at that time. It was a problem, and another thing to complain about. Of course, I had to put on a happy face for others for the fear of them judging me. Morning sickness was all day sickness, travelling by bus which triggered it even more.

Arguments with hubby continued. I was in default complain mode; complaining about him being illiterate and how he was supposed to look after me, drive me. He clearly did not fit my "expectations" of a husband then!

Yet, he was patient enough to stay with me through that time, his time to rant about me was at work with his colleagues!

By pregnancy month 4, I was starting to enjoy being pregnant, sickness had stopped. I was on holiday from university, I think it might have been the Easter holidays as we are in March by now. One night, hubby was at work, I started getting pains, heavy cramp pains. I was 19 weeks pregnant by then. I thought I was safe, most pregnancies miscarry before 12 weeks, according to National Statistics. 80% of miscarriages happen before 12 weeks. Only 0.5% happen at week 16. Well, I'm 19 weeks, baby should be safe I thought.

I called the midwife, telling her what I was feeling, she told to come in for a check up, and they found I was dilating. They couldn't stop me from giving birth, I give birth to my first child at 19 weeks. He was fully formed, I can still remember his little face and body.

The story of my life was now this, "I got married when I wasn't ready to please my mum, I deferred my University to get married, I didn't ask for any of this! WHY ME?!"

If I was hard to be around before, I was the worst to be around for the next 10 months while I was trying for another baby only to make me feel better for the baby I lost. Every month was an emotional rollercoaster until I got pregnant again and by then, me and hubby were always arguing, almost weekly over petty things.

I conceived again, lived the remaining months in fear incase I lose this baby again. I was at the hospital every 2 weeks for a scan to make sure the baby was safe. 3 days after my scan, at week 20, I started feeling pains, this time I was in denial, "It can't happen again." … It did!

I again give birth to a beautiful little baby, this one looked so much like Zaf. That hurt me most when I saw his face in the baby. By now, I had an inclining, it must be me, my body has done this.

Emotionally, this time, I was feeling different, not angry or blaming others, more so angry at myself for behaving in the way I had been for so long. For the first time I had the realisation of how arrogantI had been up until now. Now, I was in a helpless state, looking back, this event humbled me for the first time in my life.

That night when they got the baby ready for burial was the first time I prayed and did not ask "why did this happen to me?"

I asked God for help, I hadn't prayed like that in years, and as far as I remember as a child I always asked for help. I remember I was maybe 8 or 9 years of age and anything little would happen like if one of my brothers didn't come home after school on time, I used to pray he was safe and comes home quickly. There were no mobile phones then and all I needed to see that mum was worried in any situation, I would raise my hands in prayer.

That night I prayed with the intention of healing, of letting go of wanting something that I should not have, to find the wisdom in this problem, to feel peace again. For it is peace we all want and we look for it in people and things.

> *"For those who believe and for those who find comfort in the remembrance of God, surely in the remembrance of God do hearts find solace"*
>
> *(Quran 13:28)*

This was when I started to make the shift from victim to feeling empowered and grateful.

I just lost another baby, how could I feel grateful?

I started researching, as far from my faith I had been all my teenage years, I was 20 years old now. I knew God was loving and that He always gives us good even in the problems.

My first call for gratitude was knowing that my babies will be a means for me in the hereafter if I was patient. This was enough for me to have my first breakthrough, I cried in gratitude when I read this. I then realised that it was not just me who had to deal with other's problems, I had people around me who had to put up with my bad attitude. My mum, my siblings; and most of all, Zaf, he had to deal with my diva attitude!

After confirmation from the medical team, it was him who had a wife whose body could not keep his babies for the full term and not once he complained about this to me, but I always made sure I complained about him not being literate.

He was someone who naturally looked at the best in most situations in life, he always said "everything does not stay the same in life, things change, every time is not the same" were always his feedback when I complained about him to him. I started to look up to him, I mean this was a man who may have had a harder childhood than me, he came from a broken home, who rarely saw his mum growing up and then lost her when he was a child. He never studied because of the poor education system where he lived and he was not ready to be educated either. This is when I made the next emotional shift around my marriage, as before this society was telling me, "you're too good for him" which was so wrong, I have to write a book on this topic itself.

I had to marry this guy, he had so much of what I did not have, in terms of wisdom and submission to God. I started to look at him and us as a couple, he gives me what I lack and I give him what he lacks...

> "They are as a garment for and you are as a garment for them"
>
> (Quran 2:187)

So here I'm talking, maybe 3 weeks into loss, all this was coming up.

My school friend, Ayesha, who used to visit me frequently to check on me, she told me to read this

> *"Which of the favours of your Lord will you deny?"*
> *(Quran. Surah Rehman)*

I didn't know why I needed to read it, she just said, you will feel better.

More awareness opened up to me, I realised how ungrateful I had been for what I already had.

We decided to stop trying for a baby and focus on us. I had to start living in the present moment. I wasn't suddenly happy, I was still grieving, I was still crying almost every night, yearning for the babies, but I was content, I felt content with resentment to life.

Making this shift was not easy around my family, they didn't have the breakthroughs that I did, they still wanted me to try for another baby. Get help and from my extended family I was the "poor girl" who couldn't have babies; that became my introduction at one time.

I was praying again, and I felt amazing, finally we could focus on our marriage and each other.

Gratitude drove me through this time in my life, I did get some counselling which for me it didn't move me forward and process the grief. I found a coach, and had calls with her which helped me process the loss.

Life was going good, we were going out together, really acknowledging the good we have in our life, I mean, we had problems but with the problems we had so much to be grateful for. So much good also happened since we got married that I overlooked because I was so busy complaining about what's not good. My focus shifted to gratitude and my blessings started to increase as I became more conscious of them…

> *And ˹remember˺ when your Lord proclaimed, 'If you are grateful, I will certainly give you more*
> *(Quran, Surah Ibrahim)*

I can't say this without still being in awe, that 7 weeks after losing our second baby, We conceived!

We didn't plan this and had accepted we should stop trying, but we welcomed with gratitude, by now, I had not attached the fact that I will be happy if I have a child, I was content anyway. This is the key here. God does not want us to be attached to people or things for contentment, feeling contentment is something we need to feel anyway.

I knew there would be good in this, my Lord is merciful. He will do what's best for me in this world and for eternity. I'm grateful for the growth I had, I went back to University, my tutors were ready for more maternity risk assessments.

I had many learnings that came up with losing 2 babies, if those didn't happen, I would have still been in a resentful state, holding onto past negative emotions and causing more harm to my mind, body and the people around me.

I always use this mantra with myself and clients "when you've taken the growth from your problems, the problem disappears."

As a problem is only a problem when it causes us to feel anything less than happy/content, otherwise it is "just a thing we need to do."

"God does not burden a soul beyond what it can bear"
(Surah Baqrah)

In all situations that I've gone through from them to now, I always had the solution to the problem, I just had to remove the mind blocks and become more resourceful within myself to take the required action steps.

So this was my first shift, back then I wasn't actively into self development, I was up and down emotionally for years from then. Until 2014 when I actively started self development by coming across my spiritual mentor who has guided me to self development since then. Now I have a plan to follow, I have a daily routine to follow where by any problems that come, I make myself resourceful enough to solve that problem. So I urge you today to make your shift, It is okay to feel angry or sad, or hurt about a warranted situation but not okay to stay in those mind blocking emotions.

Going back to my third pregnancy, we went through strong in faith and took the required risk management procedures for the medical team, we had our beautiful daughter. We have have been blessed with two now; Our blessings. Alhamdulilah.

Nazreen Zaman - Emotional Mastery Coach.

Website - www.flourishonpurposewithnaz.com
Facebook - https://m.facebook.com/flourishonpurposewithnaz
Instagram - @nazreen_zaman
Email - naz_zaman@outlook.com

17

OMG . . . My Face! The Day my life changed

Oh no! My face felt awful, I could not fully open my eyes. I could not open my mouth properly. I jumped out of bed and rushed to the mirror. Something had happened to my face overnight.

What greeted me in the bathroom mirror was horrific. My whole face was swollen like a football. I had no cheekbones, no chin, it was totally round. My eyes were tiny slits and my nose, well it was totally flat. Panic ran through my veins. Not knowing what to do or wanting anyone to see me looking, as I felt, so, so ugly, I did what most people would do. I hid in my room and worked myself into a depressive storm.

My face was not always like this.

When I was asked to write about my journey I felt that I had a very ordinary one, but then I got thinking about how I came to be where I am right now.

As you know, I am a Physical Health and Mental Wellbeing Coach and right now I am sitting in my upstairs office in front of a large window facing the garden. The sun is streaming through the trees and I feel truly grateful for the journey that has brought me here.

So how *did* I get here?

My mother tells me with a scowl on her face that I was a difficult baby, not the ideal type for a first time mother living away from her close knit family, and having been away from her own mother since the age of eleven. I was constantly sick with diarrhoea and vomiting; a skinny scrawny child that couldn't seem to keep any food down. My mother was at her wits end but my father refused to take me to the regular doctor. You see, my father had recently qualified as a homeopath and he was totally committed to this 'new' way of treating diseases and symptoms. So despite my mother's constant pleas he refused to take me to the conventional doctor and would 'try' one homeopathic remedy after another, wishing that I would soon recover.

Alhumdulillah, I did - but obviously I can't remember when. So let me fast forward to what I can remember. I remember being at primary school which, incidentally, I loved. I also remember feeling envious of some of the children around me. You see, they had sore throats and as a result they would be absent from school for a day or two. I, M*ashaAllah*, was never absent. It's funny the things we long for as a child. I really, really, wished to have a sore throat! The idea of having a raspy voice was enticing. But at the first hint of any symptoms, my father would tell me to open my mouth and pop in a sweet pill. And before I knew it my symptoms were gone.

When we are young we truly take good health for granted.

My school days and subsequent college and university years all passed by without any serious illnesses, A*lhamdulillah*. Over these years, I never paid attention to the constant stream of people that would visit our house with small gifts. My father was such an enthusiastic lover of homeopathy that he would pick up potential "patients" everywhere. I use the word patients very loosely because he never charged anybody, neither for the consultation nor for the homeopathic medicines. I found out, much later on, that he had treated an incredible variety of long term ailments. Without exception, all these 'visitors' had struggled with chronic illnesses, going from doctor to doctor, clinic to clinic without much difference to their symptoms.

I was now in my twenties, staying at my parents' place as my husband had recently got a job in Saudi Arabia and I had to wait for my residency visa to come through. After a while of brewing in my depressive storm on that life changing day, I sheepishly went downstairs, where I was met by my mother. The look on her face spoke a thousand words. A mixture of fear and shock. With panic in her voice she asked me what had I done, why was my face like this? This was followed by my sister who looked at me and exclaimed, "Oh my God, your face looks terrible! What have you done?"

After much discussion, I decided to go to the GP. I had not seen my GP for years since as a family if we had any medical problems, my father would whip out his magical pills. He was always ready with a pill. They all looked exactly the same. They all tasted exactly the same. Nice and sweet.

The GP said it was an allergic reaction and wrote me a prescription.

I took the prescription without collecting the medicine and went home deciding to find a professional homeopath. This pleased my now very worried father. All medical professionals know that it is quite unwise to treat your loved ones, especially during a crisis, as emotions get in the way and patience and logic seem to go out of the window.

Having found a homeopath, I went for the appointment. He gave me some advice and remedies and reassured me that things would get better in due course. *Alhumdulillah* they did.

My face got better albeit very slowly. However, it was too slow for me. My papers had come through. I had been away from my newish husband for several months. He had got a job in the Middle East and, as was the procedure in those days, I had to wait for three months whilst my documents were being verified. It was a long three months and our first time apart since our marriage a year earlier.

The waiting was over. My flight was booked. But I was not happy. I felt scared and very, very ugly. My face was still two times its original size. It was still very round but now my skin was peeling. My face and neck were oozing a sticky clear fluid and I smelt awful. I could smell a horrible odour around me the whole time. I would constantly ask each member of my family, "Do I smell?" "What can you smell?" Their replies were always the same, "I can't smell anything," "You are imagining it," "Honestly, there is no smell."

I was not convinced. Not only did I look ugly, I also smelled bad too! I had no idea how I was going to travel to see my beautiful husband. I was afraid of how he would react. This was going to be a new phase of our life. We were going to be expats in a country where I did not know a single person.

I said goodbye to my family with stinging tears. In those early days, the whole family - and I mean the *whole* family - would turn up to the airport to say goodbye. Usually those airport trips were such fun, but this time it was horrible, as I was consumed with myself, how I looked, how I smelt and what others would think of me.

Earlier, before leaving the house for the airport, my father handed me one of his favourite homeopathic books, *Lectures on Homeopathic Philosophy* and suggested that whilst in KSA I might actually find time to read it.

I devoured the book on the five and a half hour plane journey. It was fascinating. The book presented the concept of health as being in total alignment with nature. I had never realised that sometimes we have stinging tears because of the *type* of tears. I thought my tears were stinging because my face had tiny little cuts. But my face, although it did have cuts, was not the reason my tears stung. It was because of the nature of the discharge. They were, what we homeopaths would refer to, as excoriating discharges, as opposed to bland discharges. Bland discharges don't sting, even if you have cuts. This was just one small realisation of how different our bodies are. We have been designed by the Supreme Creator, Allah Subhana wa talah. Our bodies are designed intelligently and every symptom that we suffer from, has a purpose.

The more I read the book, the more I was grateful that my father had 'grown' us all homeopathically. Wow. *Masha Allah*, I really was lucky. I had forgotten about my swollen weepy face for the duration of the journey. As I came to the end of the book, it was time to prepare for landing.

Having got off the plane I eventually came out of airside. I quickly spotted my husband. He was standing in anticipation looking wonderful and happy, but I don't think he had seen me. I went up to him and he jolted back in shock. He had not recognised me. He knew that I had been suffering from an 'allergy' of some sort but obviously had not realised how bad it was. His eyes welled up with tears and he gave me a big hug. We walked to the car holding hands tightly. It was a long emotional journey to my new home which was beautiful and spacious.

Now, let me fast forward. *Alhumdulillah* my face improved. I became more interested in health and wellbeing and started reading and listening to all things medical. My fascination with health continued with my new friends and their families. I was intrigued by their health stories and how they got to where they were.

I decided that I really wanted to study homeopathy and, as fate would have it, we returned to the UK some years later where I started on a course. I have to say, without exception, I loved every single day of it. I felt like a sponge soaking it all up and my homeopath was such an encouraging person that, with his and my fathers' help, I gained confidence in prescribing medicines even before I was fully qualified. That was over twenty years ago.

Since then, I have treated hundreds of people from all countries and walks of life with a huge variety of ailments, although now my speciality is mainly but not exclusively treating anxiety. Healing my client's mental and emotional disturbances.

Anxiety comes in many forms. Worries about the future, worries about one's finances, worries about how you look, worries about what other people think of you, worries about what you say, in case you hurt someone, worries about showing your true feelings, in case others think badly of you, worries about your health, worries about your children's health, their education, their upbringing, so, so many worries. There are an infinite number of things we could worry about but what they all have in common is that they arise from the power of thought.

Once I understood the power of thought and that at each moment we are only ever feeling our thinking, something changed for me. It was strange. Everything had changed and yet nothing had changed around me. I had changed from the inside. I realised that nothing on the outside could affect how I felt.

By now, how I viewed illnesses including any of my own was different. I gained a deep understanding of the impact of our mental and emotional state on our physical health. I now show my clients how to deal with their problems. I treat them successfully *mashaAllah* with homeopathy and coaching and my clients end up with many new insights.

I can totally relate to all those patients out there suffering from skin problems and those with anxiety. I help them to understand the cause of their symptoms and show them how to deal with their anxious thought forests.

My work is so rewarding *Alhamdulillah.* I help people get energised and become healthy by bringing about change. A change that can alter your life. A change to become re-empowered. New possibilities become tangible realities. All because my clients can now see life for what it really is. Life from the inside out. Life without fear. Life without anxiety. Life without suffering, *insha Allah.*

I would love to help you with your journey and alleviate your suffering, so that you too can live life from the inside out. You can contact me via raha@rahahf.com to gain a new perspective and to take charge of your thoughts, your life and *God willing* regain complete wellness.

Raha H Farnsworth - Physical and Wellbeing Coach

Instagram - @rahahf7
Website - www.rahahf.com
Free Gift - www.rahahf.com/gift
Facebook - www.facebook.com/raha.farns

17

When I gave myself permission to be ME...

I'm the eldest of four children, 3 girls and 1 boy. My parents came to England from Mauritius and settled in Essex in the 70s. They were both in the nursing care profession and looked after elderly and vulnerable patients in hospitals and then later in care homes. Both were uneducated and both my parents worked full time to send money back home.

I lived in a little town in Essex. Growing up in a very Conservative, British society I struggled to reconcile my faith and culture with my surroundings. I attended a Church of England primary school and there I was 'Faz' but at home I was Faranaz. Nevertheless, I loved school and at times I was eager to show my differences but at other times I just wanted to fit in.

Education was a big thing for my mum and if I could breathe I could go to school even if I wasn't feeling well! Surprisingly my dad was the lenient parent when it came to education but in all other matters he was the boss and had that stare that could stop me dead in my tracks. It was in no small part down to my mum that I was the first in my family to go to university to read French and Business Studies at Queen Mary & Westfield college, University of London.

2 months into my 2nd year I became ill. I was violently sick and had severe diarrhoea to the point that I was so weak and dehydrated my dad had to carry me to the toilet. My GP, a lovely Muslim man, suggested

going straight to A&E. It was unknown what was making me so ill and so I was admitted to hospital. During the night rounds a local Muslim Doctor noticed my file and rang the alarm. She woke me up and told me that I needed to be taken to surgery straight away. It all happened so quickly. My parents had been called and I was prepped within an hour. I was sent to have investigative surgery but during the op my appendix burst. This led to peritonitis which meant that all my organs began to fail as the peritoneum envelopes everything in your body. My body shut down and I was in a coma for 9 days. The doctors told my parents I had a 5% chance of survival and that it was now in God's hands.

My younger siblings and friends prayed for me and made dua and my mum fought with the doctors when they suggested turning the life support machines off. By the grace and mercy of Allah I awoke from the coma 9 days later completely unaware of what had happened. I thought I had been out of it for a few hours only. The time in the coma had led some of my hair to die and the skin on my hands and feet was peeling off in large sheets.

I was transferred to White Chapel Hospital where I needed a further operation because I had developed an infection in my kidneys. After this op I was told that my organs were all badly damaged and that during surgery my right ovary had been removed and the fallopian tube to my left ovary was badly damaged. I was told at 19 years old that It would be near enough impossible for me to have children naturally.

With the duas of my parents, I was out of hospital exactly one month after I had gone in. I couldn't walk properly and the question of dialysis was raised but Alhamdulillah by the end of the year I had returned to my part time job, I could walk properly and all my organs (except my reproductive system) were absolutely fine.

I tried to return to university that year but I felt I'd missed too much. I continued working as a care assistant looking after people with learning disabilities and mental health issues and tried to get back to normal. I felt really unsettled and out of sorts and longed for some stability and security so I did what I thought would make me feel stable and secure…I got married! Much to my parents' dismay, they wanted me to finish university and get a job but I wanted to be a wife because I felt that would help me feel rooted. In the end they gave in and I had a 5-day circus wedding. Being the eldest and first child to get married, they invited everyone they'd ever met to the wedding. My husband was also the eldest of a very big family, born and brought up in Mauritius and passportless!

I was lucky in many ways that his parents had bought a house which was financed by letting out rooms to lodgers. I was never a fussy or a picky person and I marvel now about how I didn't really think anything of having no bedroom furniture or even a real bedroom for the first year of marriage. I spent my wedding night on a mattress in the loft 'converted' by my husband who was a bit of a bob the builder but not as good.

I returned to university after getting married and assumed my husband would return to his studies but he never did as his visa had expired and there were restrictions as to working and studying... he did neither whilst I worked and studied full time. I found the first year of marriage hard and thought if I took another year off uni to concentrate on finding my groove and helping my husband find his that it would be ok. I took a year off and worked full time and overtime. My husband 'grooved' and did little else. I did go back to complete my studies and graduated without honours and only a lower second class degree. Not wanting to leave my husband behind I encouraged him to get back to his studies but he wasn't interested. He had his parents' house and rental income from the lodgers so he was ok. I wasn't. I continued in education and completed a Master's degree in Human Resource Management whilst continuing to work full time. My husband knew I couldn't have children naturally and took me on anyway. I felt indebted to him for that and felt I owed it to him to stay... even when he hit me. It was very subtle and it wasn't until very recently that I realised I was a victim of domestic violence and manipulation. A slap here, tap there, degrading me in front of his family, causing a scene when I wanted to visit mine, never coming with me to family gatherings which led me to not going out much because everyone else was with their partner and I was sick of being asked where he was.

When I broached the subject of fertility treatment his response was very much that's your gig. He never came with me to any appointments except for once when the fertility nurse said they treat the couple not just one person. His anger and moods grew worse the more he stayed at home wondering what I was doing all day whilst I was at work or at uni. He grew more and more jealous and suspicious and his anger outbursts were always unannounced and unprovoked. He got less worried about who saw and shouted and hit me in front of his parents and my younger sisters. He was too much of a coward to really hit me hard but managed to give me a black eye and stubbed a cigarette out in my face. Both times I covered for him and said I'd walked into a door or fallen down. I did this not because I loved him but because I felt sorry for him and I also felt that because I had pushed to get married I couldn't back out now. I'd made my bed…I thought I had hidden it really well from my family but they knew something was wrong, they just didn't want to say anything because I hadn't.

In the 7 years we were married my husband worked for 6 weeks and used the money he earned to go on holiday. I paid for everything in the house, the mortgage, bought him cars, bought food, bought tools and materials for the house and shared my home with lodgers the whole time. After I finished my Master's degree I was sick of waiting for him to do anything so I got another job to plump up my cv. I began a job as a check-in agent for British Airways at Gatwick Airport.

During this time, I was receiving fertility treatment and 'we' were trying for a baby. I began to pray more during this time and asked Allah for me to be happy with my husband and to be grateful for what I have and not crave what I don't. I thought a baby would help us and that he would see a child as someone to work and grow up for.

One day I asked him if he would like a house of our own. He laughed and said he had a house. I thought this was really weird because his parents had worked really hard and they were still working in Mauritius. He just said they have to die sometime and then it would be his! I couldn't believe I'd been so stupid. My husband wasn't an inherently nasty man. He had anger and self-confidence issues but his outlook on life was so different to mine.

I wanted to have children and live in a house we had both worked together to buy. I was told I needed IVF and something clicked at that moment. I didn't want kids with him. I didn't want to be with him but I felt I worthless. Who else would want me?

I spent the next few months praying harder and harder to be happy and content... I was on a check in desk one day and someone said something really funny. I looked up and was met with a stunning smile and beautiful green eyes. All that day I kept bumping into those eyes. That evening I went out with my training class for dinner after negotiating a strict curfew with my husband. When I got there, Green eyes was there and I legged it to the loo. I didn't know what was wrong with me but I literally couldn't stand. My heart was racing and my heart was pumping. I tried to compose myself and walked back out. I sat with my friends and then green eyes appears out of nowhere. We begin to talk and 4 hours later I realise my life is going to change. Green eyes is a half Palestinian, divorced, father of 3 and a Muslim.

I went home that evening and questioned my life. I would never have in a million years have spoken so openly with a stranger, let alone divulge my most inner feelings. I went to work the next morning after a telling off from my husband for being an hour late. I was so tired from the worry and all the thoughts rushing around my head, but I knew that my life was about to change.

I came home and told my husband I was leaving him and went to my parents' house. I told my parents I couldn't do it anymore and my dad was amazing, he said stay home as long as I want. My mum wasn't so supportive but she was ok. I think for her it was more about what would people think.

That night I went to work at the care home. my phone rang. It was green eyes. His name is Tarek. I told him I'd left my husband and he asked why. My answer was, I stayed for 7 years because of what I didn't feel then, I'm leaving because of what I do now. The fact that I allowed myself to 'feel' anything for anyone whilst being married scared me because that should be sacred to marriage. Feeling it for someone else just made me realise that I had crossed a boundary for myself and I couldn't turn back. He said, well if you're not going to be married to him then, will you marry me? I said yes.

In my head it was easy. I don't want to be with my husband, he knows that so we'll get divorced. In reality it wasn't so plain sailing. I was tricked into attending what can only be described as a hostage marriage resolution meeting and after hours of being 'asked' to reconsider my decision, it was blatantly obvious that I wasn't going to be allowed to leave until I'd said I was going to go back. I finally said I would just like to get away and I was presented with a massive bunch of flowers which I chucked at my husband once I was outside.

I am not proud of the way I handled things. My Husband told me he would change, get a job, go to fertility meetings but I couldn't go back. I even continued paying the bills for a year after I left out of guilt and I have prayed for forgiveness many times. When we divorced I asked him to repay the money I had given to him from my student loan and the money I had paid in mortgage payments. He was reluctant at first and said I had taken more out of the marriage than I'd put in. I explained he had British citizenship through me, cars and all sorts. When he revoked the first talaaq he gave, I told him I'd met someone else in the hopes that he would be so angered he'd leave me straight away. It took a while but I left with only my car and a few bags of clothes and never looked back.

Moving back in my parents was a hard adjustment to make and for 6 months I tried to convince them to meet Tarek. They didn't like that he was a white Arab and had 3 children. My dad said I couldn't trust dodgy Arabs and my mum said I needed to choose between Tarek and her. After a night long 'discussion' I said that I was not prepared to lose or give up either and that I would have both. They just rolled their eyes.

During this time Tarek and I became Air cabin crew for BA and went off around the world and I moved out of my parents' house to live closer to work. My mum came round after she had a dream that he was right for me and then she made my dad meet him. She decided that a 'small' family gathering was the most opportune time to make Tarek's introduction. They got on like a house on fire, Subhanallah!

I got divorced (talaq) and married Tarek exactly a year to the day we met. We got married with our closest family in one day (90 on my side, 10 on his!) and it was the most perfect day in my life. I had told him that I couldn't have children and he loved me anyway. We went to fertility meetings together and worked together to buy our home. I had my step children over every other weekend and my life was blessed.

We'd just bought our house and were saving up for IVF when I found out my good friend was pregnant. I was sincerely pleased for her and I remember making dua for her to have an easy pregnancy. A few days later it was my birthday and I felt a bit ill. I jokingly asked Tarek to get me a pregnancy test. He returned in 5 minutes with one! That was May 28th 2007, the day I found out I was pregnant! Subhanallah I had fallen pregnant naturally and I gave birth to our first child on February 1st 2008.

After having my first born, Zakariya, I felt like I needed to show Allah my gratitude in more ways than dua. I began to wear the hijab as a thank you. I was the only uk based BA crew to wear the hijab and salwar kameez. Tarek and I now have 4 children and have been married over 15 years. I am a Parent and Child Coach and my life is a blessed one, Alhamdulillah.

I do not hate my ex-husband. The life we had feels like it was lived by someone else. He asked me for forgiveness a few years after we divorced and apologised for his behaviour. I just felt sorry for him and wished him well. I pray he finds peace and happiness. He remarried too but that didn't last very long. He's now remarried again, perhaps 3rd time lucky!

Farah Halabi - Parenting Coach. Helping stressed out mums uncover their awesomeness leading them to parent in peace, not in pieces.

Facebook - www.facebook.com/farah.halabi14
Instagram - @farah_parenting_in_peace_coach
Email - connect@farahhalabi.com
Website - www.farahhalabi.com

17

Wrestles With My Mind

I was 5 years old when I became aware of my social anxiety. I had no name for it but I knew I felt fear and panic around large numbers of people. My parents were very sociable people and their culture (Alexandrian-Egyptians) is a culture that prides itself on hospitality and a great sense of humour. Their culture includes physical contact, hugs, kisses hello and goodbye, pats on the back and little to no personal space, all of which caused me huge discomfort.

I soon learned to adapt to what was expected of me. I gave the impression that I was a confident extrovert, I complemented people constantly to win their approval and the approval of my parents, especially my mother. She was a social whirlwind. My house growing up was always full of guests and they were fed nothing less than a banquet of Egyptian and Middle Eastern dishes every time.

My environment was not designed to suit my mental health. My efforts to "fit-in" left me exhausted, but like so many other sufferers I learned ways to disguise my stress and anxiety. I developed an outer image of strength, wit, confidence and extreme kindness. I always put others needs before my own. The perfectionist in me took the facade to another level. This was the path I chose for myself, thinking I had no choice. My mother had very high standards and it became clear to me that I would have to be "perfect" to meet her expectations and win her approval.

My journey however, taught me that there is no "perfect" and her approval would never really ever be mine to keep for long.

My parents divorced when I was 12 years old. As a child in my very early teens I blamed myself, as children often do. Their divorce was very messy. A bitter battle through the courts and many attempts to turn me against one-another. They spoke cruelly of each other to me, not realising that by tearing each other down, they were tearing me apart.

The court granted Sunday visitations with my Dad which consisted of him ranting and raving about how unfairly the court case was going, how my mother was using false evidence against him and accusing him of things he was innocent of.

Often solicitors letters were shown to me as evidence of his truthfulness. Not exactly a fun way to spend my Sundays.

Upon returning home after visiting my Dad I was met at the door by my mother with a list of questions. "What did he say, did he ask about x, y and z? What was your answer? And on and on. I realised that whatever answer I gave would not be the right one. I was often met with anger and sometimes a week or two of the silent treatment for "saying the wrong things". I wondered if it was even possible to ever say the right thing when your parents were bitter enemies. I think not.

I was an only child, so you can imagine the loneliness I felt when at times I literally had no one to talk to or share an understanding look with or even blame for things going wrong as siblings do sometimes.

During my parents divorce I was aware that I was losing my self. My mental health was taking me to places I couldn't understand. My mind found ways of coping that were just not understood by people around me or even myself for that matter. I knew I was disconnecting with myself but I had no idea what to do about it. I knew if I described my symptoms to my mother she would share them with her solicitor, and I would hear about it from my Dad. So I learned to keep quiet and internalise everything. This caused me to disconnect with myself. I became numb.

This was my earliest experience of **depression.**

When you constantly ignore your feelings, show no respect to your own needs and give up your right to be heard, the doors of despair open allowing depression to manifest. Again, I didn't know at the time that there was a name for what I was feeling or what I was going through, but I was aware that something wasn't right. In fact, something was very wrong.

I wanted to disappear but I couldn't. Nothing brought me pleasure, even the sunniest of days. I continued to go through the motions, "people-pleasing". I did what was expected of me. I got myself through the day, not particularly grateful for a new one. I noticed we didn't have so many visitors any more. Again a symptom of "the divorce".

I wanted to sleep and never wake up. I never felt suicidal but I just didn't want "to be" any more.

My Dad, whom I had enjoyed a good relationship with earlier in my life became bitter, angry and very distant. I took this to mean "I am unlovable". I interpreted my Dad's negative behaviour and lack of expression to mean "I must be difficult to love" or even "unworthy of love". This manifested in me attracting men who were not capable of expressing themselves or their feelings.

At 19 years old I married a good man who struggled to express himself. I thought I deserved nothing more. You can imagine how that ended. Yes after 20 years I left. Why? Because I finally realised that I shouldn't be in a marriage or any kind of relationship if I am disconnected with myself and am not capable of loving myself or even understanding who I am. I also realised that this was a toxic relationship that was holding me back and stunting my growth instead of nurturing me and allowing me to thrive.

I struggled with my mental health and **wrestled with my mind** for around 30 years of my life, trying to make a dysfunctional marriage work, trying to win my mothers approval, trying to get my Dad to love me, trying to fit-in to an impossible culture for my condition, trying to be someone I am not, trying to make everybody happy and comfortable, but not myself, trying, trying, trying.....

I finally reached breaking point at 40 years old. By now I had 4 children. I was a mother, wife, daughter, half-sister to two young men, step-daughter to a woman I couldn't acknowledge or accept as she represented the hate between my parents(in my mind), and I was a friend. A very good supportive friend according to my friends. I was all those things, but I had no idea who I was. None. My life had been consumed by loving and caring for others at the expense of myself and my mental health.

My breaking point manifested itself in different ways. I went from comfort eating to extreme fitness. I went from not speaking to anybody for weeks to socialising daily. I went from being afraid to leave the house to travelling. I guess extremes made me feel alive. I was proving to myself that I wasn't a failure. Until I gradually realised that I couldn't function any longer. It took all my mental and physical strength to get out of bed in the mornings. I took the kids to school, went home, back to bed until it was time to pick them up in the afternoon. I was the kind of person that felt panic if my day wasn't very busy with a long to do list. Now I found myself unable to even look in the mirror.

I reached out to a friend of mine who told me something that changed my life. Until that point, ending my marriage was not even a consideration. I vowed to never put my children through what I had gone through. I hid my pain to give them a happy childhood and family-life. I had decided that as a mother, my children came first. My needs and happiness were not important if they conflicted with their needs and happiness. I believed that a "happy life" was 2 parents under the same roof for the children's sake, even if their was no happiness to speak of.

My friend told me how when she was in her teens her parents announced that they had decided to separate. My friend and her siblings didn't take this news very well. In-fact they stopped talking to their parents and made it very clear they would not accept this. Due to their reaction, my friends parents decided to stay together in a loveless and cold marriage. Not only was it loveless, it was dead, but they stayed together for the sake of the children. This sounded all too familiar.

Years later, my friend told me, that she wished to God that her parents had divorced when they wanted to. She regretted standing in their way and told me that there is nothing worse than growing up in a household with parents who don't love each other. In a house where negative energy and cold lovelessness consumed everything. Where every sentence was passive aggressive, every word sarcastic with no humour, where every look was bitter. Children feel everything. We think we are hiding the truth, but they know when there is no love.

I made the decision to end my marriage but I knew I had a huge battle to fight. Not with my husband but with people from my community, friends and family. Most of all my mother. I knew that my reasons were not good enough to convince her. There was no physical violence. No cheating. No drinking. What possible excuse could I have.

Meanwhile I knew that to make a huge decision like ending my marriage I would need strength both mental, spiritual and emotional. I connected with a friend of mine who although was in education, counselled women who had disconnected with themselves and felt lost. I asked her for guidance and she took me through an exercise that reconnected me and started me on my journey of self-discovery and self-love.

She asked me to close my eyes and relax. To take deep breaths and to allow my mind to go back in time to a moment when I was a child and was feeling hurt and abandoned. I remembered myself as a 9 year old girl who had just been beaten by my mother for being "disobedient".

My friend asked me if anyone in that moment or on that day had comforted me or helped me in any way, I said no.

My friend then asked me to hold the hand of my 9 year old self and invite her to sit on my "adult" lap. I hugged my 9 year old self and told her all the things I wished someone had said to me at the time. I comforted her and told her that she was beautiful and deserved love and respect. I told her she was special and promised her that I would always be there for her. I told her I loved her.

From that moment, everything changed for me. I finally connected with my self. I did that exercise many times since that day and each time I could feel a shift. I felt a deep respect for myself that I never felt before. I realised that I am a beautiful person worthy of love. I realised that my feelings did matter and my voice needed to be heard. I learned that I can heal myself by going back in time in my mind and giving myself what I needed. I don't have to wait for an apology from others to begin healing myself. Most people don't feel the need to apologise and most people have moved on.

I learned that day that I had the power within me all along to heal myself, love myself and tell myself all those things I had longed to hear from my parents and others. I learned that my approval is enough. My love is validation enough. The day I hugged my 9 year old self was the day I stopped neglecting myself. The day I connected with my 9 year old self was the day my journey to mental health and emotional healing began.

Aya Attia - Mental Health Advocate. Mindset and Wellness Coach, Personal Trainer, Proud Mum, Author and Teacher.

Instagram - @ayafitness
Email - ytaya2001@yahoo.com
Facebook - www.facebook.com/ayafitness

17

Perseverance can take you anywhere

When life gives you lemons you make lemonade right? Well I did something like that but replaced the lemons with eggs, flour, sugar and butter. I started baking in 2010 it was something I admired but never had the time or knack for, this was new territory and I was ready.

So, baking as a hobby was great, I would wait till the evening when the husband got home eagerly passed the kids over and experimented lots of recipes and ideas I would write down during the day. Cakes were made in different sizes shapes and flavours for friends and family. Every time I visited family, or someone popped round I would bake a cake and decorate. This continued till I had a relative over who suggested I should sell my cakes, sell my cake I thought they were not good enough for me to sell to the public. Where would I start? I'm not business savvy, I don't even know how to sell! I don't have a shop a name or any funds?

Looking at my three kids Haaris, Zohaib and Inayah were growing up so fast and with them so were their needs, the weekly budget was just getting tighter and tighter. Taking everything into consideration I spoke to my husband about selling cakes, he laughed it off and thought the same as me HOW? With no knowledge of the business world, no funds and no proper support I was a little defeated, I went to sleep that night thinking this will never happen.

I still remember it was a Thursday I woke up and felt I had to do this. Whatever it takes, call me stupid but I wanted this. I thought one day it would change my life and my families, a little optimistic I know but I'm a dreamer and I was dreaming big.

Fast forward a few weeks and I opened a Facebook page. I put on all the cakes I had made so far in my journey I was so proud of myself. Looking back at my work now, it was so awful so wonky and I see the progress. I went on to vista print and invested in some simple business cards. And that was it I could feel it, this started the rush of excitement for what was to come, the thrill of starting a small business on my own.

Two years on and I was selling cakes, I was making money, but the excitement and the thrill had left. I just didn't see much growth, I was making cakes but, in my eyes, not making much improvement on the design side or the income side. The reality of raising three kids running a house tending to an extended family and trying to make my dream come to life was all getting way too much as well as not enough of an income after putting all those hours in. I was exhausted to say the least. I Wanted to quit many times in the coming months but I persevered and kept going selling two tiers cakes at £60 no wonder I wasn't making enough. I couldn't share the disappointment I felt with my better half I felt like it would be a told you so, it was as if this wasn't a business I was running more of a hobby that just covered the costs, still frustrated I pushed on.

Sitting one evening flicking through my phone I had an idea to type how to price cakes on You Tube, lo and behold so much info on how to price and run a cake business. Why didn't I do this earlier! I told you I wasn't business savvy I just loved baking and putting a smile on peoples faces. I buckled down that evening with a pen and paper and made as many notes as I could and took in lots of info and made a costing list and then a proper price list, something I had never done before. Suddenly I was stimulated again, the passion the love and thrill were returning. I decide to sell at school fairs to get my name out I did free cakes for charities, free cakes for a few Instagram influencers who promised a huge following but no I was still stuck but this time even worse off than before. I started to lose my original customers because I raised prices. Seeing other bakers who started after me or alongside me flourish was disheartening, I felt like a failure.

I closed my shop on Instagram and that was it for a good few weeks. My sisters pleaded for me not to, but I was fed up and frustrated with the whole process, I was done.

During the next few weeks I focused on everything else in my life, my father's health deteriorated and my priorities changed. Everything in my life was turned upside down. Nothing else mattered but my father. My Abu ji (dad) didn't make it. For us that was it life ceased to exist, happiness was nowhere in sight, after losing my mother in 2001 dad was all we had. How do you make a come back from so much heart ache? I mourned my dad for months. I guess I'm still in mourning, but I guess time is a healer and you begin to come to terms with life.

Going through my Instagram I noticed I had a few unopened messages I thought they would be condolence messages, but these were from random people praising my cakes asking me why I closed, how they don't want to go elsewhere for their cakes. It hit me THEY WANTED MY CAKES and not a handful 20 odd customers. Baking when I started was an escape mechanism for me, away from the housework, away from the kids and everything else. Just me in my little kitchen enjoying my own company and doing what I loved. I needed that again in my life I needed some time alone, some time to ignite my love for creating again.

So, I took the plunge for the second time this time with a little more experience and a lot more knowledge a know how of the cake business. I was going to price everything up set up a professional page get a proper logo and invest in myself to learn some invaluable skills. Investing in new tools gave me a new mindset and new sense of belief in myself. And then I got it, it's not about how beautiful my cakes are (I mean thats a part of it). I need to believe in myself and my ability, this thought bought about a new hope and new passion for baking that

I never felt before. I stuck to the prices. I didn't under charge from that day onwards and I believed the right customers would come along. Slowly but surely this started to happen, and I was happy with the way things were going I was finally making a profit. I was getting better at designing and better at creating and giving a clean finish to my cakes. So, I set out to look for cake classes that would help me reach the finish that I wanted. It's a small world I was flicking through my WhatsApp stories when I came across a cake a wedding cake picture, it looked stunning exactly the sort of finish I wanted on my cakes. I messaged the lady and asked who made the cake and she said it was her sister in law. I took the details and emailed this lady she turned out to be a fellow baker who's children attended the same school my children did, what a coincidence. I felt like the it was meant to be...

Tahira turned out to be a great blessing for me, she not only taught me how to create beautiful cakes, she did it all for free! Just to help a new business grow. What a wonderful human. From that day I started with confidence and created many beautiful cakes, the more I created the more I fell in love with baking and creating cakes which was great as far my passion goes. But I was a small business and customers looked bleak. I only got orders for small cakes and a few here and there nothing sufficient enough to make any sort of profit. All that confidence and pride slowly started fading once more, left with yet another dilemma I decided to call it quits until my sister convinced me otherwise. You really don't know how far you have come until you see it from someone else's perspective. She gave a look in from the outside and supported me and told me I under no circumstance can give up this dream I had of mine and especially not after coming this far.

I think I got a bit of a big break when an influential Instagramer contacted me out of the blue for his daughters first birthday cake. To say I was shocked is an understatement I was in awe he could have gone with anyone, but he came to me, he obviously saw something I was missing. I decided to give him a discount on the cake to create something big and spectacular to show off all my new learned skills that I hadn't utilised yet. I created a four-tier pink white and gold cake. Delivered it to his house and set it up. When I saw the reaction his wife had to the cake I was in tears. Someone was in tears due to my cake WOW.

Something clicked that day, and something changed in me I don't know what, but I found a new belief in myself. That day was the biggest turning point in my baking carrier. I got up the next morning chased the council again and begged for them to inspect asap. They had left me hanging for far too long. Along side sorting out the inspection I contacted wedding cake exhibitionists and booked two of the major shows for the following year.

This journey is still going its not going to come to an end yet hopefully. I'm learning as I go, I pick up things as I go and I'm creating a new sense of belief in myself and my abilities as I go. But that's the best part about the process its not the getting there it's the journey in between. Self-doubt, lack of knowledge and perfectionism took a lot out of me, it left me quiet bare at times but you know what? I got up every time stronger than the last, because if I hadn't, I wouldn't have met some of the most amazing people I have met in my life. I have come across some amazingly generous people; I have come across some souls that have blown me away with how much love they have to give. I've had myself supported by complete strangers who have never met me, there was this one customer and the cake was to be delivered in Mayfair London, she messaged me just before I left to ask if everything was fine, I responded with as well as can be and I really hope you like the cake. Her response was amazing she told me to take a look at my work and let her know if I was proud of it, I said yes and she said that's, it will be perfect! For her she might have just said those words for me, but they were the most important and confident boosting words ever.

I've not looked back and am hoping to take this business to new heights. I manage a small business and its booming so far, I look after three kids and I manage a house which include cooking, cleaning and the rest of it. But I will not back down and achieve what I need with patience and time. I will be where I need to be when its my time to shine I will.....

Shezana Majeed - Founder of The Vanilla Cake Shop,

Instagram - @vanilacakeshop

17

Pains Of Womanhood

The year is 1976 it's the 30th day of July, a tiny baby is being born. She is a baby girl. She is beautiful and she is worthy of love. Within a few days she has contracted the worst strain of German measles. Her mother and grandparents are so worried about her. They don't know what to do. She eventually ends up in an intensive care unit within two weeks of being born, and she spends the next six months in the intensive care unit. The baby I describe is me. And this is my journey through health.

As a young child I started my period very early at the age of 10 years old. Ever since I started my periods I have bled heavily to the point where I had to wear two sanitary pads and a tampon, and I still bled through my clothes. With the heavy bleeding came a lot of pain in my back, my stomach and in my reproductive areas. On top of that I used to suffer really bad headaches and eventually I became very anaemic. Later on this period pain and the prolonged periods lasting between seven and 10 days went on to cause numerous issues in my life, which included endometriosis, adhesions in my reproductive area, and a long-lasting battle with fibroids.

I suffered with fibroids for the best part of nearly 20 years of my life. Never did I ever imagine that there would be a natural cure for fibroids. At the time everybody that I spoke to just kept telling me that there was nothing more they could do for me especially the medical profession. From my own personal recollection I remember having at least four operations just to remove the huge fibroids that were making me look pregnant even when I wasn't. At one stage my stomach actually resembled that of a six-month pregnancy.

The heavy bleeding and prolonged period pains persisted throughout my 20s and early 30s. It eventually came to a head one year shortly after Christmas day, when my daughter who was around the age of 13 at the time found me laying on my bathroom floor in a pool of blood cradling myself like a baby that was about to be born. I was in so much pain she took one look at my face and one look at my surroundings and decided to call her grandmother. My mother turned up to the house and an ambulance was called, and before I knew it I was in the accident and emergency department of Stepping Hill Hospital. The bleeding and pain was so severe that I had passed out on the bathroom floor unable to move, the ambulance men had to carry me out on a stretcher.

Upon arrival to the hospital I was examined by a Doctor Who then gave me the devastating news that the fibroids they had removed only a few months ago had actually grown back. This time they were more aggressive than ever. I was told by my consultant that the only options I had open to me, were either I have another operation to remove the fibroids with no guarantee that they won't grow back again, or I would have to have an operation in order to remove my uterus. I was also told that this operation would then mean that I could never have children again, and within a few months or even years I will have to start taking HRT (Hormone Replacement Treatment) to balance my hormones.

Bearing the state of mind that I was in at the time I was ever so confused and wasn't sure which decision to make. Whichever decision I made would continue to affect me for the rest of my life. I consulted my boyfriend at the time, as he already had three children, he was not very keen on having any more children. However I went on to think about the fact that there was still almost a 15-year age gap between us and I still really wanted to have children. Even if it wasn't with him. At this point I had already had two successful pregnancies. My first child a boy called Chris, died at a very young age of 14 months old from a cot death. My second child a girl named Olivia was now 13 years old. I still felt like I did not want anybody to take away the option of me having children in the future. However at the same time I really could not bear the thought of continuing my life with the prolonged anaemia from the heavy bleeding as a result of having fibroids.

To this day I still believe that my condition at the time, of prolonged heavy bleeding and fibroids was responsible for the breakdown of my relationship at the time. I gradually became this miserable person who didn't want to go out socially because I literally could not be out for more than two hours before bleeding through everything including my clothes. I could only wear black clothes. My wardrobe was just full of black clothes. I could not bear the thought of wearing anything with colour in case it showed through the bleeding. If I sat down in one place for more than two hours I was frightened of getting up because every time I stood up I had to look back at the chair where I would often see the a patch of blood from where I had bled through everything.

Roll on the next day in hospital, this was now day two and I was still unable to make a decision either way. After much deliberation, I eventually made the decision that I could no longer live the way that I was living. Heavy bleeding, prolonged period pains, and fibroids had literally taken over my life and turned me into such a miserable negative person. Something that I would never wish on anybody else. When my consultant came to do the rounds, I signed the consent form, and I signed away any chance I ever had of ever having any more children. And with one stroke of a pen my uterus was gone… Just like that!

I remember the day I was wheeled down to the operating theatre. I was so emotional, so confused, and so tearful. Even though I'm trying to hold back the tears as much as possible to keep everybody else around me so strong. The first thing I remember after coming round from the operation, was just tears. I actually woke up in the recovery room crying my eyes out like I've never cried before and I just could not stop crying.

A follow-up appointment with my own GP then revealed that I would have to take HRT at some point in the next few months or the next few years for the rest of my life. I remember saying to my GP that there is no way on earth I am ever going to go on HRT. And to this day, I do not take hormone replacement pills or any form of HRT. I manage my health and my hormones simply through the use of food as medicine. This is what I teach and this is what I believe in. And that is how my journey in to writing the period Protocol began, by losing my uterus, and then later doing the research to find out that I actually did not have to have the operation, fibroids and heavy prolonged periods are actually treatable naturally without modern day medicine or brutal hospital operations that leave you without a Uterus, and for some women in some cases their ovaries are also removed. Even though this was not the case for me as my ovaries were left intact.

The work that I do now aims to inspire and empower women to heal the world and heal each other naturally. This is why I feel so passionately about gifting each and every single woman in this world with the gift of my e-book, The Period Protocol so that they can take their health into their own hands and learn the very simple methods that they can do, starting today, in order to help them get rid of the issues that they face during each monthly cycle. Period pains, heavy bleeding, prolonged periods, and getting hormonal prior to your period is not the normal way of life.

Before writing this book I actually tried this protocol on a number of family members and friends who suffered with long prolonged period pains and on top of that they were extremely hormonal at least a week or two before they came on their periods. This of course did not just affect their health but also went on to affect their relationships, their work, and other aspects of their social life. The protocol that I gave them and the protocol that I'm about to give you changed these women's lives forever. Not only did they get rid of the hormonal tendencies, and premenstrual tension, but they were also able to significantly reduce the blood flow to just spotting, and they also reduced the number of days they were on a period.

Some of the women experiencing a period between seven and 10 days were able to reduce that to between three and four days of just spotting with no pain and no symptoms that they were even coming on a period. You too can benefit from this very simple protocol that I am now going to provide you.

There is no catch as to why this protocol is free. All I ask is that you share the link from where you got this protocol with your friends, family and loved ones. On top of that I would very much appreciate it if you could give me some feedback, and a testimonial if possible. By sharing your period story you will also be helping other women around the world. Many women do not want to talk about issues they have with their reproductive systems, because we have been taught to be extremely embarrassed about talking about such issues. However my belief is that the more stories we share, the more we can actually help each other. So please remember to share far and wide, your period story will also be helping other women around the world.

So just to recap, heavy prolonged period pain affects millions of women across the world. We need to break the silence in order to overcome this health challenge. My experience ended up on a hysterectomy but yours doesn't have to, and that's why I have launched the One Million Women Appeal, so that I can help as many women as possible around the world by allowing them to download my Period Protocol for FREE at this link: https://www.venus-club.org/heavy-period-protocol

Please share the link far and wide so that together we can help each other to heal. Apart from giving birth, there is nothing more beautiful and powerful than women who inspire and empower each other with knowledge. "Be The Change You Want To see In This World" Gandi

Namaste

With Love and Gratitude,

Helen Nachintu - Natural Health Coach & Mentor
Website - www.venus-club.org
About Helen Nachintu: https://www.venus-club.org/about-helen-nachintu

Period Protocol FREE Download: https://www.venus-club.org/heavy-period-protocol

Facebook - https://www.facebook.com/venusclubhealth/
Twitter - https://twitter.com/venusclubhealth
Linkedin - https://www.linkedin.com/in/helen-nachintu-85aa7a38/
Instagram - https://www.instagram.com/venusclubhealth/
Youtube - https://www.youtube.com/channel/UCY6SqLQdOop4SaKfyM3wZhg?view_as=subscriber
Pinterest - https://www.pinterest.co.uk/VenusClubHealth/

17

Resilient to find true love

What makes you want to jump out of bed happily every day? Do you have to drag yourself out of the bed to brace the day? Or does the very thought of starting with a brand new day fills you with energy?

As a young girl, I used to ponder upon this question. Unlike other teenage girls, these questions used to take me back 1400 years ago. I would often sit on the stairs in my family home and wonder how would my life be if I was born during the time when Prophet Muhammad PBUH was alive! Maybe because unlike most little girls my mother raised me by telling me bed time stories of Prophet Muhammad 'PBUH', Sahabas RA and friends of Allah also known as Awliyas (saints). I would often ponder upon my existence and what (if any) legacy I can leave behind?

Later on I learned that my core values were seeking knowledge, making a difference and leading by example. I wish I had known them before as they would have saved me from so much emotional pain and trauma but this very trauma made me who I am today. My lack of emotional maturity at the time used to project me as an introvert, shy with a hidden touch of boldness and a book worm.

Later on I learned to leverage these skills as a Coach. Everything my mom would tell me about the companions of the Prophet Muhammad SAW and brave Muslim women would make me want to be more like them, but most people around me lacked such exemplary character. I had most of my teenage years avoiding guys despite of their attempts to get my attention, studying Islamic history, singing nasheeds, writing poetry, hosting school and college functions and counselling friends who would feel torn between their dreams and realities (little did I know I always had a coach within me).

I grew up in a middle class family in Lahore where people were too busy trying to make their ends meet and practice Islam without really understanding the soul of Islam. Majority of my class mates will focus on fashion, forming groups to make others feel good or bad, secret (sometimes not so secret) crushes and studying almost near exams. For me, I resorted in burying myself in seeking knowledge in order to be one of the best students and modest fashion (of course). Love was a sore subject for me and my sub conscious judgement about love caused me more pain than I could ever imagine.

My mom would often describe true love to me with this metaphor. A true love brings you closer to Allah. When the lover loves his beloved, he doesn't just buy her a shirt. He plants cotton wool and makes a shirt from scratch, using his hands to sow the seeds and nurture the plant so he can loom the cotton and stitch the shirt. In every step of this creation process he falls more and more in love with his beloved hoping she will accept this present. This yearning in his heart brings him closer to Allah, so he prays more to find his beloved in this world. This love starts from the eyes but it's roots are based in the soul. The only remedy for this kind of love is praying to Allah that He brings you closer to your soul mate. I would often feel myself feeling this kind of love every time my mom would share true love stories. The girl in these love stories will often look like me but I was too shy to tell my mom (spoiler alert: she still doesn't know).

Fast forward 18 years of my life, my family found a suitable husband for me. My mom knew my love for knowledge so she made sure my future husband will honour my commitment. This turned out to be the only thing he committed with. Allah had other plans for me and made me go through series of trials, hurt, trauma, pain and sorrow that I wouldn't wish upon any one. I was living in one of the richest countries of the world but felt one of the poorest women in the world. Hollow, sad, deceived and full of guilt. I would question my imaan and if Allah even loves me? I felt like a victim and blamed myself for being in an abusive marriage. I prayed and even tried killing myself (may Allah forgive my sins). Allah had better plans for me and despite of my transgression in my desperate emotional state, Allah blessed me with a son. It truly was one of the happiest moments of my life. I still remember my son's nurse's words 'You look really beautiful' (despite of feeling like a total mess few hours before birth). It was the glow of true love that made me forget every pain I endured during his pre-mature birth. I nearly lost both of us due to my domestic situation (don't need to go into the details as I left that part of my life with Allah and my ex).

Through that adversity my family helped me getting out of my abusive marriage and I moved from USA to Lahore for a few months. I decided to never let myself be treated like a victim again and completed my masters while fighting for my divorce. I had no idea how else I could have thrived if it wasn't for my desire of seeking knowledge and my family's support. I went into full time work, while nursing my son at night time and preparing for my post grad exams. I couldn't deal with constant pity and questions from society for my divorce despite of never sharing the pain I endured during my marriage. This never stopped my beloved Asian society to assume and judge me for my divorce. I decided to move to London so I can raise my son in peace and independence. Alhamdulillah it was a success until I got re-engaged with a different version of my ex. It took me a while to realise that I have to resolve my inner conflict before embarking into any other meaningful and successful relation. It was the moment of emotional awakening and my journey towards becoming a coach. It took me years to scratch the surface of emotional mastery and tons of courses from NLP, Motivational interviewing, mentoring and paradigm coaching.

I learned the truth and myths about sub conscious beliefs and how they have been one of the reason for self-sabotaging my dreams. My childhood definition of true love didn't subconsciously believe in that love and I ended up being in personal and professional relationships that would somehow feed into my fear. I learned to remove the word victim from my dictionary and turned that victimhood into ownership. My passion and zest of knowledge never faded Alhamdulilah, so I kept on investing into my personal and professional development. I became a mentor, health trainer, personal trainer, a coach, an educator for the national health sector and a Navigator also known as community social worker. I switched my career focus from business administration and marketing to community and social work. I always wanted to make a difference in people's lives but I forgot about that dream when I got married. Allah brought me out of that abusive marriage and gave me opportunities to study in the best colleges and universities in Pakistan, USA and UK. It's easy to forget your purpose when you go through trials and turbulence but through the pain Allah makes us the best version of ourselves.

I had to go through these trials to help my clients whether they were single mothers trying to come out of abusive relationships or repairing their marriages, single professional mothers wanting to balance their personal and professional lives or someone who had lost hope in finding true love. I had to learn the true meaning of resilience myself before showing my clients how they can achieve it. As mother Teresa said, "One must really have suffered oneself to help others". Allah was showing me his mercy, though always protecting me even when I couldn't see that due to my ignorance and emotional pain.

Now I am blessed to be working with clients from all walks of life and show them their own blind spots of excellence. I truly feel humbled and blessed to be running my coaching business and connecting with people globally, appearing on Islam channel to show people how they can understand their emotions and resilience while showing them how to experience true love.

Now when I get out of bed, my day starts with gratitude and prayer that I become a source of guidance to help someone around me.

I still ponder upon what would have happened if I was born in Prophet Muhammad PBUH's era and I am sure a lot of Muslims wish and pray for this. Allah is all knowing all seeing. Allah knew that I am best served in this day and age so He chose this time period for me. He gave me freewill to use my life experience to help others or feel disempowered by it. Not a single leaf falls without His permission. He wanted me to experience everything I did and learn on my own through His mercy. So I chose this experience and knowledge as a Amana (trust) and gift to help others and show them they too can be heroes and sheroes by taking ownership, instead of choosing to resort in hurt, guilt, shame or a victimised mindset. My clients are doctors, entrepreneurs and working mothers as well as stay at home moms. They are all unique and serve a unique purpose in this life. When they come to me they usually can't see it for one reason or another. Allah blesses me to become part of their excellence by dusting off the unsettling emotions and pointing them towards their right direction. Towards their true self. This true self is never broken, incomplete or hollow.

I facilitate spiritual transformation by bringing in western psychology and Islamic values together.

As a young girl, I would never have chosen psychology as a subject as I was more into science and mathematics but Allah put me in situations where I had no choice but to learn human psychology. I am blessed to learn the secrets of Western Psychology and combine it with my Spiritual upbringing and Islamic knowledge. This helps me to experience love whenever I want to and showing others around me that they can too. I could never have done it without experiencing this love myself first. Today I can honestly say I am grateful for all the things that happened in my life. I am humbled to admit they brought me closer to Allah and to my clients and become part of their unique journeys.

You too can experience true love. The kind of love story my mom used to share with me. Little did I know at the time, the true love always existed within me. The very fact that I feel love for others is the reflection of how well nurtured and loved I am.

As Rumi RA says, "Become Love and Love will find you". I find love whenever I chose to. How about yourself? Do you want to learn how you can learn to love yourself and others unconditionally? Do you want to experience this love and resilience in your personal and professional lives? If so you can connect with me through my website www.Ayeshaikram.com.

Ayesha Ikram - Transformational Coach

Website - www.ayeshaikram.com
Facebook - www.facebook.com/transformativeCoachAyesha/
Instagram - @coachayeshaikram

17

A Shy Pakhtoon Girl

Swirling around slowly
In the rain.
And enjoying every rain drop
As it fell on my face
A calming effect it brought,
As it refreshed my thoughts.
The scent was of a fresh new rain
My brain started to free itself
From the surroundings.
This serenity made me dream
Of becoming a successful
And influential woman one day.

For I was only a young shy girl
From a Pakhtoon family
Of an Afghan origin
Born and living in Mardaan,
A city of Khyber Pakhtunkhwa Province
Of Pakistan.

Girls around me
Rarely got educated,
Let alone

Successful and ambitious
And I had already dared to dream big
Little did I know,
I would be going through
What will feel like
Fire, at times
To become
Pure Gold…

Wearing the traditional salwar kameez
And dupatta as a school uniform each morning
I draped a chador around me
And waited for the bus.
To attend high ranked school, far away
My parents wanted to raise
Me and my siblings
With first class education.

Snuggling with my grandmas in the afternoons
From both my Madar
And Baba's sides
I remember their advice
To be strong
And fight for my rights,
For as long as I was alive.
Going to the local shops in the evenings
With the neighbouring friends
And playing hide and seek.
In the local streets
Of Marian,
Have become a fond memory now

Those golden childhood days
Brings a natural smile on my face.

A luxurious lifestyle
Where servants are waiting for their master
To return home and knock.
And the door is opened immediately
To welcome you inside a beautiful house
With meals already prepared and ready at the table
My parents left all that and much more
Just so we can have a bright future,
Full of stars, they said.
While they began to sacrifice their own stars
One by one.

Being in Australia over ten years
The journey feels so short at times
As if it happened within a blink of an eye,
Or at times it feels so long
As if a thousand years have passed.

It was my mid teenage
I landed in a new country,
Among new people.
Started from a small rental apartment
And watched Baba apply for jobs everyday
For five continuous years
But not giving up
And Madar attending English classes
Eager to learn
The new language.

Saving every penny
For there came financial problems
A family to feed,
And issues too many to resolve.
Much like a rebirth
As at times it felt like learning to breathe from scratch.

Going to a girls only high school
With my broken English
And a thick accent
I was called a FOB,
Fresh off the Boat
With no friends.

Fast forward
Two years later
Achieved a scholarship towards university.
To study Civil Engineering
A non-traditional field for women
And questions started to raise,
If I would be able to continue?
Since I was a girl
Studying a degree
For which was apparently meant to be only for boys.
But nothing stopped me
For I was determined to continue.

Suddenly Madar got sick
And I cried that day
As I didn't want to lose her,
Here I was standing
In the middle of my studies,

And younger siblings.
I reassured everyone, every single day
It will all be okay.
Where inside
I was longing for someone to tell me
It will all be okay.
It felt like I was walking on fire
My feet started burning.

A while later came the day
Completion of my civil engineering studies
It was a happy day.

Started working
In a male dominated field
Where it's full of challenges,
A women is seen weak
And her strength is tested
From all directions.
Not too many women are seen where I was
My resilience was tested on a different level
For I was a Muslim girl,
From a Pashtoon Afghan background
In a field where not many women choose to go.

But I continued to strive
And progress further.

Enhancing my creative side
In the evenings,
I started studying beauty therapy and makeup

To free my mind and heal my soul
And colour my life.

And then came a storm
Which took away my savings in a glance
Within a day I had lost a big chunk,
I walked out the door that day
And fell on the road.
Had an injury
With a scarred face.

A lot that cannot be described in words
But can be reflected as it felt like
I was riding a bike uphill,
Through rough terrain in bushy mountains
While an earthquake was shaking my ground
And a thunderstorm was disturbing my sky,
My heart felt like a broken piece of a star
And my soul felt empty.

It took me a few months to re-gain my strength
To rise up and continue,
And start again.

Today
That's me standing in front of the mirror,
I see in it,
A young woman
Working as a civil engineer in a male dominated world,
Who has walked over all the challenges
One by one
Some nearly took my soul away from my body,

But I continued
And you can too
Fight for whatever is it that you wish to achieve
It is well worth it

You will find me around you
If you search and look…

Sadaf Khan Muhammadzai

Instagram - @SadafSoul

17

Dream...Plan...DO!

Would you like to get a glimpse into my world of creativity? I am Naila Ahmad, I am a wife and mother to very active 4 children. I was born in Sialkot a city in Punjab, Pakistan on October 1983. I spent all my teen years in Middle East and then moved to Pakistan in 1997, I came to live in the Uk in 2004.

I come from a very liberal and educated family. Our parent's emphasis was always on education and acquiring skills. We used to read and travel a lot. by travelling and reading I as a young girl imagined a lot. I used to imagine the architecture and the lifestyle of the older generation and civilisations. Hence I took up three subjects at college that mattered to me and were my greatest interests, Islamic studies, English literature and Home Economics.

As a young girl I was always fascinated by my grandmother's skills of crochet, embroidery, thrifty lifestyle, my parent's knowledge and wardrobe. All of this around me had instilled the love of creating & crafting. With my father's encouragement I started to pursue my hobby of sewing & my mother's love of embroider. I began playing around with beads, threads and fabrics. I remember I was found with an embroidery hoop or something on a summer's afternoon & on a winter evening with BBC URDU playing in the background.

After I was done mothering our four beautiful children, I started thinking about myself and in the hindsight I wanted to make the connection where I had left some years ago. I found myself asking one question to myself (prompted by the lectures of Asfaque Sahib, Bano Qudsiya, Qasim Ali Shah and readings of Zia Mohiuddin). Naila what are you good at? What can you do to earn a living by being a stay at home mum? What skills have you got to earn a pocket money or simply find a way to express myself? I came up with few answers and on top of the list was, sewing! There it was I had got the answer, because sewing was the one thing that i never ceased doing. I realised I loved stitching up literally anything! From my my first house curtains to my children's nurseries, from my outfits to my daughter's birthday dresses.

After a little research, thanks to all the handy technology these days it wasn't too hard, I came to a conclusion of starting a business making cushions, novelty cushions that are not found on the high street, something unique and bespoke.

With lots of encouragement from my family, friends & few doubtful comments from here & there my little business www.londoncushions.co.uk came into being in 2016! I became self employed for the first time. It was a very emotional step and a huge leap of faith, as I never went into employment or work before.

From a small school fair to some major ones, exhibiting at all the boroughs of London to my new venture of co-running a local market in East London, called THE CREATIVE SIDE OF LONDON,(providing a platform for small businesses) we are growing from strength to strength.

I began with using hight street fabrics, remnants & very renowned designer textiles, now i print my own fabric! In 2018 I took up block printing inspired by native Pakistani handiwork that i used to see in my grand mother's village. It just fascinated me, how with few paints and blocks one would create a whole new design. I love playing with colours, textures and patterns. My small business has evolved with time. I also use the art of Lino Printing with my self carved stamps. My LONDON DESIGNS have proved to be very popular. I make iconic

British Landmarks on stamps and print one by one on fabric, it's pure labour of love & joy.

I have been blessed by a few features too like being published in a worldwide selling magazine called SIMPLY SEWING, winning the #SFL winner award by Lady Karen Brady on Twitter,

I was chosen by our local council to have a pop up shop for a whole one month in 2018 in Leytonstone. My interview published in the local newspaper as a budding entrepreneur and being interviewed on Islam Channel Urdu by Musart Ellaahi!

I have been blessed in becoming an ambassador for SIMPLY GREAT BRITAIN in London (a small company that celebrates small businesses like myself) and having few stockists too of my work on your high streets. I can't thank Allah enough for my successes.

I often get asked was it hard to start a business? I reply, No. Its' harder to continue, to flourish, to make a brand, to keep going with the same energy and passion. All one needs is honest passion, a drive to reach their goal and fulfil their dream. The importance is having the ability to evolve with time and requirements. I wish everyone the best of luck on achieving their goals and finding their niche.

Naila Ahmad - Founder of London Handmade Gift Shop, London Ambassador for Simply Great Britain.

Instagram - @londoncushions.co.uk
Website - www.londoncushions.co.uk

17

Death, Divorced and Dismissed

"Mum's dead" 344 missed calls, 153 messages. My Mum (Rahimullah) had returned to Allah, in the early hours of Saturday morning. Heart wrenching. Gut wrenching. Destroyed.

I was miles away, in Saudi, living my dream, working as an English teacher.

I'd just found out I was pregnant with my third child too. I can't believe she's dead. We just spoke a few days ago, about having another girl and how amazing it would be, for my children to grow up with their Nani.

I rang my sister unable to speak. I could hear my siblings sobbing. My whole family were there except for me. Guilt and shame overcame me. I was living my dreams, while my Mum was suffering. The last time I had seen her was 3 months ago, in hospital. She had been admitted for kidney failure with fluid in her lungs. She was slowly drowning in her own fluid.

As I sat on the phone sobbing, my mind wandered back to a time when I was 6. I cried to my Mum, because I was so afraid she would die and I wouldn't be there for her. My Mum chuckled and gave me a hug and told me she loved me always.

My heart ached. It felt as if it would explode out of my chest. My greatest fear came true that day. Here I was, sat on the other side of a phone, sobbing because I chose to live my dreams instead of be there for her.

She believed in me. She always taught me to fight for my dreams. She encouraged me to keep going, even when I felt so defeated. Now all I could hear was her voice in my head, telling me to be strong. "Rose you need to come, they want to bury her soon".

I wasn't allowed to leave the country without my employer's permission and because it was the weekend, there was no chance I'd be leaving until Monday. I told my sister I'd call her back and rang my employer, crying, asking him to let me go to bury my Mum. They agreed.

Alhamdulillah, by the Mercy of Allah I found a flight for the same night. I packed some things and headed for the airport. The whole plane journey was a blur. I couldn't stop crying. All I felt was so much guilt. I remembered all the times my Mum looked after me when I was sick.

I remember the time I was pregnant and she walked all the way to Sainsbury's to buy me fruit because I was going through depression. I remembered all the times we argued and how I wish I hadn't reacted the way I did.

I wondered if she forgave me. For being the worst daughter, for being so rebellious. For putting her through so much heartache. I remembered the times she stayed up all night crying because I had left the house and spent all night with my friends. I remembered the times, I wasn't there for her when she needed me the most.

I remembered the times I told her I hate her, because she wouldn't let me hang with certain girls. Now I realised she was only protecting me. I remembered the times I was so angry at her for not coming to my school events and realised now, that she had her own problems to deal with.

She was a single mother, raising 6 kids alone. She buried 2 sons in her life and still carried on strong. She was a warrior and my kids will never know just how amazing their Nani was.

"Why didn't you just quit Rosy"?

"You should've left and stayed with Mum"

So many thoughts, emotions and guilt filled inside of me. She'd been there for me my whole life, and I couldn't even be there, in her last moments. When I arrived at my Mum's home, I felt my heart sink into my gut. Usually I was met with beaming faces, my siblings laughing. Mum would be sat in her fave spot on the sofa and I'd run up to her and hug her and we'd laugh. But this time, I was met with the hospital bed that she died on.

The house felt cold and empty. Hollow.

My brother talked about how she passed. That she went peacefully without pain. That she said her shahadah and her body was full of light. I was happy to know that she was with Allah, jealous almost. I wanted to be with her. They drove me to the masjid where her body lay. I walked into the cold room and there she lay. My hero.

I felt numb to the core. As I got closer to her, I secretly hoped she would get up and hug me like she always did. She never liked to rest, always on the go. I couldn't cry, I just smiled.

"You're free Mum. I love you" I asked Allah to let her be in Jannah and left.

Washing her body was such a beautiful experience. I know it's weird to say, but it was like I was taking her home. She brought me into this world, and now I was returning her. When I saw her wrapped in her white shroud, I sighed with relief. I hadn't abandoned her, just as she had brought me into this world, I had the honour of returning her to her Lord.

We buried her, on the same day my son was born. 21ST March 2017. I returned to Saudi feeling solemn. I was still grieving but I felt something shift inside of me.

And then things took a turn for the worst. My employers made me redundant and I had 2 months to leave the country. Talk about a low blow to the gut. I was devastated. I had sacrificed being with my Mum for this job. For this dream. I worked so hard and now it was like the rug had been pulled from under my feet.

I felt angry. Bitter. Grief. Pain.

With little to no savings, I returned to the UK, with 2 kids and 34 weeks pregnant. My marriage at this point was non existent. Having to deal with grief whilst in an abusive marriage, was probably the hardest thing I ever had to do. When you have to manage your emotions as well as stay in a situation that is *only* causing you harm, I'm telling you it's torture.

After I gave birth, we divorced and I could finally grieve for my Mum, for losing my job. I could grieve for me. That woman who sacrificed so much to keep others whole. I found me.

I woke up for Tahajud one night and cried my heart out to Allah. I never once doubted His Qadr, I knew something amazing was going to be born from this. My mum raised me to get right back up and keep my head up. I begged Allah to guide me down the right path. To guide my feet and my heart, to what's best for me in my religion and Hereafter.

I was already working as a health coach, but I wanted to use my experiences to impact others. So Allah guided me to my first mentor (Hind Adebago I'll forever be grateful for your guidance) and then I studied Rapid Transformational Therapy, which changed my life and the life of my clients forever. Through this my 5 figure business was born, I unearthed a part of myself that I had hidden for so long, because I was so consumed with abuse and turmoil.

I wanted to help women thrive after abuse. I wanted to help women build businesses they love, whilst being deeply connected to Allah. I wanted to show women that anything and everything is possible. I wanted to use the example of Khadijah RA and show women that the power of our Sunnah. That we can be wealthy and firm in faith. Nothing can stop you as long as you have Allah. Because when you have a vision, it's from Allah. When you have a yearning to serve and help, it's from Allah. So who are you to say it's impossible?!

In 3 months I went from:

> *Government assistance, to a 5 figures business. I'm recognised as a Transformational expert globally. I have been on TV, podcasts with thought leaders and radio. I've 10x'd my fees. I've helped 100 women in 25 countries overcome trauma. I'm recognised as a Thought Leader (mind blown). I'm a part of this book (again mind blown!). I've been invited to be a paid speaker at a global event. My videos have gone VIRAL (over 40k views) and the likes of Lewis Howes and Kimra Luna have given positive feedback. I'm no longer working FOR clients, they're coming to me!*

My goal is to impact millions worldwide and open an academy that teaches women how to build successful legacy-driven businesses and to also give back. My deepest desire is to build a charity for young girls who are growing up without a father. I'll be holding Transformational workshops to help them overcome bullying, the pressure of beauty, peer pressure, drugs and sex. I want to show them, that there is hope.

I'm so grateful to Allah for going through the most excruciating pain, in 2017. I am so grateful that I'm still standing here today.

I wouldn't be here, if I was still working in Saudi. I wouldn't have come to the realisation that life is so short, and the only time you have is *now*. I wouldn't be here, thriving, if I chose to stay in an abusive marriage for the sake of my kids.

Anything and everything is possible. And you are only one decision away from living your best life. I'm here because I didn't quit. And I believed Allah was Greater than my problems.

I say this with all my heart, you are stronger than you think. You are never a victim. You are a warrior!

Rosalean Batool - Transformational Expert; I help coaches, healers and therapists, heal from trauma, without years of therapy, to make more money in business. I use a combination of powerful therapy and coaching to help women get results in business and gain mastery in all areas of life.

Instagram - www.instagram.com/rosaleanbatool
Facebook - ww.facebook.com/rosaleanbatool
youtube - www.youtube.com/rosaleanbatool

If you're a coach and finding it difficult to sell your services download my Free eBook 5 Ways to Sell Your Services without Going Broke https://mailchi.mp/55b665cf6f06/5waystosell yourserviceswithoutgoingbroke

17

Tawakkul (Trust In God)

Have you ever wondered what the true essence of faith means? Or perhaps wondered what driving force is out there that fills that void in your heart and gives you hope to see light at the end of the tunnel? Such has been my journey since 2017 of finding myself through having faith but learning from other's experiences, in a journey that connects us all for lessons that we each need to learn through experience.

I have always sought to understand the power of collective dua (supplication), had heard about miracles and other people's success stories, but it was about time God showed me what it truly meant. Having complete tawakkul (trust) in God can have such 'mountain moving' affects for humans and their faith in seeing miracles come true. I am not talking about holding the moon in your hands (however with today's technology anything is possible). I am referring to having belief and faith in what it is you desire in your daily life and the obstacles you face can be overcome through the level of trust (tawakkul) you have as an individual in your Lord.

So what is tawakkul really? It is an Arabic word and derives from the Islamic concept of having full reliance on God, trusting in God's plan. Now this should not be mistakenly thought of in such a way that one is unwell and just twiddles their thumbs hoping to recover speedily. It does not mean to act lazily. One needs to first make an effort, seek out the possibilities and options out there that can aid this that are all within the permissible remits and then have that reliance and trust in God. Thereafter whatever the result may be, a desired outcome or something that was not hoped for, having the faith, the trust and the acceptance that this was what was decreed is the true essence of Tawakkul. It is through this that one attains a spiritual connection with God, and thus inhibits the element of a Sufi.

There is a voice that speaks within us, when we are troubled, we are seeking answers and looking for a sign of hope or guidance. This voice or call it intuition, your gut, is your true self speaking to you. Is it ourselves that hold the guidance within us when we seek it or is it God guiding us in which direction to go? In order to understand this, God put me through a journey and connected me with thousands of people who each had a story to share and needed some kind of direction in life.

It's as if it fell into my lap and was meant to be. A sign so strong and yet so clear, a door that opened so wide that I was pushed to walk through it. When I was in my teens, I always knew that whatever I did in life I wanted to help others. I wanted that to be my main path. I wanted to make a difference in the world in at least one person's life that when I am no longer alive, I have left some good in the world. Two years ago I felt to create my own social media group on Facebook specifically for the purpose of helping others. I already had a growing following on social media and was often asked by my followers to create a private group. They seemed to be inspired by how I used to address common issues. However I never knew how quickly that prayer of others would manifest. My Shaykh (spiritual teacher) was in the city in the summer of 2017, and although super hard to catch him one to one, I somehow bumped into him and asked him one question; if he thought I should begin with this endeavour to help others. He glanced at me from the corner of his eye and said yes immediately, blessing me and making a prayer for success in this path and all that would connect in it. The very next morning the group was formed, in fact I received a strange notification to become an admin of a group that was unmanaged, upon investigating I found that many people I knew who were connected with myself for already proving them support were a part of this social media group. And that is where this journey began, the birth of this group in August 2017 called 'An-Nur Al-Haqq' (the light, the truth).

Life then changed for me, and I began being faced with listening and supporting so many people's issues, that I forgot my own. I felt more grateful about all that i had and what i was blessed with, and realised my issues or struggles were in fact nothing compared to what was being brought to me. The attachment, the love, the encouragement, the empowerment and that motivation that others received from me was phenomenal and something that i was so not aware of in black and white. Of course there were the keyboard warriors, those that hid behind a screen and did what they could to try to put me down. I just continued with my work, someone wanted to share their problem or someone wanted guidance on how to deal with a social matter, I was there to provide that support. In all situations my purpose and goal was to direct these people towards their faith, guide them so that their trust in God increases, make collective supplications for others that needed support in the group. The group became a community, connecting people all over the world. But amongst all this I was the one who's faith and trust in God was being tested, God was testing my strengths through helping others.

There were many examples right before my eyes; people being jobless and finding a job all through collective dua and prayers, some dealing with serious break ups, some finding a spouse and being happily married, others recovering from an illness. The beauty was everyone coming together and supporting each other. I began noticing a pattern, those that made effort, and then group members praying collectively were then being relieved from their problems. It was like this positive energy, this force, coming together and increasing one another's faith and trust in their Lord. I began to observe and it was refreshing to see that so many people began to relax and have faith. I felt that my mission was accomplished and problems began to decrease. Yet there was a problem, an emptiness inside me. Why was I unsettled? I was helping hundreds come together yet I was falling apart inside on my own. I began to become confused. So many success stories and what was mine? Why wasn't God answering my prayers? I began to assess myself, and as I did I became so isolated and deeply lost.

I was always spiritual, had always lead a disciplined life, good grades, degrees, good health, good job, a social and confident butterfly. I was a girl of faith, I would pray on prayer beads and ensure I lead a good life by giving charity. I used to dream and wish for having a family of my own, to sing to praise the Prophet PBUH, travel as one of my passions, have my own website. Yet my wishes and desires were not coming true. No matter what I tried it would fail. I fell into depression, feeling like a failure and lost with no progression, I fell into a battle within myself.

Almost a year went by in this dark hole, of being cut of from a social circle, having a new job but being stuck in an office, working around my working life to help others I very quickly forgot myself. I became lost. My confidence and self-esteem was on an all time low. Having to face people became too daunting and anxious about the 'what's new with you' questions from others. Everyone around me was happy, everything was working out for them. I was mocked and bullied by people I thought were lifelong friends, who didn't want to know. Instead of receiving support or to be heard I was called names and was made to feel low about myself. The person that was there all the time during her own pain was socially bullied and mocked for not being married. I had everything but not a husband. No one to turn to, being shunned off and then scared of my reputation, I closed off. Having an image of being the strong and brave one, others always expect you to get on with it, such was the opinion of my family. And with parents ill-health I could not turn to them for support. Equally the pressure was high from them too. Living a straight forward and disciplined life, insecurities began to form.

Something was clearly wrong with me I kept thinking. Throughout 2018 I felt I was worthless but the only thing that would make me forget this was helping others. I would still pray I would still praise my lord, but I forgot about loving myself along the way. I felt like a robot, getting up daily going to work, trying to have extra activities but not wanting to see people, I would rather help someone who came crying to me with their problem. They relied on me, I couldn't let these members down. My belief in God was always there, but I began to question whether my God was listening to me and why what I truly prayed for wasn't being answered, yet everyone I guided and helped was finding success.

No body wanted to listen, everyone was just wrapped up in their happiness, I could not speak out about my issues and fears. I was left on my own yet i continued with my daily routine. Keeping everything bottled up inside and not having anyone to talk to and not being able to trust became a huge barrier and cause for being anxious and low. Everyone around me was either too happy to care, or struggling with their own issues. I began to write down my pain and why I felt lost. And soon God crossed my path with some great people who have become very close friends, which for me in all essence was enough to which I am grateful for this day. It was God's answer, if one door closed another one opened.

I had realised that my journey of being lost within myself was the biggest purpose and test for what was to come next. Through loss I had also gained what was more serving and beneficial to me, goal orientated and positive people became my inner circle. What was removed was not healthy for me and God had cleared that from my path for a reason. I had to form the group as a starting point of what was to come next, as that inspired me to create my own YouTube channel, write motivational blogs and launch my very own website www.atiyabhutta.com in 2019.

At the end, life will always test us, the struggles will always be there, at each moment we will continue to learn, but amongst this God made me realise that everyone is connected and has a purpose. These individuals had to cross my path, and through helping them, each one helped me. With a bit of patience and faith, God had bigger plans for me. In essence he had answered my prayers as now I am also in the travel business which has been one of my dreams come true. And with time, having tawakkul in His plan, he will bless us with more.

Some wounds are visible however we often forget about the strong people who could be struggling within themselves as there are high expectations of them to deal with things alone. Everyone is going through a journey of their own at their own pace, but be sure to be kind to everyone that you cross paths with, as they could be battling with something behind closed doors.

Atiya Bhutta - Motivational and Inspirational Speaker, Blogger, Leader, Founder of Facebook Islamic Dua group 'An-Nur Al-Haqq' & Senior NHS Manager from London UK.

Instagram - @Atiya.b.official
Website - www.atiyabhutta.com
Youtube - Atiiyah Bhuttah
Facebook - www.facebook.com/AtiiyahBhuttah

17

The Story So Far...

If you're reading this, you must be very bored, so for that, I do apologise. I like to joke around, and entertain those around me. I gain the upmost pleasure from giving pleasure. My exterior radiates confidence, assurance and spirit. Those who know me will tell you that I am the calm before the calm. But there's much more which sits quietly hidden behind the mask that I sometimes force myself to wear. In my journey so far, I have learned that life is not always easy, everyone is fighting their own battles, and that Heaven is not on earth.

My name is Aukash, and this is my story...

****

I'm now 23 years old, but it was my teenage years that changed my life forever. I was once an incredibly shy, awkward 15-year-old. My social anxiety defined my youth, and stopped me from living a normal childhood. At the time, I thought I was normal, but as I was getting older and entering adulthood, I could acknowledge that I had a serious problem – a very serious problem.

I attended Chesterton school in North Cambridge. I was lucky to make friends by chance, and I was comfortable around them. My school days at first, were "normal". I could never pick up the courage to speak to anyone outside my circle, but that didn't bother me so much to begin with.

However, I remember in Year 10, when I was 14, my English teacher picked a few of us in the class to read a book out loud. Instantly, my heart dropped. I was used to feeling this way, but on this particular day, I felt worse than I usually would in such a situation.

Whilst dying inside knowing that I would now have to read out loud in front of my class mates, the teacher called my name and asked me to start reading. I could feel my heart beating at full throttle. It felt like I had a 1000 faces staring at me, waiting for me to make a mistake so that they could all laugh at me in harmony.

Just a few words into reading, I stutter. I froze for what felt like a light year. I locked eyes with my teacher. She saw my red tomato face, and she knew I could no longer continue. I wanted to leave the room, runaway, and never have to see anyone's face again. All because of a little stutter whilst reading a book. Ridiculous? I know.

These "episodes" became worse as the days went by. Unfortunately, society teaches us (especially men) to "man up". I didn't have the courage to tell anyone about my social anxiety. I just thought to myself "no one would understand".

Year 11 started the same way that year 10 ended. I was a year older, and a few inches taller, but my confidence was still at an all-time low. The Christmas holidays that year, however, changed my mind-set forever. I got back from school, and I opened YouTube on my dad's phone. I saw this video in YouTube's suggestions called "Muhammad Ali highlights". I clicked on it, as I had all the time in the world to kill.

Just two minutes into the video, I was blown away by what I saw. "I'm handsome, I'm pretty, and I can't possibly be beaten. I am the greatest", said a 22-year-old Cassius Clay in preparation for his fight against the indestructible Sonny Liston. I was mesmerised. I had never seen such confidence. How could a person be so sure of themselves? How could someone be in love with themselves? How could someone be so bold and brash?

Everything about Muhammad Ali had me on awe. He was tall, handsome, quick-witted, incredibly charismatic, and above all, he was confident. He was of course no prophet, but I was convinced that he was the pinnacle of modern day humanity. I wanted to be everything he was, and by that, what I really meant was, I wanted his confidence. I wanted to be able to go to school, and comfortably speak to anyone I wanted to and live a normal teenage hood. My friends would often invite me on the weekends to hand out, go swimming, play football etc. It would be easy to get permission from my Parents, but it was impossible to get permission from Mr Social Anxiety.

Through-out my five years at school, and my two years at college, I never socialised outside of school hours. Not even once. It was now time I forced myself to get out of my shell, and show the world my true self. Muhammad Ali was the foundation for my journey to finding confidence. The journey had many different routes; I just needed to decide which one to take.

I began to study Muhammad Ali very closely. I played close attention to his figure of speech, and his body language. He walked up-right, and he would often speak in rhyme. His poetry was a work of art, in itself. I knew I could never make it as a boxer, so I thought why not give poetry a go? One evening, all alone at home, I decided to write a piece. This is what a 15-year-old me came up with:

You Said He Was A Nobody

You said he was weak,
But yet he had a heart of steel,
You said he was dumb,
Is it because you didn't know the pain that he would feel?

You bullied him always,
And gave him less respect than a dead dog,
You were the cause of his suicide,
As all his memories were just depressed clouds of thick fog.

You made him lose all his confidence,
And called him an attention seeker when he searched for cure,
He drowned in his tears,
As he was left all alone and insecure.

His family mocked him because he was very shy,
Little did they know about the pain he felt inside,
He tried to tell his school,
But all his wounds were just brushed aside.

Then the day eventually came,
When your harsh words became too much for him to take,
He overdosed on some pills,
Knowing that he would never awake!

Now, before we jump to conclusions! This poem did not reflect how I was feeling at the time. Suicide was never on my mind. I have always been a believer that no soul is burdened more than it can bare. Having said that, I still don't understand why I wrote something so dark. Could it be that I had inner demons at the time, but my brain refuses to accept that today? I honestly don't have an answer for that, and neither do I want to think about it.

I had just recently joined Facebook, and my first post was this poem that I wrote. Within a few hours the poem went viral, and I was receiving messages from all over the country. I was amazed by how many people said they could relate to what I wrote. It was the first time in my life that I received praise for what I did. I saw numerous messages demanding me to write more and have my work published. And so I did. All praise be to God. I had my first poem published in a book called Through the Eyes of a Poet. It sold in retail stores and online. I was just 15.

I even had the opportunity to share my work with the MP of Cambridge at the time, Julien Huppert. He encouraged me to get in touch with radio and television shows to see if I could get the chance to showcase my work on a wider scale. To cut a long story short, soon after I turned 16, I was invited by BBC Radio Cambridgeshire to be interviewed and to recite my poetry live on air. This was the toughest decision of my life.

The success God gave me through poetry helped my self-esteem (albeit, only a little), but my social anxiety was still hot in its prime. I convinced myself that if I didn't do the show, I would never be able to overcome my fears. So, I went back to watching Muhammad Ali's highlights on YouTube to gear myself up. Eventually, I accepted the offer, and I told none of my family or friends. It was the fear of making a mistake live on air, which stopped me from telling anyone.

Fast forward to the moment of my radio debut, and I was a bag of nerves. I shaved, wore my best suit, and drowned myself in my dad's aftershave. I have always been content with my appearance, and I enjoy dressing smart. Externally, I felt I was ready, but internally, I was the complete opposite. Before I could dwell any longer, the radio show began, and so did my usual nervous stutter. I was interviewed for 15 minutes, and I recited my poem about bullying. Looking back seven years later, I think I put on a decent show, considering it was first time speaking to 30,000 people live.

At the time however, I gave myself a tough time. I have always been my greatest bully, my biggest critic, and my most harsh judge. That night I couldn't stop thinking of ways to criticise myself. There really wasn't much to criticise, but I was able to find my ways.

For a few months, I stopped writing, and I ignored all media invites. For me, it was a time of reflection. I felt lost. My confidence was playing hide and seek, and I had no idea where to find it. And the worst part was that I saw most of my friends at the time move away from me. I'm not saying they were jealous of my work outside of school and college – certainly not. I think they were just confused, and couldn't quite understand what I was doing with this new "career" I was pursuing.

Four months into my hiatus, I received an offer from Islam Channel TV, to make a live appearance on their flagship chat show, Living the Life. This was the first time I had the chance to showcase my work on television – it seemed too good to be true. I knew it was an opportunity I had to grab with both hands.

Once again, I gave myself a pep talk. I knew that saying no would hinder my journey. So, on Monday the 25th March 2013, I made my television debut under the bright lights of the Islam Channel studio. This was the turning point. My self-confidence grew a mile overnight. From being a kid who couldn't even ask to go to the toilet in front of class, I now performed live in front of a world-wide audience.

I give all praise to God. Not everyone is given the opportunities that I was fortunate enough to encounter. God is kind. God is the most powerful. God is the GREATEST! Seven years later, and I still have my bad days, but I have now learned how to deal with them. Social anxiety is no joke. It can ruin lives. It disturbs me how mental health is still a taboo subject in society. Always push yourself, strive for greatness, and never give up. Life is not always easy, everyone is fighting their own battles, and Heaven is not on earth.

Smile

A smile is an effortless gift to give,
And can improve someone's day,
During tough times,
A smile is the best thing to display.

A smile can be used to hide your pain,
And your worries and tears,
A smile can be used as a blanket,
To cover up your fears.

A smile is your enemies worst nightmare,
And your haters most terrible sight,
If ever in doubt or darkness,
Use your smile to make the room bright.

So if anybody ever says you're not good enough,
And makes you feel miserably and grey,
Just keep your chin up,
And smile away!

Aukash

Aukash - Author and Event Host

Instagram - @AukashZ
Twitter - @AukashZ

17

Rebirth after trauma

When I was 16 years old my father died suddenly, traumatically. He was literally here 1 night and gone in an instant the next. The biggest shock of my life!

The second biggest shock of my life was my divorce after 17 years of marriage and 22 years in a relationship. When I lost my father I was completely devastated and traumatised, because my father was the love of my life- the first man I ever loved. The first man who loved me.

You could say…I lost myself in grief, but I never really found myself. The only Identity I knew was attached to him. It was like he was my oxygen and now I was suffocating and couldn't breathe. That's what the panic, anxiety and fear felt like.

My marriage was one of the most wonderful gifts I received from my creator at the most perfect time in my life. He was exactly what I needed when I needed to help build a successful life. He helped me to focus on life and not get distracted, "stay on the straight path" if you will to success. My husband grounded me, cared for me, and comforted me. He allowed me to be me or so I believed at the time. We had an amazing life: of wealth, health, happiness, status and success. All the things, anyone looking in from the outside would say we were the perfect couple and had it all. We were married for almost 17 years and have 3 amazing children together. Most of our time together was good, however we grew on separate paths in our own journeys. The most constant thing for me was my faith and connection with my creator.

Always there for me and never letting me down, as we unintentionally do to each other as humans. People change, make mistakes and have limitations. God is limitless

Each time I had a loss of a significant man in my life, my identity was lost too. I didn't know who I was, because it was attached to another in an unhealthy, toxic and destructive way. One wrong move and I would collapse. My existence was dependent on him emotionally holding me up. I was like a leech, I needed to latch on to someone who could define me and give me permission to be.

For me it felt like I was reliving the trauma of losing my father all over again except this time I was the mother of three children who needed me to be their emotional rock. They were my dream come true. They were my purpose at that time in my life. My co dependency stemmed from beyond the loss of my father at a young age. It stemmed from not knowing how to live any other way besides being controlled. Looking for people to tell me what to think, feel, how to behave and make decisions. So now you can see why I was ripe for attract a partner that needed to control everything and everyone in his life. My natural disposition was to comply, always to comply. That is how I knew I was good enough, that I mattered, and was deserving and worthy of love.

Having a superficial relationship with God, allowed me to somewhat hold my own emotionally because I had some attachment to my real, solid, rock. Not the one I perceived to be my rock, (my husband at the time). I am referring to My spiritual connection to my Creator. I had no choice at this point but to turn up rather than turning to people to save me, as I did my entire life. I don't know how I made it through, because in May 2013, just 6 months before…I was unraveling as I sensed my marriage collapsing, and then by November 2013 I could stand on my own. Nervous, uncertain, shaky legs, but yet I knew I would be OK with The Source that would never leave me.

Little did I know that the excruciating pain during this time was from the lifelong layers of toxic behaviour patterns and negative ingrained beliefs pertaining to my value and worth. It manifested through subconscious negative self talk and Self loathing in the form of self criticism, judgment, and punishment. This new journey of rebirth began. My spiritual and emotional rebirth with my foundational and essential relationships. Discovering my identity for the first time through my relationship with God of love, forgiveness, kindness, compassion and mercy as my Protector, Provider, Maintainer, Sustainer. I did not just believe this on the surface level but absorbed it at the core and started living it. I lived it in a manner that brought about self awareness and consciousness to give my self the love, kindness, forgiveness, and compassion, that Allah gives to me. Understanding that the word identity has the word 'I' in it, I was able to find my light and connect with my real purpose here on earth.

My husband was one of the best gifts, I was divinely gifted. He was exactly what I needed when I needed it. You see after my father died, I was searching for another man to fill the void, to validate me, to dignify and make me feel like I mattered, that I was good enough and important enough for some body to love and value me unconditionally. Any man that gave me the slightest bit of attention, I lost my senses for them.

Actually I was searching for all this even before my father died, and was heading down a path of self destruction. I guess you can call it a divine intervention. Because the pain, grief and darkness from the loss of a parent propelled me to a man who took care of me. Actually I looked to him to fulfil all my needs: Emotionally, physically, spiritually and intellectually. He grounded me to stay focused and on the path of success. I was on a path of self sabotage just to get noticed, to feel I mattered, that I was someone important in this world. My marriage, my husband saved me and protected me from myself during that time of my life. That was a Divine gift from my creator that I will always be immensely grateful for.

After 17 years in my marriage I found myself dishonouring and compromising my values and I was willing to sell my soul to stay attached, safe and secure in my marriage. My divorce was also another divine gift that once again saved me from myself. You see No BODY, no Human call fulfil all your needs, nor are they meant to by design. That fulfilment of the void can only be filled by connection to The Creator. It's absolute, unconditional, and never ending. And when I realised I was worshipping the means rather than "The Source", my path was altered setting me up on a trajectory to reach and express my full potential.

Another thing I realised is that trials and tribulations would keep showing up in my life in excruciating ways until I learned the lessons Allah was trying to teach me. I wasn't a very good student at the time and could not head the signs, being so disconnected to Allah and myself.

On this newfound path I was able to find the unending source that I was searching for since my early teens. I found the direct link inside of me, directly connected to me. The spiritual connection that each human being has to his or her Creator. It's part of our composition our DNA, a natural GPS to guide us through life.

It is expressed through self love, self respect, honour, and dignity, through self discovery.

Don't be afraid of the pain. I know it hurts. The negative self talk hurts. You have to go through it, release and heal to get to the other side of your potential. Don't numb or escape or get busy as society tells you to, or it will spread and grow like a cancer of self hate inside you. Don't avoid, mask or drown it with drugs, alcohol, media consumption, sex, any destructive behaviour.

You can't will yourself out of the heartbreak, you have to feel yourself through it. When my father died I was searching for my Identity and lost it with his death. I kept looking outward for somebody else to fill that for me, then I lost my husband through divorce and had to search again and this time I hit the jackpot!

Identity has the word 'I' in it. It is inherent and intrinsic. You will keep experiencing the same struggles bundled in a different packages until the lesson is learned.

So I invite you to ask yourself, what is it that I need to learn in this struggle? So, what can I do, you may ask. How….

1. Don't be afraid to spend time alone with yourself without your phone or electronic device. Do a regular digital detox. There is so much messaging that goes on everyday we are bombarded with. Everyone has an agenda. Figure out what yours is first. Spend time alone in nature, pondering and journaling your thoughts, ideas, pains, dreams.
2. Have real, raw, vulnerable conversations with yourself (self acceptance) and then with family and friends. Don't hide and stay at the surface level
3. Don't be afraid to speak up, speak out and express your voice, ideas, feelings, contributions. they matter. Not in a rebellious or defiant way, but in an authentic, vulnerable, unapologetically you way.
4. Take baby steps. Start in your comfort zone or safe spaces and build your vulnerability muscle and take that strength go outward into new uncharted spaces
5. Get comfortable being uncomfortable. Train and condition yourself to seek it out. That is where the growth happens
6. Don't be afraid of the pain. Go through it to get to the other side of resilience and growth. Then you will be able to weather any storm and come through at a higher level.

Remember you are here for a purpose. We know the purpose of our creation is only to worship our Creator. So it is your own personal responsibility to know and love The creator, as part of worship. In getting to know and love Him we get to know and love ourselves. That is the journey. It is your responsibility to figure out how you are going to worship your Creator besides personal obligations of worship such as prayer, fasting, charity and hajj. For example, I only became conscious of having a purpose when I became a mother. What spoke to me was to raise God conscious children who live as productive members of humanity by serving with the gifts and talents Allah blessed them with.

So when we divorced, it triggered the pain and loss of my father's death. That petrified and initially sent me in to a panic. I didn't know how I would live without him. It was impossible for me to breathe and all the flashbacks from the death of my father were being re-stimulated. This period strengthened my faith and connection with God, because I knew that he would never let me down or abandon me.

This newly attained strength helped me to focus on all my blessings and only the positive aspects of my life. I realised that God was trying to teach me a lesson. A lesson that HE was the source of everything and where I had placed my husband in my heart only belonged to God. That the more I chase people and things the more they run away from me. But if I connect with my creator as the source for everything and live my life to please Him then everything I need and want comes to me at the perfect time.

There is a saying our prophet Muhammad PBUH said: "How wonderful is the affair of a believer, for his affairs are all good and this applies to no one but the believer. If something good happens to him, he is thankful for it and that is good for him. If something bad happens to him, then he bears it with patience and that is good for him"

There is good in every situation. We all know that challenges, hardship, and adversity build, grow and develop our character. We look back and say I got through that and had I never experienced that I would be so patient or skilful or.... They are custom tailored for us.

"What has reached you was never meant to miss you, what has missed you was never meant to reach you"

These teachings really helped me to look at the positive and ask myself, this perceived "bad" thing thats happened to me. how can I use to to grow, develop and better myself. What can I learn from it? I perceived "bad" things such as death, loss of people or material…

I HAD A CHOICE:

TO BE UPSET, DEVASTATED, ANGRY, SAD DEPRESSED AND THEN TAKE IT OUT ON EVERYONE AROUND ME, BLAME EVERYONE BUT MYSELF

OR

Realise this was a test with a purpose…what am I to learn from this. How can I look inward and see how I can improve myself, my character to please my creator.

How can I worship my creator by serving his creation?

Two things happened: I decided to work on myself, to grow develop and educate myself to be the best person and example for my kids as rising independent, kind, free thinking people who benefit their community and society was and is my goal. Help people and serve in whatever capacity I am able

I didn't know at the time that I was designed to help people in a grander capacity in changing their lives. Through their mindset, hearts and bodies and inspire them with the tools to reach their full potential and have a ripple effect in their own families and the people they touch in their lives.

"Love The Source more than the means you will be gifted" That's my biggest LESSON

I feel I am the richest person in the world filling myself up from The Ultimate Source that never ends so I may give to His creation.

Through my journey I found that in order to live, really live the life of fulfilment and of feeling on cloud nine you have to know and discover yourself first. Before going after anything else. Meaning you want love, which WE, all humans want. You have to give it to yourself first. Self love, care, acceptance and forgiveness. The only way to give it to yourself is to get it from an unconditional source, which is The Creator, The Ultimate Source.

I don't regret any of it…because without that journey I would never have arrived to where I am today. I relate my story to you, because if I could do it all over again, knowing that I matter simply because I breathe, that's enough validation. Knowing that I was already equipped with the answers I was seeking, would have allowed me to focus on myself first, develop myself, understand myself, my psychology. All this could have opened doors for me FOR more peace, contentment and fulfilment. The feelings not the material gains. We think the material gains will make us happy and fulfilled, but that only comes from knowing and loving yourself, imperfections and all. If you love yourself, meaning you talk to your SELF the way you talk to your BFF or someone you care deeply about, you have compassion and kindness for them, you don't hate on them. What are the things we say to ourselves? I said to myself… You're too fat, too dumb, too brown, too Muslim, not Muslim enough, not witty enough.

All my life I hadn't been the one making decisions for myself so I never really knew how to make decisions on my own. When I was in my parent's home they told me what do and made all the decisions for me. My obligation was to listen and obey at all times. Then I got married and my husband made all the decisions so it was much of the same. The only patterns I knew were of control.

5 years ago I found myself going through an unexpected divorce coming out of a co dependent relationship bordering on shirk (associating partners with God) I had no idea how I was going to survive and be OK on my own.

I was left devastated not knowing how to make decisions on my own. I didn't know that I had a voice much less how to use it to speak up and out for myself or for what was right or wrong for me and my children. Every decision no matter how big or small left me debilitated and in agony, not feeling like I had the ability or capacity to make decisions. I couldn't say NO, set healthy appropriate boundaries in my relationships. {EX, Kids, Family, friends, etc} co-parenting post divorce. I felt powerless and stuck in insecure self destructive thinking and behaviour patterns that lead to parenting challenges where my children were expressing aggressive, defiant and withdrawn behaviour stemming from hurt and fear due to being stuck in the middle of their parents conflict.

Caught in a web of Parental alienation, I blamed my ex, felt victimised and disempowered to take charge of my relationship with my kids.

For everything else I blamed myself stemming from not feeling good enough, total Victim mode, pitying myself, helpless, powerless, and utter despair. I felt like I was carrying the weight of the world on my shoulders

With no where else to turn I turned to The Ultimate and only Source that would never let me down or abandon me. I turned to Allah in a way I never turned to anyone in such desperation and humility. I focused on my two most important relationships: 1. Allah 2. Myself.

Allah sent me all the people and resources to help me with my relationship with myself and identity and all the areas I was struggling in. When I asked for courage, strength, clarity, confidence and HELP to feel OK alone on my own. The help came through experiences I needed to go through to develop all those attributes that were already within me. Allah does not change the condition until people change themselves.

One of the resources Allah gifted me with is the Inside Out Paradigm (IOP) which is the understanding of how we psychologically work as humans. And that my feelings are coming from my thinking in the moment. Knowing and understanding this truth empowered me with clarity and confidence in my communication in co-parenting with an ex who made all the decisions in the marriage and expected the same post divorce. If it didn't go his way he brings out all the stops of intimidation, threats, emotional manipulation with kids, and blame, empowered me to know that no matter what he does I am in charge of my relationship with my kids and Allah is in control of the outcome (back to two most important relationships)

IOP taught me that my thinking was shaping my experience of my life moment by moment. Not the people or circumstances in my life. It wasn't my EX that was disempowering me. It was my thinking around him and the thinking around my situation.

As a result of this understanding… I had such clarity I could make really good decisions on my own, quite confidently, based on what was right for me and my kids. I didn't have any hesitations due to how he or others would react second guessing, self doubt, to speak up and out for what I needed using my voice, speaking my truth. I could just BE ME and that was good enough. I could say NO where I wanted to, Say Yes to myself and my truth, set boundaries and limits with my EX, which before the IOP felt overbearing and looked impossible. It allowed me to break 2 decades of controlling, oppressive, abusive behaviour patterns and set new boundaries and way of interacting in a parental relationship on level playing field. Equal footing.

IOP understanding gave me the ability to: Be my authentic self with courage and fearless confidence to show up as the imperfect, messy good enough ME I have increased connection to and consciousness of Allah (taqwa) Tawakkul and reliance on Allah has allowed me to thrive where I've been planted, accept Allah's qadr and plan for me without resistance even though it wasn't how I was seeing the direction of my life.

I've been able to have ridaa (happiness and contentment) with what Allah has chosen for me. It looks like I've lost the relationship with my two teenage sons due to parental alienation by their father but I've gained and been gifted a redo with the relationship I have with my mom through serving and caring for her. A relationship that was filled with a lot of misunderstandings growing up.

It's allowed me to thrive where I've been planted and focus on the path Allah wants for me knowing that He has control over all things and having the faith He has the power to bring us all back together and heal our relationships as he's allowing me with my mom.

This may sound too good to be true but it's real. Because we are not alone and left to carry life on our shoulders. when we understand the facts of how the mind works and that our thinking is shaping our experiences and we have control over that this is all possible.

This is possible for anyone. Available to everyone. I feel like it is my miracle and it can be yours too because I am no different than you.

Rayesa Gheewala - High Performance Coach. The Divorced Muslimah Coach.

Website - www.rayesagheewala.com
Free guide on coping and healing from divorce http://bit.ly/2KVaGNX
Instagram - @rayesagheewala
Facebook - www.facebook.com/rayesa.khan.5

17

"And he found you lost and guided (you)" Quran 93:7

I was raised in a Catholic family in the 1980's, in México; my father was practicing more than my mother, as Catholics we attended church early every Sunday. I remember at a very young age I had my own opinion about what I believed when it came to religion.

Later in life I refused to do a first communion, refused to confess my sins to a priest among other things, the reason why I didn't do these things was because I felt deep in my heart like a hypocrite and it wasn't what I wanted to do nor believed; that always felt uncomfortable but the saddest part would be I lived in a broken home.

Dad had drinking problems, mum unfortunately took years to put an end to, so growing in a home like this was very hard; many arguments, shouting, violence, abuse, sleepless nights and fear were the common feelings in my life as a child.

I always wondered if dad was religious why he would behave like this. Now a days Psychology would say my dad was an ill man that he might have been through a big trauma in his life and developed alcohol dependence to the point of becoming diabetic blind and dying in a hospital due to multi-organ failure of all the years of abuse. Yes sadly my dad past away when I was 25, he was 56 and had no will to change his life and he succumbed this way when he had many chances in life to be and do better for himself. Despite this I will always be grateful to Allah for letting me do peace with my dad before he died, forgiving each other, taking care of him in the last 3 years of his life, Subhanallah.

This taught me that you do have the time and chance in life to be better, to strive against things that are not good for you; at that time I had no idea what Islam was, I had only seen and heard about the 9/11 attacks but nothing else, so after dad past away I dedicated myself to "improve" my persona; but that was in fact a facade of "improving" in my comfort zone, meaning I was inconsistent and all depended in my mood, time or energy.

Over the years I lost other family members, little by little my family circle was becoming smaller and over time many things would come to mind, unanswered questions & doubtful thoughts. I guess you can say I got tired of running round in circles when it came down to religion, but once more I let those feelings be buried for years to come…

The Muslim Switch

"And he found you lost and guided you" Quran 93:7

Years continued to pass by and I forgot about religion at the same time as having the conviction that there was a God blessing me in every aspect of my life. Made many mistakes but tried my best to overcome and grow from that. So after the birth of my first child, my 7 year marriage came to an end and I began to feel more and more disappointed about life, regardless of having a home, a car, my basic needs covered, an education, friends, family everything and anything you can think of this dunya (world).

I had that miserable feeling, I felt lost and I had a terrible need to find that, that would make me feel whole. So one day after months of being like this I had no choice but to end up in bed crying, I didn't know what was happening to me, I would ask myself how is it possible that a 30 year old having it all feels so empty, so alone!!!!!; After hours of crying in the darkness of my room late at night for many days it eventually hit me when I asked God and said: please help me and show me what I need, all of a sudden then I felt a strike in my heart that hit me like lightening making me shiver and feel a sensation of calmness and warmth and it became clear and said: "I need God!" It was shocking to realise I somewhat forgot about God, his blessings and the fact that he was there with me every step of the way through challenges, tests, ups and downs.

Next day I began look into different religions; meanwhile I got a Facebook friend request which I accepted and eventually spoke to him in several occasions when one day I heard the Adhan (call to prayer in Islam) coming in from his flat window in Argelia where he lives. I asked him what that was and he said "you don't know what that is?" He then said "I need to pray I will be right back" after ten minutes, he came back and started to explain.

It amazed me how much respect he had for his religion and the prophet (peace be upon him), how he would speak and address the conversation about Islam, I had never heard of this before and it made want to learn more about it, the only thing I knew about Islam was the 9/11 basic information everyone seemed to know.

I started learning about Islam, found many helpful and beautiful websites but also came across very disturbing ones (not part of Islam); I couldn't help to be confused and that gave me more curiosity to try understand why "if the world has Muslims all over only a few are doing these atrocities?"; I felt I had to get to the bottom of it without becoming a media sheep following everything they say.

Days later after visiting four different book stores with no success I decided to come back home, then I remembered on my way back a shop I could go to; blessing in disguise the only Quran copy was there on the shelf waiting for me. Bought it took it home and immediately started to read. As I continued to read it I felt drawn to it and in two weeks' time read I in full and realised this was a religion of love, understanding & respect with a deep connection and to god.

With more research I found an established mosque in my city, I drove there in order to seek more knowledge or information; I walked in had all my questions answered and with certainty I knew that this was what I was looking for all along, three days later I did my shahadah, Alhamdulillah.

By that time I had already made changes in my life such as wearing more modest clothes, stop drinking, clubbing, lowering my gaze, praying, however the one thing I thought was going to be the hardest thing for me was to stop smoking because I had been smoking since I was fifteen, I tried to quit many times with no success. One day whole heartedly prayed and asked Allah to help me quit this negative addiction, Subhanallah from one day to another I took the last pack of cigarettes, binned it and until today I have lived smoke free for 9 years.

As months went by I continued my transition, started letting my friends and co-workers know about the decision I had made. Shockingly I received rejection, disgusting comments and a lot of criticism; one of my closest friends said to me: "you are going to regret it because these women live oppressed and they are going to control you, not let you do anything". Long story short our friendship after this no longer existed; this person sent me an email giving me an ultimatum to either choose our friendship or to profess my religion and yes I chose Islam and let that person continue his journey.

Because of the negativity and how misinformed people are about Islam I knew it would be hard for mum to understand. Funnily and sooner than expected she asked me on a very hot day "Why are you wearing a long sleeve top on a 32° degree heat?" I said "I'm not hot mum" avoiding the topic . Then she asked me (as she knew I was looking into other religions.) "Have you found a religion that you like?" That completely caught me off guard, as I had planned to tell her over a cup of coffee.

I answered honestly yes I did and I'm happy with what I've chosen, then she said "Don't tell me you have become one of those crazy people that blow themselves up!", I stood there stone cold, my heart started to beat so quickly, my mind flashed a thousand thoughts per second. I looked in her eyes and said "Yes mum I am a Muslim" Instantly I saw rage and disappointment in her eyes, I knew she felt betrayed.

The consequences of me telling her did not wait, she stopped talking to me, her face was as cold as ice and her overall look at me was so different, I could see she was frustrated and hurting. Weeks passed by and I guess she couldn't handle the fact I had become Muslim by conviction and that nobody brainwashed me into it, that one day she bursted.

That moment was horrible because, sadly there was mocking, shouting from her part and it seemed as if our relationship would never be the same. After the rant I continued to learn about my religion and to nurture my soul; so within time I could answer all her questions if she ever gave me the chance. Eventually she spoke to me, noticed serious changes in me as mentioned before.

Being a Muslim in Mexico is hard because you start to realise how deprived we really are when it comes to halal (as there′s none), clothing, books, etc. I even had to order my first praying matt from Turkey as there are no shops that sell Islamic articles; when it came I was very happy.

You also have to deal with the Islamophobic stigma, the stares and criticism, not being allowed to work with a headscarf on etc. Overall having all these challenges every day did not put me off to continue to be a Muslim and continue to improve myself as a person; so I lived life as best as I could to avoid haram, developed my knowledge about Islam and the relationship with those whom were a part of my life.

Sadly few of my revert sisters succumbed to the pressures of society and their non-supportive families and stopped practising. Seeing this made me really sad and pushed me once more to fight even harder to remain Muslim.

The way I started to see the world through Islam enabled me to be better, to be different, to care and certainly more grateful and humble till this day; I've had many moments of struggle, many challenges, teary moments but despite all this process I achieved what I like to call "THE MUSLIM SWITCH". To me the Muslim switch is to connect to the deepest level of awaken consciousness; where my actions and intentions are always in sync in my daily life.

This connection is within all of us, we just have to develop it, achieve a high level of Imaan, to accept and believe that all chosen for us is for the best and trusting Allah with undoubtable certainty. It's definitely a work in progress and it needs to be maintained. So don't ever quit!

I hope reading my journey will captivate your heart, your mind & also make you feel contentment with the tests you have had and faced, the tears you have cried, the pain you have endured in order to become a better Muslim. Surely Allah knows your heart and belongs to him in good or bad, so stay steadfast do not lose faith as Allah loves you

May Allah (Swt) grant us understanding.

Ameen.

Karla Nagui - Charity Worker.

Facebook - www.facebook.com/karla.nagui
Instagram - @k_nagui

17

Spread Your Wings, and Fly

Guided by instinct, steered by nature, and blessed with a little luck, a miraculous journey begins ~ every day.

}i{Butterflies mesmerise us with their beauty, colour and graceful flight. They signify transformation, renewal and hope, throughout their miraculous metamorphosis.

}i{Against all odds, a tiny egg transforms into a caterpillar, expanding in size, up to one hundred times. Assuming several forms during its brief lifetime, it emerges into a magnificent winged creature.

}i{Butterflies are sentinels of good news. It has been said that wishes whispered upon a butterfly's wings will be granted. Some people accept the message from a loved one from the other side, when a butterfly appears.

}i{In 1972, MIT professor/meteorologist Edward Norton Lorenz

Presented a doctoral thesis entitled, "Predictability: Does the Flap of a Butterfly's Wings in Brazil Set Off a Tornado in Texas?" Yes, a butterfly's flutter can indeed affect the weather pattern on the other side of the world.

}i{Butterflies are important to the environment:

as food sources for insects, birds, and bats, as caterpillars, they consume weeds, plants and tree leaves, they pollinate, increasing yield of flowers, fruits, and vegetables, their presence/absence is a barometer of environmental change.

Butterflies entertain, as they engage in a colourful courtship dance. Dipping, darting, and flying in spirals, they seem to defy gravity. If all goes well, the successful suitor leaves her with all she needs. They flutter off on their separate ways. Tasting with her feet, the female carefully selects the best nursery for her precious cargo. Her sensors are two hundred times greater than our taste buds. She makes prudent choices, favourably stacking the odds for her offspring. Eggs are fertilised, as she thoughtfully places them. She arches her abdomen, depositing an egg on the underside of a leaf, to protect them from predators, parasites, and rain; or upon the tender, new shoots of the host plant. Have a plan. Consider the future.

Milkweed is the exclusive host plant for monarch and queen butterflies. Zebra long wings, Gulf fritillaries and Julias opt for about any type of passion vine. Swallowtail butterflies aren't as discriminating, and have good taste. They deposit their eggs on carrot, celery, parsley, dill or fennel plants along with the leaves of certain trees, including citrus. Making good choices improves chances for success.

Butterflies can lay a dozen or up to a thousand eggs. The average is a couple hundred, in her scant lifetime. Even with those large numbers, not everyone makes it. Some eggs may be washed away by rain, or become food for other living things, succumb to fungus, or never even develop. The butterfly doesn't waste time worrying about what she can not change. She goes about her business, pollinating flowers as she drinks in the sweet nectar of life. She maintains hope, trusting that those tiny eggs will transform into barely visible caterpillars. Her life may be days, weeks or months; dependant upon climate, species, weather patterns and luck. What can you do today to create momentum/ positive change?

In a few days (or weeks), lucky little larvae emerge, and feast on their eggshell. The host plant becomes their food source. Caterpillars do three equally important things: eat, poop, and sleep. The host plant provides sustenance and water. Sometimes caterpillars chow down to the stalk to maintain their voracious growth spurts and energy. Some plants, including milkweed have the unique ability to release a distasteful hormone as if to say, "That's enough! I need time to grow back". Speak up. Don't wait until resources are diminished.

If there is an army of caterpillars present, they have to eat what they can, when they can. They must expunge anything that no longer serves them, whether that's frass (poop) or old, too-tight skin. This is exhausting. Time to rest and recharge is a must. With some luck, the smart and the strong will survive. Have a plan, and keep moving forward.

Caterpillars can grow up to one hundred times their size, depending on the species, weather, and food source availability. Unknowingly, they have big jobs ahead of them, with impacts greater than they will ever know. For a couple weeks, they're just hungry caterpillars, enjoying the gluttony. Eat, poop, sleep; all important. Take care of yourself.

Some caterpillars are smooth-skinned, while others are tufted, bristled, horned or hairy. Others can be poisonous. Swallowtail caterpillars have a unique defence mechanism, an osmeterium. When threatened, they display two gel-like antennae from their heads, with an unpleasant odour. Most butterfly (and moth) larvae are defenceless against birds, lizards, frogs, toads, bacteria, fungus and human interference (pesticides and loss of habitat). Life can seem like an uphill battle. What can you do to protect yourself?

After they've shed their skin four or five times, or exhausted their food supply they reach a crossroad. Do they stay, go, or change? There's no guarantee there will be food, if they leave the safety of the host plant. They put themselves at risk to predators, parasites, and the unknown. Some heed that inner calling, confident in the timeless wisdom of nature guiding them. Using several pairs of tiny legs and pro-legs, they crawl along. Claspers serve as suctions, holding them to the surface as they scale. Some will travel great distances. The adventurous settle on a safe, dry place. Using their back set of claspers, they anchor themselves. In a day or so, they face another major decision. Attached by a thin silken thread they created, evading gravity, the brave let go. Upside down, from the inside out, they begin another miraculous transformation. The old, useless baggage (final skin) falls away. A chrysalis forms and hardens. What can you release, freeing yourself from your story, habits, past?

Did I make the right decision? What are the others doing? What if…..? There is no rewind, no looking back. For now, they focus on the moment, rest and hope for the future. If all goes well, in a couple of weeks there will be a wake up call. Prior to sunrise, the new life form must make a conscious effort to burst from its self-made constraints. There is a feeling of euphoria. Walls are broken through. A rush of air fills new lungs. Three pairs of new legs grasp for something solid, above. The plump lower body, attached atop the chrysalis lowers. Breathe. Hold on. Everything will be all right. A rush of adrenaline flows. Two sides of the proboscis must be zipped together. This appendage at the chin works like a straw, and is what the butterfly uses to drink nectar from flowers, feeders or juice from fruit. The insatiable caterpillar feast is now only a past memory. Are you willing to live mindfully, in this moment?

From the shoulder area, there is movement and weight. Breathe. Believe. Flex. Good things are coming. Right place. Right time. With every breath and stretch, fluid pumps from the body into the shoulder area. Magnificent, colourful wings slowly unfurl. The butterfly is damp and vulnerable for hours, as s/he adjusts and gets used to its new body. Two compound eyes provide multiple views of everything in sight - except for their own glorious wings. What magnificence do you not see in yourself?

As the sun gently warms the Earth, the butterfly gains strength and confidence. When the time is right, s/he will execute a few fast flutters. Solar power assures the butterfly, there's hope on the horizon. Facing into the wind, s/he lifts off, with joy. Floating on the breeze is indescribable, with spectacular views! Like advertising billboards, brilliant blossoms beckon the butterfly to sample their bounty. This is a symbiotic relationship. The flowers provide nourishment and energy, while benefiting from the pollen gathered on the butterfly's antennae, legs and body. This results in more flowers, more beauty, more fruit, and more vegetables. Are you contributing to your environment/ relationships, positively?

S/he will scan the landscape for movement and scent to attract a mate. Miraculously, they find each other. The dance begins; lasting minutes, hours or days. She is left with everything required, and may have gifted him with nutrients to assist him in further sharing his gene pool. A process begins anew, every day.

Whether caterpillars become a beloved monarch, a giant swallowtail, or a tiny sulphur, their very lives matter, as does yours. Everything we think, do and say (even to ourselves) matters. As illustrated by Edward Lorenz with The Butterfly Effect, the flutter of a butterfly's wings can affect weather patterns far away. Small, seemingly insignificant changes can indeed create monumental changes. With every thought we give attention to, every bite we take, every dollar we spend and every action we set into motion, we are creating momentum, choices and results. Some, we may not live to see.

Like beautiful butterflies, we are here on this wondrous Earth for just a brief moment in time. Eat, poop and sleep. Eat healthy, take care of the body you were given. Stay light, float on the breeze. Eliminate anything you don't need and that which no longer serves you. Is that an item, a house full of stuff, a toxic relationship, or a bad habit? Make the time to rest and recharge. Self care does not make you selfish.

Before your feet even touch the floor, have you envisioned a day overflowing with infinite, joy-filled possibilities? Or did you revert to the comfort of the familiar, and made excuses why you're not where you should be, or with whom you should be? Maybe you already wasted time, by worrying about stuff that might not even occur? While we agonise over a situation, we rarely consider the multitude of people whom would gladly trade places with us. Life presents us with an array of options, every day.

To attain and benefit from the lessons we came for, we will endure metamorphosis, many times. We imagine better outcomes, had we made different choices or been offered other options. This may require multiple attempts. Sometimes it's better to choose being happy, than being right. Agree to disagree. Life isn't always fair. We don't always get what we feel we deserve. Bad things happen to good people. Desired results may evade us, even when we have done everything right. We can choose the woe is me approach, refuse to engage, procrastinate, or look for the butterflies, rainbows, opportunities, lessons and unicorns. Success mandates us to push past barriers and self-imposed circumstances we create - just like the butterfly.

Trust the wisdom of nature, listen to your instincts and know that just by being here ~ YOU are living miracle. What are you waiting for? Spread your wings, and FLY!

}i{"Your talent is God's gift to you. What you do with it is your gift back to God" - Leo Buscaglia

Tina K VaLant - Extraordinary Photographer, Speaker, CBD Transdermal Squares. Founder of Extraordinary Photography.

Facebook - www.facebook.com/tina.valant
Instagram - @tina_valant
Website - www.TinaValant.com
CBD transdermal squares
for pain/anxiety relief, helps the body heal itself

17

Will there be hope?

What I'm about to share with you I've only shared in talks, but I would now like to reach out to a wider audience, as it is my intention and passion to let you know that *there is hope.*

When I think back, it seemed that all was going well in my life until the age of five-and-a-half. I remember kindergarten well: the toys, the games we played, and the other children. It seemed to be a happy time, I can still smell and feel the leather bag I used for my packed lunch and the little packets of sweets we got for our birthdays. But then things changed. At that young age, my existence was taken to a different level; one of fear, hopelessness and despair. The twinkling star within me suddenly lost its sparkle.

My father could be very funny and had a caring side to him. He was a hardworking man. But, unfortunately, he was also an alcoholic. He drank from a very young age, and was still drinking when he met my mum. In fact, he never stopped. During his drinking sessions, his personality would change. He would become an unpredictable, nasty man, becoming aggressive and violent towards my mum and us (my brother, my sister and me). We'd constantly be treading on eggshells, trying not to upset him. Over time, he became spiteful even when he wasn't drinking.

The day he changed my life, I was five-and-a-half years old. It happened when I was trying on my new school dress, an exciting time for many girls at that age. My mother needed to make some alterations, so she stood me on top of the kitchen table to save her crouching. She left the room for a moment to get something, and as she walked out, my father walked in. He saw me standing there, walked towards me and started speaking to me in manner that made me feel very uncomfortable.

I was hoping that my mother would come back into the room any second, because from the way he was speaking to me and from what he was telling me, I knew something was wrong. There was nothing I could do. Then he touched me in a way he shouldn't have. I knew that what he'd done was wrong and, by this time, I was praying for my mother to come back. It all happened in a very short space of time. Not only did he touch me in that way, but he also managed to scare me into keeping what had happened from my mother.

That was the first turning point in my life. One moment, I was five-years old, excited about my new dress and looking forward to going to school, and the next I was on a completely different path: a path of abuse, shame, guilt and feelings of disconnection. In that moment, my innocence was destroyed and the sparkle I'd always had just disappeared.

My father started to 'groom' me and my life took a different turn. He made the abuse sound interesting and exciting, so he would get me to touch him and please him. It was a gradual process that didn't feel right to me, but since I was then only six years old, I had no alternative but to go along with it. He also threatened me and kept me in fear, so that I wouldn't say anything to my mother. In this way, he continued to manipulate me.

The abuse wasn't just physical, but emotional, too. I must have been about seven or eight-years old when my father told me that, when I grew up, I should be a prostitute. This, I think, was going to be more for his benefit than for mine. I was devastated. I was so scared and horrified, in disbelief that my father could say something like that. This only led to feeling even more worthless and shameful. I remember being very upset, and when my uncle asked me if anything was wrong, I started crying and told him what my father had said. With kind and gentle words, he told me not to worry, that it was not going to happen, that my father was probably drunk when he said it.

Drunk or not, it had been said, and the words were very powerful. However, over time, the thoughts and fears I had about what my father said fell to the back of my mind. Life carried on as normal (well, what seemed normal for me) and on the surface I forgot about it. Subconsciously, however, the seed was planted.

It was rooted deeply in my mind.

Six years passed until my dad's abuse was discovered by my mother. She caught him touching me in forbidden ways and all hell broke loose. Shortly after that, he left the house, though he still lived in the same town. At first, I felt scared every time I left the house. If I saw him, I'd hide in a shop across the road because I couldn't face seeing or speaking to him. This continued until one day, when I was about twelve or thirteen-years old, I asked myself whether I really wanted to be scared of him for the rest of my life. And the answer was NO! I realised at that very moment that I had a *choice*.

So, plucking up all of my courage, I decided to visit him. I knew that I was going to be safe, as he had a new partner, so I went to his house. I can't remember what I said or what the conversation was about. All I know is that when I left his house, I felt truly liberated. I 'felt the fear and did it anyway'. In my opinion, that was the first step of accepting what had happened to me. Of course, that one action alone didn't unravel or heal the deeply traumatic emotional experiences and their effect on my belief system. The question is: how can anyone want to accept something so bad and wrong? However, later I learned to accept him for who he was by understanding his background. That helped me to eventually forgive him. Someone once told me that not forgiving is like wishing someone else dead, but drinking the poison yourself. The anger, the sadness, the negative feelings that you hold inside do not harm the other person: they harm YOU.

Looking back at those dark times, it felt as though the real me was disappearing. I knew that things were not the same for me as they were for other children, but because I'd never experienced a loving, happy life, I didn't know how much better other children's lives were. A child forms its belief system in the first six to seven years of its life, when the brain is like a sponge, taking in all the negative and positive messages. It forms beliefs about the 'self', about others and about the world. The beliefs that I was developing about myself and the world around me were not positive at all. I had to learn to accept my awful experiences and to take responsibility for what I was thinking and how I was interacting with the world.

Making changes from within takes time. It's a gradual process and I'm grateful for that. If the changes had happened faster, I think I would've gone mad; I wouldn't have had the time to process everything as I went through the stages of learning how to be more self-accepting. It would have been an explosion of emotions sending me over the edge, rather than a process of growth, reconnecting with who I really am. It's like gradually getting rid of the weeds in a dark, dead, unloved garden and putting the love and light back into it, allowing the flowers to grow. It has taken me a long time, but I am so grateful that I've managed to make changes within me and that I've been able to forgive both him and, most of all, myself, as what happened to me was not my fault.

Accepting what my father did and accepting my father for who he was started me on my journey to freedom. I began to recognise that I could be free to be me, free from the demons of thought that I was not worthy of love. In coming to understand that it was not my fault, I could then begin to change the terrible feelings of guilt and shame and, with it, accept that I'd been dwelling on the past.

Over the years, I have learned to accept and not to pass judgement on people, because I don't know what experiences they've had that have made them become who they are. I believe that no one who chooses to have a sense of self-worth would choose a path of self-destruction or choose to intentionally harm other people. For my father, it was almost as if the dark side had won him over. It can take time to overcome and accept what's happened to you and what's been said to you, but you have to keep trying and never give up.

I wish I could give clear instructions on how to gain acceptance, like a set of road directions: 'take a left turn, right over the roundabout up the hill and take another left and you are at your destination'. But it's not as simple as that: there are no instructions for how to reach acceptance. You create the experience of finding it and getting there yourself. It's an individual process of inner growth. To find acceptance you have to look at people and situations from a different perspective. You have to find the mental agility to bend and guide your thoughts to a different and more positive way of thinking. Allow yourself to look for the positives and learn from what has happened to you.

Our belief system defines how we feel about the world, and governs how we behave and interact with others. How we perceive ourselves has a lot to do with the beliefs we created from the experiences we had from the day we were born.

I grew up with a negative belief system about myself and suffered silently from the effect it had on me. Nobody knew how I really felt about myself, and I couldn't tell anyone. I felt upset and alone with my emotional pain. I think, even if I had found someone I could have talked to, I wouldn't have had the words to explain my feelings and thoughts at that time. As a result, I grew up with emotional insecurities. I was rebellious and I made some bad choices as I didn't know how to trust my instincts. I did all the normal kid stuff; staying out too late, exploring life. But I also started to express my anger and frustration and nobody knew why. It must have looked as if I didn't care about anyone or anything, even though I did. I simply felt that I was misunderstood by the people around me, since no one knew what had been going on pretty much all of my life. I wanted to be liked, loved and nurtured. I longed to feel safe and wanted, as I was not experiencing any of those feelings at the time. I knew that my mother loved me, but she didn't know what was happening. I couldn't tell her because my father had threatened me that if I told anyone, I was going to be put in a children's home. So, life continued and I kept on praying for a better one, praying for help, and for someone to come and rescue me.

I was never any good at school. I had to repeat a whole year at the age of eight, and in my school report they wrote:

> *'Angelika tries very hard but she just doesn't seem to be able to do it.'*

What a soul-destroying message for a child, and a very negative one for my parents too. What my parents and I didn't know at the time was that I was dyslexic. I didn't get the support dyslexic children have today - in my time, dyslexia was not recognised, so children like me were just called 'stupid' and were made fun of. I was only diagnosed with dyslexia in 2002, and up until then I believed that I simply didn't have what it takes to learn and study like other people.

When I left school, I went to the job centre for careers advice and instead of leaving full of hope and courage, I felt that I'd had another doomed day. The advisor remembered my brother, who had done very well in school, and said something like, "What has happened to you? Your brother has done really well. Why haven't you done well, too?" I felt my heart sink and I wondered, "Does *everyone* know how stupid I am?" I was feeling so hurt and frustrated that I couldn't express my feelings, nor explain what I was forced to put up with at home. However, I think it is fair to say that I had a lot on my plate during my school years, and this played a big part in how I did at school. At that time in my life, the belief that I couldn't succeed, and that I was unable to learn and better myself, was still very deeply engrained. But I didn't give up. I left school at the age of fourteen, and with the qualifications I had, I could have done good things or started a career. However, my mother's belief was that I didn't need an education, as I was going to get married and have children, and with my history at school I had no chance to get any further education anyway.

So, it was decided that I should do an apprenticeship, learning to make fur coats. I succeeded in my training, which was great, but I didn't want to stay in that kind of work. In fact, I wanted to become a nurse, but I was told that I needed more qualifications. So I tried attending classes at evening school, even though I was told from the beginning that I wouldn't make it, or that I couldn't do it. I tried anyway, but didn't get the support I needed to succeed so, eventually, I gave up.

Despite the negative comments that were made about me, I never stopped trying to learn and educate myself in the best way I knew, in my own way. I came across books like *Siddhartha* by the German author, Herman Hesse. *Siddhartha* is a novel that deals with the spiritual journey of self-discovery of a man during the time of the Gautama Buddha. I loved this book. It inspired me and, during this time, I started my transformational journey. I read many more books and some poetry of Herman Hesse and began to learn about spirituality. I found that this was a really good way of learning; it gave me food for thought and I connected with the ideas.

Having accepted that learning in a classroom was not the best way for me, I started to enjoy educating myself in my own way, although I wasn't conscious that this was what I was doing. I also read Carlos Castaneda, and that too made a deep impression on me and stimulated my way of thinking. I realised that I'm not stupid! I'm just different, and I learn in a different way. I was going to a 'better school': the 'School of Life'. All in all, I have to thank the woman in the job centre and my teachers for pushing my buttons and contributing to making me who I am today!

When I was seventeen, my family moved to a different town, so I moved into the first place of my own. It was great, but it was also lonely. Even though it was my choice to be there alone, I felt like nobody cared. I wasn't used to living on my own and I ended up spending a lot of time with myself and my thoughts: my negative beliefs continued to dictate my life.

Nearly two years later, a man came into my life, and once more that took me onto a different pathway to a very different way of life. He seemed to be really nice and he liked me: I thought he really cared. He was older than me, and it probably didn't take him long to realise that I was an easy target. He was the person who slowly manipulated me into becoming a prostitute. He would paint a picture of how much money we would have and what we could do with it. He persuaded me that it would be for our future and that it would prove my love for him if I would do this. I didn't know any different at the time. I didn't know that I had a choice: my self-worth and my belief in myself had been destroyed from the age of five.

It was these negative beliefs I had about myself that gave me the ability to do what I did. I believed, because I had no education and felt unworthy, that being an escort girl was the only thing I was good for. I believed that 'good girls' had a good education, and therefore had good careers, and that 'bad girls' didn't have an education, and so had demeaning or meaningless jobs. It was as if my dad had prepared me for this with his words and actions and it was in my belief system that this was what I deserved. I simply didn't know any different.

We moved to a city together and from my early twenties I started working as an escort girl. I used to go to some of the best restaurants and hotels when escorting businessmen who were visiting the city. I enjoyed fine food and wine, so it also taught me a lot. I met a variety of men: good, bad, interesting, educated, but also rude and ignorant men who treated me as if I was at their service, rather than appreciating me as a person. That part of my life was another form of education which I believe gave me the ability to read people and situations.

With time, I came to realise that if my partner really loved me he would have asked me to stop working as an escort girl. In fact, he never would have asked me in the first place. I know he had feelings for me in a way, but they were not the right feelings. He'd had his own experiences in life that made him the way he was.

Eventually, my feelings for him started to change and I wanted to leave him but didn't know how. So life went on, with me working as an escort and him continually upsetting and hurting me emotionally. In all those years, I couldn't tell his or my family, which also meant I couldn't ask for help to leave him and get away from escorting. I stayed in the relationship for nearly ten years, believing that as long as I was under his influence, I couldn't get out and do something better.

So how did things change? Well, I started to believe in myself more. I started to believe that there were different things I could do other than being an escort girl. I realised, once again, that I had choices.

Once I'd started making these decisions, however, this time I wasn't going to go back to my old thought patterns. I kept on thinking (just as I had when I was a child), "This cannot be it, surely." My intention was to get out of the escort business and, after a while, my efforts paid off. I told a friend I was looking for a job and he helped me, putting me in touch with his friend who needed someone to work in customer service in the company he was working for. I couldn't believe my luck. Someone actually wanted to employ me! I was overcome by tremendous joy and fear at the same time, as escorts 'don't work in offices'. Not long after that, I started the job.

I had a new beginning, not only because of the job, but also, a couple of months later, I met my future husband there! After a few years together, we got married and a wish of mine came true: a new life, a new journey, and another new beginning for me. I'm sure this enormous change, to escape from life as an escort girl, was successful because I'd made the *choice*. I had put my heart and soul behind the thoughts and, feeling positive (and a little scared, too), I stepped out and took the action that supported what I wanted to achieve.

When we are pushed to step out of our comfort zones, we learn and have new experiences. It's about choosing to let go of those negative thoughts that lead to negative outcomes. Be aware of your thoughts and ask yourself if they are really serving you for the better, or if they are keeping you in old habits. Make the choice to create stronger, better, more positive thoughts to build an image of the best version of yourself.

In time and with practice, I learned to observe my thoughts, and when the negative chatter started I changed it to positive thoughts. It takes no effort at all to *not* be in control of your thoughts, whereas to be constantly aware takes supreme concentration; it takes time, it's a process. If you fall off the wagon, don't beat yourself up. Recognise your negative thoughts and change them to more positive, happier ones and you will start to feel better. When you feel sad, check what you are thinking about. What is your negative thinking pattern? How can you improve it? Don't let fear drive your mind; try telling yourself that it's not real, that it's just a thought creating a negative feeling, an emotion from the past that you have not managed to change yet.

We are not only affected by the words of others but also very much by the words we use when we speak about ourselves. Even small phrases like, "Oh silly me," or, "I could never do that," keep our self-doubt active and keep us stuck in negative beliefs. Choose not to get involved in negative conversations because even if it is not about you personally, it will still affect you. However, it's very important to remember that positive thinking alone is not enough to change your life. Your heart must be in it as well and you need to truly believe that you are worthy of the positive things you desire.

About fifteen years ago, I had a tarot card reading with a lady in Bath. I decided to see her as I wanted to have a glimpse of what might lie ahead on my path. When we met, I took a liking to her immediately and, during the reading, she gave me what she understood to be an important message. She told me that I had a natural aptitude for teaching and that she could see me facilitating workshops, and that I would be very good at it. I said to her, "No way! That is not something I can do!" Even so, there I was, being told that one day I would be facilitating workshops. There was no way, I felt, that this could be possible as it would involve writing. Plus, I didn't know *what* I would teach! I could see myself as a facilitator, but actually running the whole show, absolutely not!

But about seven years ago this all started to change when I was asked, "What is it that you are passionate about? What comes easily to you and takes no effort for you to do?" It was then I decided that I didn't want my challenging and 'colourful' life experiences to go to waste. I decided I wanted to work with people who were stuck, overwhelmed and feeling hopeless. I wanted to give people hope and inspiration and to demonstrate that, by sharing my story, anyone can change their life. No matter what we have or haven't done, no matter how low we might feel, each one of us is worthy of love.

So here I am, once the abused child, the dyslexic pupil, the escort girl, educated by the 'School of Life and Hard Knocks', having gone through the journey of ACCEPTING the challenges, changing my limiting BELIEFS about myself and making the CHOICE to do so, all of which has brought me to this very moment when I am writing these words. My experiences made me who I am. I love who I've become, and now I can only be true to myself.

My intention is not to impress you with what I have overcome, because everyone has a story and I just happen to be sharing mine with you. My reason for sharing my story is to give people hope that they too can change their lives, whatever the situation. We always have the choice to make some kind of change, and even consciously choosing not to make any changes for the time being is better than just letting things run their course. It's not necessarily about having traumatic experiences in order to find out what you're really made of. Sometimes, it's just a matter of realising that we may not be achieving what we would like because we're living according to other people's values. Einstein famously said, "If we keep doing the same thing over and over again, we will have the same outcome again and again." And, in my opinion, life is too short to just 'make do'.

So, what is your choice? Where do you want to be in your life? Will you let your limiting beliefs run the show and hold you back? In the workshop I have now created, I use my own principle called ABChange4life: simple, effective steps which can guide you to your path of change. The ABC steps become your building blocks from which you create the platform to change your life. The workshop is about exploring your self-belief and working through steps that can help to make those all-important changes.

This is the end of my chapter, but perhaps, for me, it's a new beginning! How about you? What will you choose? Will you let your past determine your future? What changes can you make today? As they say, sometimes your worst enemy lives between your ears.

I wish you the greatest happiness and the freedom to be you. We are all worthy of love.

Angelika Breukers - Change Maker, Speaker & Author of Free To Be Me! ABChange4life Mentor.
At the core of Angelika's work is her formula to living a life free from pain or shame, and to become full of joy: *Acceptance* + *Belief* + *Choice* = *Change*

Change your story, change for life.

Website - www.AngelikaBreukers.com/
Instagram - @angeliksbreukers
Facebook - www.facebook.com/abreukers1

Your Fresh Start...

This is a new day, a new beginning. It starts with a choice – right here, right now.

I am Alexandra Grace Scott, your fellow traveler on the road of life. The words I have written here are from my heart to yours. You have survived some of life's most difficult challenges, and it's my desire to help you. Your personal challenges may have left you defeated, discouraged and in despair.

I want you to know that I care...Who am I and why am I sharing this?

Years ago I found myself with two children, divorced, experiencing post- traumatic stress disorder, with little money, a health challenge and a bleak future. I knew that to move forward I had to rally myself. I needed to make some changes. I call these changes the Seven Healing Choices.

My aim is to help you find the power of CHOICE that exists within you. These Seven Healing Choices have been "tested" and proven to work - by me and many others faced with severe hardships.

These Seven Healing Choices will help you to experience peace and a better life. They are gentle shifts you can make through your ability to choose.

When I made these choices, they brought a much needed healing and a new way of thinking and feeling (yes, you can shift feelings!). I searched for answers to help me find some strength, have a plan and just a spark of confidence and hope.

What I found are these Seven Healing Choices. Making these choices, I was able to go forward from just "surviving" day to day. Positive things happened in my life, doors opened and I was able to find my "better self" – in my relationships, my job, and with my family. I became financially independent.

For a number of years I've shared these Healing Choices with the women at Burckle Place, a transitional housing program for homeless women founded by the Lord's Place. I have seen the positive results first hand.

If you can make shifts in your thinking, the result will be changes in what you do - and what actually shows up in your life. Making healing choices is up to us - it's an "inside job" and a choice only we can make.

"YOUR FRESH START can happen today!"

Martin Luther King, Junior - "Take the first step in faith. You don't have to see the whole staircase.

just take the first step."

Rising out of homelessness, helplessness and hopelessness can begin today. Before the outer can change, the inner needs to be looked at and put in order. That part is up to us!

HEALING CHOICE ONE - To move forward FORGIVE YOURSELF

In order to move forward we need mental, emotional and physical strength. That's why it is critical to start by forgiving yourself. We can then release these "mistakes" and allow ourselves to heal and move forward.

Holding on to regrets, shame and blame weakens our inner strength. We can become paralysed when we're drowning in guilt, self-hate and anger.

Healing through choosing self-forgiveness is a vital first step that helps us to:

- make better choices
- build healthier self-esteem
- have greater self-appreciation
- have a brighter future

HEALING CHOICE 1 - As Lucille Ball once said,

"Love yourself first and everything else falls into line. You really have to love yourself to get anything done in this world."

Negative emotions do nothing good for us, and just drag us down. We need to have compassion for ourselves as human beings surviving in this challenging world. The past has passed. Did you learn lessons from your experiences? Self-forgiveness will allow you to release shame and blame. This is key to moving on to your new life and build a healthy opinion of yourself.

Take the lessons of your past with you and move on.

HEALING CHOICE 2 - To move on with your life - FORGIVE THE UNFORGIVABLE

Forgiveness of others is crucial because it heals us. Try viewing those who have hurt you as having mental and emotional issues. Forgiveness does not excuse the wrong.

Our past frustrations, anger and rage are certainly understandable and valid. However, maintaining the outrage over life's hurts and injustices creates negative emotions that are harmful. These emotions release stress chemicals that affect the body, the mind, and weaken us.

Resentment keeps us stuck in the same place (the past), preventing us from moving forward with positive emotions.

Here's a prayer to help you remove past hurts and clear the way for healing. It certainly may be tough to say, but saying this will start healing the hurt, the anger, and make you stronger. It's worth it.

Think of the person(s) who have hurt you, and pray:

"I'm sorry this happened. I forgive you. May God bless you. Thank you."

Do this for yourself, for your own healing. This prayer will clear the path for good to come forth into your life.

HEALING CHOICE 3 - The power of gratitude - BE GRATEFUL

"When I started counting my blessings, my whole life turned around." - WILLIE NELSON

Being truly grateful daily is one of the most powerful practices. It affects your body, mind, relationships and energy all day long. When we face difficulties in life, it can be hard to be grateful for anything. Feeling appreciation every day for the smallest things increases our happiness level. Gratitude also releases toxic feelings like resentment, frustration, regret and depression. It increases both mental and physical strength.

Gratitude helps in healing trauma. Exchange self-pity for gratitude. This practice will change your day, your chemistry and your life.

Gratitude:

- reduces toxic emotions
- increases happiness
- reduces depression and stress
- improves physical health

What are you grateful for today? Think of three things you are grateful for right now. Write them down. Research has proven that if you do this for just 21 days, you will be a happier, more positive person. It works!

Gratitude is a healing choice you can make starting today.

HEALING CHOICE 4 - Your mind is yours to control - CHOOSING YOUR THOUGHTS & FEELINGS

We have the ability to influence our attitude and moods everyday by choosing our thoughts and shifting our feelings. The alternative is to believe we have no control over our thoughts and let life and our thoughts just happen to us.

"Automatic" thinking is mainly negative. (Studies have shown that as much as 75% of thinking is negative.)

The good news is we have an inner capability given to us by the Creator - and that is the power of choice. This remarkable ability gives us inner control when we feel life is out of control. We need to watch our thoughts. We have the ability to choose and create positive thoughts that provide us with power. Positive thoughts = Positive results

HEALING CHOICE FIVE - Find direction and your strength - DISCOVER SILENCE

We live in a world of constant noise and distraction, and can hardly "hear ourselves think." Being in silence has a power all of its own. Silence allows our inner knowing to flow to us.

It has been my experience that silence helps me find who I am. It brings me solutions, guidance and direction.

Silence for even a minute reduces stress, brings calmness, and provides clearer thinking. Silence allows you to discover your true self. I discovered a simple, powerful technique to experience the silence within. It's Heart Focused Breathing. Take a minute and try this for yourself.

Breathe a little more deeply than normal. Breathe in 5-6 seconds and breathe out 5-6 seconds. Imagine you are breathing from your heart. To help you focus on your heart you can place your hand over your heart. Scientists have discovered the heart possesses a special intelligence (a knowing and feeling) that communicates to us.

Discover the map to who you are and are meant to be, by practicing this daily, whatever is going on around you.

Listen to the desires of your heart as you practice being in silence. They will point the way to who you are and what you need to do.

Being in silence reveals your truth.

HEALING CHOICE SIX - Believe in yourself - CREATE SELF-CONFIDENCE

When I was at my lowest, to move forward I had to believe in myself. Moving on from a place of desperation, I had to find things to appreciate about myself.

Here's what I realised - I am a creation with unique DNA and abilities – an intelligent design created by an Intelligent Creator. You are one of a kind.

Believe in your unique self, with a unique personality and abilities. Like each snowflake and each flower, you are truly unique.

Another powerful tool to create self-confidence is to close your eyes and imagine a movie screen in your mind. See and feel yourself in the movie of your new life.

This kind of visualisation is very powerful. Athletes use it to enhance their performance with astonishing results. Muhammed Ali used mental and verbal practices to impact his performance. He shared perhaps the simplest yet most powerful statement of self-worth,"I am the greatest!"

Use visualisation to find, see and become your best self.

Low self-confidence brings a feeling of weakness, lack of energy,

low motivation and sadness. Instead, choose to feel like a child of God made of divine substance. (We possess the same properties as stardust!). Stand tall, smile! You know more than you think you know. You are stronger than you think you are. Look in the mirror and talk to yourself like you would to someone you love. Tune into what you like about yourself and your abilities.

Self love and appreciation of what is right about ourselves is essential to going forward. Rejection of ourselves is self abuse.

Our failures are events, not who we are!

HEALING CHOICE SEVEN - Believe in your future - FIND YOUR POTENTIAL, PURPOSE & PLAN

We need a plan to build anything and make it a reality. It can be as simple as writing down your goals and action steps. Decide what you want. You can start small by thinking of what you want for the day, the rest of this week, the month, and the year.

Life is a process. You have the power to choose to not give up! You can't accomplish what you want if you give up the belief that you can and will.

Without action, you aren't going anywhere. If you make a plan, you will be more motivated to take action. Your future is built through the actions of the present. So take small steps forward. It's more about going forward and taking some action toward your intended destination.

Inaction makes us feel doubt and fear, which could lead us to giving up. Taking action makes us feel hopeful and more confident. It increases our courage and self-worth.

Identify what is holding you back What can you do to make it better? If you experience a setback, believe it's part of the process and a detour leading you to another door.

99% of failures occur because someone believed that a setback was a defeat. Look for the positive in everything. It's never too late to begin. You can do it! Find support for your vision and your goals through a program, counsellor, spiritual leader or an individual who believes in you! Believe in yourself.

THE SEVEN HEALING CHOICES outlined for you in this chapter can change your attitude, energy and outlook to one that is positive. The Seven Healing Choices will make a difference in your life. Remember that small shifts in our thinking create big shifts in our lives.

Going forward, make your life count by making a difference in the lives of others – a kind act, a smile, a word of encouragement. Don't judge the future by the past. Share your story of letting go of the past and how you gave yourself a "fresh start." Volunteer to help others. You will build self-confidence and self-esteem in others and yourself.

Service to others helps you to know you are making a difference in this world.

Making the choice to incorporate the Seven Healing Choices in your life reflects your willingness to take the next step in faith (acting as if and feeling you can overcome the difficulty. Take some action! (knowing that no change comes without some action).

I have shared the Seven Healing Choices from my heart and with the sincere hope that you use them to make ***YOUR FRESH START.***

ALEXANDRA GRACE SCOTT, AUTHOR
"Forget the former things; do not dwell in the past." ISAIAH 43:18

Alexandra Grace Scott went from being a struggling secretary on food stamps to becoming an entrepreneur and CEO of a multi-million dollar company.

The business she established, International Business Forum, helped facilitate the digital world of today by bringing together venture capital investors with emerging technology entrepreneurs.

Having developed the capacity to heal from her past and manifest her goals, she is inspired to share this knowledge with others.

As the author of the chapter, Your Fresh Start, Alexandra explains The Seven Healing Choices to create a life that works. These choices are simple to understand and easy to implement.

Originally from New York, she resides in Palm Beach Gardens, Florida.

Email - agscott12@yahoo.com
Facebook - www.facebook.com/alexandra.grace.946
Instagram - @alexandra.grace.scott

17

Mind over matter

We all have a different idea of what the mindset is, where it comes from and how to use it. Each of us are right in our own way in the way we look at it. Many people believe that mindset is inherent in us and cannot be learned or changed. Where did our mindset come from? Most of the time, it comes from the environment around us. The way we grew up, what we saw, what we did, what we heard as we were developing our personalities. In today's world our mindset is shaped by social media, the news, internet, TV shows and gaming.

Have you ever thought about where your own beliefs come from, how they affect your daily life and do they affect your mindset? You can bet they do and just how much they affect you is up to you!

Did you know that you can decide what your mindset will be first thing in the morning? To feel a shift, you can set it up long before that. Have you ever had a day that you were looking forward to for months in advance? You thought about it every day, woke up excited, planned for it, you were ready to go and walked around with a big smile on your face because of it? The build up to that day is huge! You wake up that morning and you are psyched! Your positive mindset has brought you to this point. Then you walk out to your drive way that night and your world comes crashing down around you. (Sound Depressing? Maybe, maybe not.) Why would it be depressing? Because you had set your mindset. That this was going to be a huge day for you and in an instant it all went away! Mindset is tied to emotion and emotion is tied into everything we do, think and act on. It can throw you off of your game.

What happened in that driveway, does not have to be anything life changing, but it's just enough to throw off what you think or feel for the rest of your day, week or longer if you let it and there goes everything you were looking forward to. As you can see mindset is not just a long term, built in, way of life, it's also a daily occurrence. Mindset can be changed, learned, unlearned, set, reset and used in our daily lives.

I would like to expand about what happened in the driveway. I had a friend who had a dream to create a video in Washington D.C. The video was a simple one; he wanted to gather some people together and film a message for all of America to see. The message, was one from his heart. They would stand in front of the Washington Monument and while smiling and waving they would say from deep in their heats "Smile and Wave America, We Love You!" He had been planning this for months, he would soon be living his dream to carry this message of love and hope to people all across America! When he walked out to the drive way, his dreams were crushed, someone had stolen his van! He was stunned, confused, why would anybody want to take his van? It wasn't like this van was anything special; it was just a van, an older van at that!

This is where mindset takes over and dreams begin. What are the possibilities here? Do you give in? Do you accept defeat? Maybe you have a pity party or cry in your milk. This is a pretty big deal, his ride to Washington is now gone, his dreams are crushed and he can't think of a way out, that was in 2010. Back in 2006 he suffered some setbacks that changed his life. In 2006 he had a business partner that mismanaged his business, he almost lost that business, he had to jump in and save it. Five months later he received a phone call from his son-in-law that his daughter was in a moped accident with him and she hit her head and was in critical condition, in the hospital near Seoul Korea, where her husband was stationed in the Army. She spent forty-five days in the hospital fighting for her life; then his beautiful daughter passed away. His grief was indescribable.

Four months later, he took another hit when he almost lost his own life. His blood pressure had risen sharply from all the stress and was dangerously high and he ended up suffering a cerebral haemorrhage. His wife was told, "Call the family, He's dead tonight."

There was no way he could have two deaths in the family in four months and in that instant a new mindset was created. It was a never give up, never surrender, mindset. He spent two weeks in the hospital, four months sleeping in a Lazy Boy recliner, with a headache so bad that he could not sleep in a bed; and six months learning to walk and talk normally again. He lived, but recovery was slow. He felt as if he were seeing life through a fog. He fell into depression, and life hardly seemed worth living; but, he had to survive for his family.

Those nine months were the worst of his life. He questioned everything around him. He was a mess, wrecked with losses. The world seemed to be falling apart. He needed something to get himself through, but had no idea what.

About a year later, he was sitting in a VA hospital with his wife at the time, getting ready for a brain scan, depressed and mentally foggy. His wife asked him a question that would change his life. She said; "What do you want for your birthday?" He had no answer; he could not think of a single monetary thing that he wanted. All he could think of that he wanted people to get along with each other for one day. That's it, just one day. Was this too much to ask? For some reason, the idea of people smiling and waving at each other sparked something in him, he knew it was impossible to get everyone to get along. But wondered if he could touch the lives of everyone he met in a day and at least make them smile. He made a promise to himself that day, that he would share his smile with ten million people in his life time! Now, that would be something! That's why the video was so important for him to do.

He stood in that driveway, stunned. Now what? All of his thoughts were about the trip to *Washington*. He wondered how he was going to get there now? The insurance company wouldn't give him much for the old van. After the deductible, there wouldn't be enough money to buy another car and he would be left with no means of transportation. The more he thought about it, the more determined he became that nothing was going to stop him from making that trip! There was that mindset that he had created back in 2006 and he decided to create another mindset for a new journey, one where he would not be stopped.

The funny thing about the human mind is that it will go where ever you train it to go. Over time he had trained his mind to find the best situation in life no matter what! So his mind found the best in this situation. Is a little thing like a stolen van going to stop him, heck no, so he decided the best thing for him to do is walk to Washington D.C.!

This man went from having his brain wiped out and almost dying from three veins bursting in his brain and filling his skull with blood in 2006. To walking 2,000 miles up the Southeast Coast of America in 2010, because he was able to shift his mindset over and over again in those 6 years. Not only did he walk those 2,000 miles he did it with only $200 in his pocket. He did not have a plan as to where he was going to sleep each night. He did not have a plan of where he was going to eat. He did not plan out how he was going to get from one place to another he just knew he was going to walk to Washington D.C. Funny thing is, he did go to Washington and when he got there, a hurricane hit Washington on the same day he had planned to do the video!

Knowing what you now know about this man do you think that this set back stopped him? You're right, not only did it not stop him, he kept on walking all the way to Manhattan, New York! Yes this is an incredible story and it's hard to understand how he could have done this. Here is the thing, it is all about the mindset. Without the right mindset he would not have even started this journey. There were many challenges to overcome and each one was a shift in mindset. When you start a journey of this magnitude your mind has to be strong, you have to be ready for any changes and you have to create a new mindset all along the way.

How do you travel 2,000 miles never knowing where you are going to sleep each night, never mind that you are walking, even if you are driving it is a tough road. Think about having to find a place to sleep each and every night, where you are dry safe and warm for 277 days, that's nine months on the road. How do you shower and keep yourself clean along the way, with only $200? What about eating? Eating three times a day for 277 days is 831 meals. How can you do that without the mindset that you will be able to find those meals each and every day. There is much more to the mindset than we can ever imagine.

One of the things I can tell you is that when you train your mind with the right mind set, you can do anything! I am using this trip as an example because of all of the factors that go into this story, there is the fact that he never once slept outside. He took a shower every night, woke up and had a cup of coffee each morning. He always had food to eat and had plenty of snacks and water. He never once had to do without the things that he needed and there was always someone there to help him when he needed it!

You may be wondering how this story can help you change your mindset. You may think this guy must have been raised in a great and positive environment, trust me he was not. His family was good, but the neighbourhood was filled with gangs, drugs and violence. Growing up he felt that he was not good enough, couldn't do anything right and was not smart enough to even graduate high school.

One day he saw himself in a mirror and after many years of drug abuse he did not even recognise who he saw in that mirror. He knew that if he didn't make some changes he would be heading to deaths door. That's when he began to understand the power of his own mindset. You too are more than capable to shape and grow your own mindset to make your life easier. You may be wondering how I know so much about this man… That man is me. I have learned and grown over the last few years. I would love to share the tools of creating a new and better and better mindset with you and speaking at your next event. I look forward to hearing from you soon.

Edward Smile Rodriguez - CEO and Founder of The Smile and Wave Project.

E-Mail - fromfltony@gmail.com
Cell - 561-506-4607
Website: - http://www.smileandwaveamerica.com, www.TheSmileAndWaveProject.com
Videos - http://www.youtube.com/watch?v=gFoL4nEzFvc
http://www.youtube.com/watch?v=eP32Fzxkkds
Facebook - www.facebook.com/10millionsmiles

17

What doesn't kill you, makes you stronger and resilient

I am Saima Duhare the founder of Halal Fresh, UK's first halal non subscription recipe box.

I always had a passion for food, cooking and eating which stemmed from my Grandmother and Mother who taught me how to cook and were always creative in the kitchen. I was raised to eat everything fresh from meat, fish and vegetables as well as trying different cuisines, I never shied away from food which I wanted to extend to my community by offering creative meals to make dinner times an exciting table to sit at

Never had I thought I would go onto creating my own food business Halal Fresh back in 2016, I had no idea of what I was doing, was absolutely clueless, armed with passion, motivation and a mission to encourage healthy eating and bring back the joy of home cooking, a skill which I believe has been lost given the era we live in were everything is running at the speed of lightning, since eating has become a means to fuel our body oppose to considering what we are putting into our bodies. I began this journey, where I spent at least 2 years immersing myself in the food business, by surrounding myself with like-minded people, all the while learning about business as well as holding a day job

Its not been easy and along the way I'd come across numerous challenges, such as investment, no one wanted to invest since I couldn't demonstrate I ran a business; finding a chef which took 6 months by this point I had interviewed at least 80 chefs, before I found in my experience the perfect chef whom I'm working with right now in developing world cuisine recipes! In addition I had engaged with at least over 200 suppliers, knocking on doors if they would supply pre-portioned ingredients, to which most would ask, what's your MOQ (minimum order quantity) being a start-up I didn't have the buying power or finances since everything in the end was funded by my day job and my Mother, who was a huge support and believed in my vision and mission! However, the knocking paid off, I managed to secure reputable brands. Needless to say this deflated me and also made me determined, a very strange feeling! A feeling now am grateful for, tough times teaches you character

No book, course or education can prepare you for the journey of being an entrepreneur/business woman. It's a lonely place. My business was a beast and I had to find ways to negotiate with it, if that makes sense, it adopted its own personality, and I had to roll with it. In a way my business was teaching me, the only thing I could compare it to, its like having a child and you have to pay attention, be intuitive, go with your gut feeling and pray that it will all work out! Faith played a huge part.

After going through the trials and tribulations, as the saying goes, what doesn't kill you, makes you stronger and resilient. I decided I would now carry out a soft launch where I invited 40 people in 2018, needless to say this was very daunting, putting yourself on the firing line, but the 40 people who agreed to participate were absolutely lovely and fed back, which was a massive help since this helped me to improve all the findings from the user experience. The recipes, delivery and general nitty gritty stuff I hadn't even thought of. So this would take another 6 months instead of the 3 months I anticipated. Here I learned the art of patience and timing.

By this point I had a firm idea of what I wanted my brand to stand for, that it was ethical, environmentally friendly, no food wastage and responsible as well as being a fun company that enjoyed creating recipes and making dinner time enjoyable, taking the hassle out of going shopping, or thinking what to eat all the while being mindful! Being part of a cause. What makes it worthwhile, is my customers and hearing their feedback on how I've made their life easy and that they get to try different meals, or their teenage daughter now helps to cook, or their husband is having a go at cooking.

In the end it was my purpose and my WHY I overcame the initial obstacles and I'm grateful to ALLAH SWT in putting me on this journey. It's only the beginning and I have a long way to go and no doubt I will encounter more barriers and obstacles nothing in life is easy, and if it were,

I wouldn't know how to grow the business or achieve personal growth.

We are more than just a recipe box, In light of the above, I officially launched Halal Fresh in April 2019 Alhamdulilah

Saima Duhare - Founder of Halal Fresh, Dinner is sorted!

Website - www.halalfresh.co.uk
Instagram - @halalfreshuk

17

"There is nothing stronger than a broken woman who has rebuilt herself"

My name is Sarah, I am that strong woman who is still standing here today, striving and aiming high! I was that broken woman who was so tired and even lost, from all the hardships I had endured and the harsh lessons that I had faced in my short life...

God knows I've overcome everything that could have easily destroyed me for good, but no matter what, even at my lowest points of feeling completely defeated and hopeless I always told myself "just keep trying, don't give up!"

I grew up without my parents or siblings, raised by a family that physically and emotionally abused me, leaving me to fend for myself at the young age of just 16 years old...

Throughout my young adult life, I went from job to job, house-share to house-share, back and forth up and down the country, lived abroad and even travelled around the world, hopelessly searching for a sense of belonging to somewhere, something and someone...

At the age of 23, I decided to move to Manchester, hoping to have a fresh and new start... I got myself a place to live and a part time job and enrolled in college for the next two years and later got into university. It wasn't easy, in-fact it was very lonely living in a place that I didn't know anyone at all, going to college with students a good 5-7 years younger than me and working as a carer with elderly people who were either very ill, dying or suffering with their mental health.

Eventually I made friends with some lovely Muslim sisters, at the time I was surprised at how friendly and nice they were because of all the negative media and news about Muslims...

After some time of asking many questions about Islam, I took my shahada and became Muslim.

I was brought up as a catholic, my faith in God has always been very strong and sincere. However, when I was about 15 years old I stopped going to church as I was aware of many contradictions in their teachings and scriptures, because there is no "original Bible." There are various versions of the bible, because the text of the Old Testament existed as stories that were passed down through generations, before being moulded together by different authors. Over time, texts within the Bible have been changed, either added in or even completely taken out from it!

I still identified myself as a Christian, believing in one god (not the trinity) and would still pray and think about god on a daily basis! Over the years, every now and then, whenever I wanted to feel at peace and even closer to God, I would visit a church where I would light a candle and simply sit in the church breathing in the incense and would say a little prayer, but I never went to Sunday mass again or participated in any of the religious gatherings, I didn't even identify myself as a catholic.

After several years of researching and searching for the truth about Christianity and who my creator was, I was now learning about Islam. I truly believed in my heart that Islam was the true religion and that The Quran was the last book sent to us by God and is literally the word of God himself, which has been perfectly preserved and not altered in anyway to this day!

I was completely amazed and shocked to discover that many of the biblical stories were also in The Quran, as well as the Christian Prophets such as: Adam, Moses, Abraham, Isaac, Joseph, Noah, Jesus... who were also acknowledged prophets in Islam! I couldn't believe that they never taught us this in school and that it wasn't even common knowledge? Sure, as a Christian I knew and acknowledged that God sent down The Torah to the Jews and The Bible to Jesus (Christianity) but to discover that after Prophet Jesus (known as Prophet Eesa to Muslims) that God had also sent down The Quran to Prophet Muhammad (peace be upon him), was complete news to me! Prophet Muhammad (peace be upon him) is even mentioned and prophesied in The Old Testament! I felt like a big secret had been kept from me and probably most Christians...

There were many amazing discoveries I had come across and even scientific facts and proofs in The Quran that led me on my path to becoming a Muslim... but the pivotal moment for me in my decision to sincerely accept Islam was regarding the story of Moses (known as Prophet Musa to Muslims) and The Pharaoh (of "the exodus" in The Bible). In both Islam and Christianity the two stories are very much identical in both the Bible and The Quran.

Both scriptures agree that the Pharaoh drowned when he tried to pursue Moses (Prophet Musa) who led the Israelites to safety across the parting (by God) of The Red Sea, to aid their escape from the evil Pharaoh and his army, who he had enslaved and persecuted the Israelites for many years!

However, in The Quran it gives an additional piece of information in Surah Yunus (chapter 10 verse 92) "So today We will save you in body that you may be to those who succeed you a sign. And indeed, many among the people, of Our signs, are heedless"

In 1898, the preserved and mummified body of "The Pharaoh of The Exodus" was found in a tomb in the valley of Kings in Egypt.

The identity (name) of The Pharaoh in the Moses story found in both The Quran and the exodus in The Bible has been much debated by scholars over the years, concluding it to be that of either King Rameses

II or Merneptah, who was the thirteenth son of Rameses II and was the fourth ruler of the Nineteenth Dynasty of Ancient Egypt.

In 1975, Dr. Maurice Bucaille who was a french medical doctor and member of the French Society of Egyptology, along with some other doctors, received permission to examine the preserved and mummified body discovered in 1898. The findings of which proved that the cause of death was most probably from drowning or from a violent shock, which immediately proceeded the moment of drowning.

"So today We will save you in body that you may be to those who succeed you a sign. And indeed, many among the people, of Our signs, are heedless"

The Quranic verse that states God (Allah) shall save his (The Pharaohs) body as a sign, has been fulfilled! You can even go and visit the mummy at the Royal Mummies room in the Egyptian Museum in Cairo, Egypt!

This captivating and powerful verse in The Quran compelled Dr. Maurice Bucaille to study The Quran, ultimately leading him to accept Islam and become a Muslim, just like me!

It's now been 10 years since I became a Muslim, sadly over the years I have experienced prejudice, discrimination, both verbal and physical abuse, rejection, loneliness & isolation from both society, people I knew and worse of all from those nearest and dearest to me... all because I changed my faith and practice of religion. Sadly, many reverts to Islam experience this too, some end up leaving the religion as it's just too much for them, this really breaks my heart the most! I've personally had close friends that have left the religion, not because they don't believe, but because of the hardship we face here in the west...

You might wonder, why haven't I left Islam? Well the answer for me is simple, Islam is such a beautiful religion, it's totally misunderstood and only teaches peace and good morals and beautiful manners in ones character. Don't get me wrong these past 10 years have been so hard and even heart breaking for me, to the point that it literally nearly broke me!

But at the end of the day, I truly believe in Allah and Islam, whatever pain and hardship I have personally suffered and endured these past 10 years has got nothing to do with Islam or Allah, it's the individual people who have wronged or harmed me.

It doesn't matter to me what another person may believe in or what religion they may be or even not at all?... only how we treat one another: Kindness, good manners, respect, morality, empathy, compassion... basically humanity, is what is important to me!

Three and a half years ago I was driving on the motorway with my then 4 year old son, sat in his car seat behind me. A large articulated lorry on my right, suddenly hit me and was driving across the side of my car! The next thing I know, my car somehow ended up sideways in front of the lorry, whilst it pushed me along the motorway! I remember thinking in that moment, that this was it, we were going to die! In that moment, all I could think to do was to steer left... The next thing I know, my car was spinning round and round on the busy motorway, I could see cars dodging me, everything was going so fast yet so slow at the same time. Finally my car came to a stop right in the middle of the motorway! My whole body was in complete shock and shaking, trying to take in what had just happened?

To this day, I still don't understand how me and my son survived that day without even a single scratch on either of us, apart from some bruising on my ribs from the seatbelt I was wearing. My car was completely damaged and had to be written off! One thing I do know though, is that God saved us that day and protected me and my son from great harm and even death! That day something inside me changed, over time I slowly went into a deep depression as my physical health began to gradually worsen from the whiplash to my neck and back. The witness who saw the lorry go into me ended up letting me down, so what I naively thought would be a simple, quick and clear cut case, is still going on to this day! The lorry driver not only nearly killed me and my son, but now he was lying and accusing me of something I didn't do? This truly upset and angered me inside, I just couldn't and still can't understand how someone could do that to a person and live with that conscience? As hard as it's been both physically and mentally, one thing about me is I know I am a strong woman, I am a fighter and I will always fight for justice, wether it be for myself or someone I know and even those I do not know, that's just my character... I've exhausted every possible avenue I could think of to try and prove my innocence and disprove his lie against me. No matter what happens, I know I've tried my hardest, there's nothing more I can do, my conscience is clear. I realise after all this hardship, that it's just a test of patience and endurance and I leave it now with God.

I've spent the last three and a half years suffering in physical pain and was even diagnosed with fibromyalgia almost two years ago. Words can not describe the constant struggle and hardship of living with this illness, especially as a single mother with no family or support network around me. Over time my health was gradually declining, I felt like I was loosing grip and control of my own life, simple everyday tasks would become so difficult for me, even walking my son to school would literally feel like I was climbing a mountain! I couldn't be the mum I was or wanted to be to my son because I was so ill, this was really hard to mentally accept and really affected me emotionally.

One day my doctor turned to me and said "Sarah, go and get some sun and warmth, take a holiday and just rest and relax your body." So I took his advice and booked a holiday to Dubai for me and my son! The warmth of the sun was so relaxing and therapeutic. It was nice to have a change of scenery and just unwind and have fun with my son. The heat helped the pain in my body and having healthy freshly cooked food for me gave my body energy and the nourishment it so desperately needed! This was the positive turning point for me, it seems so obvious now when I think about it, but it never even occurred to me at the time because I was so consumed and overtaken by illness that I couldn't think outside the box or even beyond my illness as I was simply living my life day by day.

It wasn't until after I got back home, that it suddenly hit me... Why don't I set up my own Muslim friendly travel website? I've got ten years experience in the travel industry, I'm well travelled and as a Muslim revert that's a women, I have the advantage and personal knowledge of what's lacking and required in the Muslim tourism industry!... It was literally staring at me in the face, I'd be a fool not to at least try especially as travel is something I was so passionate about and loved to do prior to becoming a Muslim!

I didn't want to set up a travel agency or be dealing directly with the public, I had to come up with a concept that worked around my illness and my situation as a lone parent.

In April 2019 I soft launched my website: Halal Travel Escapes, an inspirational global travel search engine for Muslim - friendly accommodation. The aim of the website is to inform, inspire and bring ease upon the Muslim traveller to search for and book their ideal holiday that is Muslim- friendly and meets their religious needs and requirements, such as a hotel that serves halal food or has women only spa, swimming or sunbathing facilities.

Staring a business is not an easy thing, but Halal Travel Escapes is something I'm genuinely passionate about and truly believe in! It's gave me something positive to focus on that I love doing, but most of all it's given me back my identity and confidence. At the age of 33 I finally feel like I understand myself and who I am a person, me, Sarah O'Neill.

I am that strong woman who is still standing here today, striving and aiming high!

I was that broken woman who was so tired and even lost, from all the hardships I had endured and the harsh lessons that I had faced in my short life…"There is nothing stronger than a broken woman who has rebuilt herself"

And I am rebuilding myself, my life and my future! At the end of the day, all you can do is try and the rest is up to God!

Umm Sulaiman - Managing Director of Halal Travel Escapes.

Website - www.Halaltravelescapes.co.uk
Instagram - @halaltravelescapes - Facebook - www.facebook.com/halaltravelescapes

17

Bling lovers and magpies

I am Nasira Kasmani and I am the proud owner of Jewellery By Nasira, a sparkly jewellery and accessories boutique in Datchet near Windsor (Berkshire), which is also an online business.

I reside in the Royal Borough of Windsor and Maidenhead and I have taken a leaf out of my neighbour, the Queen's book and have a weekday residence in Bray and weekend residence in the West Midlands with my husband. Living in this beautiful area allows me to be close to the countryside yet I am still only 45 minutes from the hustle and bustle of London. I love visiting Royal Windsor and the castle, and am fortunate that I drive past it twice a day, to and from my jewellery boutique in Datchet.

After leaving university over twenty years ago, I have worked in a number of sales and marketing roles and eventually moved to business consultancy, which has taught me some invaluable lessons that I have been able to apply to my own business.

After completing 10 years in consultancy contracting roles in 2016, I was looking at a change of direction and decided to look at the possibility starting my own business. This was a huge step after being in paid employment for over twenty years and I wanted to do something that I was passionate about, that would allow me to network and collaborate with like minded business people and also ensure that I could continue working with all the charities that I have been supporting since my university days.

I have always had a passion for jewellery, which is thanks to my mother, who always made sure that I was wearing some form of sparkle from a very young age. In my younger years, my own collection was always made up of precious metals and stones, however, the expense of purchasing these as time went on was literally bankrupting me, so I started purchasing high quality costume jewellery made with Swarovski crystals and American diamonds. My collection quickly grew as it was more affordable, and I found I had something different to wear everyday. I was also no longer worried about being mugged or losing items! This became my inspiration for 'Jewellery By Nasira' as there is a huge market for affordable, good quality costume jewellery that looks like the real thing and it was something that I wanted to share with my fellow "bling lovers and magpies" and in December 2016, the Jewellery By Nasira brand and boutique were born.

I love it when my clients tell me about the compliments that they receive when wearing items from my collection, I love the personal touch and offer complimentary jewellery and styling consultations in the boutique and online via video call, which has allowed me to work with clients both nationally and internationally.

In 2018, Jewellery By Nasira was nominated for Traditional Jewellers of the Year by Britain's Asian Wedding Awards and was awarded the finalist certificate.

In 2019, Jewellery By Nasira was nominated for and won Creative Jewellers of the Year by Britain's Asian Wedding Awards and has also been shortlisted for the same category in the 2020 awards. I also won Highly Commended Business Women of the Year by the She Awards in the March 2019 for the brand.

The Jewellery By Nasira brand has become well known for the adjustable crystal tie bracelets in a gold, silver and rose gold finishing. These are delicate enough to be worn by our younger clients and if layered and stacked with other bracelets and bangles, make a huge statement!

Layering and stacking jewellery is very popular and one of the ideas that I like to promote with the brand. This alongside with guiding clients in how to style their Asian inspired jewellery with their traditional clothes has been one of our unique services that clients appreciate.

My own personal jewellery style is simple and elegant, I like to add a touch of sparkle to my everyday look with a stunning pair of crystal earrings, a drop pendant necklace and one of our crystal tie bracelets. To change this up in the evening when I am going out, I add additional bracelets to the look and go slightly larger on the size of the earrings.

What is my goal for the future? I would love to have the Jewellery By Nasira collection available in retails stores around the country and have brand ambassadors promote it from the comfort of their own home to their own client base. This, in conjunction with the online shop which is available on the website www.jewellerybynasira.com will allow anyone, anywhere in the world, to purchase their favourite jewels. I also want to continue contributing to and supporting the local charity sector which is something that is something that is very special to me. I have very close relationships with many local groups including the Slough Modest Sisters, Sakoon Through Cancer, Islamic Help and the Salam Charity that I work with continuously to raise funds and awareness of their projects.

The business journey has not been easy, there are days that I wonder as to why I left the security of paid employment but then I remember my passion and love for my brand and the smiles that it brings to the faces of so many people. No matter what happens in the future, I am so pleased that I took this leap of faith and followed my dream – I will never be left wondering 'What if......?'

Keep smiling, sparkling and shining!

Nasira Kasmani - Founder of Jewellery By Nasira.

Website - www.jewellerybynasira.com
Instagram - @jewellerybynasira

17

Triumph

She was bored. Exploring her neighbourhood was like spending three hours on a merry-go-round, after ten minutes the thrill melted into monotony: the same streets, houses and alleyways were broken only by her own movements as she kicked pebbles, hopped, skipped and jumped. Suddenly, she was mesmerised by a bright, green, open field. It was one that she had seen many times before but today was different. Frozen in time, looking out into the vast space, she began to imagine a grand park with everything she could ever dream of. The excitement bubbled over and she rushed home to express her ideas to her mum. 'Write. Put this idea in a letter and send it to the council, I will help you'. Her mother said. So she did.

I was 5 when I wrote to my council petitioning for a park in my local area, I didn't know I had a voice then, to my amazement they replied affirming that a park would be built. To this day the park still stands as a beacon of joy for children and teenagers far and wide. I kept the correspondence neatly locked away as a reminder of my first triumph, I didn't realise it then, that deep inside of me a fire had been lit.

The oxygen that kept my flame going came from my 'Coach Carters', I was blessed to have many of these. There was every teacher that believed in my potential, my championing lecturers at UWE Bristol, the friends and family that took my ideas seriously and encouraged me to go get it, girl. I believe that we can ignite our own flames, but I also believe that your circle can fan your flames or try to extinguish them.

My circle and initial positive influence started with my family. My mum is among the most strong and resilient females that I know, she came from a long line of them, famously known as 'The Joneses', she is smart, classy, astute and pragmatic. My father is a visionary, his parents left him in the UK with a £50 note, a blanket and siblings to care for, he sold Afro Caribbean products out of the back of a van and grew up in an era rife with racism. He told me of a time when he drove a car falling off of its hinges, all the while imagining that he was driving a Jaguar. He got his dream cars and currently has a portfolio of properties. All of my immediate family are health-conscious, competitive and a great support system.

If you don't have a great circle that will positively inspire you, create one. Who do you spend most of your time with? What books are you reading? What talks are you listening too? These will all influence you.

Allow me to be one of your 'Coach Carters'. I may be your first but hopefully, I am one of many. You, dear sister/brother, are capable of greatness and now is the time to dream, believe and achieve. Appreciate every part of being a unique individual, there is no-one else like you. Stop sitting on ideas and make them happen. Ignite the flame.

Permit my chapter to describe fundamental tips through the sharing of my own experiences, entwined with years of research into success theorists and some of the world's richest and most successful women to help fast-track you toward your higher goals.

The Dream Catcher
What's Your Worth?
Building Confidence.
Remove Barriers: Build Your Empire.

The Dream Catcher

"WHATEVER THE MIND CAN CONCEIVE AND BELIEVE IT WILL ACHIEVE."

All success- by the will of our Creator -begins with mind power and the definiteness of purpose. Working for money serves no-one while working for what you believe in is paramount, unearth work that ignites a burning passion within you to accomplish your higher goals.

When I left university, there was a remarkable amount of pressure on graduates to find a job, any job, especially after the media frenzy surrounding first-class degree holders scrambling to find work. I settled as a business developer for a private multi-million-pound company, I got on well with all of my colleagues nonetheless I felt the altruistic gravitation to work in a setting that helped people, so I gave in to my calling.

At uni I was in the gym six days a week, only six because a member of staff told me I couldn't continue training seven days a week, rest days were just as important; after I left the private company I found myself in the gym again, a friend and personal trainer at the time suggested that I should become a personal trainer, so I did.

What is your calling? Write your goals onto paper with your passion in mind and work towards it. Create a definite plan for carrying out your desire and begin at once, whether you are ready or not. You won't be ready to achieve your goals until you believe you can acquire it.

What's Your Worth?

"EVERY HUMAN BEING HAS A NATURAL DESIRE TO FEEL LIKE THEY ARE SOMEBODY".

The 'I am important attitude'.

Every living soul was created with a purpose. It's acceptable to value your own importance, this is not pridefulness. When you recognise your importance and the unique value that you bring to the table, people will respect you, even the ones that don't care to admit it. What you think of yourself will be felt by every person you meet, your energy speaks volumes, more resonant than your words.

Accepting your importance and recognising it is a key to your success, whatever that may be to you. How you priorities your health and the amount that you're willing to spend on yourself is an indication of your self-worth.

I'm a member of three different gyms. Two are local to my home and have a satisfactory collection of equipment, the third is the most distant, has all the equipment I need and is open 24 hours; the latter is my favourite but in case of time constraints, poor weather, or insert unpredictable predicament, I'm prepared to pay and go above and beyond to prioritise myself at my own convenience.

As director of Athelea's Daughters Training Club, the UK's first Muslim women's health brand, I have had the pleasure of supporting hundreds of women worldwide. However, a common thread is that a lot of us unwittingly value junk food more than our own heart health. Numerous women will begrudge themselves spending £30 a month for the online ADTCFit Program, but they will effortlessly spend £60 a month on takeaways, coffee shop visits and make-up. 'Saf, what if we can't afford healthy food', I hear you say. But we can, it's what we buy and how we use it. There are hundreds of recipes online that only require five or fewer ingredients.

Make time for yourself. Most women are the managing directors of their households, if we fall ill, specifically for neglecting our health, what happens? We will pay £5 for chicken and chips because we value chicken and chips at £5. When will it become second nature to put that cash aside and spend it on our health and wellbeing instead? Building heart strength through exercise is self-care, self-love and will improve your feeling of self-worth.

Building Confidence

Chuck yourself in the deep end, practise saying yes to opportunities that scare you and embrace a 'jump now, grow the wings on the way down' attitude. It will open doors you never knew existed.

At 5 years old I was one of the few black children among a sea of white in my school hence I was bullied due to the colour of my skin, I fell victim to my hair being pulled, people spitting in my food and my face being slapped. I remember turning my hand over and putting a ring on to see how I would look if I was white, I began to hate standing out. When I eventually told my family about the bullying I learned a valuable lesson: to eat or be eaten.

I was 10 years old and I watched my grandmother die before my eyes, I learned then to bury my emotions and block hurtful events out.

I was 11 years old and I was too shy to call the doctors surgery to book an appointment, I didn't like speaking to complete strangers.

I was 20 years old and I was still the girl that cringed at the idea of calling my local doctors to ask for an appointment, but I stood on a stage before 1000 students, I was in board meetings, in the winning team for local and national business competitions, pitching ideas and holding training days and an awards night, all because I made one decision to take a hop, skip and a jump in a direction that I would have never normally gone. I chucked myself in the deep end.

I am 28. I'm black. I'm female and wear full jilbab. I moved to Derby— a completely new city— after marriage, the first things I wanted to do were join the gym and meet Derby's Alan Sugar. My husband gave me the name of a self-made female millionaire, so I wrote to her on LinkedIn, eager to get the ball rolling. To my surprise, she agreed to be my mentor and before I knew it we were a week away from having our first face-to-face meeting. As much as I deeply loved my jilbab, my humble yet boldly physical statement of being a Muslimah, I was suddenly hit with worry about how seriously I would be taken because of it. I knew it wasn't wholeheartedly accepted by today's society.

What would she think of me? Would I be taken seriously? My mind was brimming with anxious thoughts and a whirlpool of questions.

But I powered on. I mentally grabbed a hold of my anxiety and put an anchor on it, I knew I had to chuck myself in the deep end, irrespective of the mental self-sabotage that I was experiencing. Once I forced myself to step outside of my comfort zone, sparks started to fly and amazing things happened. Once I showed up, big and bold and spoke with certainty, I was taken seriously.

Self-esteem is a reflection of what we think of ourselves, so be mindful of highlighting your temporary shortcomings more than your strengths. We are in total control of our level of confidence, once you accept and love you for you, your confidence will be off the Richter scale, even if it takes a bit of anxiety and flapping about, to begin with.

Remove Barriers: Build Your Empire

Running your own business-especially as a mum is very enriching. We're entrusted with the majority of daily actions, so there are 101 excuses to put your dreams on hold.

At this point, I'm a one-woman band, with a countless list of actions to complete each day, although I thoroughly enjoy being slightly stressed and very busy.

In September 2017, I enrolled on a course that would get me one step closer to growing my business and opening an Academy offering health and fitness-related qualifications. This meant that I had to wake up at unsociable hours to study child and husband free. In October 2017, I had excruciating pain in my lower abdomen, which turned out to be an 8cm beast of a cyst which caused ovarian torsion. November 2017 and I'm heading into the hospital to undergo surgery, I wouldn't let this barrier be a waste of time, so I took my iPad with me and continued to work on my coursework until it was my turn to be operated on. The operation ran smoothly, I passed my course and I now have the ADTC Academy.

I have a toddler, Aalia, and a husband, Nasir, I share the majority of my time with them, so if I need to exercise or complete some important work, I will wake up at 4:30 AM to get the job done and squeeze as much as I can out of those golden hours.

Where there's a will there's a way, it's easier to make excuses than it is to force yourself to wake up early or apply yourself when you'd rather be hanging out with friends.

Stepping outside of your comfort zone and pushing your boundaries is the only way to build your empire, envisage how you can work with obstacles if not obliterate them, believe in your dreams and you will achieve them, know your worth and as a result increase in confidence. Turn negative situations on their heads and leap over barriers.

There is a common thread in successful people, it starts in our minds.

Wherever you are, no matter your past, current circumstances, education or lack thereof, know that it's already within you. You have a certain grace, strength, intelligence and fearlessness that will propel you to where you want to be. The abundance that is meant for you will never pass you and will only cease once our time here is done, so stand tall and be excited about what's to come.

Safiyyah Henderson - Founder of Athletes Daughters Training Club

Website - www.adtcteam.com
Instagram - @adtcteam
Facebook - www.facebook.com/safiyyah.henderson.58

17

How a perpetually single lady got married

I had always followed the rules: I went to school and got great grades (one of the nerdy kids for sure), I went to university (3 times) and studied what I was passionate about, I embarked upon a career as a teacher and over the years worked my way through several promotions. I then bought my own home and lived independently as a (semi!) responsible adult for many years. However, the one thing I was always trying to do, throughout most of these accomplishments, was to just get married! Yet that was the one thing I couldn't do. It's not like I could study for a qualification that would guarantee me a husband at the end of it right?

Despite my other achievements I so wanted to be married. I was over 30 and I wanted to stop being the older unmarried lady in the family. I wanted to stop feeling like an inexperienced child in front of my married friends and cousins. I so sincerely wanted a husband, a wedding, a family and all the adventures, trials and tribulations I saw others enjoying. I often went to bed only to wake up in the dark of the night in panic and tears wondering "will I ever get married?"

Don't get me wrong, it's not like I was leading a miserable life. I had great friends, a full social calendar, a warm loving family, good health and the means to travel a few times a year. I knew I had a lot to be grateful for.

However, I also knew that I wanted companionship beyond my friends and family. I wanted growth and someone to grow with and I wanted to feel that love and commitment that comes from a spiritual union. I was tired of being my own *everything*: a one woman show. I wanted someone to share life with. How was it fair that others could have that but not me?

For those of you reading this who have *not* been in this position you must be thinking "well what stopped you?". For those of you reading who *have* been in this position you will know! Where do I start? The liars, the secretly-married men, the time wasters, the guys not interested in marriage, the guys hung up on their exes, the indecisive guys, the constant rejection over silly things like my height or my cultural background, potential in laws who didn't approve of their son's choice, unsuitable matches brought by well-meaning friends and relatives not to mention the general perverts who lurk out there online and behind their phone screens.

I spent 15 years working my way through this list until I met the one guy who totally destroyed me. He was unsuitable in every possible way. He was: childish, rude, arrogant, egotistical, insulting, judgmental, self-centred and very narrow-minded. His family didn't approve because I was older than they would have liked. They said I would get fat, old and ugly very quickly, that I probably wouldn't be able to have children and if I did they would be "deficient" in some way. It was the worst few months of my life.

"Why the hell did you keep going then?" I hear you exclaim at me as you lower your book and roll your eyes in disbelief.

Good question. The answer? Because he was prepared to get married. Despite all his faults, he was one of the few men I had met who actually wanted and was prepared to get married. By that stage I was in such a panicked state about marriage that I would have married a broom if it was sincere about marriage!

Luckily fate intervened and ended things for us. The sense of relief I felt was immense but not as immense as my sense of regret and embarrassment. How the hell had I fallen so low that I could have even entertained the idea of being with a man like that? I realised then that something had to change. My desire to get married had become this pathetic, all-consuming obsession that had clouded my judgement in every possible way and I had lost sight of what I actually needed in a marriage and spouse.

I prayed for guidance and it came in the form of a webinar led by a wonderful angel of a lady called Michelle. Michelle had married aged 40+ and when she was talking about her experiences I was like "yes she understands me!" Add to this the fact that Michelle is a devout Christian lady meant that she understood my need to stay within certain boundaries that a lot of relationship guides (I turned to a *lot* of them for help!) didn't address. I contacted Michelle and discovered she was a coach and within a few weeks I began my coaching journey. It was the moment that changed my life.

It was like my eyes had been opened to a whole world of knowledge that I never knew existed. Here's one of the most fundamental problems a lot of single Muslim ladies face: most of our lives we're told to minimise our interactions with men. I even went to an all girls' school such was the notion that free mingling between the sexes was not to be encouraged unless they were uncles or cousins. Then all of a sudden, one day, BAM! You're expected to just go out into the world, meet a man, connect and make a life-changing decision followed by a big sparkly wedding and tick "marriage" off your life to do list!

What *actually* happens is that when we meet men for marriage we have no idea how to handle the situation. So we either go into it guns blazing and hope that our boardroom skills will help us bag a spouse the way it helps us bag a new account. Or we feel overwhelmed by the whole experience and before we know it we've been duped, led on and disappointed more times than we can count.

My coach helped me to navigate all of that. She helped me to learn more about my needs, my boundaries and my power so I was able to put myself out there without the usual feelings of dread, frustration and panic. My luck didn't change overnight (there's no quick fix for matters of the heart after all) but I certainly dealt with it better. I met another man who turned out to be insincere about marriage yet I no longer obsessed about his actions but simply learnt how to move forward with dignity and confidence. I met a man who had zero concept of appropriate physical boundaries but I didn't blame myself, I simply saw it as a reflection of his manners and moved on without carrying resentment forward. I met a man who had grossly exaggerated his age on his online profile and instead of getting angry about being lied to I handled the situation with grace. All thanks to my coach.

Then came the one!

I almost cancelled our first meeting because I was so tired both physically and emotionally from my marriage search. But with a little encouragement and some sage glass-half-full style words of advice from Michelle, I went. By now I no longer dreaded these first meetings. I knew how to handle the situation, what to say and what to aim for. I felt able to get to know a man and connect with him without transgressing the boundaries of modesty. I also knew how to decide if he was right for me. And he was!

Just like that, after 15 years of searching, there he was: sitting in front of me, sipping coffee and looking rather dashing! 7 months later we were married!

I'd found the man I'd been looking for and the marriage I wanted and I couldn't believe how easy it should have been all along. I had learnt to love myself enough not to accept second best. I had learned to ditch the checklist and look with my heart. I had learned to face my fears and take a risk I learned how to compromise for marriage without compromising my values and myself. And most of all I had learned that what I had needed to get married successfully and happily had been there all along: MYSELF.

Then about a year into our marriage I started to feel restless. Here I was enjoying matrimony with the most amazing man I could ever have dreamt of marrying and meanwhile there were sisters out there who I knew were needlessly going through the exact same pain, heartache and despair I had gone through, without the kind of guidance they needed.

During my years as a single lady I realised how little support there was out there for single Muslim women and especially those of us "over a certain age". We were just expected to know how to do it and if we hadn't achieved marriage by a certain age we were expected to just marry anyone for the sake of being married. No one ever stopped to think that maybe, just maybe, we needed support.

At that moment I made it my goal to support my single Muslim sisters who were struggling to get married.

Now please don't misunderstand my motives. I don't go around assuming that *every* Muslim lady who is single must be in want of a husband (to quote the late Jane Austen…sort of). But I did know that a large proportion of single Muslim ladies did want to get married and would benefit from and gladly accept support.

And so Single Muslima Solutions was born.

I trained as a coach and combined it with my own experiences, observations and methods and before I knew it I had created something that single Muslim ladies all over the world could call their own. I created a space where single Muslim ladies could feel accepted, understood and supported whatever their situation or life story.

It's been an amazing journey though not without its bumps. I often find myself at the receiving end of backlash from those (unfortunately usually men) who claim that what I do is "haram" and goes against the teachings of Islam. However, I strongly disagree with this.

The way I see it, it's a *fact* that so many Muslims out there prefer to meet and connect with a spouse on their own terms and in their own way without the traditional family setup. We can either bury our heads in the sand about it or we can accept that it happens and give single Muslim women the support they need in making this important decision so that they can feel confident to make the right decision without compromising their values, beliefs or boundaries.

My method – *The Diamond Principle* - is simple and yet so effective. I guide ladies through the 4 cornerstones of the Marriage Search Mindset: challenging negative beliefs, managing fear, nurturing self-acceptance and creating ideal match recognition.

Since creating Single Muslima Solutions I've worked this way with countless ladies and watched as they have gone from feeling anxious, frustrated and close to giving up on their marriage search to fearlessly and effortlessly meeting and marrying their ideal match.

I've had the honour of appearing on The Islam Channel and British Muslim TV as well having articles published worldwide in publications such as Sisters magazine. I currently work with ladies all over the world from London to New York to Cape Town and everywhere in between and I never fail to feel that glow of contentment and exclaim that yelp of delight when a sister who was formerly heartbroken and about to give up tells me "guess what? …I'm getting married!"

Soraya Soobhany-Chohan - Founder of Single Muslima Solutions

Website - www.singlemuslimasolutions.com Email - soraya@singlemuslimasolutions.com
Instagram - @singlemuslimacoach Facebook - www.facebook.com/soraya.soraya982845

17

Plucking up the courage to change

I'd like to share pieces of my past in hopes of inspiring someone, that when you pluck up the courage to change, your life will start to shift in massive ways.

I'm Maryam, a mother of three boys. I was born and raised in the U.K. I grew up in a big family, 8 brothers and sisters in total.

I would say I had a good upbringing but my parents divorced in my early pre-teens and my mother brought us up alone. We travelled quite a lot to a few exotic countries, as my mum wanted us to be brought up in a Muslim country. We lived in Saudi for 9 months then moved back to the U.K for a couple of years, then moved to Marrakesh for over a year. We learned to read Arabic and the recitation of the Quran. Things got tough for my mum financially so we had to move back to the U.K. I was 15 years old at the time, and little did I know that in a years time I would be married to the person I chose and fell in love with but would turn out to be a nightmare.

My journey into entrepreneurship all started when I plucked up the courage to leave a 12-year abusive toxic marriage. I remained stuck, scared, afraid and hopeless for 12 years, hoping things would change, while continuously walking on eggshells in fear that at any moment the chaos and violence would start all over again.

It wasn't until I read a book- an NLP that I had my aha moment that changed the course of my life. Somewhere along in one of the chapters in the book, there was a sentence that read; "do you see yourself where you are now in five years time?". The answer was a profound "hell nooo!"

I literally got shivers up and down my spine and felt a sense of empowerment and choice, I had a choice! That I can take charge of my life right NOW. I didn't have to wait for tomorrow... as tomorrow was just an excuse; that kept me stuck in the past. I decided there and then with the firm belief that enough was enough and it was over and that I was going to take massive, scary action! I no longer wanted to live this abusive life cycle. I wanted a better life for my children and in order to do that, I need to make that shift now. It was done in my mind. I made a plan, plucked up the courage and executed on it.

All change starts with a decision and courage to follow through with that decision combined with massive action.

I moved to Dubai in 2015 to be near my mum and sisters to start a new life. Everything was looking up and I started a nursery nurse job at the local prestige nursery. After two weeks, I decided to quit my job. This job life wasn't for me- it never was, it drained me and sucked the life out of me. I dreaded waking up on a Monday morning, to start the whole process all over again! I couldn't be trapped to a 9-5 and ask permission to go on holidays and take days off and wait for the weekend to come around. I was missing out on life. I was living for the weekend. I was missing out on watching my boys grow up. I knew that I wanted more and that there was more to life than this. Living pay check to pay check life wasn't for me. It was scary but I took the leap into the unknown, in a foreign country and with 3 children in tow. I had to once again face a scary uncertain future.

When one door closes, another one opens. That's when I stumbled upon network marketing. It opened my eyes that I could be my own boss and make my own money. I was driven and excited about this opportunity to be my own boss. I was going to make it happen no matter what. I was making good money but unfortunately, that didn't last long as the company shut down.

But something good came out of it as that's how I met my current husband. We met at that networking event. We instantly clicked and we felt a connection, and the rest is history.

We got married and flew back to the U.K, not my home town Manchester but London as a newlywed with my children. This was a new start and a fresh chapter in my life.

I had gotten a taste of the entrepreneurial journey and the freedom it brought so there was no going back. My goal was to be my own boss and be financially independent. Being married wasn't going to stop me, as I believe women should have their own backup and create their own financial success. I wanted it so badly for myself and my family.

Since then I started many business ventures, a lot failed, and some I made money from but something just kept me stuck. I would start and then stop, it was like I was self-sabotaging my own efforts. I made some money here and there but had no focus, clarity, had the negative talk- I always found myself stuck because I was listening to my inner negative voice. It's like I was sabotaging my own success. I knew I had potential, but didn't believe in myself. I felt unworthy of success. I feared to die with unfulfilled dreams. I had a breakdown. I fell into depression and didn't really feel motivated to do anything anymore.

My husband saw how down I was, and booked us to go to Hajj, the Holy pilgrimage in 2018.

That journey in hajj is where I got to see my loopholes and it was like looking into a mirror and I could see all my flaws. I felt like a Ferrari without an engine. I was on an emotional rollercoaster. I took this opportunity to connect with my Creator on a deep level. I balled my eyes out, and asked my Creator to please "fix me". I felt broken and helpless. I think everything I went through in my past was all tumbling on top of me like a tonne of bricks. At the same time, I felt a deep connection with God, as I knew he understood what was in my heart that I couldn't even express to any being. I made sincere Dua every single day for God to heal me and show me a way out.

My journey was a true eye-opener and the u-turn I needed in order to get my life back on track. I had conviction that my prayers were answered. When I flew back home, I started to work on myself, my mindset and my healing. I was raw and honest with myself. That's when my spiritual awakening started to happen. And my mindset started to shift. I realised in entrepreneurship, its not all about the formula and strategy, its mindset. You need skin in the game. It's 80% mindset and 20% strategy.

But after my breakdown, I had my breakthrough. I realised that the only obstacle getting in my way was my mindset. I had a lot of limiting beliefs that were causing me to sabotage my own success. I knew that I needed to work on myself and mindset and not at the surface level but at the core. I wanted to get to the root cause of my issue. I knew that's where all the limitations and limiting beliefs were coming from. So I put in the work, the real work and that's when my transformation started to happen but I knew I needed to go deeper. I found a coach who I wanted to invest in but they were really expensive, I was like, what do I do? So, I decided to sell some valuables and work with this coach.

Through my pain, I found my power and that's why and how I became a mindset and success coach. I am passionate about helping ambitious female entrepreneurs shift their mindset towards success, thrive and make an impact. My mission is to empower women and I am on a journey to impact as many lives as possible.

I started to believe that I was enough and that I am deserving of success. I started having the confidence and self-belief to show up online like never before. I was taking massive action to move the needle forward in my business. I was focused and had clarity on where I was heading. I was achieving the goals I set myself. I was finally making money moves. I learned from my own transformation and coach what it takes to help others overcome self-doubt and become confident, and not let fear of failure get in the way of achieving the success to gain financial freedom. Because the only person getting in the way of success is your mindset.

Maryam Davis - Success and Mindset Coach. NLP, Hypnotherapy & EFT Practitioner.

Instagram - @itsmaryamdavis
Website - www.maryamdavis.co
Email - hello@maryamdavis.co
Facebook - www.facebook.com/maryam.davis
Linked In - www.linkedin.com/in/maryam-davis-47b455105

17

Overcoming Obstacles

Did you know that 88% of people look at online reviews before making a decision to call you about your services? Did you know that they look at reviews from the last 2 weeks only? Did you know they will read the 1-star reviews first and see how you respond before they make a decision to pay for your services?

How many times have you used the internet to find/search for a local business in the last year? Did you know that your Google My Business listing has the potential of bringing in over 200 inbound calls per month of people inquiring about your services? And yet, people are posting to social media sites and wondering why they are not getting any business.

I didn't know a single thing about marketing or what "Google My Business" meant prior to working for a high-end digital marketing company. Eight years ago, I had a mom blog, self-published a book and had no idea how to get on the 1st page of Google. I thought if you wrote once a week and posted it on my blog and to various social media sites it would grow and I'd become "famous and help hundreds of people all over the world solve problems."

Three years into writing blog articles once a week and 108 subscribers later, I realised that my dream of earning $500 per month from my blog was not going to happen. It didn't make sense to me how these famous writers were getting all these subscribers and showing up on the first page of Google. I felt like I followed the instructions the "gurus" recommended but there were zero results coming in.

At that time, I was a stay at home mom. My husband and I have three kids. I was (desperately) looking to make an income from home, just $500 extra per month, so that I can stay home raise our children and relieve my husband from some of the stress of having to be our single income provider. I wanted him to have a good nights rest stress-free. That's all I was begging the Universe for and I tried several opportunities to make this small simple dream a reality: Sales, Cold Calling for an insurance agent, home parties, and multiple multi-level marketing businesses. I made so many friends from multi-level marketing and discovered the power of personal development.

Being a stay at home mom is hard, in my opinion. Raising tiny little humans who depend on you for everything and look to you for advice and guidance about the world is exhausting. What if I say the wrong thing? What if I steer them in the wrong direction? My children were blunt and honest and very observant and I took everything personal.

One beautiful sunny day, the birds were chirping and the sun was out. The sky was blue and the warmth of the sun was enlightening. I remember this day so vividly because this is the day my husband and I got into an argument over a $35 bra.

After all, I stayed home with our 3 young children while he worked 5-6 days a week 10 hours a day to provide for our family. We were barely surviving from one check to another and every penny counted. I so badly needed a new bra and only spent $35. *The wire was poking my skin - ouch!*

I completely understand where he came from and the stress of having to provide for all of us to keep us afloat was stressing him out, kids grow out of shoes and clothes so fast and let's not bring up the grocery bill. We had more money going out than coming in.

I clipped coupons, looked for sales and went through the clearance aisle. Got donations from friends whose children were older than us and grew out of their clothes. It felt like we were in survival mode when really we have happy healthy children a beautiful home and yard for us to relish in and full bellies. My parents helped out every weekend and life was really good. My husband and I figured out a way to stay home with our children and raise them and it was worth the "sacrifice" of limiting ourselves down to one income.

After that argument over a $35 bra something in me ignited and I vowed to never have a conversation like that with him, or anyone for that matter, ever again. Or to put us in a financial situation where $35 is "too much." I wanted so badly to relieve my husband from stress and to change our family's situation. Even though our children had no clue what was going on and thought life was fantastic, I wanted to show them something different is possible.

I sat down that night in tears, while everyone was asleep, allowing myself to release my tears of sadness and anger and frustration and wrote a letter to the universe clearly defining what it is I needed to find. Something like:

> *Dear Universe,*
>
> *I need help. Will you please help me find a job that doesn't require sales and commission. I seriously am the worst person when it comes to that. I am looking for a business that offers an hourly rate (I'll take whatever you send me) and will allow me to work from home so that I can continue to work from home. A company that is on the verge of hitting it big and that my skill set is able to help give them that push that is needed to get there.*
>
> *In love and truth, Me.*

I don't remember the exact words because I burned my letter afterwards. Like a ceremony for the Gods or something. But guess what!? A few months later my good friend asked me to co-host one of her live shows since her co-host was going to absent that day. I learned about the digital marketing world and met the owner of a high-end digital marketing company that has been in business for decades who was looking to hire an account manager. I was hired the day I helped with the interview and my life changed literally overnight. I literally "struck gold" overnight.

I heard about people who "become rich overnight" and never believed it, but I get it now. Just like that, I had an hourly job, working remotely from home and meeting people all over the world learning about Local SEO and Google Ads and teaching our clients how to get on Google.

I found Local SEO fascinating and spent every spare minute learning about it. I was so amazed by all the strategies used in order to get on the first page of Google and to see the amazing results that come from it. Side note: this is a long term play for your business and not something that immediately produces "x" amount of phone calls to your business in less that one week. My little mom blog would have never made it with what I know now.

Since that amazing day and three beautiful years later, I have been recognised as one of the top local SEO experts teaching businesses how to show up on Google all over the world producing results and delivering a consistent number of qualified leads at a fixed price with a three times return on investment. Woo hoo!

So I encourage you to take a second look at your Google My Business listing, fill out the "info" tab and ask for reviews. 7 out of 10 people will leave a review if you just ask. When most businesses set out to gather reviews to their business, they'll typically mass email their customer list asking for a review. These are great strategies but these are not the best type of reviews you can get and quality counts a lot when it comes to online reviews.

When customers are researching a business online, they look at the number of reviews (obviously) but what most businesses don't realise is how important the actual review content is. The best way to get better quality reviews is to have those in your company working closest to the customer to ask for the review using the *2W review strategy*. When you text vs email these questions with your Google My Business profile link, you will receive 30-50% more of a response.

1. What benefits did you receive? &
2. Why would you recommend us?

Using this little strategy will dramatically increase the quality of your online reviews and therefore drastically increase the number of inbound calls to your business as a result.

Crystal Horton - Marketing Consultant.

Instagram - @imcrystalhorton
Website - www.crystalhorton.com
Twitter - @imcrystalhorton
Facebook - facebook.com/imcrystalhorton

17

Story of a Princess

My story is not that of a Disney account, nor that of the Princess in New York. But that of "Lalla Magou Hadda Cisse".

My full name is composed of several parts that are related to my multiple origins: Mauritanian, Malian, Senegalese and Egyptian (Aswan).

The name 'Lalla' is an honorific title given to important women or noblewomen. I find that every woman is important. Every woman should be treated with respect and dignity.

My father, Prince Cissé Zakaria Ibn Kaine, President of the Islamic Federation of Belgium, was born in 1933 in Ziguinchor, where my grandfather fought against the French colonial authorities in 1907.

On my father's side, my father comes directly from Dighna Diabé Cissé, founder of the royal dynasty of Ouagadougou and 18th descendant of Khaya Makhan Cissé, the last emperor of Ghana. Not the current country Ghana (but the Ghana Empire). Khaya Makhan Cisse was the last emperor to convert to Islam at the time of the Almoradives.

On the side of my mother (Fatoumata Keita), my father is directly related to the great Emperor Soundiata Keita, founder of the empire of Mali.

This double imperial origin largely explains the princely and traditional title which is not incompatible with the Islamic or republican structures of the different countries of the region.

We have always had a humble and modest education. My father was proud of our royal origins and today we are too.

I could write you a book about my family and my origins but today I would like to share with you my life journey, which has not always been so simple.

My world rocked when my father left us. And then my older brother. It was a real shock to me and my brothers and sisters. The question also already arose: "who was going to continue the inheritance of our father"?

I do not think there is anything that can prepare you to lose a parent. I think it's a big shock even in adulthood because that's when I understood my father's wisdom. A few years later, I lost the father of my children.

That's where I was so, 32 years old, mother of 2 small children aged 2 and 4 years old. With great responsibility and in mourning. How was I going to overcome all of this? That's exactly the question I asked myself. I never thought I would be widowed at 32 years old. So many questions crossed my mind: "the education of my children, the work that I was doing at the time, my life...".

The hardships I overcame made me the woman I am today: " Life Coach for Women". I decided in 2013 to improve my "state of mind". So I took the time to heal my emotional wounds. My mission is born...

I also expanded my academic communication, interpreting and teaching skills with NPL coaching. I embarked on a new journey of life, helping many women who want to heal emotionally to become the best version of themselves. I took courses in personal development with great coaches. I could develop techniques that helped me through the trials of life.

Today I coach hundreds of women, who are marked by a traumatic event, anxiety, depression, burnout, self-confidence and women who want to undertake action through my academy: "Soul Empowered Sisters." The name "Soul Empowered Sisters" came to me when I discovered that as a life coach I could not only continue to help women, which is the mission of my life, but I could even help them more. to reach their full potential.

My mission is to help and guide women on their journey, wherever they are, where they want to go; so that they can live a fulfilling life.

I thank God every day for giving me this way of life because thanks to that I found my gift, my passion: 'that of helping women to become the best version of themselves and to be more satisfied and to accomplish beautiful things in life.

Lalla Cisse - Emotional Health Coach - NLP Master Practitioner.

Facebook - https://www.facebook.com/groups/soulempoweredsisters/?ref=bookmarks
Instagram - https://www.instagram.com/soulempoweredsisters/

17

For the love of words

A READER, A PUBLIC SPEAKER IS BORN

It was golden and it was spectacular. The first medal I ever earned was when I was 7-years-old. My second-grade teacher in the Bronx, New York, gave me the medal for outstanding reading skills. From then on, I realised my love for words in every aspect whether it was reading, writing and/or speaking, embracing different mediums of communication in my development for self-expression. It was a challenge I had to overcome as a little girl who was in her last year of learning English as a second language considering my mother tongue is Bengali. It was as if I had hopscotched over the stones of doubt and continued uphill with a possibility of going downhill. However, I stayed uphill and instead of going downhill, reached toward a rainbow, vibrant and hopeful.

My second-grade teacher also gave me my first-ever public speaking role as Queen in the school play, "The King and His Daughters." I wore a big dress with puffy sleeves and a golden crown on my head. At the time, I felt that in order to memorise my own lines and perform them at the exact timing, I had to also memorise the lines of the rest of the cast. Noticing that I had indeed memorised the entire script, my teacher gave me the responsibility to remind the rest of the cast members in case they had forgotten their lines Opening Night. I remember feeling like it was a huge honour rather than something one would consider a huge burden for such a little girl. However, responsibility is something that can begin at any age, another precious lesson I learned from my teacher.

Teachers. They have the talent to encourage and inspire, showing us the golden opportunities that life has to offer. That first spectacular, gold medal and that first spectacular golden play gave me an insight into something I could grow to love-words. For the love of words, I am where I am now-a published author, writer and an English teacher.

I was asked to write about my journey, a topic as vast as the ocean, as high as the mountains and as wide as the valleys. I journeyed through them all and through time to start at age 7 and will make my way through the pivotal moments in my life where I developed my skills in reading, writing and public speaking.

A WRITER, A PEACEKEEPER

Plaid, blue and white skirt, up-to-the-knees. Light blue shirt. Dark stockings and black shoes. Hair up in a ponytail with a matching scrunchy. This was my daily uniform for the private, Catholic school I attended in the Bronx, New York. From ages 12 to 14, I experienced no peer pressure to "fit in" a specific wardrobe style except for the occasional "Dress Down Fridays" as per American tradition.

"Dress Down Fridays," for me, entailed baggy jeans and a baggy shirt. While my classmates believed I was just being a "Tomboy," it was really my mother who chose my clothing as I, myself, had no personal style or as they call today #ootd. Yes... Mommy bought my clothes for me and I happily wore them, without any argument. What I wore did not define me. I let loose my personality through other means.

My nerves never failed me. They crept up on me right before my name was called to go up on-stage. Every time the flutters began their battle, I just let them do it because I knew that they would disappear without a trace as soon as I began to speak. A sudden confidence overcame me as soon as I opened my mouth. I used every facial expression that matched the letters, words and sentences flowing out of my soul. I let my hands fly up and down, all around, inviting the audience to take a journey with me.

I had been chosen every year as a representative for my class for the public oration (speech) competition, whereby I had to write and memorise my own 10-minute speech about a given topic. If it were, for example, "my imaginative vision of a futuristic world," I played the role of a tour guide and took my schoolmates, teachers and school staff on a trip through time and space, all from the comforts of their seats. At this point in my life, I developed an imagination that I could also translate into both written and oral communication. It only confirmed what I would one day, some day, decide to do with the rest of my life.

When you read the words "Private Catholic School," you probably think I felt left out of social circles because I was only one of three Muslim students there. But, I felt just as included as any other Catholic student there. Religion was not an issue. At one point, my teacher even chose me to give a speech at a church, competing against other private school students, on the topic of "religion and peace." The words "Muslim" and "Islam" were definitely in my speech, but what I had hoped the audience took away from it was the word "peace." From then on, every opportunity I had to clarify misconceptions about Islam at a public forum, I held onto it as tightly as one would try to hold onto a melting snowflake, with vigour and hope. I knew very well that I would risk losing the competitions, that snowflakes inevitably melt. I finally realised that winning a competition was not as important as the effect that words have on people-written, read and/or spoken. In trying times like we experience every second on Earth, I hope some people remember my words, remember the peace that we experienced together, being in the same room, sharing the same stage, even sharing common interests.

A POET

Stars. That was the title of my first, original poem. My aim was that of romantic nature. My doubt was that it would ever win. It was, after all, my first time and it was short, concise, yet meaningful. Much to my surprise, Stars won first place at my high school poetry contest.

In addition to being the first poem I had ever written, it was also the first poem I had ever performed in front of an audience. All of this was thanks to the encouragement of my creative writing teacher.

Every week, my classmates and I strolled down the long, wide corridor, admiring the vibrant and diverse paintings on the high ceilings, a sign of a historical building that was once an all-boys boarding school. It eventually became and still is a public co-ed high school in the Bronx, New York. We would then climb up a narrow staircase into the attic. The attic was big enough for an entire class of 20 or so and there was a large circular window looking over ever-changing seasons, beginning with the drama of fall. I would often admire the leaves that tumbled to the ground, some following the wind, others being trampled beneath the soles of ruthless teenagers.

In this attic, my creative writing teacher inspired and encouraged me to write stories, to write poetry and to realise my dream. In fact, it was after one of these classes that I had finally decided, architecture was not for me. After all, I deplored numbers despite being an A-student in math and devoured words, also an A-student in English. I eventually became the editor of the high school newspaper, using it as a platform to continue clearing misconceptions about Islam.

A few months after winning the poetry contest in my Bronx high school, I moved to New Jersey. At my new high school, I continued my aspirations. In fact, I became the Editor for their high school newspaper and joined public speaking competitions. One of these was The National History Day Contest, whereby we researched, wrote and performed about a given topic or person related to the theme.

Fortunately interning for The Herald Newspaper at the time, I also utilised that opportunity to gather research on my historical topic, Florence Nightingale. I created my own stage props, my own costume, my own script and performed on my own as Florence Nightingale in front of a panel of judges made up History professors at William Paterson University. There were contestants from schools all over New

Jersey. The winner had the opportunity to go to Washington D.C. to compete on a national level!

Scene 1. A black dress, 19th-century white nurse's head cover, a desk, a chair, a journal, a feathered pen. I sat down and performed my original monologue, inspired by true historical events. Out came a surprise: I performed in the British accent over my American one, beginning with the words, "Dear God, why?"

After having performed all of the scenes, including a costume change into that of one of Nightingale's soldier patients, the judges asked detailed historical questions about her. I knew Nightingale as if I had traveled back in time and met her. It was a pleasure because when it came time for the winners to be announced, I felt as if I was 7 again: it was golden and it was spectacular. It was in my hands!

From the age of 7, I had begun to develop my skills in reading, writing and public speaking. By junior high school and high school, I had begun to enhance those skills by participating in intense competitions. Through these pivotal moments of my life and with the encouragement of my teachers, I learned that my words can be impactful.

Getting a message across, attempting to inspire a positive change through my love of words, became far more important than winning contests or debates. Sure, winning is something, but it isn't everything. Everything or close enough is when I see a person smile because of my written words, a person nods in agreement with my spoken words or my daughter laughing because I just read her a funny bedtime story. For the love of words. Nothing more. Nothing less. Just that.

Rumki Chowdhury - Published Author, Journalist and English Teacher.

Website - www.rumki.com (official author website & blog) www.
hayatimagazine.com
Instagram - @rumkic
Facebook - @rumkitheauthor
Twitter - @rumkichowdhury

Rebuild after a Collapse

A dot on the map, this is where I was born: From an island which appears as a dot on planet earth, so tiny, but named the paradise of the Indian Ocean.

At the time of writing, I have just come back from the best places on Earth, Makkah and Madinah. Having taken this journey all by myself and my 11-year-old daughter, a journey organised within 2 days of travelling, Alhamdulilah. I am ready to give you a detailed account how it all started.

Well, let's dive in. I know many will read my story to get inspired to become an entrepreneur. I want to ride you with me on this rollercoaster journey. Would you like to know how starting my journey with a simple doll costing £1, had finally led me to a serious online business with a 6-figure revenue within a few years, with absolutely no experience at all in ecommerce?

The journey started after the 4th baby was born. So, why did I choose to leave my secure job to start a rocky journey and throw myself in the unknown? Has it been worthwhile? Would I do it all again if I had the choice? You will get all the answers, I promise.

The idea behind me telling my story is to inspire you, to show you how a completely broken person through domestic violence and suffering from health issues, can be successful with the trust in Allah and determination to never give up – Has it been easy? No. Did I enjoy it? Yes!

So, it was in October 2004 when I realised I was pregnant with my 4th child in UK, still a very foreign country at that time as we only arrived here towards the end of 2002 with no close families to help in any way. At that time, thinking of my situation, I completely pushed away the idea to leave my children and go back to work after the birth of a baby. Yet I have left my 3 children to go to work full time previously and I have suffered doing so. I repeatedly told myself there should be an alternative, even though I had no idea what I could do at that time. It was by the mercy of Allah that someone mentioned Ebay as a website to buy second hand stuff as we were struggling, and I joined as a buyer to buy a few things, starting with bidding on 99 pence stuff. After only a few months, I very timidly thought I maybe could sell a few things too. But I never did it as I could not visualise myself as a seller.

Life was tough. Most weekends I was busy with sewing dresses for my daughter, as I could not afford to buy any dress for her. The sewing machine was one that we won for £1 at an auction! It started to get interesting as I thought, maybe I could be sewing something to sell. But sewing what? No idea came immediately. I could make so many things I have been making in my teens, like purses, skirts, baggy trousers etc but as I said before, I could not see it working for me in any way.

Interestingly enough, with my big belly, seated on my comfy sofa and sewing a dress, I suddenly got the idea of making hijabs for dolls and the whole Muslim doll idea just kept flashing in my mind. Due to our financial strain, I was in the mode of saving everything (pennies mostly), I have been saving the cut fabric that were left over from my daughter's dresses. So, I used these left over fabrics and tried to cut out a tiny hijab for a doll one day and next came the doll's jilbab, all from various fabrics that did not cost me anything. And dressed up in hijab, that doll looks absolutely gorgeous. That was indeed a lightbulb moment for me.

So I headed to the Pound Shop and bought 5 dolls for a total of £5 and dressed them all in Islamic clothing and started listing them on

Ebay for £5. A timid approach, a hand stitched hijab and a jilbab was on a slim doll and ready for a Muslim child. There was no business plan, no future project but this gave me so much confidence, I had no idea what are profit margins for online sales, I read about Ebay fees. It was just the fun and the excitement, seeing the bids coming in, the watch item from Ebay buyers and finally the first sale! I am grateful I kept the momentum going. From the first sale, I knew it is not going to be too difficult to push products on that marketplace, I started thinking ahead, and let my creative juice work to get me Muslim products ideas. This was in 2005.

"Modest fashion" was born. I started researching products I could sell related to the Muslim world and there was no competition as such. I was googling "wholesalers + abaya + hijab" etc and random results were coming, none from the UK. I had no idea how to buy from abroad. No one to advise me either as I was no British citizen back then. I carried on working my part time office job, heavily pregnant and head bursting with ideas by the minute.

The best thing I did at that time, was duas. Sincere duas. And Al Fattah (The Victorious) guided me to success. I laid my hand on a factory, producing abaya and kaftan in Saudi Arabia and offering me door delivery. The minimum order was £500 and I have a baby on the way. I could not gather this sum of money, I took the risk, sacrificing the baby's essentials which was planned and took my salary to put this order through.

At that point only a few dolls have been sold and the profit was reinvested in purchasing more dolls and some black fabric for abaya. My first order for ladies Abaya and Kaftan arrived and I started listing them on Ebay.uk but they were also appearing on Ebay.com. I was selling 3 to 4 abayas a day worldwide and my motivation to serve people with Islamic clothing was my driving force. I was not bothered by profit as much as I was by my desire to bring good quality abaya in the UK. They started selling fast, no advertising needed. The delivery date for my baby was fast approaching too. In no time, I was an Ebay PowerSeller.

I knew at that very moment that I will not go back to work. I knew that Allah SWT has answered my duas to stay full time with my child and I never looked back. I run forward with new ideas, every penny was invested back into the business, it was not a massive business yet it was just replacing half of my salary from the office but there was lots of baraqah in it. Alhamdullillah.

So, I hear you saying, how on earth did you scale to 6 figure revenue a year? As you see above, I dwindled on the details of how it really started with the intention to motivate sisters to start small, to invest with their pocket money and learn the steps, baby steps will bring you far. Another tip is touch your business daily no matter what the circumstances, keep moving forward, implement new strategies, test and see what works. Surround yourself with positivity.

Now I will tell you how I transited from owning modest fashion into a website to selling in a completely different niche and growing far bigger. So, here is a detailed journey to inspire you to scale your home business to a professional business, generating real profit.

My Ebay business grew fast and I decided instead of giving Ebay a share of my profit, I will have my own website and sell various products, my range grew to salwar kameez, Islamic DVD's, Islamic gifts, kids books etc and things were pretty good. However, life came in between and I was pregnant for my 5th child just after performing Hajj.

That last pregnancy was causing me morning sicknesses which lasted till 3pm every day and for months. My business suffered and I also wanted a more automated business where I can be free to be at home and not having to do any packing daily and trips to post-office.

So I carried on learning, buying courses online, one of the books that really changed my life was "Day Job Killer" by Chris Carpenter. I read cover to cover and applied the techniques, soon I could see Allah's infinite Mercy once again in my life. I do not need to be shipping abaya and hijab every day to earn a profit! There was another way, affiliate marketing! I became passionate about online marketing until today.

I BECAME A SPONGE! I was devouring a book a day! I studied harder, learned, applied, and analysed data, it was another learning curve, but my digital marketing skills grew and I was developing into a top online marketer. I was marketing big brands online, getting residual commissions and I lost myself in that journey by closing modest fashion instead of selling it over. An unforgivable mistake.

I never stopped, it was unstoppable, I studied niche and got onto several marketplaces at once and saw the profit potential. By 2010 I knew what an online profit margin was, how to get traffic to websites, how to scale and how to talk to suppliers, negotiate prices and maybe you reading this would think I was on my way to become a millionaire.

I was once more tested in more ways that you could imagine. By then I was a mother of 5 kids, working enthusiastically around my kids. Things took a sour turn. Domestic violence has always been part of my marriage, I was "managing" it with patience. However the abuse multiplied by an unimaginable factor! I was suffering daily abuse in all its forms. I could not figure out the reason nor could I stop it. I could not escape, I was trapped. My children's father had an operation and his mental health started deteriorating fast. Of course, the business plateaued. I stopped learning and focusing as I was then diagnosed with severe pain which might have been rheumatoid arthritis. In reality it was my body's response to traumatic events.

I lost momentum. I saw no future. I abandoned all of my sources of revenue one by one as my mind was messed up and depression took over. However, you will be amazed to learn that my lack of concentration and focus lead me to a shocking career choice. I decided I needed something entertaining to keep going and I became a childminder for 2 years. I enjoyed my time around kids, it healed my suffering, and took one day at a time. I only worked with a handful of children, the love and affection I received was all worth it.

Would you believe it if I tell you there were more tests waiting for me? Unfortunately, I cannot give you more details but my marriage had to end finally due to safety reasons. Which also ended my temporary escape of being a childminder!

I want to tell you, that I have had to rebuild *several times.* After losing it all and never losing hope. In 2011, I relaunched online with a children's e-book. I had experience in everything digital marketing, search engine optimisation and building websites but my anxiety level was high, I was suffering from trauma, and pain. I had no energy and no confidence. I could only survive life at the bare minimum.

It was at that very moment that Allah opened His Doors of Mercy once again, I rebuilt from scratch, I restarted my ecommerce business and built up my Marketing Agency while also having a Network Marketing business for which I achieved the level of Eagle Manager. I was helping lots and lots of sisters achieving success, life was busy but rewarding. As a business coach and mentor, life was good.

I reconnected with my life goals and decided that Jannah is too precious and I have to restructure my day to achieve my greatest goal which is Jannah Ul Firdous. I prioritise my ibaadah and Zikr and my legacy to help my sisters worldwide. As a Muslimah we have to learn to work smart, to free ourselves for ibaadah, serving Allah first. Can we be both, an Entrepreneur and a Muslimah? Yes definitely. With a positive mindset, proper guidance, we can indeed achieve success in both worlds.

I spoke about my mission to help both individual sisters and businesses earlier and you can see how I do them both by visiting www.muslimapreneur.com and www.aminabibi.com I wish you a successful journey as an entrepreneur and invite you to connect with me on Facebook anytime.

Amina Bhoyroo - CEO at MuslimaPreneur.

Website - www.muslimapreneur.com, www.aminabibi.com
Facebook - www.facebook.com/aminaflpuk

17

Blossom Into The Real You (BITRU)

I never thought I would be this strong, many years ago. Many people heard my story and would tell me how strong I am. I would be a trillionaire if I had a penny each time I heard that from people accompanied by the look of awe on their faces. I've started to forget that like Xena the warrior princess I now have a strength that the whole world can see.

Truth is, my strength comes from a lot of lessons learned, mistakes made, pearls of wisdoms received. I now know that my soul knew exactly where it wanted to go, knew exactly what I needed to know to be who I am today.

I am now engaged to be married to a man I call my soul mate, though this blessing came after many years of being caged in toxic trauma bonds with abusive narcissistic men. I was the magnet for those who take, take, take until all that was left in my cup was only drops left which no longer seemed like thriving but it put me into survival mode.

Through out my single mum life, I have been judged by many, as I have a unusually youthful appearance paired up with being a shorty. As I walk down the road, or call an Uber, people stare with many questions for which I wished always to say "I may look young, maybe you think I'm spoiled but my body hides inside it years of bruises, I may look so happy with my signature smile but unbeknown to many, memories of past abuse linger. I'm sure you have heard of celebrities who smile on camera though suffer in silence. I am not one to stay quiet, my extroverted thought reflective, creative nature is always looking for another outlet for which to express itself. People see you smile but have no idea what you went through to get there.

My journey of healing started when I realised that it wasn't love I felt for any of my toxic past but it was a trauma bond connected to my narcissistic & toxic connections, mother & ex husband. It felt like the rug was being pulled under my feet when his mistresses came to me with evidence of his unfortunate infidelity for over 8 years, it led me to question everything I believed was true for me at the time, I was in a shackle of the mind, therefore my soul was trapped and unable to take me to the next levels of growth.

Fast forward to the divorced single mum with sole responsibility of 3 young children, all under 6, youngest being 4 months old, I had to think carefully, as I switched onto survival mode. I did not have time to cry, because the babies would suffer if I didn't do something fast. I used my last savings to get myself a coach for the first time, that was how I realised how powerful it can be, when somebody else believed in me. One day I watched a youtube video on co-dependency, and from then on, I realised why I had been an energetic attraction for an abusive narcissist, one realisation led to another, I would describe it like a domino, where I kept growing continuously without a break for over 2 years straight!

I was adamant to to get myself back on my feet after such a life altering let down, I learned as much as I could about business online and started to focus on looking for my life's purpose, which I knew deep inside had something to do with healing others. I already had gone through things and came out the other side alive, people would ask me questions like how do I do this, how do I cook healthy meals to lose weight. Even though I loved staying healthy, I felt inside my heart that I had a bigger purpose and just the healing of the physical body was not enough.

I was in London without a village of supportive sisters, no grandma as the family rejected me due to my marriage to a person outside of the cultural norm so I was alone for 5 years, no sisters, no mother, no aunty, no uncles, no cousins.

In my pursuit to escape an abusive family I fell into the arms of an abusive narcissist who initially felt like my guardian angel until his true colours came out in many toxic ways and who would leave me by myself to go on holidays abroad in Africa while I had a lack of support and therefore had the most traumatic and difficult childbirth experiences. I sat and wondered why women had to go through so much, was there another way? I grew up seeing my mother suffer so much that all I knew was suffering after childbirth, but something told me to keep looking. I then found an online course on Ayurveda for women, where I discovered ancient knowledge on how women in the past used herbs, special diets and a strict confinement period of rest and rejuvenation for women, usually alongside a supportive network of women who helped with the baby. I realised that women were not supposed to be weaker after birth or postnatally depressed, but instead they were meant to be treated like Queens for they are bringing in life to the world. They should be nourished, supported, well rested meant that they were able to bond with their babies and husbands.

This is not what happens in the west and actually studies prove that there is a postpartum epidemic which doesn't exist in countries where the cultural norm is to practice a confinement period. It gets even worse, some women suffer the most during this time as this is when they are the most vulnerable, there fore a narcissist starts the abuse. This type of trauma has several serious results such as mental health issues that can last for several years unless treated. There is an obvious need for this practice to be applied as part of a women's healing after birth therefore I originally created a group called KYINAT VILLAGE support group to see if there was any interest in this and if other women were going through this. I learned that women all over the UK and abroad were suffering as there was no concept of rest for women. Most women started to clean and cook right after giving birth and entertaining family who were not cooking for her! I decided that I would create a course called “ A Pampered Postpartum”.

In the west women are expected to have a baby and go back to work the next day. This is actually a massive detriment to women and children. First of all the female body after giving birth goes through many processes, the joints are looser, the body is weaker, the chemicals in the brain are all over the place and require a specific type of diet which enhances the bodies ability to heal and therefore bring back the mother to strength. If this process of healing is missed out, the mother faces the consequences for years to come. Sadly it is not only the back pain, or fibromyalgia from c-sections, it can also severely affect mental health. There are vast amounts of studies that have shown a link between postpartum depression and childbirth, there are severe levels which can also put baby a in danger. The most serious part of all of this is that it is proven that some mothers develop bipolar, and even severe psychosis after child birth. Some women have harmed themselves and develop on going Ptsd symptoms and long term depression.

I was looking for the link between the body and mind. By feeding women the correct diet during postpartum they have an opportunity to allow the brain to relax and feel loved. I wanted to learn more so I embarked on a journey to study naturopathy. The struggle was real, imagine trying to find baby sitters for 3 children as a single mother, with no support from a narcissist ex who would just as well use this as an opportunity to put me back into his abusive cage. With Gods help I managed to find a way. Boy did I learn who my real soul family were at this crucial time. I travelled out of town to learn medicine from as far back as Ibn Sina, Galen, going all the way back to hippocrates. I discovered how the human body is literally a self healer but what was most astonishing was that I realised that while the body healed, emotions were also being healed, I realised that we cannot heal a person without healing all three parts, mind body and soul. I found that women would do better if they had a nourishing sisterhood to help them cope with the demands of a new child as this is a very sensitive time where women can literally lose their minds.

As I studied, worked double harder then anyone else, balancing my three children, bills, running a home, I prayed and I pushed through, I was still feeling God guiding me to a much deeper place. Every person I met on my journey taught me something so precious, sometimes it was a person I met on the train, or a colleague at the college. It was taking me to a place that I may have been unconsciously ignored for many years.

That place was my childhood. I learned that my current state was a result of an unhealed childhood wound. There I was waking up to the next level, gradually I'm growing, blossoming into the real me! I wanted to help others so badly but a healer must heal herself, love herself, in order for her cup to be full and spilling, then heal others.

This is when I realised that God was taking me to my purpose, as soon as I started healing, I was able to truly accept me, the whole me. I started to sing and write songs again, I started to write my book again, I started to live again. I believed in love again, though I left my choice of partner to what I believe to be Gods choice. I wrote exactly what I wanted, how my ideal husband would make me feel in a lot of detail and left it to faith, that the right person for me will be there in the correct time. To my surprise I was gifted with this person who I believe to be my soul mate, best friend and husband and soul father to my children all in one!

My healing and self discovery work goes on up until today, what I learned which was most profound was that the correct parenting is crucial for betterment of humanity. I was raised by a single mother who had severe mental health issues which seemed like I was being raised by Dr Jekyll and Mr Hyde. The abuse that came with that was not her fault as she was unhealed, and had wounds that run deep which she never successfully healed. Her mother forced her into marriage at the age of 14 and she gave birth to me at 15 and a half. She was raising a child while she had a history of abuse and was a child herself. I forgave my mother as she was a victim of abuse from a horrible family who mistreated her and it is the only way to truly heal and now I have the tools to raise my children as best as I can. My father was non existent, so I was the proxy parent and missed out on most of my childhood because I was responsible for all the household responsibilities at home whilst trying to study. It was unfair but at the same time I learned how to cook like a pro and in my privacy I wrote poetry and practised my passion of singing. Music and writing was therapy for me which helped ease the neglect I felt as a child. I thank my mother for the times she treated me with love when she felt normal and able to. Single mothers get it hard and she did the best she could, I pray the world sees how detrimental it is for children when being raised in hardship. I love my children but I always wanted to have them when I was able to give them the best. Sometimes God plans better and we have to accept and make do with whatever support we have available.

I guess single mothers get it hard, I always wondered why relationships did not work. Now I understand that two people who were not only decades apart in age, but who also were unhealed and incompatible were bound to end in misery. Looking back they were forced by cultural norms to do what their narcissistic parents wanted. Truth is that was uneducated parenting and people with subconscious programming that did not serve nor their children.

What this taught me was If more women and men looked inwards and did the inner child work, took parenting classes, I believe less children would be abused in our societies, we would have loving two parent homes to grow up in and this would prevent the cycle of abuse and generational trauma which I broke as a Bangladeshi woman. I am so glad I fell upon an amazing book called the human magnet syndrome which put sense into me why I had attracted one narcissist to the next, it was all about my childhood.

This is the reason I teach people what healthy love is supposed to be. Healthy love does not give you anxiety, it accepts you with your shadows and all. I would push men away and go into trauma until I realised that my inner child is protecting me from anymore pain. Even if a man in front of me was healthy, the inner child would get triggered and run which lead me to the song " running". I learned that real love from a good propel can actually help you heal faster and reach your inner most potential, which abusive relationships prevent. My ex's and my mother put their own insecurities on me and hindered my success and my healing because they couldn't deal with my shine.

I am still learning but now know what healthy parenting is supposed to be, while I heal my own wounds and ptsd like symptoms. I am switched onto healing mode when I teach my children what I know and work with my patient and kind, whole, fiancé on ways to constantly grow and evolve together. We are both parents and we realise that compassion, patience and our own healing as parents is the most important thing we can do for our children's future. If you can't understand your emotions such as anger or repeated automatic behaviours then reach out and get some help. Don't let you be the reason you and your children are prevented from having a nurturing relationship where you don't raise your kids to be the best YOU, because its not supposed to be about you but instead raise them to be who they are individually.

The journey has only just begun, I am now using my knowledge and experience to help others become repellents to negative energies, abusive and especially narcissistic relationships and advocate real, happy & healthy relationships, heal their own wounds and instil strong healthy boundaries into their lives.

Each time a person contacts me to ask me if they are with a narcissist, I see myself in them all those years ago, and I tell them that they are not crazy at all. They are in a trauma bonded relationship, seeing their mood turn from despair to hope is priceless!

The idea of creating an urban village "because Queens raise nations" made me realise that its not just a postpartum support they need. It's community issues. Studies have shown that women thrive better with a group of strong women behind them, the importance of sisterhood and women being around feminine supportive energy is vital for true thriving, not survival. If we look at women's health issues, most of them are due to high cortisol levels which are burning out, the oil of the lamp of life reducing. These women therefore develop both mental and physical health problems due to always using the fight or flight stress response. The men in these relationships need to be more empathic and to be honest, educated about how a woman brain actually shrinks after childbirth, if that is not enough to bring about compassion for women after childbirth I don't know what else will!

I want to create a movement where I see sisters helping sisters, which is why I created private Facebook group "BITRU SISTERHOOD" where I create awareness of childhood wounds and how to heal them. My message to women out there is that if you love yourself completely, there is no limit to how wonderful your life can actually be. Therefore, even if you were not loved before, once you love you, the real you flaws and all, then you create space for more healthy relationships whether platonic or romantic that actually serve you rather than deplete you.

I am the living, walking truth, If I could go through years of struggle, with no support system at all, no knowledge of why I kept attracting toxic relationships, then imagine what you can do with the knowledge, support and healing! It is extremely fitting to add the quote you find yourself in the service of others by Gandi, for that is exactly what brought me to this day, now I can help others heal and find themselves through my BITRU PHILOSOPHY to "Blossom Into The Real U"!

If it wasn't for my children I would never have the desire to heal my wounds, or strive to give them a better life, my Two Expresses and One emperor have been catalysts for my growth, they kept me moving on the tough days with their smiles, I had something to live for, it was never easy to raise an empire alone but I am grateful for all those lessons I have learned that have boosted my spiritual growth, I have had the true mind, body and soul healing bootcamp and pray I can help others too.

I forgave all the people who caused me pain as many hurt you because they are hurt themselves, but this doesn't mean you allow people to continue to hurt you. I learned lessons from all my struggles and this is only one chapter of my life, I thank God for the training I got to get to the next chapters of my life.

Much love

Rabia Kyinat - Founder of BITRU

Instagram - @Bitruwithrabia
Facebook - www.facebook.com/rabiakyinat

17

Creating your freedom life

Sometimes the most beautiful things happen just after you've hit rock bottom. I would wake up at night with my pillow soaked from tears, even though I just had the most amazing blessing come into my life. As a young girl, I never imagined that this would be my reality, after all, I was just a normal Swiss girl with long hair, who was trying to fit in, but somehow always felt like she just didn't belong.

I passed years of my life believing that I wasn't good enough without realising, that it was stealing so much joy of my life. I tried my best to pursue happiness by trying out many different jobs, traveling to various countries and then also by leaving my home country to live in Egypt.

What I found there was love, God Almighty and freedom. I was working together with my husband on a safari yacht as dive instructors and we went to some of the most beautiful dive sites in the world. During that time, bad news came from back home in Switzerland.

My mom had been diagnosed with Cancer and that surely was a shock for me. Still, I stayed in Egypt while going for a visit from time to time and also started to plan for a family with my husband. We knew that I couldn't continue diving and I was trying to figure out what else I could do to add to our income.

I applied for several jobs, but I couldn't find anything and I started to have the fixed idea that it should be possible to use the internet to work from home while being anywhere I wanted. I was trying to earn some extra money by doing surveys and even clicking on ads to earn a few pennies. In the end, nothing of these ever paid me anything, but I surely took me lots of my valuable time to figure that out. I continued my research to find something that would work.

I then thought I would need to become a medical transcriptionist, which got me to switch from my 2 finger typing system and to learn to type fast. Sadly enough, I then figured out, that I would need to live in the US, to find a job as a medical transcriptionist. After even more investigation I found a company that I thought could be the solution to my problem and I got even more excited, as when I learned about their products, I felt that they could help with my mom's health and with my overall well being.

I got started and even though I was the only person to work that business out of Egypt and the products weren't available there, I decided to make it work. And after a short while, I was earning money with it. Well, I didn't become a millionaire, but the earned money proved to me that it was, in fact, possible to earn money from home while doing something that I love.

After a while, I got pregnant and we were extremely happy about that. When we learned, that we were not only going to have one or two but three babies at once, we were quite shocked, but also three times as exited. At about the six-month mark of my pregnancy, I flew back to Switzerland as we didn't want the babies to be born in Egypt for medical reasons. I moved in with my parents, but even though I went there for a happy event, it was a difficult time.

My mom now was severely ill with cancer and the chemotherapy was taking a toll on her. It was a very hard time to have 3 babies growing inside of me while seeing my mom's health deteriorate more and more. A couple of weeks before my planned C-Section, she had to go stay in the hospital, as she had become too weak to stay at home. Luckily, my doctor's clinic was located inside the same hospital. Like this, my mom was then able to come to one of my ultrasound examinations, where she was able to see the babies in 3-D.

But that was the only glimpse she would get of them. Ever.

Just about 2 weeks before our boys were born, she died of cancer. I was so sad but I knew that I just had to stay strong. For the babies and everyone around me. The rest of my pregnancy went without bigger complications and we made it until the planned C-Section date and on the birthday of my dad, our triplet boys, Bilal, Hamzah & Sofian, were born. As they were a bit tiny and needed some more help, they needed to stay a bit longer at the hospital, but in the end, everything turned out well.

It was really hard to keep up with everything being a new mom to 3 babies and I never had the time to grief about my mother's passing. That's why I would wake up at night with a pillow soaked from tears. I felt that I had to be strong and even though that the year 2008 was the toughest year of my life, I found strength with God Almighty, as I always reminded myself that He would never give me a test which I couldn't withstand.

My life now was all about the babies and I barely had time to myself but we felt so blessed and happy having three babies at once. About 12 weeks after giving birth, we went back to Cairo and started our new life in Egypt. I already had stopped working on my business before I left for Switzerland, as I became so extremely busy with preparing for the birth of the triplets and then caring for them, that I wasn't able to continue my journey with that company.

That was fine, as this part of my journey contained some of the most important lessons of my life. I learned to be more patient, be less perfectionist and got more interested in healthy nutrition. Meanwhile, the situation in Egypt became worse and worse and we were there when the 2011 revolution happened. The aftermath of it was, that we didn't feel safe to stay there anymore and as almost no more tourists came, my husband would not have much work either.

We then decided to leave Egypt and go live in Switzerland. Just a couple of days before we left, my husband and I had an interesting conversation with friends, which got me restarted in my quest to be able to earn money from the comfort of my home, while still being there for my children. Equipped with some new ideas and after settling in Switzerland, I started selling used things online and I also got into importing goods from China.

I learned quickly that you can't trust everyone and several business transactions were a total loss on my side. But I also got successful in selling baby carriers and hammocks. Still, next to caring for triplets and with another baby on its way, that was a lot of work, as I needed to have stocks at home and then ship each order out separately, which is a lot of work.

So while somehow it wasn't that bad of business and I made some profits, it wasn't the best idea either. That's when in 2016 I decided to get involved in online marketing and even though I didn't have any idea at first about it, I committed that I would make it work. My guess was, that it would be quite easy and that I would be able to do this by anonymously sitting behind my computer.

Years later, that sounds pretty humorous to me, to say the least, but at that time I had extremely low self-confidence. I would never like to have a photo taken of me, I would never post photos of me on social media and getting on a video call with my mother in law was almost impossible. But little by a little while on this journey to learning online marketing I also fell in love with self-development. I realised that I needed to work on my mindset, especially on the beliefs about myself.

At the beginning of my journey every time I would hear someone say that it is all about your mindset, I would think that this is just some woo-woo stuff, but now I know that they were right all along the way. And if you think, that I just got involved in online marketing and was successful immediately, then you're wrong. It took me about a year to earn my first dollar online and I was always looking for the next best thing.

I would jump from one opportunity to the next, not realising, that it wasn't so much about the opportunity itself, but about my skills and my mindset. Still, I got some success here and there and I even made it to some top spots on the leaderboards including winning some contests! That was such a great feeling and increased my self-confidence by leaps and bounds. While I was working hard on getting ahead in my journey, my health wasn't doing that great. I was suffering from frequent migraines which would stop me from being able to look after my family and living life in a normal way.

I also had frequent pain in my neck from an old injury I had from being involved in a car accident in my early twenties. That pain was also the one thing that stopped me from creating the habit of working out regularly, as most of the work out efforts would end up with me having more severe neck pain again. As I was also on a journey of natural health and the thought of taking any medication didn't excite me, I was looking for a remedy for my problem. I heard from a friend about a natural product she had found and I thought to myself that I had nothing to lose by trying it.

I ordered a box of the seed-shots and just after a couple of days, I could feel a difference in my energy levels and overall well being. The pain in my neck was decreasing. I was amazed and at the same time, I came to realise, that I finally found what I was looking for. Since my first business venture in Egypt, I had become very interested in natural foods and on how to live healthier. My high-risk pregnancy and the cancer diagnosis of my mom even had more impact on me to find out how to make food my medicine instead of making medicine my food.

This was my real passion - showing people how to reclaim their health and take fewer prescription drugs in a completely natural way. Additionally, I wanted also to show the other stay at home mom's out there that there is a way to earn money from home while caring for your children, instead of dropping them off at daycare and missing out on the big milestones.

There is a way to make your dreams come true. You are never too old, to introverted or unskilled. Any skill can be learned and if I could do it, then so can you. Yes, there is another way than settling for what society tells you is normal. You can create a different life for yourself and your family by starting to do things in a different way. You are deserving and worthy of having the life you dream of. I'm truly blessed to be on this journey and even though I'm not yet where I want to be, I've come a long way and my vision of impacting many families keeps me going.

Janine El Hinnawy - Creative Business & Marketing Solutions.

Website - www.janinelhinnawy.com
Free Gift - https://janinelhinnawy.com/book
Facebook - www.facebook.com/JanineHinnawy
Youtube - http://bit.ly/JanineYoutube
Linked in - www.linkedin.com/in/janinelhinnawy/

17

A Blossoming Mum

Hello, my name is Zohal Ghafari, I came to live in Canada with my family at the age of 7 from Afghanistan. I am a mom of 3 kids. I have a degree in psychology, studied self-development since 2010, have been a mindset coach for moms in the area of self-development for the last 4 years, empowering them to live their dreams, let go of overwhelm and inspire and motivate their children. My passion is to work with moms and help them focus on what matters most to them, to have an amazing vision for their life, to take action towards their dreams, to overcome their fears and to connect with their kids and help them flourish.

At the age of 3, I had lost my mom in the civil wars in Afghanistan. Growing up with my Dad and my 5 siblings wasn't always easy. But we lived in a Country of opportunity, the opportunities are vast for little girls and women in general here in Canada. I was very ambitious about studying from a very early age. Finishing only grade 1 education in Pakistan and being put in a grade 4 class once we arrived here in Canada, basically I had to skip grade 2 and 3 while studying in a whole new system, the Canadian curriculum. It wasn't easy at all but I was super dedicated and very much a perfectionist (something that I have recovered from through self-development). At the age of 19 I got engaged and decided to get married, coming from an afghan culture, where the daughters mostly study when they are single if they do have the opportunity to study, once they are married, they are most likely not able to study, maybe because they have a baby to raise, or become a housewife, or start working instead of studying. I promised myself that I will be getting my degree after marriage. And that's exactly what I did, I prayed and committed myself to studying and getting my degree in psychology. I was also working at that time, part time as an office admin, studying French, and working on my degree. Soon after I finished my degree and started working in the government, after my contract finished, I had my baby boy.

I was enjoying every moment of being with my baby and studying self-development books, I read 40 books in that first year that I was home with my baby. It was super inspiring, I wanted to continue reading and reading, I was in love with the way these books taught you, teaching you to dream, to live a life full of dreams and letting go of perfectionism, facing your fears, facing your obstacles, overcoming your obstacles. Taking action everyday, being consistent. Planning your life, prioritising, making progress. However as I was reading, many of these books were written by men, men who didn't have the responsibility of a baby, who lived a different life, whom moms couldn't relate to as much. Especially muslim moms.

I felt really inspired but I wanted to hear all this from a mom, from a mom who is living life with her kids and still putting in these formulas and writing books and giving lectures on self-development, self-love, self-care, self-esteem-self progress. As I was continuing to reflect and study, I decided to stay home with my son, work on my studies and bring another baby. I had my daughter when my son turned 2 and a half. I was consistently taking courses in the area of self-development, started getting coaching sessions every week. Yes, before that time, I was not really familiar with coaching, who is a coach, what they do, what is their purpose.

That's when I gave coaching a try. I fell even more in love with this whole world of self-development, A coach believes in you, listens to your struggles, your hardships, and helps you overcome them. A coach encourages you to become the best version of yourself, to overcome your fears, you are in an environment of total positivity. An environment where anything is possible if you give your best and have dedication. A coach is a mentor who guides you to reach your goals and keeps you accountable. And that's exactly what I did for a good year, every week I would meet up with my coach, talk to my classmates who were in same situation as me, trying to discover their passion and achieve more in their life. I would meet up with other ladies and talk about my wins and my losses for that week and learn more and take note and get coached. It was an amazing experience. That's when I questioned myself a lot. What do I really want to do to make a difference in this world. What would I do, if I was not working only for the money, instead working on my passion and for bringing a change in this world. And after writing down the answers to these questions, I realised that my passion was to help moms get knowledge of self-development, to discover their purpose, their passion. To dream more and if they had given up on dreaming, to start dreaming again and taking action towards their dreams. That's when blossoming mum coaching was given birth. I created classes for Moms, to talk about success, to dream, to create a vision for themselves, to let go of fear, to live a life of purpose. I created these classes with knowledge and money that I had invested towards my degree, towards my books and self-development courses and coaches that I had taken. My psychology degree and the 6 years of self-development studying that I had done. It was time for me to give back and to help moms enjoy their journey of motherhood while being productive. We had an amazing time and continue to have an amazing time whenever I am coaching these strong humans called moms. I started coaching moms from different backgrounds. Some had full time jobs, working in the government, working as a teacher, having their own business, some were stay at home moms. They came from different walks of life, but they all had one purpose in common. To live their own individual purpose, to become the best version of themselves. To dream and achieve their dreams. By being the best version of themselves, bringing out the best in their kids. Connecting with their kids, Helping their kids emotionally and academically. Creating more time in their day and their week, achieving more and enjoying life.

The reason that I was so motivated to make my niche to be Moms, coaching specifically for moms is because Moms as we all know are the most amazing creatures on the face of the earth. They are so strong and they do so much. From the time that they go through pregnancy, to birth, to the newborn, the terrible twos, the pre-teen years, the teenage years and so on. As soon as a woman becomes a mom, it is a totally different world. There is so much joy, unconditional love for that new bundle of joy however there is so much responsibility as well. Your whole perspective changes, you look at everything through the Mommy lenses now. You put your children first, you have sleepless nights, and busy days, trying to balance studying, career, work life and trying to get everything done, that most of the time in the midst of it, you lose yourself, you lose your identity, you forget about your purpose, your dreams, you feel far away from a life that would match your blue print (the way you would have wanted your life to be). Motherhood and it's journey is one full of joyful moments and full of hardships. Connecting Moms with self-development help them be passionate about what their doing, help them let go of stress, get over the mommy-guilt and overwhelm.

The reality is that a lot of moms end up neglecting themselves, they don't exercise as much, they don't have "me time", some time to themselves, they don't read good books to inspire and motivate them, to help them get over their challenges, to invest in themselves, they don't have time to cook healthy food, and in the middle of all this, they lose themselves, their identity, who they were, what they liked, what they enjoy spending time on, what big goals and dreams they had. What they wanted to achieve. They may feel guilty, frustrated, but moms deserve so much more, they deserve to be told that they are enough, that they are doing enough, that they deserve time for themselves, that they are a good mom, that they are giving their best, that they deserve to be motivated and to be productive. They deserve to choose happiness and to be happy. That's exactly what happened, I said, there isn't enough of self-development and coaching specially for Moms, I will be the one to create that content, and help Moms out, help them be inspired in their daily life. Create an environment where they don't feel alone, to be sitting beside other moms and have ambitious big goals and dreams. I don't want Moms to stop right there, as soon as they become a mom, they let go of their dreams, either they become a stay at home mom, or live that same job everyday that they are not even enjoying. I wanted to open different doors and opportunities for these moms, by telling them to dream more, to believe in themselves more, to make everyday a better day then tomorrow and to define success on their own terms. What does success mean to them personally and go for that.

Lots of struggles are faced as a Mom when you are going for your dreams. Of course in the Journey of Motherhood you face many hardships inclusive of sweet moments as well, but then to transition to divert your attention for your dreams, you will definitely go through hardships but it's really important to stay strong and stay connected with your purpose. Doing anything important in this life needs patience, and lots of it. If you are going to be impatient and want things to come together right away, exactly the way you want then remember that you are setting yourself for giving up right away. Because life doesn't work that way, you have to work for your dreams. It's very important to embrace your failures and look at them as learning experiences, I love the quote that says, you either "learn or you win." So look at your situation as always being a win, win situation. Because if you are learning from those experiences it is still a win. Remember that your efforts is what matters the most, the results won't come right away, but eventually so many opportunities and results will come your way, if you stay in the right vibration, by staying positive, adapting the growth mindset. Putting in the effort and celebrating those efforts. Personally being a wife, and a mother of 3 kids, my eldest 9 years old son, second youngest almost 7 years old daughter and then my 3rd one my precious little baby almost 6 months old at the moment. I do my best to cherish every moment with them. I put in my time and effort towards them and also towards my own dreams. By balancing everything out, taking one step at a time, and acknowledging that I have only 24 hours in my day, and I need to prioritise what's important. And also remembering to forgive myself if I don't always do things right.

I try my best to Manage my time well by using a daily planner, this keeps me in touch with knowing where my time is going, and blocking time for the most important areas in my life is what will help me reach my dreams. Keep yourself accountable on your results for each week, how much progress you did. So whenever you feel overwhelmed, tired, exhausted, take a break, go back to your purpose, go back to your why, why are you doing what you are doing, why should you be putting effort towards your dreams, what kind of person will that make you in the long term, connect with your purpose. Who would you want to be remembered as when you leave this world, who do you want to have become for your kids, what kind of role model, what kind of example would you want to be for them. Do you want to be remembered as the one who lived life fully, who gave her best, who went for her dreams. This will truly give you a lift, not to give up on your dreams when the struggles become big. Focus your vision on how far along you have come, work on your dreams from a place of gratitude, for when you are full of gratitude and have a positive attitude you will not give up and you will persist until you reach your dreams.

There is no end to achieving dreams, when you finish one, create more and thrive to reach even more dreams because in the process you are growing into an amazing individual. These can be health goals, financial goals/career goals, your goals for your kids, your spiritual goals, relationship goals and so on. The list is endless.

My advice for Moms:

Always remember that you are doing great. Count your blessings, dream, create an outstanding vision for your life, do not stay stagnant. No matter what, progress, take action, work on your skills everyday, whether that is studying, learning something new, reading a good book, getting coached. Keep yourself accountable towards your vision. We all need some help in this beautiful and difficult journey of motherhood. But it doesn't have to be so hard, you can focus more on what matters to you the most, what brings joy to your life and what will help you and your kids. Choose courage over your fears. And most of all, investing in your education, in your self. Read that amazing book, listen to that inspirational lecture, learn something new, get into that life changing coaching program. Make sure that you do not neglect yourself and make it a priority to live in this beautiful journey of motherhood to the fullest. I am always here for you if you would like to reach out to me.

The programs that I run are one day workshops, (one on one coaching) online or in person), group coaching, speaking events. Coaching classes are usually 8-12 classes or sessions. You can book me for any of the above. Call me or text me to book an appointment for a free coaching session.

I also have a blossoming mum group on Facebook, just search blossoming mum group and it will show up and you can join.

Zohal Ghafari - Mindset Coach for Mums - Bachelors In Psychology

Instagram - @blossomingmum
Email - blossomingmumzohal@gmail.com or zohalg@hotmail.com
Text or Call 613-804-8416
Facebook page - https://www.facebook.com/blossomingmum/

The Gift of Sakeenah

The dreams we had as a child, the memories of planning of what we wanted to be when we grew up, the anticipation of being an adult are the few distant thoughts we seldom think about as adults. As children we had an idea of what we will become as an adult and at times we are able to achieve our dreams and ambitions, other times God had greater plans for us.

For me, I was a simple person, with no ambitions or goal's, my only aim was to please Allah Subhana wa ta'ala in this life. Due to this intention, I never thought Allah Subhana wa ta'ala will give me the most beloved gift I could ever receive. I didn't search or ever thought of doing the work Allah Subhana wa ta'ala would set me out to do.

The support work started on social media, funny as it sounds, social media got me connected to so many people, ideas and thoughts. I wrote one post regarding about the need of supporting women who have faced domestic violence in the Muslim communities. Discussions, rants and reprimanding on Facebook made me realised how deep the problem we were facing as a community. The voice I raised on social media, allowed women to stand up and speak up too.

Being flooded with messages with love and support, I was also inundated with messages of women who desperately needed help either to get out of their situation or were facing the difficulties of the after math of abuse. At that time I wasn't equipped to help as I was completely novice at this myself. I had to refer to organisations that were able to help these vulnerable women.

Due to austerity, many of the organisations were struggling to support the women; either there was no space at one of their safe houses or lack of resources. These organisations are vital to our community, and they were under huge amount of pressure. I decided to think outside the box, how we can support the vulnerable and the organisations. That's when the amazing Muslim community stepped in and helped with raising the funds to arranging food parcels or place for the women and their children to stay in.

This story is not about me, but an acknowledgement of the strength in the Muslim community. It is they who helped build Sakeenah foundation. With every share, ideas, stepping up to help, it was us. That's why I believe the foundation is the community and will continue to be the community.

Sakeenah did not come with all glitz and glam. There was a fight to make a space on the table for the community. The huge responsibility of making sure the community is heard was hard. There were times I have cried over statements, questioning, even a smear campaign of a once close friend. One day I woke up reminding myself that when you set to do something for the betterment of others, expect struggles and sacrifice. To rely on Allah alone and no one else, as He is the One that closes doors and opens unlimited opportunities for you.

The opportunities were hidden most of the time, and I had to be very patient with every decision I made waiting for the answers that at time took months. The challenges and opportunities are the ones that made me grow as a person, and who I really am as a whole.

Sakeenah came through not just for sisters in need, but also for me. Amazing how Allah sets out your life. This has to be the biggest gift I have received from Allah, and will always be grateful. Sakeenah gave me the motivation, the belief, the self-esteem when I was going through the test of losing my best friend. My best friend, who encouraged me, supported me, challenged me to think outside the box, who gave me ideas that helped Sakeenah grow and make what it is today. My best friend, who I am always forever grateful and will always love for the goodness that they have brought; their mark on Sakeenah will always be there.

The marks that we all carry ourselves and the marks you imprint on others, is a story we leave behind. With Sakeenah, I wanted to leave a somewhat a positive, life changing story behind for those who need it. I wanted the community organisation do what its name suggests. To bring tranquillity to others who need it.

Tranquillity is not only for those who are vulnerable but hopefully to the community we all live in. The changes will come if we are all proactive in caring, kindness, love and upholders of truth. To bring justice, strength, inspire and change matters that have held the community captives through workshops, collaborating, raising awareness, campaigning. The more we speak up, the more we all become a Sakeenah.

Sakeenah will grow only if we want to grow ourselves. Ready to make those difficult changes within us and our communities. This is just the beginning for me, you and those who are touched by Sakeenah. Wherever there is darkness, we bring the light. Wherever there is injustice, we will bring justice. Wherever there is silence, we will bring the noise. Wherever there is despair, we will bring hope. Wherever there is pain, we will be Sakeenah.

Thaminah Aziz - Founder of Sakeenah Non-Profit Organisation.

Instagram - @sakeenahcommunity

17

The Ladder Against the Wrong Wall

Have you ever really wanted to pursue a dream but doubted yourself? Maybe you've made some excuse as to why your dream isn't possible for you. That voice in your head has told you all the reasons why it won't work. You're too young, now too old, too thin, too heavy, too this, that and the other.

And before you know it. You're listening to that unhelpful inner voice. You're questioning who you even thought you were for entertaining the idea. "Why did I ever think this would work?" you say to yourself.

Can you relate? Me too.

In fact, this was something that held me back for a long time.

You see, it was just a few years ago that I had a dream to start my own business. At the time I was working in a corporate career within the world of legal recruitment. I had done well at College and University, gained a law degree and after a period within legal practice, I made the move into legal recruitment.

Whilst I enjoyed some aspects of my job, over time I found myself thinking "is this it?"

I couldn't believe that this was all there was to life and over time the long hours, office politics and corporate grind left me feeling uninspired and unfulfilled. I frequently found myself frustrated and I knew deep down that I was meant for more, but the problem was I had no idea what that "more" looked like.

I wondered if it was all a pipe dream and whether I was asking for too much. After all, wasn't this the way things were supposed to be? You go to University, get an education, work for 40 years and then retire with your carriage clock and pension. If you were lucky, you got to enjoy a bit of your life after retirement.

And what then? Was that it? Was that all there was to life?

I knew I didn't want this for myself.

Eventually, I got to the place where I was so over my corporate career. I was sick of making money for someone else as well as not being appreciated. The negativity, micro-management, long hours and constant moaning about my life got me weary and sick of the sound of my own voice.

I was just another voice in the "everyone hates their job" chorus of my work colleagues and it was draining me and leaving me down.

But despite all of this, I had no idea how I could change my circumstances.

On the one hand, I felt as though I should be grateful, I had a decent job and salary and I was comfortable, but it wasn't enough. There was something missing.

During this time, I often dreamed of having my own business and working for myself. BUT, I didn't have the confidence to make the move.

All that fear and self doubt I was talking about earlier – that was kicking in big time.

I often dipped my toes into what it would feel like, being more in control of my life, living life on my terms, doing work I love. I spent many lunchtimes in Waterstones reading through the business books. Planning my escape strategy. But, my limited thinking at that time led me to think there was NOTHING out there for me.

That I was destined to spend the rest of my life looking out of the office window, dreaming and wishing for better things. I thought everybody felt this way about their job and that was just the way things were.

But I was determined to open myself up to the possibility of a better way of life for myself. Do something so that at least I would know that I had tried to pursue something that felt more meaningful and passion driven to me.

I enrolled on a few evening courses after work and had fun making new connections and learning new skills. It showed me that there was so much more to life than the corporate grind. I started to get excited about life again.

It was around this time I discovered coaching. I remember vividly that sunny autumn day, at my Introductory Weekend, when the teacher mentioned a quote by Stephen Covey

> *"Most people spend their whole lives climbing the ladder of success only to realise, when they get to the top, the ladder has been leaning against the wrong wall"*

Suddenly it all made sense.

The Ladder Had Been Leaning Against The Wrong Wall This Whole Time!

And as I embarked on my coaching diploma, I realised how much I loved coaching. I loved how it empowered me and would do my future clients. I definitely didn't feel that way about recruitment and it was no wonder I had so much apathy towards that.

I started to realise that I could do anything and recognised many of the thoughts that were holding me back as limiting beliefs. Armed with this new found confidence, I finally took the plunge and left my corporate position and started the business I thought I had been dreaming about.

Only It Was The Wrong Business !!

I had been so exhilarated to finally realise that I could do anything that I didn't give any thought to what I actually REALLY wanted to do! I had just moved the ladder a little further along the same way and started climbing up the same wall!!

So, while I threw myself into getting my own recruitment business under way, the demands of starting a new business meant that there was not enough time to focus on my coaching studies and these started to fall by the wayside as my recruitment business took priority.

I remember the moment when I got my first client cheque in my recruitment business and instead of feeling elation or exhilaration, ***I Felt Nothing.***

I felt like a failure, as I realised I wasn't progressing my coaching diploma because I was working so hard building something deep down in my heart I knew I didn't want to build.

It was a hard pill to swallow.

But this time I knew that if I could change once, I could do it again. I looked at the lessons I had learnt from this and discovered that my passion *was* coaching and that was the area I wanted to commit to. I threw myself into my new coaching business and got over any feelings of failure.

> *I figured that when I was old and grey and looking back on my life, I would rather have tried and failed than to never have tried at all.*

I Realised That This Was My One Life To Throw Caution To The Wind And Really Go After My Dreams.

I also changed my outlook on life. Gone was the negative, worst case scenario outlook and in its place came a new attitude to live life as if everything was in my favour. I enhanced my spiritual practice, started to meditate and do more yoga and journaling and focused on becoming more present and enjoying the now.

I became my own spiritual restoration project. Initially, I started working with women in the corporate world and those within professional services which fit my background. I set my business up so that I was able to work from anywhere and I got the chance to do some travelling and building my business at the same time.

I Loved The Freedom That Came With Having This Sort Of Business.

I also loved the transformation in myself. I noticed I was more confident, more empowered, more in control of my life and how it was being shaped. As I started working with more and more women, I started connecting with those that were in a similar situation that I had been in.

They were sick of their corporate careers, they were tired of conforming to society's views of how they should run their working lives and they felt that the old ways of working were not right for them.

They too wanted to build a life and business on their terms. But the fear and doubt was holding them back and getting in their way. They were sick of being and thinking like an employee and they wanted to create their own legacy.

The more I worked with these women, the more I realised this was my purpose. This was the work I was meant to do. Work that didn't feel like work because it felt so aligned and fulfilling.

Finally, The Ladder Was Against The Right Wall.

I've come a long way since the time I was an unfulfilled employee following society's script working with amazing women who refuse to settle for less. Who don't let the fears and self doubt get the better of them. Who aren't afraid to follow their dreams and women who dare to do things differently.

So, if you are where I was when I was questioning and doubting myself and wondering whether I had what it takes, I want you to know that anything is possible for you. That dream you have, that big desire – it's meant for you. That's why it's in your heart and mind right now.

And I encourage you to follow your heart's desire. To push past the fears, the stories and the unhelpful inner voice and to know that you are meant for great things. Start with small steps if you have to. Get help and support. No woman is an island and we are not meant to do this ourselves. Before long, your dream will be a reality.

Tasmin Sabar - Personal Coach

Website - www.tasminsabar.com
Instagram - @tasminsabar
Facebook - www.facebook.com/tasmin.sabar
Pintrest - @tasminsabar
LinkedIn - http://uk.linkedin.com/in/tasminsabar

17

A Life Most Ordinary

I'm nobody! Who are you?

Are you nobody, too?

Then there's a pair of us -- don't tell! They'd banish us -- you know!

How dreary to be somebody!

How public like a frog

To tell one's name the livelong day To an admiring bog! - *Emily Dickinson*

I've been asked to write about my story - a life changing, road to Damascus moment; Light, Clarity, Purpose all in one flash! For me, it didn't happen in quite such an apocalyptical manner; "it came to me quietly and grew as does the best love per Mama Cass." (It's Getting Better - song by Cass Elliot)

This is a celebration of the quiet life, the ordinary life, the ordinary happenings and occurrences which nevertheless lead to extraordinary shifts, transformations and richness beyond measure.

An ordinary life, which I deliberately curated. Growing up, in my world, everything was extraordinary: my parents, my background, the people who gravitated towards my family, my ethnicity, my name (in a world where the phrase 'ethnic minority' and all its connotations had not yet been coined) was extraordinary..... in that I stuck out like a sore thumb. I didn't like it......

And thereafter all my endeavours were directed to be the Ordinary.

I hankered after anonymity; not to have to answer the question- where are you from, not even where is your family from? How do you say your name? Why do you speak with an English accent? My world picture was cosmopolitan white. I was not quite born but certainly a bred, north London child, having moved gradually north from Golders Green via Temple Fortune to North Finchley.

We then moved right out to Watford in the late 60's and boy was that a culture shock- yes I wanted to retreat to ordinariness, and walk close to the wall, because the alternative was the racism and misogyny which lived in these outer areas, better documented by others.

Retreat into ordinariness seemed to be the order of the day!

Time went on - I desperately wanted to fit in, or so I thought. What I actually wanted was not to be quizzed, and to be just accepted without having to explain myself. I wanted to be in a place where every-one knew how to say my name, and there wouldn't be the same repetitive questions, and I could be without fear.

So, Reader, I did go through the marriage! I married him, went to live in Pakistan to lead a life most ordinary; to be liked, for assumptions to be positive ones, to blend in. But no extraordinariness hounded me. I was English speaking, didn't really get the hang of the reality of the local culture, my husband and in-laws were extraordinary and wanted to be more so. I just wanted a quiet blending in life. Whats wrong with that I want to know? I certainly didn't want to be extraordinary to order!

There was a mismatch there and clearly a difference in aspiration; alas, Reader, as I married him, so I left him, or rather I prefer to use the narrative of, he left me!

I came back HOME to England with my 2 year old precious daughter, and set to constructing A Life Most Ordinary.

I started work with a Local Authority, in what I thought was a very ordinary role, I worked to managerial level, and brought my daughter up. The irony is I wanted **her** to be extraordinary in all the right ways

Evidently, secretly I do value the extraordinary. Truth to be told all that I did was extraordinary. I brought my daughter up, whilst dealing with a narcissistic mother and forged my seemingly ordinary career. I Managed to remain in the same organisation for more than 25 years. My daughter grew up, and has forged an extraordinary career as a city lawyer.

My humdrum life continued until.... drumroll, I met someone! Yay! I was a humdrum no more, if I was to be extraordinary, I could do it with someone else - and there lies the rub: I was afraid of standing out on my own, scared of being seen, scared of ridicule, scared of being exposed, scared of failure, scared of being asked todo stuff, taking on responsibilities that I wouldn't be to or couldn't fulfil - Scared! But with ANOTHER, I could: I could be seen either in the light or shadow of someone else. I wouldn't be solely responsible, I would be able to share.

As with most organisations, whether in the public or private sectors, the dreaded

word 'reorganisation' was being bandied about. With sheer hutzpah or complacency, I ignored it. I thought, I had my chap, I had been there for so long, what could possibly go wrong? Well, Reader, wrong it did go, with a crash, bang and a jolly old wallop!

My relationship floundered, burnt and crashed - for the most common of reasons: he wanted to go back to his previous paramour - I was as crushed and deflated and hurt and humiliated as any 17 year old. I wanted ordinary - I got the ordinary and most certainly common!

To add insult to this humiliating injury, my role was indeed made redundant. I endured a painful interview with my manager where the word 'redundant' was actually uttered to me, about me, in the cold light of day and with cold breath. I had never actually heard the expression in reality and in relation to me - thus far it had been a mere abstraction, heard on the news, known of other departments and hapless colleagues. Like death, I never thought it will happen to me.

Let me just dwell on this for a moment: death, redundancy, divorce/ separation, evictions. all final, endings; to experience these events is very different to hearing about them, imagining, sympathising, empathising; the private thought is, it won't happen to me.

But, Dear heart, it does and it will! And when it does, it doesn't put a comforting arm round your shoulder, it does not utter whispered words of wisdom, it does not offer warm space of an alternative, it does not offer a sustaining drink.... it is cold, hard, unyielding in its truth, and tests you as it thinks a grown-up should be treated. The blow is delivered without flinching and you take it, internally crouched, but on the chin, pretending its not wobbling.

It leaves you feeling bereft, floored, weak, cold.

At least that is the effect it had on me. This coming hard on the heels of the break-up, rejection as I chose to see it at the time. I took a few days off work to 'compose myself' and collect my thoughts'. I wandered around the local shopping mall in a daze, and the thoughts started to form themselves, with the vocabulary of worthlessness, rejection, defeat, misery, despair.

I was not new to this: the last time I had been assaulted on all fronts was when my marriage broke up, no husband, no job, no home - because he wanted to be with someone else. How banal?

I didn't go into free fall then because I had my daughter for whom I had to rise and be strong, provide sustenance, a roof, education, - everything that parents do for their children. I could not afford to crumble into a heap. At that time I shed a few crumbs but then rallied, got up, dusted my self down, nursed my bruised feelings and then got on with it.

This time around? Where was my reason for being up? I had everything but nothing to rise and be strong for. Through the fog of shock and grief (yes, I was grieving for my job, my love, my purpose) however, I knew that if I didn't get up, however wobbly, I wouldn't have the strength to ever rise.

My Damascus moment came in that shopping mall, where I was on the verge of breaking down - tears, sobs, snot, possible physical crumple as well as the emotional tsunami. As the familiar personal admonishments and chastisements were swirling in my head and my heart felt as though it could not beat any more..... a voice, a small but resonating voice whispered NO, No you are not going to crumple, don't listen to them, listen to me. This voice and words..... for that's all they are words and thoughts which you bring out, like a tried and trusted outfit, for occasions such as these.

I listened to the voice, and replaced the words swirling, with anything else: poems, nursery rhymes, the few Muslim prayers I know by heart, and the Lord's Prayer to which I often turn in times of trouble. Anything to drown out the debilitating effects of the words.

And THAT, dear Reader was my Damascene moment, in a shopping mall, in Watford. What could possibly be more ordinary than that. But in that very ordinary moment, an extraordinary strength entered me, such a strong sense of self that I hadn't experienced in all my 58 years.

My next step? I went clothes shopping as is the most sensible thing to do when faced with redundancy. But with the resolve NOT to be judgemental when trying on garments, I decided that it would be the garment that was wrongly cut and shaped, not me. There would be no 'does my bottom look big in this?' questions, no judgements about being too short or the trousers too long; how many millions of short-legged women there are in the world.... we cannot all be misshapen, the fault is with the manufacturers.

This one moment of revolt against the dictatorial words, and act of sartorial defiance set me on a new path which has led to an extraordinary birth of an extraordinary life. I embrace the extraordinary in myself and others. The ordinary circumstances and realities of ordinary life are to be celebrated - I'm not jetting off to Bali or Milan every month of the year.

What I am doing is working, on my coaching practise, adoring the challenges of business and family life, explore the courage I'm sometimes reluctant to show, own my fears, rages, hesitancies. Before I habitually say 'NO' to opportunities to stand out, I explore what 'YES' would look, sound and feel like.

I said YES to travelling to the mountains in Pakistan earlier this year, Himalayas, Hindu Kush and Karakoram mountain ranges all meeting, showing me an extraordinary beauty and lesson that there are no borders. I said YES to public speaking, extraordinary for a life-long stammerer. I said YES to overcoming my habitual shyness, and reaching out to other business women, to meet for lunch.

I said YES to an extraordinary life, while celebrating the power and loveliness of a life most ordinary.

Extraordinary things happen in the midst of the Ordinary...... Allow them

Exercises

1. **Mirror work** At least once a day I look at myself in the mirror keeping my gaze on my eyes for at least a minute (start off with 30 seconds as this can be quite challenging at first). I move from my eyes to my whole face, taking two minutes. I look at myself without any thoughts at all, neither approving nor judgemental. This is just ME with ME. I look at myself with kindness and love without discernment. This exercise bonds me with me and gives me all the acceptance I require.
2. **Journals** I have taken to keeping a Success Journal where I record all the successes of the day, however small that may be: sometimes doing the weekly shop without slip-ping in cheap biscuits is a success, alongside completing a piece of writing, doing a Facebook Live, running a workshop. I also record where I've noticed a hesitancy or negative feeling and have recognised

and managed or overcome it. Whatever I know has tested me in any way, I note in this book. I now have a compendium of my own success stories and events.

3. **Vocabulary check** Banish particular words from your vocabulary. The first two to begin with are "ought" and "should". These words smack of an action which has its origin in an external imperative. whenever you use it, to yourself or aloud, just pause and ask " who says I ought or should". If the answer is: journalists, social media wisdom, your friends, colleagues or your mother, then DON"T. If the answer comes back as 'me". then use "I want to" or "I will ".

When we don't do as we "ought" or "should' it makes us feel, at best, infantile (ooh I'm being naughty) at worst, fodder for manipulation and reinforces the sense of not doing what you think every-one else is doing, or what is expected of you.

To finish I would exhort all of you to embrace yourself, your life, your loves and enthusiasms, every-thing you are - therein lies the extraordinary.

Sylvi Hussain - Transformational Coach and NLP Practitioner. Owner of Sylvi Hussain Coaching and Training. Founder of *Yes You Can* Workshops.

Website - www.sylvihussain.com
Facebook - Sitwat Asad
Instagram - @sylvihussain

17

Stepping into Happiness - My Journey out of Victimhood

I've always wanted to live a life that was full, outrageous and full of abundance since before I embraced Islam. I always pushed the limits since adolescence, I realised at that stage of my life that I had some level of control with the results and outcomes in my life. As a Catholic, my faith in God was always strong and my love for Jesus was deep and profound and yet so many things about Catholicism didn't make sense and I began my search to reach the truth. I explored many aspects of Christianity and still I felt a huge void in my heart. I explored and practiced Buddhism and Hinduism and I learned about meditation and going inwardly. Meditation was a practice that felt like a glove and gave my heart so much comfort and still there was a void in my heart. Many practices within Buddhism and Hinduism just didn't feel right and I returned back to Catholicism and I accepted that I was born a Catholic and therefore I needed to learn how to be the best Catholic in order to fully please God. By this time I was married, I had my first child and I was filing for divorce after being married for 5 years. My exploration of God gave me the insight to my own abilities and my own power and how I could not just settle. I had a responsibility to be my best, teach my offspring to be her best and surround myself with likeminded individuals that would keep me on a track of growth and expansion.

At the age of 24 I was a single mom starting college with a clear goal of always expanding my knowledge to live a life where I could please God and receive His blessings. In my first semester in college I took the general education classes needed to receive my bachelors in order to work towards receiving a degree where I could be self-sufficient. My goal was to be the best role-model for my daughter and live a life where I could make a positive difference for others. As I stepped into my Speech 101 class, I felt a bit vulnerable as I was the oldest in the class and my insecurities engulfed my mind and yet I still needed to focus and achieve success to keep myself moving towards my desired goal. After a few class sessions and group activities I felt comfortable and I acclimated to the college scene. As I mingled and I got to know more students I began to feel more and more comfortable even though I was about 4 or 5 years older than the students I was meeting.

When I entered college as a divorced single mom I had not intention of getting involved in a relationship as a matter of fact I had set the intention to not even think about being in a relationship until I completed my college degree. The unexpected definitely happened, without my knowledge the love of my life and my life partner was in my Speech 101 class. Even though I was adamant about not getting into a relationship he swooned me off my feet with his good looks and sweet talk and we engaged in deep conversation that intrigued me to find out more about who this Arab student was. After a few weeks of talking in class he asked me out and I said yes, it was as if I had not the will to say no.

We talked deeply about religion and this was my first introduction to Islam. He shared about his faith and I shared about my faith, we talked about the similarities and the differences. The more I learned about Islam the more I wanted to know and the deeper I feel in love. I was brought up to be a "good girl" so dating for a long time was not something that was part of my DNA, as we spent more and more time together I broached the question, "what is your intention?" and the response was, “marriage?” and I smiled. I guess you can say I proposed, I was never the one to beat around the bush and I always wanted to be clear with intentions. We were married after 3 months of dating in 1988 and the real adventure was about to begin.

I have always been an optimist and at times that has set me up for heartbreak and disappointment, not necessarily because of being an optimist and actually for being naive. After 1 year of marriage I embraced Islam and my mother-in-law died of breast cancer. During my first year of marriage I was pregnant twice and both pregnancies were lost. This was the most devastating year of my life and I was thrown in a direction that was an unknown territory. My husband is 4 years younger than me and the influence of his family on him was very strong and powerful and I saw all my insecurities and weakness emerge to a level that overpowered my thinking. My heart was broken and my spirit was broken and my goal was simply to get through each and every day without having a breakdown. I suppressed my true feelings and buried them deep in my soul and I put on a smile that got me through many years in a very robotic way, just going through the motions and doing what others expected of me.

The next 5 years were long, lonely and a time where my mind was confused and detached from God. Five years prior I had stepped into the truth of Islam and I allowed life experiences to throw me off track disconnecting me from my Creator and things needed to change. I was tired, frustrated and worried about the future and it was time for me to take a new approach. I began to learn more deeply about my rights as a wife and as a woman and I had to drop the victim mentality in order to step into my true power with the will of God. I was no longer afraid of judgment and criticism and I was ready to speak my truth.

As I recognised the power of my own mind and as I lost the fear of what others though about me I began to feel myself pull closer and become more aligned with Allah. Allah had created me to be great and to do great things and once I began to believe this my whole world began to change. The change that was ahead of me was not easy and not streamlined, many people in my life were shocked by my new outspokenness and my new ability to go against the grain of the status quo. I knew and believed, as Allah taught me, if I was not willing to change myself nothing around me would ever change and I was no longer going to stay stuck in the negativity of others. As I began to heal the wounds of the past and as I began to forgive others and myself more and more opportunities began to show up and I learned to ask what I wanted.

It was time to have a family or to make a decision if my husband and I were a family at all. He had many fears about having children and I dreamed about having a child. We sat and talked openly and after expressing that if he was not interested in having children I was not interested in staying married. Soon after we got rid of all birth control methods and the blessing arrived shortly afterwards. I was grateful to give birth to our son in 1995 and the first 2 years were a blissful and peaceful time that bring memories of joy and harmony. My son was healthy and energetic and my oldest daughter from my first marriage was happy to have a sibling to play with and everything seemed perfect.

As my children grew up and began to have their own way of thinking, I noticed I became more rigid in my own thinking. I wanted the best for my children and the only parental guidance I ever knew was the guidance I grew up with, tough love and corporal punishment. I had sworn I would never hit my kids and that I wouldn't repeat the parenting patterns I had learned from my own upbringing. My temper shortened each year and by the time my son was 6 years old and full of energy I began a pattern of abuse that I could not stop and that I didn't recognise as abuse. It took getting reported to child protective services for me to wake up and look in the mirror. I had unhealthy authoritarian parenting patterns that need to be broken and it was not an easy fix. This was my moment to return to school and to help myself heal from my past abuse and to stop abusing my own children. I studied Human

Development and I felt so ashamed of all the harm I had inflicted on my son and my daughter. I wanted to break the cycle of abuse in my own family and I wanted to help other families to the same.

I learned to understand the feelings behind my own thoughts to better understand the different states I would get stuck in. As I learned to ask myself about my fears, my worries and my insecurities I learned to forgive myself and I became courageous enough to vulnerably ask my children to forgive me. This journey of self-reflection opened up my mind and my heart to connect with Allah at a level I had never experienced in my life before. This is when I made the commitment to myself to never again allow circumstance to determine how I showed up in life especially when circumstances became challenging. I was committed to do my best to live in the present moment with gratitude and compassion.

It not easy to live in the present moment always in gratitude and with compassion, as a matter of fact I fell off the wagon many many times. I am grateful that I always did find a way to jump back on the wagon living in the present moment with gratitude and compassion even if I had to heal my bruises afterwards. It has always been in those temporary low moments that I learn the most. I began to learn that happiness is a feeling I always have access to even if the circumstances are challenging. I gradually learned that it was good to feel good and that feeling good helped me navigate through difficult challenges with grace and with ease. By making up my mind that I was going to be happy no matter what, I truly experienced Allah's wisdom of experiencing ease after difficulty. That was the secret to stay in a state of happiness even when things got really hard and ease when things arrive sooner than later.

We have been taught that happiness is a reward one that we need to suffer for in order to acquire and this leads many to believe that happiness must be earned and that is false. We all deserve to feel good and there is nothing that has to be sacrificed in order to live from happiness. The opposite is true, happiness and good things can come easily and you are worthy of experiencing happiness at any moment of your choosing. What you must do is open your heart to the universal abundance of love that Allah instills in our hearts. Try this approach, close your eyes and imagine what it looks like to feel happy. You might feel yourself smiling and you imagine and that is where it begins with a smile on your face. As you close your eyes imagine your favourite place that makes you feel happy. Can you feel happiness surging through your body with this simple practice. No matter the challenges you have endured you have the ability to heal your heart and live from happiness every day.

Estela Rodriques Jebril - Therapist, Founder of The Passionate Muslimah Academy.

Facebook - https://www.facebook.com/estelarodriquezjebril
Email - estela@SpiralUpConnections.com
Website - www.spiralupconnections.com
Twitter - www.twitter.com/Estela_Jebril
Instagram - @estelarodriguesjebril

17

Resilience is NOT bound to circumstance!

I was 31 years old, I can remember it like it was yesterday. It was a rainy April morning and I was sitting with some friends, as my 3 year-old-son at the time was playing. We were all having coffee and chatting like our usual play dates, but something was off with me that morning. I remember that we were having a conversation about possible baby boy names for one of my friends who was expecting. I was trying to recall the name of my brother-in-law, and I couldn't recall it for the life of me. That was odd to me because there was no reason why I shouldn't be able to recall it, I knew his name very well, but it just wouldn't come to me. I shrugged it off thinking that perhaps I was just tired.

At that time my husband was very busy with his studies and I was fully occupied with my son and all the household tasks. I knew I had a list full of things to do that afternoon, so I had decided to gather my son and head back home.

Once home, I started making lunch for my son, while preparing for the following day's meal in advance, I knew I had to go to the hospital the next day for an iron infusion. Being the multitasked person that I was, and organised too I could handle many different things at the same time. While the meal was cooking in the oven on low, I decided to quickly jump into the shower. No sooner after I got out, everything started to change. I recall feeling odd and called my mother to let her know that something was off, I remember my mom was quite concerned and she advised me to call the local medical information number to speak with a nurse. I hung up with her and immediately made the call, I to get in a nurse on the line and I started to explain to her that I wasn't feeling very well. All I remember is that as I was talking to her and at one point she interrupted me and told me to call 911 emergency services, she had also instructed me to open the front door and turn off the oven. I probably told her that I was cooking something at the time.

I hadn't realised that by this time, I wasn't making any sense when speaking to her, I was hardly able to speak and my words were slurring. I probably passed out, because within what seemed like minutes later I came to and found myself lying in between the threshold of the front door of my apartment and felt the heaviness of something on top of me. I could see from the corner of my eye that it was my three-year-old son who was lying on top of me, staying very close. The ambulance had arrived, and all I could think about was what's going to happen with my son, how will they lock the door, what about my husband.

I immediately tried with whatever strength I could gather, to ask them to call my mother, as I struggled to get her phone number out of my mouth, with each word almost impossible to pronounce, they somehow managed to figure it out and contacted her assuring me that she was going to be meeting us at the hospital. I was relieved that she was there to take care of my son and I also knew that she would get in touch with my husband to let him know what was happening, although, I didn't quite yet know myself what really was happening.

My son holding his little stuffy tightly in his hand came into the ambulance with me and the first responders. With the sirens blaring, we quickly headed off to the hospital. When we arrived my mom was already there with my brother and my son went directly into my brother's arms from the ambulance. I remember feeling very tired but relieved that he would be okay and safe. Not long after that, my husband too arrived at the hospital. He had been so concerned and wanted to understand what had happened, I still didn't know what had happened to me, nor had I been aware that I couldn't move half of my body, not until the doctor came and lifted my arm, and as he let it go, it fell smackdown to the bed. Then for the first time, I understood that I was paralysed on my left side, quickly I realised that my speech was slurred as it was difficult to communicate and to be understood.

That first night in the hospital seemed so challenging for me, it was the first night I slept away from my baby boy, I had never left his side before that, but the exhaustion with what just happened on my body took over and I fell asleep.

Days flew by as I would drift in and out of sleep, with an intense migraine, I remember the moment when the doctors wanted to have me stand up to evaluate my physical ability, they brought me in front of a mirror in the physiotherapy room, then stood me up with the support of a lift mechanism that I was secured against. It was the first time I saw myself, I was taken aback by the reflection of what I saw staring back at me in the mirror. Half of my face was just hanging, half of my body was also hanging, I had no control over it, it was just heavyweight pulling me down. I remember hearing the doctor say to my husband as they returned me to my room, that they did not think I would ever walk again. As I saw my husband take that in, for myself, I didn't believe it to be true. Although this whole experience was surreal, that possibility did not make sense to me, not because I was in denial, but rather intuitively I knew it was not true for me.

After months in the hospital with intensive rehabilitation, physiotherapy, speech therapy, and occupational therapy, I recovered from that episode. I left the hospital being able to walk although, with a very slight weakness on the left side, but I recovered.

Although the doctors were still not quite sure about the entirety of my diagnosis they had suspected I had a neurological condition that was very rare and it could come back at any time. Only time would tell more. I spent several years without any incident, until shortly after a little accident that left me on my back for several weeks; my body began to shut down on me. My health drastically deteriorated with so many new issues coming up; debilitating migraines, seizures, muscle weakness, muscle pain and stiffness, dangerously low blood pressure, that it eventually left me debilitated, and bound to a wheelchair.

The doctors were very concerned, and after seeing over 10 different specialists, they all pointed to me that I would now need to accept that this was my prognosis and that I will need to get comfortable with my new life, with all its physical and functional limitations, yet again, intuitively it did not seem what would be the truth of my reality, still I wasn't able to walk or stand without blacking out, as my blood pressure would drop dangerously low and I could just drop to the floor at any given moment. I was stuck at home most of the time because having to walk up or down the stairs from the second floor I lived on, was almost impossible.

At times all I could manage was to walk from the bed to the bathroom and sometimes with that too I needed assistance. I have to admit, it seemed impossible at times to imagine something would just shift and take me out of that place where I seemed trapped in. However, I did not believe that was impossible, intuitively I knew it was possible. It all started with a prayer, I prayed to my Creator, for complete healing, and not only did I ask for that, I wholeheartedly believed it would be answered.

I started to seek out alternative medicine for healing my body, such as; hijama (cupping), acupuncture, consulted with a Naturopathic Doctor, followed a whole new way of eating, and incorporated supplements that would help my body heal from this illness. That year, as Ramadan began, I started to drink Zamzam water every single day with the intention and conviction that it would heal me completely, physically, emotionally, psychologically and spiritually, by the will of Allah.

By the end of that month of Ramadan, my healing journey began, I started to walk 5... 10... then 15 minutes assisted with a cane. My blood pressure stabilised, my debilitating migraines and seizures stopped, my muscles gained back strength and healthy function so that I could now finally leave the house. This continued and progressed to the point I regained my autonomy, I was now physically capable of living my life again.

Soon after this, I had a life-changing moment. It was right then when I first heard this one statement that completely changed my life.

'Feelings are coming from thought in-the-moment.'

This is when I learned about the Three Principles of Mind, Thought, and Consciousness as a Paradigm, and it was when my journey into understanding how we have a psychological and spiritual experience of life, began. This is where life became simplified. This is when my answer to complete healing was actualised.

The more I insightfully understood how it only works one way- that feelings are coming from thought in-the-moment; the more how it did not work, that feelings are coming from something other than thought in-the-moment, was revealed to me. Every single time I insightfully saw this in-the-moment, it evolved me, and it did all the heavy lifting for me. Categories of thinking, the past, and whatever looked like a challenge or a problem to me, effortlessly fell off my mind.

Redefining resilience.

Before coming across the three principles; this pre-existing system that accounts for all human experience, it often looked like circumstance was happening to me. It appeared like my experience was coming from whatever 'life threw at me'. Even so, somehow it had not been the case when it came to the prognosis of this health challenge.

It may have appeared as though every step of the way 'I got through' any moment of this health challenge because I was strong and resilient. People always told me you are very resilient, but I never even knew how I did that. I could never answer and state what I did to be resilient, as it never even occurred to me on my own that I was being resilient, so it only finally made sense to me why that was, after understanding this pre-existing system of how we have an experience of life works.

Resilience is that feelings are NOT coming from something other than thought in-the-moment. Experience is independent of circumstance. There is no cause and effect when it comes to adversity and our feelings, therefore it wasn't something I did or achieved in the face of adversity to be resilient, that is a misunderstanding.

Resilience is NOT bound to circumstance!

This completely re-defines resilience from what I had understood it to be, or what most people assume it is.

What people saw in me was the inherent quality of resilience, built into the thinking I had while in alignment with how my experience of life works. Even though all of this happened before I learned about the three principles, that system has always been what is accountable for all my experience of life since the day I was born into this life... unaware of it or not!

I just happened to be aligned with how I was experiencing my circumstance in-the-moment with the prognosis of my illness. I was not in a misunderstanding of how I was experiencing that prognosis... I did not believe that the prognosis given to me with this illness was creating my experience in-the-moment.

The more insight I have into understanding how this pre-existing system works, and insightfully seeing this in my day-to-day life, it continues to evolve me. I still get some physical symptoms, and once in a great while I still get migraines accompanied by loss of vision, speech and physical paralysis, but now whenever I get them, I am completely at ease with my experience. It takes its course and then recovery is no more than a few days at the most. I am so grateful.

In the Quran 94:6 Allah Exalted be He tells us: إِنَّ مَعَ ٱلْعُسْرِ يُسْرًا ***"In hardship there is ease."***

Things happen in life, there are challenges, but understanding how this pre-existing system works, allows me to rely on it for reference of how I am having an experience of those challenges in-the-moment, allowing me to show up with my common sense and a deeper understanding in dealing with whatever is happening in my life.

Freedom is that circumstance can never affect the way you feel. Resilience was never bound to circumstance or the past. Rather, resilience, confidence, mental well-being, motivation, are just some of the qualities that are inherently built into your thinking when you happen to be in alignment with how your experience of life works in-the-moment. This my friends is the best gift I can hope to share with you or anyone!

Zaina Della Porta, n.d. PCC - Co-Director and Lead Facilitator of Professional Coach Certification at CoachWhizz Coaching Academy; Zaina Della Porta is a Transformative Personal and Professional Leadership Coach and Mentor; Three Principles Paradigm Mentor and Facilitator; ICF Credentialed Coach and Coach Mentor; Co-Director and Lead Facilitator of Professional Coach Certification at CoachWhizz Coaching Academy; Naturotherapist and the Founder of Serene Lifestyle Coaching.

She supports innate leaders who might at times feel held back by uncertainty and doubt, debunk how they are experiencing life so that they emerge in their inherent qualities of resilience, confidence, creativity with flow.

Website - www.SereneLifestyleCoaching.com
Instagram - @serenelifestylecoaching
Facebook - https://www.facebook.com/serenelifestylecoaching/
LinkedIn - http://linkedin.com/in/zaina-della-porta-pcc-41319b167
Professional Coach Certification - www.coachwhizz.com/coaching-academy

17

A ROLODEX of Dreams

(Currently: Independent, Authentic, Filmmaker Shorts for the Internet.)

First let me tell you some of my weird story of events that all transpired from feelings within a fertile, ambitious imagination that hopefully will inspire you that the impossible can become the possible

My visions for the rest of my life in this world started when I was at school and were very grand indeed. I could clearly see/vision myself doing it all...with the single belief it was all waiting out there for me to take, seducing me to come and fulfil what life had on order for me for the taking and I was first in the queue.

School days dreamer: maybe I could be an athlete - Javelin & Discus? Or the next Wimbledon Tennis Star? Everyone loves an Astronaut! Or that Hollywood Film Star, The next James Bond...Who knows? I would most definitely love those cheques though! An Airline Pilot? A unique Diver (Sub Aqua) I might have found Nemo and Dory at once! A Chauffeur to the stars, hearing all their gossip and selling it for millions! Famous Rock Band...I mean I have the hair anyway...

some chance . . .

Left school –

What did I want to become, what was I going to become? Certainly I was more ambitious than most of my secondary modern school chums for sure.

First ever Job:

Worked with my father in a Precious Metals Factory for one year.

Is this my future? - NOPE. Spent every lunchtime day dreaming, how am I going to get out of this place and where do I want to go from here as soon as possible – my destiny is waiting.

ROLODEX -

I want to be rich and famous, I want to be in a band and famous like the Beatles - I want to be playing in a band driving all over the country and people/fans going wild over our music, recording albums in the studio and touring worldwide. That's too ambitious don't you think.

Action:

Put an ad in national music publication – 'Bristol Drummer seeks local band'.

Result:

First band: West Coast Union - Very amateur - Youth Clubs and weddings etc. Duration 6 months (Part Time)

I wanted more . . .

Second band: Papa Wesley (Bristol) Played Working Men's Clubs – Duration 6 months (But we went full time) Yes! Full time, on the road, just as I wanted but not with these guys.

I wanted more . . .

Third band: Johnny Carr & The Cadillac's - nationwide nightclub circuits – Duration 6 months (Fully Professional) this train wasn't going in the right direction.

I wanted more . . . I wanted a band that wrote 'original' songs.

Action . . . I put an ad in a national music publication.

Fourth Band: I found like a miracle and local to me, these two song writer/musicians looking to form a band and so we did and called this band Stackridge (Bristol) – we played at universities, rock clubs, main music venues across the country. Every venue wanted to rebook us back again and again as we drew bigger and bigger audiences.

Then this happens within the next five years **...**

STACKRIDGE

The band to open and close the very first Glastonbury Festival ever!

TV - The Old Grey Whistle Test x 2

BBC Radio 1 - In Concert x 2

BBC Radio 1 John Peel Show (Big Stackridge Fan)

BBC Radio 1 Bob Harris Show (Big Stackridge Fan)

The Marquee Club London (Regulars). Where the best of the best played by public demand. The Who, David Bowie, Jimmy Hendrix, Pink Floyd etc.

MCA - Record Deal

Three albums and various singles

UK & European tours with TV support appearances

Reading Festival two consecutive years running

then . . . . the unbelievable miracle happens

Beatles Record Producer George Martin wants to produce our fourth album.

ROLODEX – This is it! We are standing at the door of everything and more a band could ever dream to happen to them. I don't want my musical career with this legend George Martin to ever end.

I want more . . . global, musical fame and fortune for our music.

In the studio one evening as we were completing that Album, I had a major disagreement with the song writers who had approached me to say they felt they wanted to take a different musical direction with the band and a new on-stage lineup of additional musicians.

At this critical part of our five year journey I told them I was not prepared to compromise everything we had built and achieved to change direction now, "You guys are not famous yet" I reminded them. – Their stubborn stance and my personal viewpoint would force me to make a decision to have to leave this band in the hope they would reconsider the possible consequences of such actions with the fans, the record label, the promoters and the venues all who had fallen in love with who we were and the original music we made.

Everything I had dreamed ever be possible in my lifetime, I was now going to walk away from it all, the music success and the thought that I will never work beside this musical legend every again.

I questioned everyday have I done the right thing – will they become famous now working with George and have global success?

Within the next few weeks I was looking for a job in the West End as a professional photographer. Little did I know that George had been looking to find me and one of the band members got in touch to say to call his office as George would like to see you.

When I went to his office he asked if I wasn't doing anything else and if not already committed to other work, would I be interested working for him, looking after him, his wife and two small children as his personal aide/driver.

This would encompass, taking and collecting him to and fro from the recording studios and the office, driving his wife where she needed to go and at weekends driving them to their country home. This was a 'live-in' proposition and I from that moment became the fifth member of his family for the next ten years including:

- Living in Beverly Hills California
- Skiing with family in Lech Austria
- Sailing in the Mediterranean on his family boat
- Recording and visits with Paul McCartney
- Driving Rolls Royce's and Bentley's
- George's caribbean island studio Montserrat West Indies

Question: Did Stackridge go on to become the next Beatles and did George record any of further albums?

No! Phew!!! Their new direction and line-up was not popular with the record company, the fans or promoters and venues. Audiences declined rapidly, the record sales fell and the record company let the band go.

During my time with George, I had other dreams and goals . . .

ROLODEX - I want to Scuba Dive - (I couldn't swim at the time)???

Action: Joined a London Scuba Club (nearly drowned myself at my induction)
Loved the experience and dived in and around many UK coastlines

ROLODEX - I want to fly

Action: Joined a flying club
Achieved Private Pilots Licenses:

Fixed Wing & Helicopter

After ten glorious years, the children were grown up and off to boarding school, the time came where . . .

I wanted more . . .

ROLODEX - I want to have a new career being a filmmaker

Well here I am - I have been making short films for many years and loving it! I don't have enough paper to tell you some of the awesome brands and projects I have filmed and TV projects I have created.

IN SUMMARY . . .

What am I saying . . . There is a 'feeling' inside of everyone of what they feel most connected to and drawn to in life - and there is never just one - it can strike you at anytime in your life and if you choose to pursue it, it can be yours.

Doctor
Solicitor
MP
CEO
Change Maker
Nurse
Rock Star
Film Star
Charity Worker

Teacher
Business Owner
Tennis Player
Athlete
Astronaut
Policemen & Women
Train Driver
Weight Lifter
Fashion Designer

The list is endless . . . .

I believe that it is about 'feelings' of 'what do I want to become or do' in this life, a seed of a 'feeling' planted in the imagination of every human being - and if you keep watering these feelings they grow a little bigger and stronger each and every day and take you a step further, closer - and just like a magnet, attract opportunities heavily disguised as something else I have found you could never imagine, concealed, not always obvious and yet you 'feel' they are connected in some magical way to the end game you want for yourself in this life.

Sometimes we may miss them but it will come round again in a different form and sometimes it's our GUT feeling, intuition that tells us that this feels good and we are drawn closer toward that feeling whatever that feeling/ambition/goal/career/life choice is.

Of course some, may not desire to become great in the ego or material way but just be content with the simple pleasures of just enjoying life, family and friends, building relationships with people, doing good, helping others, standing up for something or making positive change happen in the world for the betterment of mankind where happiness lives.

You could say that life is what you want to make it. All things are possible, we see it everywhere. Dream on! Take action! Hold on! Never let go!

William Blake - Producer - Filmmaker

Website - www.williamblakefilmmaker.com
Facebook - www.facebook.com/williamblake.filmmakeruk
Linked in - William Blake Producer Filmmaker 4 Internet
Instagram - @williamblakefilmmaker

17

Change your mind

One of my earlier memories is as a young child of five years old in school. We were planning the school play, something every child of that age is excited about. I overheard one of the teachers of another class suggest to my teacher

"How about Naheeda for the part of Snow White?"

My breath stopped for a moment in excitement thinking I was going to be Snow White. The star of the show. After all she was my favourite Disney princess and character. But my short-lived dream was shattered as I overheard my teacher reply no, Naheeda is too dark to be snow white. I was puzzled. Was I not good enough as I was? With mixed emotions I took it all in and buried the feelings. Yes, I had raven black hair like Snow White, but I was lacking the white skin and rosy cheeks. I have never been able to forget the way I felt that day hearing my own teacher diminishing me because of the colour of my skin. You might think a small child would not be affected by something like this, but I did. I felt ugly. I used to dream of being able to wipe the darkness off my face so people would 'like' me. It was from that moment onwards the seed of feeling inferior was planted. My confidence was shattered. But the play went on and instead, I was given the role of a saucer.

Throughout my childhood I grew up with this feeling of being extremely ugly. I developed a way of thinking where I put myself down not just because of the colour of my skin but my features too. I grew up hearing aunties in our Pakistani community discussing what they considered to be the picture of beauty, which was everything I am not. They considered light skin attractive, I was dark. Thin lips were considered beautiful and elegant, mine were full. Straight small noses were delicate and feminine. Mine had a hump. I was only a young child, but I really believed it. I was ugly and dark skinned, I was rejected. I was not wanted, and my very soul was wounded by those easily spoken, thoughtless words by the people I looked up to the most. The people who were supposed to guide me and teach me, my own teacher and elders in my community. The effects of all these negative comments stayed with me forever. Or at least for a long time. This set the tone for the rest of my childhood and young adulthood. The human mind is a very impressionable thing. It just completely takes everything in. Consciously or subconsciously. Good or bad, it doesn't matter. My mind held on to those negative suggestions for most of my life, impacting on my mindset.

Going through my school years I found my self-esteem to be rock bottom. I would look in the mirror and see an ugly face. I was desperate to feel accepted. I would buy myself presents. I would wrap them up and pretend my 'friends' had given them to me. I was trying to fill a void. There I was a young child of early high school age, desperate for people to 'like' me. When anyone wanted to befriend me, I felt I had no value and my self-worth simply did not exist. I became a second-class citizen in my own opinion. Little did that teacher know, she shattered my self-confidence with that simple comment, and marked the beginning of my self-loathing and low self-esteem journey. My self-esteem was hanging by a thread. But life went on. The seed of worthlessness was planted and growing fiercely.

From then on whenever things in my life didn't quite go to plan, I would always find a way to blame myself. It was always me. My fault. My lack of knowledge, my flaws. I was convinced I was a failure. I became a people pleaser. I would be kind and friendly, helpful and generous, and I thought if I did this people would treat me better. I went out of my way to please all the people around me, but it was not enough. I was searching to fill a void, to fill a hole in my life. There was something missing. By then I had realised I lacked something within myself. I would never have filled that void with the validation of others, but little did I know that. It wasn't easy to realise thats what it was. This was when I discovered, I needed to work on myself and heal from the past. You see, when we are children, we can be negatively affected by the environment around us. I managed to uncover my feelings that were buried away which were still affecting me to this day. When you are affected by things from your past, or childhood, however long ago, it can often leave you with a deep void. It's like something is missing. But you just can't put your finger on it. Your subconscious blocks you from progressing in life, in relationships, and even business. You feel unworthy of love and receiving money. You have money blocks, can feel like an imposter and have no idea how to love yourself and accept these things into your life. I managed to turn all that around for myself and overcome these blocks through healing therapies and my personal growth mindset way of thinking. Now this is what I do to help my clients. I help them heal themselves on a deep level to achieve self-love, tranquillity and acknowledge their worthiness of their success. When you focus on inner healing, it opens doors and allows you to be able to live your life authentically and achieve the things that are important to you for your own personal success. You learn to value yourself, love yourself for who you are and become more resilient, without compromising your values. You don't feel like an imposter anymore, you feel worthy of all your successes instead.

The past decade I have gone through some of the most trying and darkest times of my life. I have struggled immensely with numerous aspects of my personal life. I have faced many difficulties which threw me to the ground, which I choose not to share in great detail, but I managed to pull myself through. There was a point I struggled with my finances so much I was counting pennies to buy food. Through these trials I kept my faith that God Almighty would provide for me and thankfully, he did. My prayers were powerful because I believed in their power. I believed in the Hadith where God says, "I am as to my servant as he thinks I am." I asked, he heard, I believed, he gave. Simple. My prayers were answered at times of my greatest need through the unexpected help of others as though they were sent by God Almighty himself.

Due to my past experiences I have come to welcome the grey clouds because there is always a silver lining that comes along with them. In that silver lining there is a lesson to be learned and implemented. I have grown to recognise this more and more as time has gone on. With every hardship I face, I now LOOK for the silver lining. Through my prayers God Almighty has opened doors for me out of nowhere. I learned; the help of God comes WITH the test. Don't forget that. If something is going wrong or if any negative thing happens to you, even if someone criticises you, think of it as a blessing. You are getting a chance to improve yourself and be better, to rise above the level you are at, and climb on to the next, it's a privilege and you need to thank that person at least in your heart if not to their face. Yes, it may hurt at the time, but just try to look at the bigger picture. Look for the silver lining in the dark cloud. I promise you it will be there. You just have to feel it after you find it. One really important thing I learned is this, If I have a problem of being corrected or if I have an issue in hearing something negative about myself, then it's most definitely an ego problem. The key is to crush the ego. And yes, it can take time, but it's all part of the struggle. This does not mean let people walk all over you. On the contrary, it just means, be humble, have boundaries, correct people if they are wrong but in private and with kindness, but never get into a dispute. Always be aware and mindful of your action and words, words can destroy people, so choose your words wisely and be kind. If you are someone who reacts instantly and negatively instead of thoughtfully, then you need to have some inner work done on yourself. It means you are shackled by your own emotions. If this is the case, then reach out and seek help. Being a therapist myself I knew of the powerful transformation that takes place through therapies which work with the subconscious mind which is phenomenally more powerful than the conscious mind. For me it was life changing. Now I help others to overcome their past traumas or negative past experiences which are holding them back from achieving their dreams and goals. I help others to overcome past hurts, abuse, pain and sufferings whether self-inflicted or caused by others, to help them move forward in their business and life, in order to achieve contentment, and confidence to massively increase their income. Through my work I have learnt, it's the inner pains, traumas, abuse, criticisms and knocks on your confidence that hold you back. When you do the inner work with a therapist you break the barriers that hold you back. That's what I did for myself. I invested in my professional and personal growth. I removed my limited thinking with the knowledge and experience I gained through my work and self growth over the last 12 years.

Don't be a people pleaser. Learn to say no. Have your boundaries. Know your weaknesses and your strengths so that you can use them to your full advantage. Always be kind and grateful. It literally changes your brain's wiring. If something is holding you back in your life or your business but you can't quite figure out what it is, If you have money blocks and feel like an imposter, chances are, you need to do the inner work. I help people to transform their lives just like I transformed my own through working on my emotional, physical and spiritual health. I help people heal from the same struggles I healed from. I wouldn't be the phenomenal therapist and coach I am today having a ripple effect on my clients, and their relationships and business if it wasn't for my own childhood. I am blessed to have a deep insight and empathetic understanding of of my clients issues and needs thanks to my own personal and professional experiences over the last 12 years. I have always had a resilient nature and ability to turn my deepest struggles in to successes, for me it was my survival method. Now thanks to these personal experiences I help others with this too. I have developed a strategy and holistic program. My transformational program which I developed from my 12-year experience of life changing therapies can help you achieve clarity, confidence, high self-esteem, healing from the past and removal of the blocks to unveil your full potential, so you can be a high performance achiever in your life and business goals. I did this through Prayers and effort. As a transformational mindset coach, I now help coaches, therapists, mums, entrepreneurs and professionals gain back their power through deep inner healing to achieve a powerful mindset and Super high self esteem and super sky high confidence to heal them from their past and help them excel in their business.

Naheeda Ahmed - Holistic Transformational Coach - NLP Practitioner - COSCA Counsellor - Mindset Coach - Detox specialist - Deep Emotional Healing Therapist - Clinical Nutritional Therapist - Meditation -Therapist - Life and Business Coach.

Email - transformingmecontact@gmail.com
Facebook - https://www.facebook.com/MyBodyMyAmanah/
https://www.facebook.com/groups/656096061576916/
https://www.facebook.com/groups/3033849309977938/
https://www.facebook.com/Transformational-holistic-Life-Coaching-by-Naheeda-141426663213251/
Instagram - @imindsetmastery

17

The Most Precious Gift

Born to an Australian convert father and a Cocos/Christmas Islander mother in Port Headland located on the north of Western Australia in 1985, I was raised closely connected to the ocean and nature. My parents were a free-spirited couple who overcame the challenges and stigma associated with being from different races and cultures. We would spend most of our free time as a family camping and hunting out in the bush or by the ocean fishing and swimming.

Islam had more of a cultural presence in our home than anything. With my father only having access to limited Islamic learning and literature in the 70's upon his conversion to the faith and my mother and her family only having a limited understanding. Mum was originally from the isolated Cocos Keeling Islands which is located below Indonesia in the Indian Ocean and populated by just a few hundred people. My father was what you'd call a very 'Aussie bloke' and my mum had also embraced a very relaxed 'Aussie' attitude and way of living.

We grew up very outdoorsy, very adventurous and would still commit to daily prayers, eating halal, fasting in Ramadan and other essential aspects of the faith. Overall, we lived very freely with little awareness or concern for a deeper understanding of the Islamic faith.

It wasn't until later in my childhood that Islam became much more of a focal point for our family. At the time I was about ten years old and we were living in the capital of Western Australia, Perth. My parents had started attending regular classes taught by a lady who had moved to Perth with her husband and family from interstate. She began right from the basics and taught my parents and other community members about the essential components of Islamic belief and practice. This was my parents first exposure to actively learning from the authentic Quran and Sunnah as opposed to passively reading a few poorly referenced books that they were able to obtain or listening to Ahmed Deedat cassette tapes.

Witnessing their increased passion and practice of the Islamic faith somewhat confused and worried me. I didn't quite know what it meant for us all as a family or for me as a ten year old. I didn't want the religious changes to impact my social life at school as fitting in was of the utmost importance to me at that time. My parents didn't make a lot of effort to pass on what they were learning to us kids, so our learning and understanding was only happening sporadically as we were exposed to some of their new friends, social gathering and discussions on various topics. I could see that my mother was the most enthusiastic in implementing the things she had learned and was making changes in her personal practice as well as within our home. My dad started to catch on and increased in enthusiasm once he started learning too.

At the age of about eleven, I started to reflect about how my grandmother had passed away a couple of years prior and my thoughts led me to wonder how this loss had impacted my mother. I then realised that my mother and father too would one day pass away and I was struck by grief and fear at the thought. My thoughts then continued to wonder to the realisation of my own inevitable death and I was further struck by grief and fear. I realised at that young age that I had to take responsibility for my own life and to prepare for my accountability on the Day of Judgement. Through Allah's guidance and insight (and my minimal Islamic knowledge and understanding at that age) I started to feel a heartfelt consciousness of Almighty God and a desire to do good and to be good. The awareness of death, accountability and God-consciousness resulted in my decision to pray the five daily prayers at the age of eleven as a minimum commitment to my faith and I continued on with this habit into my adulthood Alhamdulillah.

As I was on the verge of turning thirteen and about to enter my teenage years, our family moved from the city to our country beachside property which was two hours away. Isolated from the Muslim community (and any sense of community really) I had to attend the nearest public high school which was far away from the safety of being 'part' of the majority in a Muslim school. It was terrifying and daunting as I was the first Muslim that most of the students and staff had ever met, let alone the fist Muslim in a hijab that they'd ever seen. As hard as the couple of years of being 'different' were, it was pivotal in teaching me how to connect with others and help them to see the real me aside from my hijab and faith. I had to realise that I was more than my assumed 'difference' to my peers – and whilst I felt like I didn't totally belong, I did manage to establish some trusted friendships and I even excelled in my academics (which had previously been deteriorating at the Islamic school back in the city due to my social distractions).

My first exposure to a deeper, evidence-based understanding for the beauty and value of Islam took place in my year of home-schooling (at fourteen to fifteen years of age) as we moved back to the city from our country home. I was taught Islam from the very basic foundations by a home-schooling tutor that my mother was good friends with. I was also blessed to witness a living model of the Islamic teaching by the family in whose home I was tutored as their home dynamic was truly beautiful and centred around a connection with Allah SWT in every aspect.

Learning the basic teachings of the Quran and authentic Sunnah confirmed what I had felt in my heart as a young child and so my instinctual beliefs now had a solid basis and foundation. I dove further into learning as an insatiable appetite for Islamic knowledge had emerged within me. I would listen to all of my parent's limited audio and video tape lecture collections and I also read much of our families' Islamic book collection.

Unfortunately in my teen years many of those closest to me from my friends and cousins strayed into some of the common social ills, mainstream pop culture and experimentation with drugs, alcohol and partying. I have to be honest that on some instances I too at times was swept into some poor decisions however it was the Islamic learning which I had benefited from which prevented me on countless occasions from taking things too far. Alhamdulillah my faith had grounded me and solidified my sense of purpose and identity so that I was able to resist peer pressure and temptation on many instances.

Two of the most vital things that strengthened me in my teens were the prayers and wearing the hijab. Both of these practices helped me to become strong enough to separate myself from following others and from becoming careless in the decisions I made when in social situations. When presented with opportunities and situations of youth 'fun' and temptation I would contemplate as to whether I would be able to comfortably pray on time in that place or environment and also whether a girl in hijab would be suitable to be in that kind of place. More often than not, it would lead to the decision not to attend or to leave early before things got too wild Alhamdulillah.

This verse of the Quran serves greatly to remind us of the protection from wrongdoing and sin that prayer provides:

> ***Recite, [O Muhammad], what has been revealed to you of the Book and establish prayer. Indeed, prayer prohibits immorality and wrongdoing, and the remembrance of Allah is greater. And Allah knows that which you do.***
>
> ***Quran 29:45***

I was sixteen when a good friend of mine (who I didn't see often) phoned me out of the blue and had questions about what had made me decide to wear the hijab despite the majority of the girls around both of us deciding not to. She revealed that at eighteen years old she had been diagnosed with a serious brain tumour and she was so very fearful of death that she wanted to start practicing Islam. That phone-call and her journey with battling (and ultimately losing her life to cancer (may Allah have mercy on her Ameen), served to remind me once again that the Islamic principles were worth striving and sacrificing for no matter how hard the struggle and however intense the temptation.

The spiritual grounding within my childhood and teenage years resulted in my decision to settle down, marry and start a family early on in life Alhamdulillah.

As I continued my learning of Islam I felt a strong drive to pass on the teachings within my home and community. I remember in 2005 when Shaykh Khalid Yasin (an outstanding dawah speaker and African American convert) had come for the first time to my city to do a speaking tour. He presented Islam in such an articulate, relevant and soul inspiring way. I was so spiritually and emotionally moved by what he said and the way in which he said it. Not only did his talks greatly affect the Muslim attendees but dozens of non-Muslims also attended and were impacted with quite a few non-Muslims who embraced Islam after his talks. These talks had greatly boosted my faith and sense of purpose and mission.

As the years passed, I would try to volunteer when I could to do to support dawah (sharing of Islam) causes, by writing articles, holding information stalls and helping at dawah events. Eventually I started to teach the Islamic basics to converts, non-Muslims interested in Islam and born Muslims as I wanted to share the guidance and goodness I was blessed to learn and benefit from with others.

I continued on to study, complete and teach a Quran Tajweed Ijaaza course. I studied youth work, an online Islamic Studies Diploma, a fitness instructor certification as well as many other short courses in personal and spiritual development. I was passionate about faith, purpose, education, leadership, community, health and the connection and growth of myself and others.

As time passed and as I saw the need, I (along with other volunteers) established youth programs, various classes and workshops, Islamic events, a convert support group and more for my local community. Eventually we housed all of the programs in a permanent Islamic centre Alhamduillah which still exists until today.

Over the years I was blessed to make the Hajj and had five children with my husband Alhamdulillah. Our life has been a mesh of home-schooling, family time, community work, learning and teaching Alhamdulillah. We moved to another state of Australia at the start of 2018 and I launched my business Developing Diamonds at about the same time. Through my business I am able to teach from wherever I am in the world as an online coach and teacher supporting women and youth in their identity and path to success in this and the next. I speak at events and conferences locally and around the world and am able to meet, teach and connect with countless sisters in Islam and remind them about Allah, Islam and important aspects of life that I too am working towards improving.

Day to day, life does have its constant struggles. I battle as I always have, my own nafs (desires) and the natural human inclination to stray from the path of Allah but just as I battled when I was younger, I ask Allah to give me the strength to continue to battle with the same resolve (and help others to do so as well) until my last breath, Ameen. Allah has thrown many tests my way (as He tells us in the Quran that He will test those who believe) and I know that it is inevitable that we will be tested within our personal lives, our relationships, our children, health, wealth, communities and more. But I try to accept and embrace the tests and strive to find the lessons and wisdoms from Allah SWT within them.

Over the years I have managed to acknowledge many of my strengths and weaknesses and have been able to increase my emotional, psychological and spiritual resilience greatly through my Islamic learning, personal development and understanding of the Inside Out Paradigm (which teaches that your feelings always come from you thoughts) Alhamdulillah. Allah SWT has been so very kind in steering me towards beneficial learning and good people, for which I am extremely grateful.

As I continued on in life, I truly feel that Islam has been the greatest treasure and blessing. For me, Islam was the essential ingredient to feeling a sense of purpose, fulfilment, guidance, hope, optimism and meaning. Having the Quran as the divine speech and miraculous word of Almighty God (the Quran) and the Sunnah (teachings and example) of the Prophet Muhammad SAW to help me understand what this life is all about has been a true and priceless blessing. Through this blessing I have been able to discover what my deepest identity is and how to navigate every aspect of life as a human being. I realise that being a Muslim and the journey towards properly understanding and implementing Islam is most definitely an ongoing process for myself and every Muslim. Islam is and always will be my most precious gift and guiding compass in life.

The many important realisations, learnings and life experiences throughout my life have resulted in a deep sense of mission and resolve to teach and support others in their life journeys too. For as long as I can, and for Allah's sake, I intend to help my fellow Muslims around the world towards owning their identities and aiming for sparkling success in this life and the next inshallah!

Calisha Bennett - Motivational Speaker - Developing Diamonds - Coach -

Facebook - https://www.facebook.com/calishabennett
Facebook - https://www.facebook.com/developingdiamondsofficial/
Instagram - @calisha_bennett
Linked In - https://www.linkedin.com/in/calisha-bennett-39236923/
Twitter - https://twitter.com/CalishaBennett?lang=en

17

After the storm comes the rainbow.

I grew up with two loving parents, an exceptional family and clowns for friends. My life was regular and I could not ever imagine the devastating turn my life would take...

2010 was so long ago yet to me it feels like yesterday because that was the year I lost myself and my "rosy sunglasses" perception of life was tainted forever.

That year was the year the Family Court ruled in favour of my parents for custody of my dad's long lost son. The family was ecstatic and I was happy to have another sibling.

It was strange having a new person in the house and I will be the first to admit that I was finding it very difficult to adjust.

Coming out of foster care, He "needed love and attention". Our parents did everything for him and I was extremely jealous. I was not jealous because of the things he was getting, it was the fact that I was a 7-year old girl, who was afraid of being forgotten.

Life went on and everyone was happy. I began get used to the fact that life was not planning to always be pleasant...

Just as I thought life could not get worse it did when my "brother" began to make me feel awkward with inappropriate comments, gawking with evil eyes...

It was a tough living situation as my brother and I were forced to share a room because the house was full.

Let us fast forward to the night that would change me forever...

I had just had a delicious dinner with my family and I was ready for bed, so I had greeted everyone and made my way to the bedroom.

In the bedroom was a double bunk bed which my brother and I shared. I can clearly remember how jealous I felt when I was first told that he got the top bunk.

Being the child I was, I had way too much energy to fall asleep immediately. Anything could excite me and on that particular night I was very intrigued by the Mickey Mouse light on the ceiling.

I was so consumed by the light that I barely noticed my brother walking in. He kept glaring at me and I cringed as he began changing into his sleepwear. I swear I could feel the sweat forming a waterfall along my spine as he never failed to break eye contact with me.

In attempt to release the attention I hopped off my bed and went to the bathroom until I heard him getting in his bed. When I returned to the room he was pretending to be asleep and the silly little seven year old me actually believed it.

By this time i was extremely exhausted and could not wait to hit the hay. I got into my bed, said a prayer and I hoped that I'd dream of how glamorous my future would be... But what happened next was far from glamorous.

I was awoken by hot air on my neck and I felt a strong load on my chest. The unbearable load was my brother... At first I thought and hoped I was having a bad nightmare or something but my hopes quickly came crashing down when I felt his ice cold claws grip my mouth.

He undressed me... while I was fighting, while I was silently crying my eyes out and shaking my head in an attempt to make him stop. I tried to reason but to no avail. My heart was pumping out of my chest, I couldn't breathe, formulate a sentence or anything and then I swear my entire world just froze.

I swear I heard a deafening silence as he forced himself into me. The pressure between my hips became so hard that I started losing consciousness and I could feel the blood oozing from my vagina.

I awoke the next morning frantically as needed to get rid of all the evidence because I felt guilty and dirty. He just smiled and told me how good I make him feel. That honestly disgusted me to my core.

You see at that time in life I wasn't educated on rape and sex in itself so i did not say anything about it... Besides why would they believe me? I was not a virgin anymore at the age of seven...

My life would take a more drastic toll as I would end up getting raped every single day(several times each day even) for seven years. For seven years I had been living with a sexual predator and I had begun to lost all hope, faith and I had lost myself.

I was so traumatised that I had turned to drugs and alcohol to ease the pain and help me to forget but nothing worked. My life had become meaningless and I kept on fantasising how it would have been better if I were dead.

I just lost my marbles one night and I told my aunty everything, it was either that or slitting my wrists... At that time my brother had been on the run and everyone was shocked and traumatised when they heard. We followed all the correct channels, went to the police, did an internal examination etc but I was not feeling like myself.

One day I got sick in the bathroom school and courtesy of a home pregnancy test, I was positively screwed. Being a fourteen year old ninth grader and pregnant was not even a joke.

I wanted to keep the baby so badly but people were advising me otherwise, however my heart was made up. I was warned about risks of deformities and mental illness that my baby could be born with but I did not care because it was mine.

Unfortunately on one fateful day i began violently bleeding and upon arrival to hospital they had informed me that I had possibly suffered a miscarriage and a pregnancy test and ultra sound confirmed it. I was broken...

The trial started and I was so hopeful and had put all my trust in the justice system but as time progressed that trust would be destroyed.

I was treated like I was the criminal, I was accused of lying several times, I was just extremely mistreated.

Court was agonising and the trial had been running for about two years when the judge decided to just pardon him due to lack of evidence and the fact that "he was young, he did not know what he was doing".

It was in that moment I felt like truly hurting myself but I could not let him win so I began picking myself up. I had more than a dozen psychiatrists and therapists but none seemed to be able to give me the help I needed. I changed schools and was in desperate need for a positive change in my life.

It was at my school that I met the most supportive, crazy and loving friends any depressed girl could ask for. Things started to look up for me because I started smiling more and I started being confident self again.

Depression is real and it can throw us to the wolves but with great people in your circle you can learn to manage it better.

I could have given up but I did not so why should you? I could have let him have everything. He might have taken my virginity but he never took my courage and will power to never surrender.

At the moment I have just been given the news that I have passed to the next grade, twelfth grade actually so I am officially about to complete my final year of high school. I have written poems which tackle real problems in SA particularly, done extensive hours of community service at various institutions, helped other victims to start their healing process, had a good job experience, went on holiday, met people, I grew as a person and there is so much more things that I have done for the community as well as for myself.

I'm currently 16 and although he still harasses my family and I... I just remain strong and remember that after the storm comes the rainbow.

Bilkees Armien

17

Yasin and his gift of Autism

Autism is a word that used to conjure up so many mixed feelings for me, lots of inaccurate assumptions and more often than not, a lot of confusion as to what it actually meant for a person to be Autistic. Over the last 5 years, we as a family have been on a rollercoaster ride of tears, joy, tantrums, and celebrations, and have come to not only accept, but also embrace Autistic Spectrum Disorder! This is because our wonderful son Yasin was born 5 years ago and was given that very diagnosis at aged 3 ½, the diagnosis of having ASD!

At first I admit, we were a little upset by the realisation. We first noticed signs that he may be different when he was around 14 months old. It wasn't obvious at first, but now looking back there was definitely a distinct lack of eye contact from Yasin. I would have to try and make him laugh in order to take a nice 'Smiley' picture of him or create some kind of loud noise or pull a funny face just so that he'd look at me and I could then take another pic. I thought all this was normal. After all he was my first child so I didn't have any other children to compare him to.

Then Moe, his father, went to Egypt to visit family for a few weeks and when he returned he raised some concerns that his nieces and nephews, who were a similar age to Yasin, were somehow 'Different'. Different was the only way we could accurately describe it as we couldn't put our finger on what it was. It just seemed as though Yasin was in his own world. He didn't share toys or bring us toys to play with and he would never look at us when we called his name. Even when given a toy to play with that interested him, he would focus on it intensively, almost oblivious to everything else going on around him.

So I started to google my concerns and time after time the word 'Autism' would come up. I slowly began to accept that this may be a reality for us but I was still apprehensive as to what the Autism diagnosis would mean for us, Yasin and the future. We had absolutely no idea what to expect.

Around this time, I used to take Yasin to a local playgroup once or twice a week and at first he seemed to play much like the other children at the groups, but I remember one day in particular that really stood out to me. We were at the toddler singing and dancing group, whereby all the other children, mums and dads would join in and make a huge circle and would all sing nursery rhymes together and dance to the music. But Yasin had other ideas. He had absolutely no interest at all in what we were doing and instead wanted to walk round and round the edge of the hall for the entire session. What made it worse was that he was the only child out of about 12 who was doing this and I just couldn't understand why? I could see the other children smiling at their parents, saying some words and overall enjoying the group activities, but Yasin wasn't interested in the slightest. Even when they brought out the tambourine and triangle, he point blank refused to even look at the instruments, let alone hold one. It wasn't even due to him being younger than the rest of the other children either, because he wasn't. The group was for his age group. I just didn't know what on earth to do.

Then came the melt down. When it was time to leave he didn't want to go and had a full on kicking and screaming fit, banging his head on the floor with absolute fear in his eyes. I can honestly say that day was probably the most helpless I had ever felt in my life. I had absolutely no idea what was wrong with him or why he was acting this way. I could see that all the other children were putting their coats and shoes on and quietly walking towards to the door, whilst staring at us! I felt like a bundle of mess on the floor trying to contain a frantic child, hysterically kicking and screaming for no obvious reason. This went on for a good 10 minutes and I knew that it was much longer than any tantrum I'd seen before from Yasin or any other child.

Yasin's tantrums became more regular around this time too; he also started to display repetitive behaviours and ticks. Lots of arm flapping, repetitive humming and looking sharply out of the corner of his eye at passing objects as he walked by. I was fully aware of the glances from other parents and stares from other children but I knew they probably weren't malicious. I just assumed they were just as baffled as I was as to why Yasin was behaving this way, and so I would always let it go over my head. Thankfully, the children's centre staff recognised Yasin's behaviours straight away and invited me to their SEN group where they employed specialists SEN teachers. We'd finally found a group where there were other children just like Yasin, where we could just relax, play freely and Yasin could be just be himself.

Around this time I began to raise my concerns with the health visitor but because Yasin was so young at the time, I was constantly told to just 'Wait and see'. It was a very frustrating time for us; we knew that his development wasn't quite on par with other children his age but no one we spoke to would get the ball rolling and push for a diagnosis. I felt like I had to keep pushing and pushing for the authorities to take us seriously. Eventually however, we did get the appointments we'd been waiting for, and after many assessments and observations both at our home and at the children hospital, they finally gave us our much awaited diagnosis.

Our minds were filled with misconception after misconception. We worried about his future and what it would mean for him to live as an autistic individual. But as time went on, and we could see how our lives were unfolding as a family and how well Yasin was adjusting to nursery and his new school we knew he was going to be alright. He was given a wonderful one to one support teacher to help him with his development at nursery and then went on to attend a specialist school for Autism, both of which we are forever for. Gradually we came to realise that Autism is definitely not a disability or something to be ashamed of. We completely changed our perspective and I'd say we've come to pretty much embrace Autism now and every challenge and milestone it brings. We now see Autism as a blessing and this is why...

If there's one thing I've learnt about Autism over the last 5 years, it's this: Autism doesn't have to be a burden. Yes it does come with a lot of challenges, but if you change your perspective and social conditioning as to what Autism is, you start to see it as a gift and from this amazing gift you can then start to appreciate all the wonderful experiences it brings. So Instead of expecting an Autistic child to be a part of our world, be a part of theirs. Being a part of their carefree, imaginative world can be so liberating!

We just need to open our eyes and see some of the amazing accomplishments Autistic individuals have achieved. A quick Google search will bring up tens if not hundreds of people who have Autism and are famous or who have done extremely well in life, and not just in their personal careers but in their contributions to the Arts, Sciences and society as a whole. Darwin, Einstein, Ludwig, Tesla and Newton are just some of the well-known household names that spring to mind.

I've come to the conclusion; it's not them who need to learn from us, it's we who could learn so much from them. If we could only allow ourselves to enter their world and try and see things from their perspective, then our eyes would really be opened.

To experience such joy over the simplest of things and not have a care in the world or any awareness of what others think of them, can be so absolutely liberating! To be so pure hearted, to be so gentle in nature, and to become ecstatic at seeing the same episode of a favourite TV programme for the thousandth time and still finding immense joy in watching it, as if it was for the first time, truly is freedom.

Yes, in the early years it was hard and very challenging. It was hard to see your friend's kids talking and interacting, developing that little bit more week after week. It was frustrating to have to constantly chase after Yasin wherever we went because he liked to 'run off' and not turn around to see where we were, even for a second as it just wouldn't occur to him, each time we went out.

There were many things we tried in the early days with Yasin that we still do even today. Such as changing his diet and using complementary therapies. It seems that there is a huge divide within the Autism community as to whether Autism is genetic or environmental. I've read and researched a huge amount of books and research papers and am of the belief that only in about 1-2% of cases is it solely genetic, although there may be a genetic disposition that can be said and can apply to almost any condition. I firmly believe that it is more often than not environmental and that there is a very definite gut brain connection. However, even though this may be the case, I don't believe it necessarily means Autism is a disability. In my opinion Autism is the body doing what it's supposed to do given the circumstances it finds itself in, which in my book mean's its working exactly as it should.

I find that Yasin's diet does make a difference to his wellbeing, mental health and focus. When he eats well and supplements his diet with fish oils, probiotics and lots of green smoothies, amongst other things, there is a very obvious improvement in his development and overall mood. I also try to use natural cleaning products around the home and toiletries so as not to expose him to harmful chemicals. We diffuse aromatherapy oils almost daily and herbs and homeopathy are a very significant part of Yasin's healthy lifestyle. The two books that I feel have changed our lives the most are The GAPS Diet and The Body Ecology Diet. Both of which I'd highly recommend.

I've also learned that Autism is very much a spectrum and that autism spectrum disorder is perfectly named. No two people with Autism are the same and there is in fact no such thing as mild or severe autism. Autism is autism and where one can be at a certain place on the spectrum in one area; another may be in a completely different place. For example, Yasin is considered non-verbal – only in these last few months has started to say a few words, yet he's always slept soundly throughout the night since he was a baby. Others have struggled with sleep right from the start but may be "age appropriate" in their speech. Neither is more "severe" than the other, they are just experiencing their autism differently. Then there are those that face additional challenges or health concerns as well as having autism, and those like Yasin, who don't. It's all very individual.

Plus Yasin's sense of humour is wonderful, his laugh is contagious. He will chuckle at the most random of things - such as someone falling over! But then on the other hand he won't understand a joke that's been told due to his lack of speech and understanding.

I've found that the stereotypes surrounding Autism are very rarely true. Yasin is very sensitive and kind. Never showing any kind of malice, but very much aware of others and is always gentle with his siblings. He's even had moments where he'll rock his sister's bouncer when she cries as he knows it's a comfort to her, and although sharing isn't his finest quality, he will never snatch or purposely hurt another child or adult. He also makes amazing eye contact to friends, family and strangers now and will reciprocate a smile which is just fantastic.

So, the message I really wanted to share by writing this piece is that for anyone who is going through the same concerns or has a child close to them on the Autism spectrum, that everything will absolutely be ok! It may not be the outcome or life that you once envisioned for your child, but once you meet Autism and see 'possibility' instead of 'disability' a whole new world will open up to you.

Autism really is a gift to them, you and the World.

Peace.

Rachel Hannah Gee - Aromatherapist

Instagram - @organic_blu_aromatherapy

17

A New Day...

I noticed its softness of the prayer mat under my feet. It was my grandmother's. My feet fitted perfectly into the groves worn by hers. How I wished she were here to comfort me. I was so lost, so torn. From upstairs in my parent's home I could hear the chatter and commotion downstairs. My mother was preparing dinner for my children. The smell of chicken curry wafted upstairs. Mother's cooking is always the best. If it wasn't for my parents I don't know where we would be.

I escaped my marital home begging them for help. I couldn't function, not even to perform basic tasks. I was a mess. My whole world had crumbled and my brain had short-circuited. I couldn't understand what was happening and especially why it was happening to me.

Didn't I do everything right? Didn't I do enough? Didn't I pray enough? Wasn't I good enough?

Why me?

I was a good Muslim woman. I did everything that was expected of me. I did my duty to everyone. I obeyed my husband. I kept silent to keep the peace. I didn't burden others. I put everyone else's needs before my own. I gave as much as I could. I covered everything and didn't expose anyone's sins. I forgave. I was kind even in the face of malice.

I was also desperately unhappy and confused. Nothing made sense. I lived my life thinking that if I did the right thing I would be ok. If I looked after other people, Allah would look after me. I ticked all the boxes. And yet... here I was.

My heart was broken. Every part of me ached. I tasted the salty tears as they ran down my face. A wave of nausea rose up and I put my hand on my stomach. I couldn't remember the last time I ate, was it 6 or 7 days ago? The thought of eating sent another wave of nausea through me. It was all too much.

I stood up and prayed my salaah. It had become reduced to just a series of movements, of actions devoid of any connection to myself or my Creator. But I did it anyway. I raised my hands in dua but no words came. I was empty. Anger, fear and disillusionment consumed me. It wasn't fair. It didn't make sense.

Then finally the words came, strong and clear. "Is this what You want from me Allah?"

Was it my purpose to be so full of despair, to struggle in this way, to try so hard and to have it all go so spectacularly wrong? Is this really my purpose in life?

I had struggled in my marriage for over 15 years. Then one day discovered that he was not the man I married. Confused and hurt I looked in the mirror and found a stranger staring back at me. Her eyes once bright and full of joy were dark and empty. I didn't recognise the woman I had become. The unimaginable things I went through. Did it really happen? Or was it a dream?

The unbelievable cruelty of it all.

And yet, the love was undeniable. Wouldn't my love for him fix everything? Wouldn't my devotion to his happiness make me happy? Make our children happy? Did I just have to try harder? Love more? Do more? Be more? I wasn't afraid of hard work. I could do it.

I always thought that if I did the right thing I would be rewarded. I researched my duties as a wife and daughter in law. I made sure I did all that; it should have worked. I should have been happy. But it didn't and I wasn't.

Here I was with a disintegrating marriage, a failure as a wife and a mother. All of my dreams, hopes and expectations crushed. The grief at this loss was devastating but the real casualty was my relationship to my Creator and Sustainer, my Allah. I felt so alone, disconnected and despondent. I couldn't even pray. I didn't know what was real and what wasn't anymore. My compass to the Truth was spinning. I had no direction. I felt hopelessly lost, directionless and adrift.

In all that confusion there was one thing I did know for sure. I didn't want this life. I didn't want any part of this. I would rather die than continue this way. We learned that praying salaah, fasting, doing thikr and reading Quran guaranteed our safety and happiness. I tried hard. I thought that was enough. I thought I was a good Muslim, a good person. Why couldn't it work for me? What was wrong with me?

I fell so far from the woman I wanted to be. I neglected the ones who needed me the most - my children. They received so much less than they deserved. All my time and energy was spent fixing their father. It was my responsibility to take care of him, to make him happy wasn't it? Once he was ok we all would be. Right? I couldn't do it anymore. I was used up and empty. I wanted it all to end. It was too much.

Is this really all that You created me to be Ya Allah? Is this my purpose in life?

These words swirled around in my mind until I was dizzy. I lay my head down and closed my eyes, trying to shut it all out, hoping it would all go away.

The door opened gently. My sister entered and asked if I was ok. Unable to find the words to explain I stayed mute, motionless. She gently kissed my head, so lovingly and left. I was completely alone again. Desperately wanting comfort and connection so but utterly incapable of reaching out. I was trapped in my misery.

The sun shone brightly through the open window. Its warmth on my face gently woke me. As my eyes opened the light seemed a little brighter. I felt a little lighter. The heaviness was lifting. Allah had heard my prayers. Allah had witnessed my struggle. The ease that Allah had promised was coming. My shattered world was reforming one piece at a time. Dare I hope?

The fog was settling. New thoughts began to fill my mind, hopeful and optimistic. Thoughts of a new possibility inspired me to question everything that I once held close. As I began to let go of what no longer made sense I was making way for a new reality to emerge.

Maybe I was wrong about everything. Maybe this is not all I am created for. Maybe Allah is Loving and Merciful. Maybe my idea of Allah and Islam and my place in the world was misguided. Maybe I am allowed to be happy. Maybe.

And thus began my real relationship with Allah - honest, open and based in love. From this darkness new truths blossomed and new beliefs took hold. I know now without doubt that Allah loves me. I am convinced that everything that happens is FOR me. I believe with absolute faith that when things are not working out it's only because He is guiding me to another way. I am certain that He is not punishing or vengeful but lovingly guiding me to something better.

I misunderstood. I put all my trust and faith in others as I searched for love and happiness outside myself. I blamed and wallowed in victimhood. I begged from others what wasn't theirs to give. I was starving and settling for crumbs.

My duas were always desperate pleas for my situation to change or for others to change. I begged Allah to change everything outside of me. I never considered praying for ME to change. Once I did that my life transformed. I finally got it! The whole point of life is not to change my circumstances but to have the circumstances change me.

Making the decision to leave my marriage was difficult but I was determined to put my full faith and trust in Allah. I prayed for signs and I was guided. Every step of the way was shown. I knew Allah had brought me to this and that He would bring me through, He would take care of me and He did. He is the Source of All and all is in His

Hands. All the misplaced faith and trust I had in others I now rightfully placed in Him.

I moved into the perfect home where I felt safe and happy. Everyday, I wake up feeling alive, vibrant and free. I had never felt so much peace and joy in my past. Due to my divorce I had to give up so many things but the rewards have been priceless. When I pray now it is with conviction and concentration, my relationship with Allah is deepening. My duas now have meaning; I feel the words in my heart. I pause and in my heart I feel Allah's Presence. When I speak I know He is listening to me, responding to me and loving me. I continue to ask for signs and guidance and I pray for the strength and courage to follow them. It has never failed.

I remember that no matter how badly I feel He will guide me through. I see now that a gift is sometimes wrapped in pain. A gift of transformation, patience, wisdom or forgiveness is waiting for me in anything that hurts. My journey has allowed me to know Allah on a much deeper level. Had I not gone through my marriage and divorce I would never have felt this peace. The greater the pain the greater the gift. I had to let go of everything that I thought I knew to allow this new reality to emerge. I unlearned the shallow understanding of my relationship with Allah to discover a new deeper truth about myself, my worth, my purpose in life and especially about Islam and Allah.

I can't always choose what happens to me but I can choose how I show up, who I want to be. It is not my responsibility to make others happy. It is my responsibility to make me happy. I learned to be honest about my feelings, my intentions and my expectations. I took responsibility for my own life, for my feelings for my experiences and for my relationships. I realised that the only person, THE ONLY PERSON, I can control is me. I learned how to love, respect and care for myself. I can only give to others what I give to myself first. In developing self care routines and practices I discovered what was truly important to me. I learned to eat again and to enjoy life again.

Now when I look in the mirror a resilient, courageous woman looks back at me. With Allah's Grace I am passionate about using my experiences to change the lives of as many women as I can. I love helping women find the love within themselves and deepen their connection to their Creator. If I could give the world a gift it would be that each and every one of us sees the value and power within us that is our gift from Allah.

This morning my eyes opened and felt a surge of gratitude for my life. My relationship with my children is better than ever and we share meals, laughter and support. I made a decision to be 100 percent committed to being the best version of me. I vowed to do whatever I have to do to heal and be the mother they deserve.

I am reminded that Allah's Plan is always so much better than my own and I open my hands now to receive His Gifts.

Firm in my new belief that I am supported and loved by Allah I pray:

Please take care of me Ya Allah.
Heal me so that I can be the best I can be.
Heal me so that I can forgive and let go.
Heal me so that I can recognise that You are the Source of All.
My happiness lies only in Your Hands.
Heal me so that every situation is a way of deepening my faith and trust in You.
Heal me Ya Allah so that Your Will is mine.
Heal me so that I am Yours completely.

Safeera Sabdia - Life & Relationship Coach at Safeera Sabdia Consulting.

Email - safeerasabdia@hotmail.com
Website - safeerasabdia.com

Facebook Page - "Safeera Sabdia Consulting" https://www.facebook.com/safeerasabdiamentoring/
Facebook group - "Self Care Secrets for Phenomenal Mums" https://www.facebook.com/groups/154473905091712/

17

Phoenix Rising

"I'm nothing special, in fact I'm a bit of a bore", the opening lyrics to one of my favourite ABBA songs as a child of the 70s. The truth is, we are special, each one of us, sometimes it takes a lifetime to work that out, especially if we are raised in an environment or culture that constantly demeans our existence.

This brings me to a rather fitting quote by Jeffrey Fry, "To realise that everything in the universe is connected is to both accept our insignificance and understand our importance in it." There is so much extraordinary contained in our simple and ordinary existence, that in itself, is our significance, yours and mine.

I am one of five children bought up in East London to migrant Pakistani parents with strong prescribed cultural expectations and an ingrained work ethic. We had a simple life with a constant social standing and brief bursts of good fortune. In addition to the generation gap, balancing cultural identity and social norms was a huge frustration and challenge throughout adolescence and adulthood.

I married quite late according to Pakistani standards; I had negated countless prospective suitors thrown in my direction and my parents had almost given up on me. Then I met Nadeem. He knew straightaway that I was his "one", and I knew he was to be someone special in my life. Nadeem was a good, kind, honest, and a decent man, I knew instantly that he would be a fine husband and father. We got engaged and married within months, shortly followed by the arrival of our beautiful son and daughter. We were married sixteen good years; content with a wonderful family life balanced with the usual trials and tribulations.

Let me take you back to New Year's Eve 2012. That fateful night still feels surreal. It remains a constant blur yet also etched in our hearts and souls for all of time. After a wonderful day with friends, Nadeem told me he didn't feel well, and collapsed in my arms. I called an ambulance and he was taken to hospital. Through the fog I recall feeling that something was seriously wrong. I felt to my core that something bad was going to happen that night. Nadeem died unexpectedly in the ambulance en-route to the hospital, we were left behind, me and our two beautiful children aged twelve and fourteen.

Nadeem was only 47 years young when he died. The impact of his passing was huge in our local Muslim community, so much so that we had two funeral prayers for him, one in our home town of Newbury, Berkshire where we had raised our family, and one in East London where Nadeem's family lived, which was to be his final resting place.

My children and I had become part of a story, our lives and our circumstances had become a sorry tale that others would speak of. I was hurled into a situation that was out of my control, forcing me to tread through life on a journey I had not anticipated I'd be navigating alone.

You never get over losing someone you love, you never stop loving them. You find a way of living with the grief and sadness so that it no longer consumes you. When the tears flow, you let them; even years later I still struggle with the fact that I will never see his face, that I can't gently slide my hand into his, that I can't sink into his broad shoulders and feel the comfort of his strength. He's not here.

I cry mostly for my children, who will never get to call out to their "baba", share with him their exciting journeys and adventures, tell stories of their day, send him silly memes and groan at his terrible jokes. I am sorry that he will always be missing from us, and I often wonder, now that they only have me, am I enough for them? Life is vastly different from how we had planned it, but somehow, with no choice, we had to find a way to make it work, just the three of us.

I have learnt so much about mental health, about teenage depression and anxiety, about drugs, and about truly loving unconditionally, through the anger, resentment, fear and tears. One of the hardest things to accept as a parent is that I cannot make everything okay. I cannot take away their pain and I cannot make my children happy. Happiness comes from within each of us. My greatest gift is that I can love them, that I will always love them. Through all the ups and downs I will simply hold my children close to me and tell them, "I love you".

I remember shortly after Nadeem died, some aunties (distant parental friends) made a few statements that stuck with me. One said, "You should now marry the Quran", and another proclaimed, "Now you must make your children your focus". Both these statements angered me and cemented the notion that we still live with such patriarchal double standards.

How is it that a man, upon losing his wife, the mother of his children, wastes little time in bringing another woman home, a replacement; which could be to the detriment of the children and family, but on the whole acceptable nonetheless. I was angered at the comment that I somehow needing reminding that my children were my priority, as though I was unaware of this, as though they never were before. Was there a very real fear that I would neglect my responsibilities, abandon my children and start looking for a new husband, and God forbid, start dating?

I am so very proud of my children who are making their dreams happen and are currently in their final year at university. As young contentious adults, they are kind and compassionate with a real sense of justice and empathy, their baba would be so proud. I applaud all the lone parents fearlessly raising their children without a partner, it is no small task, and at times physically and emotionally exhausting.

Since 2013, beyond the disbelief and numbness, I have tried to reconnect with my inner creative voice by re-igniting old passions and discovering new adventures pulling me out of my comfort zone. Redefining myself as *just* me has been a difficult journey and I still struggle with calling myself a widow. There seems no escape as Arabic speaking acquaintances keep reminding me that the name "Waheeda" means "alone", and that it has been many years now and I must think about becoming "itnan", which means two, a couple.

I embarked on a postgraduate course in a community engagement and development the year after Nadeem died. This is a sector I had been working in for almost ten years. I later joined a local community radio station as a presenter, armed with just my voice and an intrigue with other people's personal journeys and stories that connect our communities, I launched myself into a series of live talk show broadcasts with a sprinkling of world music.

I have been very blessed to be involved with a grassroots refugee charity that supports the resettlement of our families in the district. This is a humbling and rewarding role and I am in awe of the courage and resilience of these families. West Berkshire Action for Refugees is a fledgling charity with a small team of committed and passionate volunteers.

In July 2019 I joined a team in climbing Mount Snowdon in Wales. I had never before embarked on such a mission; I hadn't prepared greatly for it, and I must confess, I totally underestimated this challenge and had to really push myself to what I thought were my limits. I hope to trek the two remaining UK mountains of the three-peak challenge at some point; Scafell Pike in England and Ben Nevis in Scotland.

My upcoming expedition is a fundraising solo road trip across Pakistan, to raise money and awareness for two women's empowerment and development Non-Governmental Organisations (NGO). I will be travelling by car from Karachi in the South to Gilgit in the North. En-route I hope to deliver motivational talks to women and girls, and also attend the centres where NGOs and charities are delivering their great work. I have connected with people on social media who are keen to become part of this journey with me, and I am amazed by the support and warmth I have received from Pakistan and the UK.

According to the World Economic Forum, Pakistan is the second worst country in the world in terms of gender parity, with women hold fewer than 7% of managerial positions. Early marriage remains a serious issue in Pakistan, with 21% of girls in the country marrying before the age of 18, and 3% marrying before 15. More than five million primary school age children in Pakistan are not in school, most of them are girls, according to Human Rights Watch. There were 35,935 female suicides between 2014 and 2016 according to figures by White Ribbon Pakistan.

Education is the single most important route to development, tackling poverty and reducing vulnerability. Education provides families and individuals with financial independence and personal growth and both the NGOs I am supporting are undertaking numerous projects to address this (www.imchf.org and www.behbud.org).

My aim is to raise £20,000, here is the link should you wish to support:

https://www.justgiving.com/crowdfunding/waheeda-soomro

In addition to fundraising for a worthy and transformational cause, I hope to show Pakistani life, culture, love and generosity to the UK and wider, to dispel some of the myths and preconceptions perpetuated in the media, and to an extent also challenge some of my own perceptions. I will be v-logging and sharing my journey on social media throughout, and I hope to publish a book upon my return.

By sharing fragments of my life journey, I hope that I am able to offer some support or inspiration to you. Our journeys differ, our destinations vary, even our experiences, challenges, and how we rise to them differ. So how is it all so relatable? How do we feel so much for others? I guess in the end we're not really that different in our core. Our pain, our healing is relatable even if our back story isn't. We hand pick the elements of one another that fit with us. This helps us to connect and to know that we are not alone.

We are all a work in progress. Constantly evolving and growing. Trying to find that level of peace and contentment that allows us to accept our authentic self in the life that we are living, trusting the universe to deliver all that is good for us and allowing us opportunity to be good to others.

I absolutely am a believer in the Law of Attraction; it makes perfect sense that whatever thoughts and vibrations you emit, will be reflected tenfold by the universe in everything around us.

I leave you with these words, and I urge you to believe in yourself; you are worth so much more than you think you deserve. You hold immense power within you, be brave, be strong, you are not alone.

Phoenix Rising

The keeper of fire in all of creation,
Contained in your fire lies eternal transformation,
She boldly rises from the flame engulfed ocean,
The ultimate symbol of strength and perpetual incarnation.

> *...She was destined for great things, far greater than she could have imagined. Greater journeys, challenges, infinite learnings, boundless experiences, and of course the greatest love. The generous unconditional kind that would breathe life into her soul awakening the essence of her being, the kind of love we all yearn for but rarely find. She had plans, big plans, but the universe had even bigger plans, for at last, with heart and mind wide open, she simply had no idea of the abundance awaiting her...*
>
> (an extract from my forthcoming book).

Waheeda Soomro - Activist - Author.

Facebook - https://www.facebook.com/Fundraising-road-trip-across-Pakistan-112321833585691/
Instagram - @waheeda.world

17

Pain to Power

Each one of us has the potential to become the very best version of ourselves and create the life of our dreams.

I am **Razwana Yousaf** and I am the boss at the **Muslim Boss Movement,** personal and professional development program. Prior to starting this project my life had come to a point of chaos, and I just felt stuck and exhausted with Intrusive thoughts. On the surface I was a happy bubbly person with all the gifts of life you could want in this world, but yet there was a deep sad empty space within.

Heal your emotions so that you can transform yourself for a better life.

I was working and I had very little time to myself for myself and unfortunately that's when burn out kicks in and brings you to a halt. So you have no choice but to stop and change direction from daily habits that no longer serve you. I realised I hadn't been prioritising my relationship with God, I didn't pray regularly and the Quran was only opened in the month of Ramadan.

I felt the very worst in emotional, physical and spiritual health one year and that year during the blessed month of Ramadan, I decided to pray like I had never prayed before. I **reached out to God in Despair**, asking him to help me. And Praise be to God surely my relief came, and all I had to do was ask, yet how often do we stop and ask our Creator?

I had gave up on myself, but GOD didn't. I turned wholeheartedly to God, all my Duas manifested into a reality, so to show gratitude to God the following year I embraced the Hijab (Headscarf).

Now I am on a mission to raise personal and professional awareness to other people who feel shackled by their current circumstance.

You can release the pain and trauma and you get to weave a new future for yourself one step at a time, one day at a time.

My issue

You maybe wondering what my intrusive thoughts were? And why they felt so heavy on me that took me into complete burn out.

First of all I think it's the Mercy of my lord that brought me to a test that made me want to turn to him for all my power. I didn't rely on any other power apart from knowing he is my creator and he is the all seeing and hearing. Second of all I was working full time, had a young family and although my husband was super supportive I had taken on too much, and as women we don't tend to slow down, we just pile more on.

But none of the above were the main issue within. The main emotional intrusive thoughts had began when I started my first business, and I felt **immense guilt for charging clients for my passion.** I always had a brave face on and no one had known what was going on deep within because I had bottled it up. I had no professional platform or coach I knew of at the time that I could turn to and share my thoughts and emotions and fears.

Hence this led me to creating a solution and movement such as the Muslim Boss Movement.

Temporary Situation - the present

Often we find ourselves at a crossroad in life. Our past no longer serves us, our future creates anxiety, and we lose trust in ourselves to do the right thing.

Maybe this is something you are currently going through, the good news is that this is a wake up call for you to realise you were made for MORE and to shape you into seeking more peace and serenity.

Don't get stuck in the temporary pain, how often as Muslims are we reminded that life is temporary and we shall be tested? And yet when the test comes we become so emotionally consumed by it that we can no longer work out a solution for ourselves. Alhumdulillah we are living in an era of self-development and when we lose faith in ourselves we can hire the right mentors or coaches to help us. But before anything PRAY like you have never prayed before, as the power of prayer is not comparable to anything else. The miracle will come from the pain in your prayers.

THE PAST…

TRAUMA

I am going to get a little scientific with you but stay with me. Most of the clients I work with have had a previous trauma either in their childhood life or adulthood, and when they think of that incident they relive that memory or pain and your body feels the emotions as if it is happening again now in the present, so you attract all sorts of disease and inflammation into your life.

So in order to heal you have to learn how the thought process works, how that triggers an emotion and how NOT to react to past events because your brain and body cells are being traumatised by YOU THINKING OF THAT.

I promise you if you really want that to change it absolutely can. But often we are a victim to our own pain, all you know is that feeling of sorry for yourself and comforting yourself with bad habits. That then becomes engrained into your sub-conscious and to change that a drastic change of action is required which is very uncomfortable to us humans since we are creatures of habit.

But you having picked up this book for a reason so we are not going to let you give up on yourself.

NO TRAUMA

Perhaps you have had no trauma but you are feeling like you currently have no drive or purpose, then I beg to ask the question when did you last pray?

The gift of Life was given to us to worship our creator, and count this as a blessing that God is reminding you that you need him. That void you feel will only come from the love and devotion of Islam and the teachings.

FEAR & FUTURE VISION

In order to attract a different outcome in life a different course of action is required. Makes sense right? You cannot continue to do what you have been doing in life and attract a different outcome. This takes bravery and courage and I know you have that in you.

So now you must conquer your dreams. When I first started out in business I made so many mistakes and they turned out to be stepping stones of wisdom to move forward and help me personally grow and my business. If I had paralysed myself of fear I would never have experienced the unknown and been able to make the impact that I only ever dreamt of. Day Dreams need aligned action.

FORGIVENESS IS HEALING

Maybe you made choices in life that now in hindsight you regret so you relive that moment, but you cannot go back and change the past, you can decide how you show up today and tomorrow and thereafter. Honour your healing process. It is now time to heal.

Intrusive thoughts can only create an emotion for you if you give them power. A thought is like a bubble, you blow this bubble and it will float away and pop. But as soul centred entrepreneurs we often over think a thought, then thought multiples into many bubbles and it's only when we listen to them thoughts and react to them that we give them power which trigger all sorts of hormones and panic emotions from within. So anytime you have an Intrusive thought take a deep breath, do not fight it, let the bubble float away. There you go, you are safe and strong.

Go live your dreams, if you want help in creating a business and life you deserve then come and find me.

AUTHENTIC MARKETING

My main passion is helping entrepreneurs take a vision for their business idea and make it a reality. Most entrepreneurs that come to me are highly conscious and ethical entrepreneurs like myself and they don't want to compromise their integrity when attracting profitability into their business.

Unfortunately we have been conditioned to believe people who have a lot of money have gained their fortunes through ill-manners. And wanting money makes us evil and greedy. This could not be far from the truth. As entrepreneurs we get to give back to the world, we follow Islam and help the less fortunate, and God does not have an issue with you fulfilling your own desires as long as you fulfil your obligations.

So the first pillar of business I work on with my bosses is their mindset around money and ensure they create a beautiful foundation to flourish from.

My free gift: www.muslimbossmovement.com/bossbrain

It's your duty and obligation to live the best life regardless of your circumstances, make a decision to heal and then honour that decision and you will become unapologetically happy and strong God Willing, regardless of your current environment.

Razwana Yousaf - Business Coach - Founder of Muslim Boss Movement.

Facebook - www.facebook.com/muslimbossmovement/
Website - www.muslimbossmovement.com

17

"Sticks and stones may break my bones, but words will never hurt me."

This is a phrase I heard a lot during my childhood and teenage years as a response of my teachers to the taunts of bullies. I was called fat, ugly, Fag, Tony and gay, nerd, four eyes, weasel, gorilla and many more names. I remember a particular girl in my class whispering in everyone's ear on the school bus about her birthday party and how I was not to be told as she wasn't going to invite me since no one wanted me there. My memory of riding that bus is that it felt like the school equivalent of having leprosy. From the age of 12, I was convinced by my peers that I was worthless. Whenever teachers said we could pick our own partners for an activity, I never had anyone who would want to be my partner.

I was that person the teacher would take by the hand and awkwardly say, "OK, Marisabelle is going to join your group today," and people weren't very excited about it. I was constantly made fun of during physical education about the way I used to run and move. Anytime I tried to express my discomfort on being laughed at, I either had "no sense of humour" or was "taking things too seriously". Some people have even used my irritation to say that they confirmed that fat people are just more sensitive. So I started just roaming around trying to be invisible. I hid in the library so as to avoid contact with my peers. I even came up with all sorts of excuses to avoid physical education classes.

And I taught myself how to smile through tears and not show how deeply hurt I was. I learned how to hide the pain. I learned how to accept being disrespected and friends betraying me and treating me badly because that is what I was told I deserved. As secondary school went on it only got worse. My self-worth was low and every time I caught a glimpse of myself in the mirror, I would only see a fat monster.

The sad reality is that words do hurt, probably more than sticks and stones ever will and their damage can extend far beyond the 'safety' of school classrooms and locker rooms. The only thing that made me feel better after long days at school being treated so badly was eating. My mum is an amazing cook and her food always gave me pleasure. So, after a long day of being called names at school, I would go home and look for food as it was my safety blanket. My mum did not want me to suffer being overweight like she was, so she used to restrict food for me when she realised I was turning to food for comfort. The restriction made me want food even more and I would save up my money to buy sweets and eat them in secret or steal food from the kitchen and eat them in hiding alone at night. This got worse as I grew older. It ranged from me buying bags and bags of chocolate and hiding the wrappers all over the house so no one could find them. To walking out in the middle of Paris in my pink pyjamas to buy chocolate because I had an urge to binge when I was 23. To eating 4 whole racks of ribs until I made myself throw up when I was 25.

How did it get so bad? By the time I was fifteen, the word 'thin' for me meant "beautiful". And since I would look in the mirror and see myself as double what I actually was I would see ugliness in the mirror. That is when I started avoiding mirrors and any other reflective surface. I tried my best not to stand out - I did not participate in events, I did not push myself. I wore bigger clothes so people would not be able to see what my shape was really like under the clothes. Even though what I wanted deep down was to be loved and be able to enjoy my teenage years. Sadly, by then, I started to believe all the things the other kids said about me and I became my own worst critic. The only thing that would numb out all the horrible things I thought about myself was food. Copious amounts of food.

My mind, body and soul were in a cage that had been constructed for me. My low self-esteem consumed me! The pleasure I got from food started turning into weekly binges during the weekend. As I started University and more stress associated with studying started cropping up this turned into daily binges. I found it difficult to stop obsessing about any kind of food, my crazy cravings began to intensify. I couldn't sleep at night until I gave in to what my mind obsessed about, and I couldn't concentrate on my studies until I had binged on large quantities of food. Again food was my saviour. It was my drug – the only thing that made me feel good. When all my clothes were no longer fitting, and the scales kept on increasing I started panicking that I was getting even more fat which to me always meant ugly.

I panicked and tried to control my eating habits by restricting food. This began a vicious restrict-binge cycle that only worsened my eating disorder. Food, whether it was a sweet, salty or fatty indulgence would send thrills to my mind.

Food is a stress reliever, a way to avoid negative emotions and a way to feel better temporarily, only to hate me immediately after doing it.

When I started working it got worse. I would be busy all day with work - made sure to never eat so no one would see me eating only to get home and consume an entire week worth of calories in an hour. I would feel hopeless, worthless and terrible.

A few years rolled on and Food owned me. The scale determined if I had a good day at work or not. My weight decreasing was a good day. My weight going up was a bad day. Even more than that—down meant I was good, up meant I was bad. I felt helpless so I stopped getting on the scale for around 3 years.

In February 2017 a man came to the pharmacy to have his blood checked I found his blood pressure, sugar and cholesterol were high, so I began to advise him on a healthy lifestyle. He did not respond but I could see in his eyes him thinking you are one to talk. You need to lose weight too.

That is when I got on the scale for the first time in ages and I was at 139.9 kg. Shock, Horror!!! That is when I decided I needed to change my life and starting to take care of me. I tried a pre-prepared food service that would bring me food and all I had to do is eat just what they brought me all day and started losing weight and I started feeling good. As the weight started coming off and people complimented me, I got addicted to that feeling. The compliments are not something I was used to. But then I would have a bad day at work and no matter how strong my willpower was I would turn to food and binge. I would eat so much I would make myself sick and then beat myself up about it.

That is when I thought ok, I need to start working out then. That is when I met a trainer who was pushing me to have abs, be consistent and strict and avoid most foods at all costs. He ended up pushing so much that I ended up on the other spectrum of the disorder. Afraid to eat, afraid to tell him if I had something 'bad' to eat. If he noticed I was bloated, he would call me out in front of others at the gym. He started using other comments about me and my body that was derogatory to me as a woman and made me obsess about my weight again. It took me ages to realise this was a form of bullying too. I was so desperate to lose weight and to feel good that I could not see the abuse in this relationship either. A few months into this I started feeling unwell and discussed all that was happening with friends who told me the trainer was abusing of his position. It was fixing one problem but causing another. And despite having lost a lot of weight I still felt worthless.

In May 2018 I got ill from eating food contaminated with some pesticide and that was the best thing that could have happened to me. I stopped going to this trainer, I sold my business and I started taking care of me. I was no longer going to fight my body and myself. I want to live and love and love myself and be happy. Since then I started a blog inspiring people about self-worth, talking about binge eating disorder and bullying. I called the blog 'Road to belle' – which means the road to feeling beautiful. I finally now am able to look in the mirror and see myself as beautiful and as worthy. I am now coaching women with regards to emotional eating and binge eating as well as self-image. I am in a relationship after years of believing I was not worthy of love. My life has flipped over and I owe it to that one patient who made me see my situation through different eyes. I am not saying my recovery has been a linear one I had falls – I had days where I binged and where I cried because I felt unworthy. But then I managed to pick myself up and love myself. I end my days with a list of 10 things I'm grateful for and a power statement. I am strong, I am smart, I am beautiful. I am worth it!

Marisabelle Bonnici - Health Coach

website - www.roadtobelle.com
Facebook - www.facebook.com/RoadtoBelle/
Instagram - @roadtobelle

17

The Blackstone

Background:

Ever since the age of 16 I had a dream and inspiration to become a Lawyer, either as a Solicitor or a Barrister.

After completing my O levels(GCSE'S and A levels) I started working in the Civil Service which I continued to do for 5 years. During this time I met someone and decided to get married much to my families horror as they knew how much I had wanted to pursue my career. However, after getting married, having children, I decided to go back to education whilst working on a full time basis. It was hard as my children were still young.

As I was in a management / training role working for the Local Authority I began my management qualifications, beginning with the Certificate in Management(CMS), followed by the Diploma in Management studies(DMS), then moving onto completing my Masters(MBA).

Legal studies/ Work.

Having completing the above, finally, I went back to studying Law on a part time basis, working full time, delivering training nationally, running a home and looking after my 3 children.

As I did not have any legal work experience, I contacted various Law Firms for some voluntary work experience for one day a week and was lucky to get some experience in a local Firm. I used my annual leave to ensure that it did not affect my post with the Local Authority.

In my role I was dedicated to promoting and encouraging other Black and Asian people in obtaining training. I carried out my research, obtained funding, advertised, and recruited 3 trainee Solicitors even before I completed by legal studies.

During my final year of the LPC, my father became seriously ill with kidney failure and only had weeks to live. I was in the process of giving up! I was blessed with fantastic friends and a supportive family who encouraged me to continue. Just before my final exams my father passed away. I was traumatised and devastated as my father had always inspired me to study Law from a very young age. (He was shocked that I did not go to university at the age of 18 after completing my A levels and that I had decided to get married.

By the time I had completed my academic qualifications (the postgraduate Diploma in Law (PGDip Law) and the Legal Practice course (LPC) I was aged 41.

I was extremely fortunate to obtain a training contract at the age of 43. Obtaining a training contract is extremely difficult and often students who have completed their academic studies cannot obtain a training contract and often give up having expended in excess £20,000 -£25,000 in course fees.

M training was in Criminal Defence and during that time I was travelling the breath of the Country for a few days at a time, leaving my young children at home with my family.

At first I questioned whether I should have taken on this role as it was against my morals as I would be representing defendants who had committed crimes. I weighed this up against qualifying and having made the decision that I was not in a place to judge.

I represented serious criminals including murders, arsonists, rapists, drug suppliers/ addicts and many more. I was visiting defendants in various prisons from young offenders to serious high security prisons, courts, police stations and families of the defendants.

At first, I was overwhelmed but as time wore on I became aware of the reasons why the Defendants had committed the crimes, rather than the act itself. This was by no means excusing the acts but rather the psychology, the mental state sand the backgrounds of the Defendants.

This experience was a huge learning curb. There were times when I would "take the work home with me," I would become emotionally upset and connected with the Defendants. Over time, like anything else one becomes resilient and takes such matters in their stride. This does not mean that I became more accepting of the crimes but I believe that I had to take a reality check and tune into other people's backgrounds. After qualifying as a Solicitor which included 2 years of vocational training, I was aged 44.

After qualification…

I worked for various Law Firms, was made reductant 3 times, then at the age of 53 I had to make a decision. The last redundancy came the day after my daughter's wedding.

Much consideration was given as to whether I should apply for employment or set up my own practice. I set up my own Law Firm in February 2010 during the economic depression.

This was either very naïve or entrepreneurial and brave. I did not have any Clients and the initial few months entailed setting up policies, procedures, marketing, completing applications for the Indemnity insurance, business plans, practicing certificates, acquiring equipment, identifying premises etc. This was all an expense and very time consuming.

I had never run a business and did not have any Clients. After much thought, deliberations and discussions with my family, both immediate and extended family I took the plunge.

Thinking of a name for the Firm was a serious consideration as the name would be represented of the Firm. I did not want it to reflect an Asian Law Firm as I was am fully versed with discrimination and prejudices against Asian Lawyers/ Firms.

The name Blackstone Law was decided upon after much deliberation. Law Firms would identify with it as Blackstone's are Publishers of Criminal law books, and Blackstone being the sacred stone in Makkah which Muslims would identify with. The name was both symbolic and meaningful.

I knew it would be very difficult to obtain Indemnity Insurance as many Law Firms had closed down during this time and even more difficult as because of other factors, e.g my age, ethnicity, experience etc. I am fortunate as I have gained a varied and extensive work experience in various disciplines. My vocational training was in criminal defence, I then transferred to civil prosecution, civil defence, then criminal prosecution.

At Blackstone Law, I've specialised in Commercial property, Franchises, Buying and selling business.

We are now nearing 10th year anniversary. This has been both challenging and rewarding.

In 2010, I took on a High Court chancery case which was extremely comprehensive, and lasted over 3 years. We had instructed to Leading Barrister, the Countries hand -writing expert, forensic Accountants and various other professional organisations. The leading Barrister had provided their legal advice setting out that we had over 75% chance of winning the case and on this basis we all worked on a "no win no fee basis".

This meant that if we won the case we would be awarded 1.2 million of legal fees. The Trial was listed for 3 weeks and a tremendous amount of work had been carried out during the 3 year period. It was a very testing, emotional and time-consuming time. Throughout this testing time my father's spirit was by my side.

Just before the Trial, a new Judge had been appointed and did not understand the complexities in the case and ordered that that we did not get our costs. This was devastating, two members of my staff team, two senior Barristers all other professions did not receive any fees after having worked for 3 years.

This nearly cost me my health, and my Firm. I was total devastated and became depressed, did not want to go work, couldn't make any serious decisions. I was very fortunate to have a supportive family who saw me through this testing time. I was blessed with a granddaughter at that time which was the catalyst for my sanity and happiness.

In 2012 -2013 there were many changes in the Law including regulatory changes fees Personal Injury. As a team we were all very diligent, hard working and came through this successfully whilst other renowned Firms had closed down during this period.

Awards and recognition

In 2015 I was shortlisted for a national award to services to Law. The competition was extremely fierce as I was competing against international Law Firms, Barristers and Barristers chambers. To my utter amazement I won and have gone on to win a few more over the years including property Solicitor of the year, Woman Lawyer of the year recognised by Legal and Finance.

In 2018, I was shortlisted by the Law Society of England & Wales for female Lawyer of the year. Although I did not win, but I was ecstatic and delighted to be shorted for such a prestigious award.

As a training provider throughout the 10 years have successful taken on 3 trainee Solicitors who have qualified and are working at the Firm and afforded several volunteers to gain work legal work experience in order for them to add to their skill set and experience. In the last 10 years I have continued to expand my portfolio of learning by becoming a mediator, a very short lived female lawyer football agent, a mentor for prisoners who wish to be released back into the community.

Mindset

I believe that mindset and attitude has been the driving force behind my aspiration. At times there were times when I wanted to give up both my legal studies and my Law Firm but have kept going despite many obstacles and hindrances that have been placed before me.

Long term Aims

My long term aim is to Franchise and or expand the Firm national and or internationally.

This requires contacts, finances, and "know how". My aim is to use the Law firm as a platform in encouraging other potential trainee Solicitors to qualify and not to lose sight of their dreams, hopes and aspirations. My advice is to keep focussed, driven and ambitious.

I am married, I have 3 amazing children and 3 beautiful grandchildren. I will continue to strive for my goals and hope to I can make a difference to other peoples lives either personally or professionally.

Bilkis Mahmood CMS, DMS, MBA, PGDip Law

Senior Partner
Shortlisted: Woman Lawyer of the year-Law Society 2018.
Winner: Property Lawyer of the year- Legal and Finance 2018
Winner: Female Lawyer of the year- Legal and Finance 2018
Winner: British Muslim Awards for Services to Law 2015
Lawyer: FA Registered Agent(Intermediary) (IMS/0000/683)
Blackstone Law Solicitors & Advocates Ltd
T: (0113) 3908510
F: (0113) to be confirmed
M: 07815 935 588
Twitter: @iambilkis
W: www.blackstonelaw.co

17

Curry, the Gulf War and 9/11 were all I knew of Islam

My journey with Islam, started 7- years ago - I took my Shahada (declaration of faith).

Actually that is not entirely true. I started my journey with Islam much longer before then, I just didn't know it.... So, the first experience I recall was when I went to senior school.

We went to a catholic school and when we studied R.E. we went to a synagogue and an old Monastery but never heard anything about Islam, Sikhism or Hinduism. Just Christianity, Catholicism and Judaism.

There was only three kids in our school that were anything other than English and white. And two of them were Asian Pakistani or Indian.

I never spoke much with them much as we mixed in different circles - I was like a GIN (Girl in between) never quite fitted in anywhere.

All I knew about one of the boys was that he lived down the road from us and his home always smelled of spices which made my dad excited. My dad would recall all of the delicious foods he had tasted on his travels with the RAF and curry was one dish he loved!

No one really ate curry back then, not in the 80's but my dad used to put a teaspoon of curry paste into our baked beans, pop it onto toast and layer it with banana! My poor sister nearly died with embarrassment one day when her best mate came for tea and dad presented her with his poor mans chicken korma.

Now we do know that not all muslims eat curry right?!! Well I would not have known that, not until I understood Islam and understood that it is a world religion, not a Northern Asian religion!

Anyway, I did not know that the lad was Muslim, not until I recently connected with one of the boys on Facebook and recognised his name being an Arabic name. HopefullyI will get to meet his wife and kids and parents soon as they still live near where I grew up. Alhumdulillah.

I later moved to another school in the Cotswolds and there were no other ethnicities there. We were all white English kids. So that was my first experience I didn't know anything about. And then the next experience I had with Islam was the Gulf War. Again, I didn't actually recognise it as anything to do with Islam. All I knew was it was on the news 24/7 and it was a big thing for me because it mean't we had the television on before breakfast.

We were never allowed TV on in the morning for the same reason I was never allowed to watch ITV kids shows - because my dad thought they were bad for us. I have to say, I now agree and I choose not to watch the news at all. The Gulf War was in every newspaper and my dad had the telegraph open double page spread on the breakfast table.

I remember it causing great anxiety for myself and for my female cousins as we shared our fears that their brothers, were going to have to go off to war. We truly believed world war three was coming. I am not sure if that was because of the media moral panic, or if it was our heightened state of anxiety which continued in all of us as we grew into adults.

All I knew is these bad guys had nuclear weapons and they were likely to kill us. Now bear in mind here at this point I did not see it as 'Muslims' I just thought it was some crazy country out to kill us.

Anxiety from this amongst many things that occurred in my childhood led to me struggling with anxiety and depression for most of my life.

That was my second exposure to Islam as later I was informed it was 'muslim terrorists '– that phrase hadn't been thrown around so flippantly back then. And then, sadly, my third exposure to Islam would have been 9/11.

I remember walking my daughter to school, my son in a pram. The playground was weirdly silent. It was an eerie silence with fear hanging in the air. The last time I had felt that deep understanding that something really awful had happened even without anyone saying a word was when my brother had died.

I asked a group of mums what had happened, and they were shocked that I hadn't heard. Do you remember I grew up not being allowed to watch tv in the morning? That habit had stayed with me. Someone tried to explain and another mother said go home and put on the news.

With the news of my brothers death and with the shock of what I had been told - both occasions had me retreating. I didn't want to speak to anyone, I just wanted to be alone to make sense of the world and the injustice. I rushed back home, turned on the BBC and there I watched in horror, in a state of total disbelief as I saw a building, a tall building and people were leaping out from high windows. I saw what looked like flags at the window, smoke billowing out, dust and people panicking everywhere, screams from the ground, faces of confusion, of grief, of panic, of fear and just like me frozen in shock and disbelief.

Then I saw a second aeroplane fly right into another tower- live on tv. My brain couldn't quite make sense of it, I watched transfixed on the film reel unfolding in front of me as that is how it felt.

Then the first tower fell. I just remember it like it literally took my breath away, like something's just hitting my stomach. And I just couldn't believe it was happening. It was just surreal. And I remember being stunned for the rest of that day.

I can still remember that clip and that feeling…

During the news and for months after I remember the word terrorist being in every headline. I don't remember it being connected to Islam at that point either, just extremists from the far east. And again, I didn't really relate it to Islam, like I said, I went back there actually a few years on, and went to the site and the museum, not just before I became Muslim.

And then my next experience of Islam was when I returned to college in my mid twenties. I met a Muslim girl there and we had become firm friends. She came to me one day and asked for help. She told me she was in love with somebody and her parents didn't want her to marry him, they had chosen her husband. They also then decided she was no longer allowed to continue her education. She was highly intelligent and had wanted to go off to university.

She asked myself and another classmate to help her escape. She brought clothes in bags for a few weeks and I kept them for her until she had enough belongings to leave. She said she could not have contact with us again incase her parents found her.

I lost touch with her after helping her escape so I have no idea what happened to her and her family, all I do remember is her saying to me it's not her religion, it's just her family and her culture. I look back now and realise there was so much more I could have done, I just had never, ever come across this situation before. I pray she is safe and well.

I still knew relatively nothing about Islam at that time but then we moved around with the Armed Forces. I knew about Afghanistan and all I knew is that we were going into a country and awful things were happening to the women there, that's all I remember really hearing about it. I recall being told we were there to help the people who were being oppressed.

One night I ended up in the pub on the base where we had recently moved. There were conversations in the pub discussing something in The Sun newspaper. They were being really derogatory towards the Afghani people and really racist and nasty. I can't remember the exact conversations, but I remember saying to the crowd that they shouldn't be talking like that. I was new on base so it didn't go down well when

I said "We are over there fighting to help these people, its not okay to be saying this racist stuff." This started a major argument and things got heated with the whole crowd against me. I got barred from the pub because I spoke up. I still didn't know anything much about Islam. I just knew what they were saying was wrong. This has been quite a pattern in my life, me getting into trouble when I speak out when I see someone being wronged.

The next thing was my sister's hen party and a Muslim friend of hers joined us for the party. I got very, very drunk and couldn't understand how this Muslim girl was having fun with us even though she wasn't drinking. I did ask her and she was very open to explaining and came across so content with her choices that this intrigued me further.

I got curious.

I soon had some new next door neighbours on the RAF base. I got friendly with the daughter and she gave me a book called Islam for idiots idiots and apologised about the name!

After this I kept bumping into Muslims and I was gaining more knowledge. I started to really look into this religion which at this point was in the news as ISIS, beheadings, oppression of women, terrorism, Jihad being on many front pages.

From what I was reading and researching, Islam was not what was being shown to us. I kept connecting with people that were Muslim and I asked them questions and I read many books, leaflets and even watched lectures.

As I read, everything in life all started to make sense.

I was actually agnostic I won't say atheist I did believe in something. I didn't believe in organised religion of any sort although I had gone to church all my childhood and a catholic school- none of what they had taught me made sense and yet Islam was making things clearer. And I couldn't understand why I was feeling drawn towards Islam, it was very confusing actually.

My heart was telling me one thing my head was saying the other. Logically this seemed ridiculous after all the things my atheist dad told me about how the world was made and how we evolved.

I discovered evidence in the Quran that no-one back in those days would know about our world today. I actually felt really torn because it felt like the man who I thought knew everything suddenly didn't. I looked up to my dad so much so it was a real torment inside of me to think perhaps he isn't the fountain of all knowledge after all, perhaps he is wrong in other things too. It really hurt!.

Yet I still got that pull, my intuition yelling to me this is the truth Sonia. It got to the point that it's like either I'm going to believe in this and got to do something about it or not. I started to understand that my life that I was leading was not Islamic and that if I believed Islam to be true I had to change.

I then kind of took it more seriously and asked God for guidance. I went to bed one night and asked Allah "If this is true, please show me, please, please show me".

That night I woke up, kind of awake and kind of asleep - can't explain it I definitely wasn't asleep asleep and I definitely wasn't fully awake.

My room was filled with a bright blue light, a really intense light and heat. It wasn't heat that was burning it was more like, like when you step off an aeroplane into a warm climate. The sort where that first breath in fills your body and you feel like you can't quite breathe fully as its not just air going in, its warmth.

This emotional intense heat had something else in it. It was a message in it, words in it, feelings in it.

This message was placed in me, I knew it was from Allah..

I couldn't see him I just knew it was him. The message was just put in my heart - This is true. This light was so bright, it was like you couldn't open your eyes, I couldn't open my eyes fully it was just so intense. And then I went straight back off to sleep again. When I awoke the next morning I texted friends and said I know this is true now.

And I couldn't deny it anymore. And so I panicked because I knew I had to change my lifestyle of sinning! It was very overwhelming. I met a Muslim doctor through my work who connected me with a revert sister. She took me to the mosque to take Shahada. I turned up in my jeans and a T-shirt.

She wrote down a few Arabic words to me in English writing, Masha Allah, and SubhanAllah. I can still see the tiny piece of paper that she wrote it on to explain a few of these words, thank God for her.

So that when the other people said it in the mosque I'd started to understand. When I read the meaning, it was such a beautiful meaning.

I took my Shahada, it was terrifying absolutely terrifying I could hardly understand the Imam who actually sounded very stern. I get the giggles when anything serious so that was a nightmare for me.

Luckily he was on the other side of the room with the door in between us so they couldn't see me stifling my nervous laughter. The more he repeated the words I was to copy and the worse it got! I got there in the end and took my Shahada, and then yes life changed.

That was really really hard, and another really hard time was the part from the loneliness, it was very lonely that year. My family weren't there, they couldn't understand it.

I let go some old friendships that I couldn't have any more, I could socialise with these but as they were mostly male friends that I had, and we would go out and drink, so my social life was gone and I was a single mom of four children.

And yes it was really a lonely time.

I chose to make changes, knowing that it was, you know, sinful of some of the lifestyle that I was living. Socialising with both men and women, drinking alcohol and wearing what Islam would consider as revealing clothing.

It was a lonely year, it really was a lonely year. Yes I had made new friends in the mosque but I lost old ones. I remember walking into the playground to collect my children from the RAF school. I was wearing the hijab and people pretended not to see me, they kind of stepped back a little bit, avoided eye contact.

And I know that that would have been hard for them, that unannounced transition.

However, I also found new friends that weren't Muslim, women who hadn't spoken to me before came up to me. They started asking questions, and I started forming new friendships. Over time some of my friendships returned when the shock and fear calmed.

I remember one very good friend meeting up with me 18 months on and saying "gosh, you're still the same old Sonia aren't you! I am glad you haven't changed."

That first year was really really tough, my family were not happy at all. It was really hard for them. It caused quite a lot of conflict between my father and myself.

He really did think that I've been brainwashed that potential is going to be a terrorist…And it got quite aggressive in our conversations, at times he got very angry. I was really shocked at my dad's response really, really shocked. I expected it from my mom, not my dad. One day I had gone to visit and somehow an argument blew up when I mentioned Islam. I decided to leave but first went and cried in the bathroom away from everyone.

My dad came up and asked me not to leave and at that moment things started to change. I shared with him that actually he was a big part of my journey into Islam. That he being so open minded and understanding of other cultures led to me not thinking all Muslims are terrorists. That him telling me never to judge someone else led to me asking questions before making opinions of the muslims I met. All his ethics he had taught me, had led me to being open minded and not following the sheep and finding out for myself that Islam is a peaceful religion.

My mum was kind of okay initially when I just told them and I wasn't wearing Islamic clothing so no-one else could tell. It opened up conversations about Christianity. I actually apologised to her because I used to take the Mick out of her belief, not nasty but teasing and that used to upset her sometimes. Now we had something in common and understanding of Christianity with the basics that are similar to Islam. It brought us closer together and it certainly makes me feel closer to my mum then ever before.

Once I started wearing the hijab, however it became really difficult for my mum. The first time she saw me in it, we were in a motorway service station. She was kindly picking up my boys to take them to her house and to give me a little break.

She was wandering around the service station looking for me, then she came up to me and was really upset and angry and red faced from embarrassment, she said, " No wonder I couldn't see you with you wearing that thing." She hadn't recognised me, and I hadn't told her I was wearing it because I was worried how she would respond.

We sat down and whispered loudly - "take it off." I replied, "Mum, please don't ask me to do that, I've never ever asked you to take your cross off." She has always worn a cross on a chain. The conversation kind of stopped there about that.

We just talked politely for a few minutes, it was awkward really awkward. I understand from her point of view because we grew up in a Cotswold village, a white village with white people, white sheep, white ducks even the houses are blooming white limestone!

There is a lot of very racist folks down there where I grew up. Some people who who have travelled or commute from the bigger cities are open minded but there is a lot of misunderstanding about Islam and other cultures.

That was really difficult, really difficult. I remember my Nana's conversation with me shortly after, HER saying "Trust you Sonny" she used to called me Sonny "Trust you, sonny. Of course it was going to be you, if it was gonna be any of you it was going to be you." Meaning out of all our 12 cousins, her grandchildren it would only be me who would embrace Islam.

She wasn't angry though, nor embarrassed, at least not openly to me. She even bought me a headscarf. We had a couple of little chats about Islam and Christianity, I asked her about what she really believed in and she asked me questions. When I shared we are very similar except that in Islam we believe Jesus is a prophet, not the son of God, she replied "I never believed that Jesus was the son of God anyway Sonny."

My wonderful, kind, happy, strong, courageous, Nana passed away not long after that chat.

I was so scared that she wouldn't enter Jannah because of her belief but I recalled that conversation and I read our last text message, which she had sent to me saying she wanted to know about Islam and we must have a chat about it one day Sonny. We never got to have that chat. But it gives me hope that she will be in Jannah In Sha Allah because she believed there was only one God.

It was really tough. But getting through that I learned about Islam, I started studying a bit more and went to some classes, I went to the talks at the mosque. I got more involved with the mosque and some charity work volunteer work and learning more.

Then the next challenge hit me.

I never ever made Dua all for anything for myself at all. All I ever asked Allah for was for everyone to be guided to Islam so all the pain in this world would stop. The first time I asked one Dua, for anything else my world came crashing down. I heard that my sister; who lived in New Zealand, had gone into labour. I just made Dua that everything would be okay. Shortly after I received a text message saying the baby had died.

And I fell to the floor, I couldn't believe it. The pain was unbearable because I wasn't there for my sister, I wanted to take that pain from her. I feared she wouldn't cope and I knew I was strong enough but was so scared she wasn't. I couldn't be there. I was a lone parent of four, and the one Dua I had made was refused.

And I was really confused, angry, I felt betrayed Astaghfirullah. It didn't make sense, such a simple Dua. I was just stunned. I remember getting the kids ready for school, I just had to pretend nothing had happened. When I returned home I opened my Quran.

I read part that I hadn't seen before. I read if a parent stays patient after losing a child, their child will call for them on the day of judgement and help them get into Jannah.

Then it all started to make sense to me that. My sister is very atheist. And that if she stayed patient in this time then I've got hope that she would want to join me in Jannah. And that gave me understanding and hope. It also gave me hope for my parents who lost a son, my beloved brother.

I wanted to take that pain from my sister, she didn't have that belief like I had and so her anger continued, her questions continued. It was and is of course very difficult for her and her husband. Atheist she is and yet she asked me to pray for her so that gave me some hope that she was getting some comfort somewhere. These were the big challenges.

And I guess little challenges have been the racism back home in the villages where I grew up. My eldest daughter left home for Uni and then worked in a cafe and a pub near my mum. She experienced racism in the village towards her because I was a Muslim. People knew thanks to Facebook and our gossip system.

I was really shocked about some of the people who were being abusive towards her, one in particular I would've considered open minded and a good past friend, he was awful to my daughter. I felt huge guilt being the cause of her ordeal. I was really shocked at his response I just couldn't believe the naivety of people and the ignorance, it made me really sad and it's really really sad that they don't understand Islam and for them to be racist like that. My daughter was just a teenager.

I became very very anxious going down there, and I still get anxiety walking around in the villages where I grew up. Yet I've got some amazing friends down there that have said to me, Sonia you know it's just small minded people. One time I was told to go back to my own country! It was an Eastern European guy who shouted this at me and I just laughed at the irony. He looked confused and wandered off. One guy pushed me in town, after an older guy he was with said something about Muslims. I let it go and when I saw him later on his own he just looked at his feet. I felt sad that he clearly hangs out with bullies that make him behave a way he maybe isn't comfortable with but probably too afraid to just fit in. Too afraid to say no to the people he surrounds himself with.

Some of my friends in the armed forces have remained really good friends with me Alhumdulilah. I now have more Christian and Mormon friends than ever before, I have many, many Muslim friends from around the world and I feel truly blessed.

The hardest thing that I've found giving up is being able to be out in the sunshine!! I love the sun so much and having to cover up when the sun is out for the 3 days a year we have in UK!! It's super annoying. Currently that's definitely the biggest challenge for me.

Fortunately I work from home, which allows me to sit and work in the garden during the summer so I can strip off. In sha Allah I will get to Jannah and I will ask for lots of sunshine and all my family and friends to be there with a glass of wine from the wine river running past my house.

Sonia Keats (Shields) - Mindset and Mental Health Coach - CEO of Find Your Freedom.

Instagram - @sonia.keats
Facebook - www.facebook.com/findyourfreedom/
Linked In - www.linkedin.com/in/soniakeats/

17

Exhausted to Energised

For many years I was blessed with exceptional health and vitality. I was a sporty child and loved physical education. This carried on throughout to my university years and I found it easy to pick up new classes and sports and loved walking. I have had two brushes with ill health and I describe them below.

I finished university and worked for a year and then decided that I was directionless and needed to find my calling. So I convinced my parents to let me go and live in Alexandra Egypt by myself for 6 months, I convinced them that it wouldn't mean I would be murdered or maimed but would grow up. To seal the deal I enrolled into an Arabic course where they guaranteed shared accommodation with other female students so my parents knew I was living in a safe space.

I boarded the plane with all my bags checked in except one, slightly worried about the how I was going to log these bags around when I got there. I mean what do you pack for a 6 months trip, so I took almost everything that I thought I would need. I had to get myself from Cairo to Alexandra were I would be met by a representative of the school. This trip was going to be the single most exciting thing I had ever done but I was also 22, I had never travelled without family or in a group of friends and I couldn't speak Arabic. My excitement was also coupled rightly with some concern about how I was going to make this work. But I wanted it badly, so it was going to happen.

I got myself to Alexandra, after a very kind Egyptian family helped me get my ridiculously large bags to the Cairo train station I sat looking at the scenery feeling overwhelmed at the fact that all I could see was desert and I could finally call myself a true traveller. I made it to the entrance of Alexandra train station where I was met by the representative after two men helped me with my luggage.

I was shown my new apartment which I would be sharing with 2 other ladies. It then dawned on me that actually as I had always lived at home I actually didn't know how to feed myself properly. As one of 7 siblings we all had specific jobs and my job at home was cleaning the kitchen. I had perfected this job but now I had to be able to feed myself as well as clean after myself. This was an oversight on my part…oops.

I suddenly went from being very healthy because I was raised on real food that was cooked by my mum from scratch with minimal clean ingredients to "pot noodles" becoming a staple in my diet. I did learn to supplement my burgeoning pot noodle diet with fresh fruit and grilled chicken. It was the first time in my life that I felt tired and not brimming with energy and full of life as I was used to.

Egypt did wonderful things for me in terms of growing me into my adult self, becoming independent, self reliant, learning to enjoy my own company and developing that everything has a solution mindset. As well as finding direction and wanting to train as a teacher after volunteering at a orphanage as an ESOL teacher.

I also came back with some unwanted side effects due to my poor diet. I developed digestive issues, random and unexplained stomach cramps but this all seem to subside after a few months of my mums foods Alhamdulilah but it would resurface now and gain.

My second brush with non optimal health It started when I fell pregnant with my first child at 28 and my skin changed overnight from dry to acne prone. My skincare routine at the time couldn't cope with my skin breaking out so badly. I was using all the wrong products and making my skin worse. But at the time I thought I was doing the best that I could.

The spots on my face would take forever to heal and leave dark marks. At my wit's end, I decided to do what I was trained to do. Research and find evidence that these lotions and potions could do what the marketing said they could do. I learned that what I was doing was making my acne worse. With my new-found knowledge I changed my skin care and adjusted what I ate, and I saw some improvements overtime

However, when I went back to my busy and stressful teaching Job, working and having a baby took its toll. I was diagnosed with adrenal fatigue and my digestive health which never fully recovered from my pot noodle days in Egypt took a nose dive again.

I was constantly bloated and uncomfortable and I had horrible hay fever every summer, rhinitis all year around, a constant brain Fog and exhaustion that would have been collapsed on the sofa everyday by 5pm desperately trying to keep my son engaged while I waited for my husband to get back from work so he could take over and I could crawl into bed.

During this time I was emotionally hard on myself, I felt like I wasn't living up to the image I had of myself. Everyone else seemed to be coping fine with juggling work and being a mum but I was struggling to do either well.

Along with my own health problems my son had a severe milk allergy and I had to make everything from scratch and watch his diet like a hawk. He was under weight and wasn't thriving as he should have been. I was nursing him at the time and worried about weaning as dairy wasn't an option for him. I tried to be perfect at everything that I had to do but all that did was put even more pressure on me and it wasn't healthy at ALL during this time, physically and emotionally I was struggling.

I was reading a lot at the time trying to see if we could do more to help my son heal from his allergy, I came across a lot of information around using food as medicine. We started making changes to our diet and supplementing with food based multivitamins which really improved my son's appetite. But being a child he got an infection and was put on antibiotics. That really set him back as he had loose stools for 3 weeks and his weight plummeted to the 4 percentile meaning that 96 percent of his peers weighed more then him.

At the end of my tether I heard about camel milks ability to heal the gut. I searched and found a raw cow milk (when its pasteurised the immunoglobulins no longer work) supplier in the neighbouring city and put in an order and got my husband to collect it. Adam thrived on it Mashallah!

As my son's was coming on leaps and bounds I started to look to my own health. I felt like I now had the head space to make myself feel better. By this point I had amassed a lot of knowledge and developed expertise in the anatomy of the skin and the best ingredients for specific skin concerns and my skin wasn't back to normal but was doing better. I had also learnt a lot about nutrition and the healing power of food.

But what I really needed was someone to help me get to where I dreamed of being. Someone who knew how to implement all the things that I had been learning about without overwhelm. When my son was 1 years old and I was 30 but felt decades older I decided to put myself first and invest in a health coach. It was then that my health improved exponentially and my skin along with it, Alhamdulillah.

I know wake up early every morning full of energy, I no longer drink caffeinated drinks as I don't need the additional energy boost, my skin has never looked so good and I thoroughly enjoy taking care of myself. My family is much happier now too as I am happier and have the time and energy to give my 2 children, my husband and the rest of my family my focused attention. As a bonus by son now 7 no longer has a milk allergy. To look at him you would never know he had a shaky start.

It has been 6 years since I started by beauty and health journey and in that time, I have worked with multiple coaches. Who have helped me with my own health and wellbeing journey as well as training me to become a coach myself. Since I hired by first coach my life has changed completely. It was overcoming my own skin among numerous problems that made me realise the power we have to really change our lives with the support and expertise of a coach.

We as woman struggle to put ourselves first, we don't make time for ourselves and thinking that self care is somehow selfish. But I am here to argue that its in fact selfish to give a poor, dysfunctional, irritable version of yourself to your loved one. By putting everyone else's needs before your own you are not being a good daughter, sister, wife, mother, employee etc, you are in fact doing all the people in your life a disservice and grinding yourself to the ground in the process.

The relationship you have with yourself is the most important relationship you will ever have. It will shape the way your feel about yourself, how you allow others to treat you and what you have to offer to your loved ones. Investing in yourself and your wellbeing needs to become a priority for us all if we are to live full lives inshallah.

Naima Mohamed - Skin and health coach BSC, MA

Website - www.theglowingmuslimah.com
Facebook - www.facebook.com/groups/446114379160558/
Instagram - @theglowingmuslimah

17

A Mother never gives up...

My baby Fatima leaked over night and was upset she says this morning crying "mama I wish I didn't exist." When we asked why she said that she said "because if I didn't exist then you wouldn't have to look after me, and you could look after Abdullah and Zehnab more." This sentence will always taunt me and my husband for a long time to come.

I am sat in a cubicle on the 5th of December 2019 in A&E I write my story.

I Myria Shoaib aged 39 owner of FAZ_Collection Original and FAZ Boutique, happily married with 4 children. Alhamduillah for Allah's blessing upon me.

My eldest daughter Maryam Aroush, my perfect baby, Alhamduillah. My life line, my little friend and little whirlwind. Has grown up before her age, read my story to find out more.

My second daughter had Infant/toddler diarrhoea. Constantly having loose stools. I was told by health professionals it will pass when she's 2 years old.

I started my journey of an online business after having my 3rd child, Zehnab Zunaira, little did I know what Allah had in store for me.

Constantly being at home, nothing to do apart from the usual household chores and looking after the girls, I decided to venture into an online business, I started to sell Avon products online. And I throughly enjoyed it. Taking the girls with me on a walk, posting out the campaign books.

I created a Facebook page and Facebook group. My little venture started, my business needed some attention along with the family, I slowly started introducing clothing. Changing my business name from FAZ Avon to FAZ Collection Original.

My daughters were growing, business had picked up, and Allah SWT bestowed his blessing on me again, I was pregnant the 4th time. Alhamdulilah.

I clearly remember one Friday evening my husband had gone to work, he rang me saying "Oh what are you doing" me being me replied sarcastically, I'm dancing. Husband: "Well stop dancing and get packing we moving."

Me: Confused.com moving??? "Eh hello I'm 6 months pregnant. Where are we moving and when??" Husband: "we moving to our other house around the corner and we moving tomorrow."

Me: "I've not seen the house."

Husband: "You can see it tomorrow when we move."

Packing started and by Sunday we had moved. We started renovating the house, working on the business having 3 girls and heavily pregnant. My life had turned upside down.

Fatima was 2.5 years by now her infant/toddler diarrhoea hadn't stopped still. It was just getting worse and worse. Back to the doctor again, was given movical to see if that will help. She started to go into depression. You would think what wait a 2.5 year old?? Is that even possible? Yes it is. They have feelings too. They are also affected with whats going around them. Small people with feelings.

Zehnab's development was slightly slow for the Health visitors liking. Regular visits became a norm in my household. 4 months passed and Alhamduillah I was blessed with a baby boy, the drama with my son Subhan'Allah, was unbelievable. Born premature, hanging off my cord, him being born alive, my Dr's were surprised with his miracle delivery. Stayed in hospital for 10-12 days, my family all over Oldham and Glasgow.

Alhamdulilah 10th of June 2014 we were finally all under one roof again. Sweet sounds of laughters of Abdullah, Maryam fussing over her brother, Fatima leaking left right and centre, and My Zeno, sat quietly rocking and observing her siblings delayed in walking and talking.

Health visitors frequent visits increased, Zehnab's development in questioning now, business growing. Kids growing, house still getting renovated. Zehnab's paediatrics appointments increasing, Fatima's infant/Toddler diarrhoea out of control and my life spiralling out of control in front me.

What is going on?! Downing into self pity, feeling trapped and beginning to become unhappy of the entire situation. Depression kicking in.

The years got worse and worse. Zehnab's diagnosis of Autism was given after a long haul. With Abdullah Muhammad being also suspected with it but was reassured its early days and not to worry. I was brave and held my head up, and said we will get through it.

Come 2017 my worst nightmare came alive, in April my son Abdullah Muhammad was also diagnosed with Autism. My world shattered, broke down at the consultants office. Walked out of there as I had watched a horror moving. Told my husband of the news, and I broke down again. My husbands words echoed in my ears, "In our hearts we suspected it but today's its been confirmed, don't worry we will get through it don't you dare cry".

In and out of hospital with Fatima. I did a lot of advertising whilst waiting to see the docs, spending one to one time with Fatima, finally giving a diagnosis of Crohn's in June 2018. My heart was shattered again. With friends and family calling asking how she is, breaking down in front of family was one of the hardest thing I've probably done, as I've always been strong.

Friends and family have discouraged me with my business, saying you have ill kids stop your business concentrate on the kids. They are not aware that this is the very business of mine that has kept me sane, helped me through my tough times. Having ill kids does not stop you from working from home or from a office. I felt and still feel my business is retreat haven for me to escape to.

Whilst I watch Fatima sleep in a A&E cubicle I reflect on the past 10 years of my life. Sept 2009 I become a wife. November 2010, December 2011, April 2013 I become a mother my daughters.

I start my business out of depression in 2013. I name my business FAZ Collection Original after my daughters names. In 2014 my pride and joy was born, my family was complete. He's completely a mummy's boy.

2016 I was asked to do catwalk shows in Trafford Centre by Fareda the organiser. I'm doing my 4th show catwalk with her now Alhamduillah.

In 2017 I take over a run down business called SNS fashions. Changed the name to FAZ Boutique and Alhamduillah its improving as time goes by.

In current date I'm a well known clothes seller with a 4.5 stars feedback from customers on my page. My customers know little or nothing of my life or of my special needs children. They don't know who they are supporting when purchasing from my small business.

I want to inspire other sisters, friends, mothers to never lose hope, Allah SWT always has a plan in store for you.

Theres no harm in breaking down in front of family, friends or even in front of a stranger. Its helps the heart to become light. Breaking down does not mean you're weak or you cant cope. Keep your faith, keep smiling its sunnah.

He's blessed me with 4 beautiful children, a good husband and a name in the clothing business.

Alhamdulilah for yesterday, today and tomorrow.
Myria Shoaib - Founder & CEO of Faz Collection.

Website - www.fazcollection.co.uk
Instagram - @fazcollectionoriginal
Facebook - www.facebook.com/fazcollectionoriginal

How I Saved My Marriage Without Waiting For My Husband To Change.

I fell in love with the man of my dreams and married him with the blessings of my family. However, soon into the marriage, we started to have problems. I am not going to list them all here but one of the biggest was communication.

I began to ask myself: why was it that my husband refused to talk about things that really mattered? Why did he always sweep everything under the carpet? Why would he not listen to what I had to say and understand how I felt? Sometimes I felt as if I might as well have been speaking to a brick wall; often left feeling ignored, invisible and rejected. This would also result in us having blazing arguments which left no respect for one another.

As time went on, our relationship got to a point where we started to become distant from each other. I began to think that I had made a terrible decision in marrying someone who refused to talk to me and understand my needs. He didn't seem to care how I felt, which left me so broken. Many times, I would cry myself to sleep, feeling terribly unhappy and alone.

But I wasn't ready to give up.

I was determined to find a solution, whatever the cost.

The first solution was to demand from my husband that, since he had a massive communication problem, he needed to get help, otherwise, our marriage was over. This resulted in a big argument, with him saying that there was nothing wrong with him and that I was the crazy one who should change. I painfully swallowed his words and continued with my search.

They say never share your problems with your in-laws but, hey, I was desperate, so my second solution was to pour my heart out to mine. I found out none of his family seemed to care what I had to say. My words only fell on deaf ears.

My next solution was deciding to turn to my friends and family. I started to become a little hopeful as I had heard lots of useful advice and tips in how to make your husband listen – this ranged from cooking his favourite meals, speaking with kindness and being more patient. Being a dutiful daughter and friend, I followed their useful advice and put it all in practice, sadly, this did not seem to change my husband.

I then switched my search to the online world, hunting down all the top relationship gurus, books and tools to find the secret to marital bliss. Google and Amazon became my best friends. I found a wealth of information that offered practical advice, tools, and techniques in how to speak to your husband and how to work on yourself, however putting all this into practice was not that easy and unfortunately brought no change.

By now I was left feeling frustrated. Surely, there must be something that would work. It was then that I decided I needed to be a better Muslim. I threw myself in daily rituals of prayer, often waking up in the middle of the night and memorising The Holy Quran. It was soon after this that I began to feel spiritually connected with Allah, The Almighty, and it felt amazing. I began to secretly beg Allah to change my husband's ways and make him a better Muslim. I prayed and prayed, hoping for a miracle from The Almighty. This went on for a while. I found myself putting all my trust and faith in The Divine, who I knew would not forsake me.

My efforts however still seem to fall in vain. There was still no change in my marriage, and the arguments and frustration continued to grow and explode. How can this be I wondered? Surely Allah could see how hard I was trying. Surely, He must be pleased with all my efforts?

It was at this point that I fell into despair. I had done everything I could think of but nothing had worked. I had completely lost the battle to make my husband listen and save our marriage. I felt helpless, exhausted and silently depressed. I finally started to accept the reality that my marriage was over, and that it was heading down the path of divorce.

It was then that the miracle came.

The miracle was a moment of a mind-blowing insight. I realised that I had been stuck in a trap. I had been stuck in the "I'll be happy when…" trap.

Now, you might be wondering, what on earth is the *I'll be happy when… trap?* Let me explain.

I had been believing all this time that *I will only be happy when* my husband will give me some attention and starts listening to me. I had been believing that *I will only be happy when* my husband starts to take some responsibility in the marriage.

This realisation changed everything.

Previously, I had been waiting for my husband to do something *before* I could feel happy. For example, I thought that if only he would do more household chores, *then I would feel happy.* If only he would listen to me more, *then I would feel happy.* If only he stops ignoring me, *then I would feel happy.* So, I waited, and waited, and waited for my husband to change in order to *feel happy.* I was stuck in this trap waiting for my husband to change and waiting for happiness to arrive. The way that I had been thinking before was that it was my husband's behaviour that had been making me upset, angry and frustrated and only if he changed his behaviour then I would give myself permission to feel happy. What a trap!

I started to see more and more that my husband never had the power to affect me in any way. I realised at that moment that my happiness was never going to come from my husband as I had been led to believe all these years. I could be happy right now. The *waiting* game was over.

Now don't get me wrong, being a Muslim I knew previously that nothing and nobody could give me happiness except Allah, but the difference now was that I was consciously awakened to see this truth on a very deep level. I felt so blessed for this awakening that I cried for days. Furthermore, I felt instant joy, contentment, tranquillity, and bliss without having to wait for my husband to change (which he did!).

Who would have thought that it could happen with a simple insight? An insight that not only transformed my marriage but my life in ways I never dreamed possible. I was no longer was suffering, screaming like a crazy person to be heard, and the constant blazing rows also came to an end.

For the first time in years, my husband started to be attentive and listen to me more. We were able to have meaningful conversations in a peaceful and loving way. He started to take more responsibility, show me more respect and it started to matter to him how I felt. The changes in our marriage were endless. You probably might have guessed by now, that we are not divorced, but, remain peacefully and happily married. *Alhamdhulillah.*

If you're feeling fed up with your spouse and want to let go of the stress and frustration, you can get a free 10 minute audio meditation that can bring the joy, love, and happiness back into your marriage, then click here: www.robinakauser.com/free-gift

Robina Kauser - Online Happy Marriage Coach helping frustrated, disconnected and unhappy Muslim wives to find joy, love, peace and happiness in their marriage.

Website - www.robinakauser.com
Instagram - @_robinakauser
Facebook - www.facebook.com/robina.kauser.1

17

My Path to Self Mastery

I believe everyone has good intentions. We all want positivity and change for the better. We want to look and feel great, be successful, and enjoy healthy relationships.

> *"In any given moment we have two options: to step forward into growth or to step back into safety"*
>
> *Abraham Maslow*

However just mere hopes and wishes are never going to make a difference. Living life in a state of redundancy and allowing our unconscious autopilot mode to lead us will not bring us success and fulfilment of souls. If we truly wish to achieve our dreams, there is a tried and true way of going about it and it is certainly the most exciting journey you'll ever take on.

There is no short cut to success and living your life to your fullest potential. It requires sacrifice, courage, discipline, self-discovery, letting go, allowing mistakes and gaining wisdom. It is the path to *Self Mastery*. All this sounds so exciting yet challenging. Many of us attend motivational speeches or events and temporarily feel fired up to change aspects of ourselves, only to be disappointed shortly after as we no longer feel inspired or motivated. The reason for this is not having clarity of purpose, in other words, not knowing your *why*!

> *"Indeed, Allah will not change the condition of a people until they change what is in themselves."*
>
> *[Qur'an, 13:11]*

This verse from the Holy Quran speaks volumes to me. What does it mean to change ourselves? We hear this all the time, but what does it mean to actually act upon that? It is a road very few travel with authenticity and passion. Some time ago, I decided I was going to be one of those people!

I began my personal growth journey a few years ago, where I realised things had to change within me. Like most people, although with all good intentions, I had some self-sabotaging limiting beliefs, a lower self esteem, a people pleasing *perfectionist* type attitude, and some thinking and feeling habits which cost me emotional pain. I began to focus on what I could tweak, what I needed to accept, what to let go and forgive, how I could perceive differently, what was not working, which new habits I needed to build, and where I could grow.

I began to change for the better version that existed within me. And as I became more and more self-aware, I realised I needed to invest in my growth and ask, firstly through prayer and then connecting with experts who had achieved self mastery. I believe in order to learn anything in life, one must humble down to realise that asking for help is a strength and not a weakness. Overcoming one's ego, which wants to keep us small and 'safe,' is essential for growth and wisdom. A self-serving Mindset needs to be cultivated. And prior to any significant change, one must discover themselves.

I am an emotional, expressive, intuitive and sensitive person who values communication and understanding. As a child, I yearned for emotional stability and often felt as if I was the problem. I thought being sensitive and 'too much of a feeler' was to be ashamed of as it was not the brave and bold thing to do. As an 80s child, where I can appreciate my upbringing with high standards and upright values, exemplified with much integrity by my parents, I was raised in an environment where being too emotional was a negative thing and therefore, I was the odd one out. Very early on in life I learned the tact to mask my true feelings. It seemed that there was only one standard of intelligence, excellence, and acceptance. I felt I wasn't appreciated for my strengths, rather compared with someone else or a standard that needed to be chased after in order to be good enough. I'm sure this isn't just my story, many people can relate to this.

As a growth seeking person, I could not settle for mediocrity and seek who I was, what fulfilled me, and how I needed to empower myself according to my individualistic gifts and choices. I finally understood what it meant when people spoke about 'finding oneself.'

It was much later into adulthood when I began to value my talents and embrace my emotional intelligence and learned to see my sensitivity as my strength. I began looking for answers for the things that were going on inside me, whether it was my expectations of others, or things from the past that I found hard to forgive, or just finding a more fulfilled life.

I began reading self development books and researched extensively as I felt some gaps needed to be filled. I wanted to feel whole and content within. Along with my strong conviction to my faith, I needed strength emotionally and mentally. I wanted to take charge of my thoughts and my feelings. Now that is a more advanced level of mindfulness that I had to acquire. It only comes through conscious, purposeful living, which is a habit of becoming. Anyone can learn and acquire this kind of blissful state if they authentically intend to attain self mastery.

I decided to take my personal discovery seriously. After all, *"Knowing Yourself is the Beginning of all Wisdom"* according to Aristotle. A few years back, I had a situation where I ended up overreacting which caused me emotional misery. It struck me hard and got me even more serious about exploring personal growth through healing. I had to heal myself. I didn't want to live in reactive mode. I wanted to feel in control with my emotions and therefore any life situation. I wanted to stop blaming anyone else and started to learn how to take responsibility of whatever was in my control. I wanted to live more meaningfully, but I couldn't get very far as I wasn't ready to be myself. It takes courage to question things and look a bit harder to find answers within oneself. Sometimes you need to unlearn things and relearn them without distortion, much rather authentically.

I grew up with wrong labels and concepts about who I needed to be. To be an Artist was useless and to be emotional was being a drama queen. And boy have I come a long way! Now, to proudly call myself a professional Artist and also an Emotional Mastery Coach. My new labels and titles are self accepted with pride and honour. They are my unique treasured gifts and ways how I give back with passion. If I didn't give back what was given to me by God, I would be doing a disservice to say the least. And how would I find my gifts if I never looked for them or claimed them?

Self discovery and acceptance helped me to step outside my comfort zone. I always found the passion to teach and nurture inside me, so I decided to home educate my kids, which took a lot of strength and ownership of my values and choices. As a full time homeschooling mom of four precious children, I became motivated to exemplify myself as my best version to my kids. Actually, that was a huge propeller for my personal growth. I decided to live by example to raise children with good morals and emotional stability.

Learning to embrace the fact that I am the only true version of me gave me a real boost inside. I was the creative minded, highly intuitive, day dreamer! I was wired differently than those I compared myself to. I had my own special talents and intelligence that many others couldn't compare to. I uncovered my gifts, embraced them and was ready to share them. I began a small business as an artist (10+ years) which brought me immense confidence, security, connections, opportunities, appreciation and so much more. It has become my retreat, my meditation and joy. I definitely made my mark in the industry for my skill, by the Grace of God.

The more I claimed my talent and put myself out there, the more opportunities knocked on my door. I discovered how independent and entrepreneurial I was. Being able to create a business out of your passions is one of the most exciting things you can do to live a fulfilled life.

On a personal level, I began shifting perspectives, managing emotions, and generated self serving thoughts for myself. As I overcame emotional blocks personally, I became more self aware and grew into a better version of me. I got to a point where my moods didn't shift because of someone else's irresponsible actions.

I connected with like minded people of passion and the community of giving back, following coaches and influential speakers. Some of my favourite people in the coaching industry that I learn from are Brook Castillo, Marissa Peers, Brian Tracy, Mel Robins, Brenden Bouchard, Joe Dispenza, Eckhart Tolle, Muhammad Alshareef, Mufti Menk and others. I worked on my limiting self beliefs, emotional healing, and mindset mastery. As my paradigm changed for the better, so did my self confidence and affairs with others. Changing my influence was massive for becoming more focussed on my goals.

I fell in love with my newly found self! Not only was I able to embrace my qualities and talents, I was also able to accept my shortcomings and was prepared to work on them. The more truthful and vulnerable I got with myself, the more I felt empowered and happier. And now I was ready to forgive myself, for not honouring me. I was ready to forgive others, for not understanding me. I was ready to let go of things that bothered me and grow through my mistakes and owned them. I was ready to love myself and grow my self esteem as that allowed me to be gentle towards myself. In doing so, I was able to overcome my habit of people pleasing and perfectionism as I learned to set healthy boundaries in relationships and expectations while letting go of codependency. It felt like purifying my heart of anything that didn't serve it. I detached myself from toxic connections or all that weighed me down.

As I learned emotional mastery on a deeper level, I uncovered my inner-most calling to change lives through coaching others in order to live more self aware and fulfilled lives. In 2017, I launched my coaching practice as I was inspired to help others through my personal growth and all the lessons I learned along the way. As I changed my own life, I began putting myself out there to bring about change in others. I began studying alongside some raw coaching experience. Getting certified trainings and certifications, gave me the experience and tools I needed to share with so many people who felt stuck, demotivated, unconfident, lost, or depressed. I began to attract the people who were looking for me. With each positive feedback, with each referral, I felt like I was beginning to make my difference. The fulfilment I get through this work is so special to me. And I know it is because I am being my truest self when I'm using my gifts and tapping into my intuition and wisdom to help others.

Our mind is designed to protect us. It likes being comfortable with the conditioned limiting beliefs, expectations and fear. It is safe to just go along with what is familiar and not question things, even if such numbness to your soul's calling might be painful. Your mind's paradigm doesn't serve you because it wants you to ride the mainstream, not question things, or take risks. In order to find yourself, discover exciting facts about you and your purpose, you must begin to challenge your mind a bit and look beyond what's customary.

If you haven't found yourself yet, well it's never too late to discover! Think about what your passions are and what you always knew you were good at. What part of you would you like to explore more? What is valuable to you in life, in relationships, spiritually, professionally? How do you think, feel, act and why? Where do you need work? What needs to heal? Which values do you want to live by and not compromise on? What works best for your personality and what doesn't? What is your ideal version of yourself? Let's find and uncover all that juicy stuff about you and expand on things that you want and need to feel whole again and become happier as a person. This knowledge of the *Self* is so valuable to us yet mostly undiscovered.

I find it fascinating to uncover the truth about the people I coach. It can be an exciting yet emotional process one might go through to really *find themselves*. You get honest with yourself. You might need to peel some layers and look deeper within. Some masks may need to be removed that you are accustomed to wear. You may or may not be ready to accept some things about you. You get to discover who you are and how you can claim your identity, values, self beliefs, perceptions and much more. Once that process is wholly accepted, I support and teach my clients to accept who they are and take pride in themselves. That is where the beautiful journey of Self Growth truly begins.

Being unapologetically yourself can significantly grow your self esteem. You have your signature way of conducting yourself. Your temperaments, relationships, insecurities, attitudes, or problems, become apparent as you begin to understand what part you play as *who you are* in that point in time. Once you know who you are, you can accept yourself as your authentic self and begin to tap into the better version of you that already exists and needs to be found. It is true for everyone who is too much for others, too quiet, too opinionated, too sensitive, too nerdy, too hyper, too anything! Don't allow anyone to put those labels on you. You are you and that is your normal. Love that. Accept that. Rock that!

For me, Self recognition was an ongoing journey which spanned over a few years. The times I felt in sync or disconnected with myself, I noticed my life reflecting that. As I connected with my authentic self and discovered my values, I began to implement my learnings into creating my life. Being radically honest with myself liberated me tremendously. Knowing your strengths is a huge advantage. When you are aware, you can build on your qualities to create your ideal life.

What a miraculous creation is this mind of ours! We have the power to change our negative patterns into positive ones, our limiting self belief systems into abundant self-worthy ones, our victimising mindsets into empowered grateful ones. God has truly given us the choice to become who we wish with all the capacity and the possibility of our unlimited potential.

Our life is only as good as our mindset. If it is fixed and negative, you will create similar results. And if your mindset is positive and progressive, you will be able to easily create the change you aim for.

What I learned is that we alone are our biggest limitation. We alone are our problem. And we alone can change that, if we decide to. Through life coaching, I help women overcome their limited beliefs and transform their lives for the better. That is my very sacred purpose that fulfils me. And it all began with the change that happened within me. Although, I do believe I have a long road ahead of me with many new things to learn and grow through, my only fear now has become stagnation. I do remember a time when I feared change, but now it excites me and keeps me motivated.

Now, a positive change sounds fun and exciting, but it comes with a price that must be paid. From needing to change your small habits to changing your whole outlook on life and expanding your comfort zone. Overcoming your self sabotaging patterns, your excuses, blame game and perhaps a fixed mindset. Having breakthroughs and cultivating a growth mindset, which invites new change into your life you never knew existed! We must learn to take responsibility for our life choices and nurture our minds towards continual growth and possibility. God has given us unimaginable potential and He already created us as our best versions, but somewhere along the way, we lose that person and must rediscover, nourish, and learn to believe in our ability to change and evolve to live our best life.

If you find any of this interesting, do reach out and talk to me! I'm here to support you on this reflective, powerful journey of Self Mastery!

Much love, light, and positivity,

Seema Khan - Emotional Mastery Coach - Empowering Women to transform and shine.

Website - www.Sisterinfocus.com
Facebook - www.fb.com/sisterinfocus
Instagram - www.instagram.com/sisterinfocus_coaching

17

Feeling the fear and doing it anyway!

I was immersed into motherhood at the age of 17 and by the age of 33 years I was a full time mother of four beautiful children. After getting married I led a very mechanical life with daily routines which I was finding very boring. I wasted a good part of my life watching films and dramas in my free time.

Once my uncle visited from the States and commented that in the 60hrs a week of watching dramas and movies, I could have completed a degree! That got me thinking and feeling guilty of all the time I was wasting. I decided to change my life! But, it wasn't that easy, the question arose 'where to start'?

In 1987 there was an opening for a parent governor at my son's nursery. My family and friends encouraged me to stand for election. I felt apprehensive and incompetent to do so. I mean what experience did I have? I was scared I would not get any any votes? I thought of the sheer embarrassment it would cause me. I had to write a personal statement and because I had no working experience or educational background, I wasn't sure what to write? I felt a real fear which made me feel sick. My family told me to write about my experience as a mother and my personal interest for their education. With clammy hands and a pounding heart, I took the pen and did just that! I wrote a true and honest statement and this was the first time that I felt the 'fear and did it'. I took the first plunge by handing in this simple statement which was going to change my life forever!

To my absolute delight and surprise I received the most votes and was elected a school governor. well now the hard work was about to begin. I remember clearly my very first Governors' meeting and how I went and sat in that meeting completely in the dark. It was full of jargon and by the end of the three hour long meeting I came out totally lost and thought to myself, there is no way can I continue this! But, how can I tell everyone this was the reason I would be resigning? All those parents put their trust in me by voting for me how could I let them down now? I decided to be brave and not let this put me off and pushed myself to attend the next meeting and the next and the next…

I continued attending meetings and training courses for Governors organised by the local LEA, which were brilliant. By the end of my elected term I managed to grasp the education system and stood for election again. I did have my reservations about dealing things at secondary level. This was going to entail a different curriculum with different problems and decisions. I would have to start from scratch and attend meetings 'sitting in the dark' again. I would have to deal with a lot of new knowledge. Do I really want to do that?

It wasn't going to be easy and I was a new parent in this school where parents didn't know me. What if I didn't get any votes or got few votes? All of these facts put a fear in me and told me not to go for it. I should be content and carry on where I was. My heart told me to stick to one school and yet, my mind was telling me to go further and help my children and the children in our community. Becoming a School Governor taught me that I had power, with a team I was involved in serious decision making. I had to do it despite the 'fear' I was feeling again.

However, to my total amazement I had won the elections by majority votes, wow! I was learning my worth and realised my abilities. I learned each time that 'feeling the fear' and doing it really can be rewarding and satisfactory if we are prepared to take a risk and go for it. I felt great that so many people voted for me and my personal statements were carrying a lot more experience and weight now.

As most of the parents voted for me I realised I had to deliver and become proactive. I started to see some people become governors' just for the name and position. But, I couldn't do that and just be sitting with a title. I started to meet parents, ask their concerns and views so that I could share their needs and help alleviate concerns. Gradually, I became more assertive and confident and helped make positive changes for the betterment of the children at the school.

I remember all the hardship I faced during this time when my opinion didn't matter or was opposed. But, what mattered was that I was able to take forward parents concerns, needs and views. I was able to fight for the right of the parents' and children of the school. This made me a strong and assertive parent governor.

In 1989 I was recognised as a 'Asian Female' Governor in the local borough. Other people from the community started asking me for advise on how to become a governor. If they were already a governor and going through some hardships, they started seeking my advise on school governing matters. I ended by providing support to other governors from minority backgrounds.

Now my role was extending to Advisor and from Advisor to becoming a Governor Trainer.

As time went by and I went from strength to strength, I began to feel good that I was able to help the community and provide some voluntary service. As mentioned before, I was the very few Asian governors plus a woman, I was approached by the Department of Education to help them for their National Campaign for recruitment of governors. I felt very nervous and thought I couldn't do it. Once again I was feeling the fear creeping in. How was I going to look on TV? what would I say? What if? etc etc.

I fought off the fear and decided to take it in my stride and the same thought popped into my mind 'feel the fear' and just do it again!

I gave my interview and came out thinking I had so much to say and I had missed the important parts. But, by this time I had learned that it doesn't matter, if you don't do well or if things don't happen the way you want them to, its all experience and good experience!

I was interviewed by the BBC and my photo and statement appeared on national leaflets. This led my to be invited as guest speaker for various organisations to inspire other 'Asian' Women especially, to become governors too. I remember going to the event and seeing my name as 'Key Speaker' and feeling extremely nervous. I went through fear again, thinking can I do this or not?

I overcame my fear and marched forward each time.

I pushed myself to join a few adult education classes such as Machine Knitting, Asian Dressmaking. I really enjoyed these. I thought of joining more academic classes. Since I had been out of education for many years I lacked the confidence and felt fearful of joining these classes. I felt inadequate to go back to studying after such a long gap, not forgetting the embarrassment I felt of sitting in the class. However, this was another stage of 'feeling the fear'.

I completed my English and Urdu GCSE's whilst being a mother of 3 children.

In between my governorship, I started working as a School Clerical Assistant, which gave me valuable experience and as more positions came available, I felt the fear and applied for them.

I progressed and worked as a Bilingual Support Teacher on a unqualified basis for 3 years. By this time I felt the urge to move on and go further. How could I do this with 4 children, a job and a school governor? But, before I could enrol on the degree course, I had to either complete a year of study at the college or produce a portfolio with a combination of work and voluntary activities. This seemed like such a difficult task at the time and I felt that I really couldn't manage that! To juggle the family, home, school and governorship seemed impossible! After fearing all these struggles, which were on a different level now as you can imagine, I asked myself, Me go to University? No it was going to be too much. However, once again I took the decision and decided to work part-time and embarked on a degree course which were the toughest three years of my life or were they?

One of my units was IT. Can you imagine a person who isn't IT literate going to the first lecture on IT? I came out petrified thinking that I couldn't do this, I would fail! I didn't want to fail, I felt scared.

I completed my degree in 3 yrs and yet was an inspirational in the community. Many other mothers embarked on degree courses after me.

After working and training other qualified teachers, and yet, being on a unqualified teacher status myself, led me to go a step further again. This time to go back to university to embark on the PGCE Teacher Training Program to become a qualified teacher. In order to do this I had to completely quit my job. How would I manage, financially and with a responsibility for four children. How was it going to be possible? Fear was creeping in again!

A good friend of mine, recognised the pattern I had set in my life and for my birthday gave me a book by Susan Jeffrey titled, 'Feel the Fear and Do it'.

I read the book with great interest and once again took the plunge to complete my PGCE. Wow! what a challenge that was, but, through sheer hard work and determination, I managed to qualify and become a fully fledged Primary School Teacher.

After my experiences, I couldn't sit still and was ready to move up and further up the ladder to better mine and my families quality of life.

After teaching for 3 years in mainstream, I had the opportunity to move abroad. With heart pounding and many sleepless nights, I drowned my fears and moved abroad into International Teaching. This was again, something I had never done or had any experience of. Teaching a different curriculum in a different country, but, I did it. I Learned a new way of teaching, living within a new community, culture, language and climate! Despite the fear!

I returned to the UK and couldn't settle, so decided to go back to International teaching again. Having spent a further 3 years abroad, I came back to settle here again. I made sure my life wasn't at a stand still or stagnant.

I applied this principle to other matters in my life and took on projects for my home. I was able to manage home improvement and expansion projects. Again, there was the fear of taking decisions. I feel so happy to say that I am now confident to take decisions and tell myself 'you can do it'!

During my development over the course of 15 years, I am still ready to take on challenges and move on in life. Just recently, with a 13 year old boy to bring up in the Streets of London, with the stabbings, shootings and drug related crimes. I had to make a very important decision - move on, but where?

I visited Turkey for a holiday and decided to look at some properties. Having checked many properties, I chose one, but, felt the fear of investing abroad. Should I take the risk? Well guess what? I felt the fear and did it! Telling myself it is worth a try.

Few months later I felt the fear again about making the move and I took the step of moving to Turkey with my family. Why? I wanted and my family to live in be in a safer place with better climate, scenery and good living. I had no idea of what the curriculum would be in schools' as it is all in Turkish. My son was coming towards GCSE's and he would have to be immersed into a new language, new system, new teachers and new friends. I can honestly say as a holiday destination this was the place and I liked it very much, but moving here was a whole new experience. Even now I am going through moments of fear. Have I done the right thing?

I have no idea where this is going to lead to, but I know that I will need to feel this fear and persevere! I am and have always been optimistic about my decisions, and hope and pray for the best.

My friends always say to me 'you are lucky, you can do it' my answer is 'you can if you give it a go'!

My children today are grown up with their own families. They tell me 'Mum, you're lucky, you've moved on in life, there are people at a standstill, they are where they were 20 years ago, but you have seen the world, experienced life and achieved so much and we are proud of you!'

My message today is 'Feel the Fear and Do it Anyway'!

Rukhsana Nawaz - A Woman of No Fear

Facebook - www.facebook.com/rukhsana.ansari.9

17

Journey through depression and beyond...

14th January 2017, the day I gave birth to my beautiful son, Musa. A day that is etched into the core of my being for a reason greater than the obvious. It is a day that catapulted me into an inner journey of self-discovery and one which I would like to share with you for the purpose that maybe what I write here will resonate with some of you going through something similar and maybe help you on some level.

Was This The End?

After having an emergency c-section and losing a large percentage of my blood during the surgery, I was grateful that my little boy was safe and well. Before I could even hold my baby close to me, I was rushed back into surgery for a second time due to internal bleeding. The cause was unknown and the worry that I didn't have enough blood within me to clot the inner bleeding was a massive concern for the doctors. Non-the-less, there was no choice other than hope for the best. Being wheeled out to the theatre I said my farewells, not knowing if I would come back around. I remember so clearly the panic of the doctors in the operating theatre. As the doctor held the oxygen mask over my face, I just wanted to shout. 'Please stop! Let me think for a moment! Let me get my head around this! What if I don't wake up! What if this is it! I didn't expect my life to end like this! There is so much I still need to do! I've not lived my life yet! Oh God – please forgive me'! No time to reflect I was put to sleep. I woke up several hours later to the sound of heart monitors beeping, oxygen mask on my face, drugged with morphine, wires coming out of every part of me. The surgery had been successful but I was in excruciating pain and could barely breathe, speak or move. Those days after the surgery were a blur. It became all about survival, about healing about getting my energy up and getting back on my feet. God had given me back my life but those early days were a great test on my health. I surprised the doctors on my physical recovery and was out of the hospital within a week.

On the Mend – The Real Test Begins.

I moved in with my parents for a few weeks after surgery. So here I was, being pampered, well looked after, 'back on the mend', grateful for life and a healthy baby. But why was I feeling this sense of loss inside me? This emptiness? Why was there an inner part of me wanting to scream and shout for life to slow down and stop for a moment? I just wanted to reflect yet life was moving at the usual fast pace and I was being pulled back into the commotion of reality. After moving back home several weeks later, I threw myself back into the daily routines and chores of being a home educating mum and housewife. This is when the real test began and one that took me to the lowest and darkest places of my inner world which I didn't know existed. The more I tried to get back into the 'swing of things' the more resistance I was experiencing inwardly. Why was I struggling to do what I had done so effortlessly for years? This wasn't my first baby. Musa was baby 5! Pregnancy, birth, motherhood, home educating – I had done this for time. I was a pro – wasn't I? Why was this time any different? I should be grateful for my life, my health and a beautiful healthy baby. So what was wrong?

I showed up every day in my life – I got changed, put on the makeup, smiled and was courteous. My children saw the other side. I would break down emotionally in front of them. I would use language that shocked and revolted me. A language I had never used before. I would simply abandon them at home for hours and go and sit in a café or a park bench for hours, crying or simply staring into space out of guilt and shame for not being able to hold it together. I would come back home and my children would tiptoe around me. Make lunch for me. Look after the baby while I slept. Leave little love notes, apologising that they will be better behaved next time. I was the adult yet my children were being more responsible than me. I would feel bad, apologise, promise to myself that I was going to get myself together – only to find that I had done the same thing again the next day and the next day. I simply wanted to book a one way to ticket to a Destination Unknown and simply disappear off the face of the Earth without causing a fuss. I didn't want drama. I just didn't want to exist. Why? I didn't know. I didn't know why I was feeling like that but I just did. After many months of staying in this downward spiral of thoughts and emotions, I realised that the only person who was going to help me – was me. I needed some focus back in my life. I had always studied formally and informally and for several years now I had been studying the nature of reality and how everything is governed by precise and accurate laws including our thoughts and emotions. I knew I had to get back on track with studying, understanding and applying the tools of what I had learnt in theory so I could change my life.

Project – Me

For many months after, I simply worked on one project – ME. Everything else became secondary. If I was going to do justice to any of my roles – I had to find me again and bring myself out of this dark place. If I was going to be more productive in life, I had to take some time out from the hustle and bustle of life to develop myself. How is that even possible as a mum of five you wonder? I took advantage of the sacred early hours of the morning. While the world slept – I woke up to be with myself. I meditated. I tried to silence my inner world.

I reflected. This was one of the most powerful practices which gave me many insights and openings of what I had up to now overlooked. My body and mind would rage with me as I tried to tame it. I knew it would. I had studied this and so was experiencing it. I stayed with it. The struggle was so difficult initially. Many times I wanted to give up and crawl back under the rock as a victim of life. I was on my own in this. The pain was real, the journey was hard but it was a path that could have only been travelled by myself, on my own.

The journey was both an outward and an inward one. I was purging everything and everyone in my life that was not conducive to my healthy functioning. Some people we cannot detach from physically so I learnt to detach from emotionally. I went from being a hoarder to living like a minimalist. I literally detoxed my home environment and all my belongings. I felt free. Felt the shackles both mentally and physically being thrown off. I could breathe again. The mind fog began to clear. Slowly things began shifting in my inner world and I felt as if I had been reborn again. I was carrying less baggage on all levels of my being. A new self, a new Sayyida re-emerged. With a greater sense of clarity and focus, I realised the value of my test and the importance of what I had learned as a way of helping others. I was qualifying to become a coach but now I had found my niche. From what I had learned to help myself, I became a specialist in health and wellness and I understood the mind-body-spirit connection from a place of greater empathy, understanding and wisdom.

Reflection.

Reflecting back now, I know what had happened. I can see why I felt the way I did and why I was struggling to get back to 'business as usual'. The trauma that I had experienced was more than the physical trauma of surgery. It was emotional and mental in nature also. Unfortunately, we see the person physically looking well and forget that they have an inner part of them that also needs some love and attention. I had experienced a massive paradigm shift, a massive shift in my thinking as a result of the surgery but I was trying to go back to the old way of life and thus was finding an inner conflict and resistance. This is why I kept breaking down. My inner was not aligned with my outer actions. This was so overwhelming for me that I was unable to think clearly and so life became increasingly difficult and seemingly easy tasks became the greatest challenges.

A year and a half later, I am a different person entirely. Yes, I may look the same, but the old Sayyida died on the 14th of January. The new one has more structure, balance, direction and focus. I am stronger emotionally, mentally and spiritually and can detach from the drama of life and find my own inner peace and happiness which is not dependant on external people, circumstances and situations to be the way I want them to be. I still have my challenges, don't we all? No one is immune to that. However, I can deal better with those challenges which is what we all simply want to be able to do. Life is like a tide. Sometimes the tide will go out and sometimes it will come in. We can't stop the tide but we can control ourselves from being dragged into without floaters on and the skill to swim through it.

Check-in On Yourself – Life is Blessing.

It is so important that WE are able to recognise the signs of what is happening to us on an inner, deeper level so WE can help to get ourselves out of this when the need arises. We need to be able to check in on ourselves. There is no external emotional or mental monitor or app which we can download that can tell other people how we are doing so it is important that we have the knowledge, skills and understanding to steer through life with greater ease and understanding. We have no choice about what life decides to throw at us but we do have a choice of how we overcome and deal with what is thrown in our direction. Life is ever so precious and the greatest gift we have. My wish is that we can all truly experience the blessing of this and really live our lives to our greatest potential as God has intended.

Peace & Love.

Sayyida Bano - Health and Well being Coach, CEO and founder of Freedom Institute.

Website - www.sayyidabano.com
Facebook - www.facebook.com/SayyidaBanoCoaching/
Instagram - @sayyidabano

17

Learning to deal with Dis-Ease the natural way

Six years ago, I lay in my hospital bed, alone, alternately shivering and sweating. This was my fourth day in the hospital and I had just been transferred from the intensive care unit, having been treated for the third time in just over a year for large blood clots in my leg. Twice before, pieces of clots had broken off and traveled to my lungs causing pulmonary emboli - those scary blockages that can literally stop your heart. Now I had a filter in my vein so the clot couldn't go any further towards my heart than my waist, but thick blood filled my entire left leg.

My left leg was swollen and bruised all the way up to my hip, but this wasn't what was bothering me at the time. Instead, the intravenous line in my arm was throbbing and my left hand was red and swollen. While I lay in the bed, I slowly became less and less aware of the room around me until all I noticed was a mild, faraway pain in my left arm. Although I knew something was seriously wrong, I couldn't think or act. I couldn't call the nurse. I couldn't get out of bed or move. And then, this dream/ fugue state actually became very comfortable and I began to relax into a floating nothingness. After some unknown time, I vaguely heard a voice in the background calling my name and then slowly felt someone shaking me. I was told later that nurses had come into the room, started a new IV and begun giving me a strong antibiotic.

Over the course of the next few hours, I began to return from that distant state and began to return to the world around me. The voice I had heard was my husband who had come to visit me late that evening and, when he saw how disoriented I was, had frantically sounded the alarm with the hospital staff.

It turned out that I had an infected IV coupled with a dangerously low blood count - I had bled a lot into my leg over the past few days - had caused me to go into sepsis, a life-threatening medical condition. And, in fact, if my husband hadn't come to visit at that exact time, I probably would not have survived that evening.

As I mentioned, this was the third time in a little over a year that I was being hospitalised for blood clots. Each time, my health and stamina had declined, but, as soon as I was partially recovered, I had returned to work. This time, though, was my true wakeup call.

At the time, I was a busy plastic surgeon in solo private practice. I was married, had two teenagers who were active in sports and school activities and I volunteered both with community organisations and our church's youth group. Yes, I was tired, yes, I was overweight, and yes, I was living on coffee. but I was a surgeon and ran my own business. I didn't have time to slow down, to rest, to…be "weak."

Instead, as soon as I could walk again, I had gone back to standing long hours in the operating room. I even had my staff move a small couch next to my exam rooms so I could rest between patients rather than walk down the short hallway to my regular office. I relied almost entirely on sheer willpower to get things done because I had nothing left to give.

I considered this refusal to rest a badge of honour the first two times I developed clots.

The third time, I finally got the message. It was time to take care of *me* if I wanted to be around to take care of others. *That* was truly honouring my self and my body.

I began by reflecting exactly how I had ended up a three-time visitor to the ICU in just over a year.

I come from a family with "PPP" – "piss-poor protoplasm" – medical slang for those who have a genetic tendency towards health problems. Three out of four of my grandparents, both my parents, and many of their siblings and offspring died relatively early due to various conditions.

Of all of my relatives, my mother was very much into healthy living, way ahead of the recent trends towards wellness. So, our family did better than her brothers and their offspring, but we still had our medical issues.

Long story short: My mother and father died within 5 months of each other, at an age that was a mere 6 years older than I am now. Mom was a previous smoker and died of emphysema, so it wasn't completely unexpected. Dad, however, died suddenly shortly afterwards of a pulmonary embolism, seemingly out of the blue. We now know that the tendency to develop blood clots is hereditary as my sister is affected as well.

At the time of their deaths, I was a surgical resident and experienced a lot of personal guilt because I felt I would have been able to save my parents if I was more experienced and knew more about medicine. I vowed then that I wouldn't let that happen again to someone I cared about and I threw myself into my work and patients.

Then, my own health started to suffer.

To understand the root cause of my present state, it's necessary to look even further back. Although I knew at the age of six that I wanted to be a doctor so I could help people, before I went to medical school, I had been a professional ballet dancer for 17 years. We worked out for 6+ hours a day and I stayed on a pretty strict diet during the week trying to stay around 100 pounds.

Weekends, though, I would eat pretty much whatever I craved – chips, bread, cookies; I'd get bloated and uncomfortable, but I was always better by Monday. I got away with eating this erratically because I was young and very active, but this was the start of some of the inflammation and gut issues I would develop later.

When dancing and touring the world became more painful than they were fun, I had returned to my first love, medicine. After having two children, sitting in medical school classes all day, and then a move to North Carolina in 2002 (with all the fried foods, grits, and biscuits that meant!), I gained 35 pounds, developed hip arthritis, and eventually had to have several surgeries, culminating in bilateral hip replacements.

But as I mentioned before, I kept going…because I *thought* I had to. I went back to my heavy schedule at work and at home, neglecting myself and my own self care in my desire to make a bigger impact much like many other woman entrepreneurs and leaders.

And eventually, the stress, excess weight, genetics, and the surgeries led to the blood clots that had nearly caused my death.

Now seriously motivated to heal myself, after much experimentation, I changed my diet to Paleo, focusing more on whole foods, fruits and vegetables, which rapidly decreased the inflammation and pain in my body. Then, drawn by its blend of strength, flexibility, and spirituality, I began yoga. Within months, I lost most of the weight and felt a lot better as my body began to regain its strength.

However, I now began noticing issues with new food sensitivities – I couldn't eat bread, for instance, without getting severely bloated, reminiscent of my dancing days, so I became more aware of which foods caused an upset stomach or other GI issues and avoided them.

Although I was eating "clean" by now, I developed an itchy, migrating rash that lasted for months. I was placed on high-dose steroids by traditional medicine which not only didn't cure the rash, but had me so dizzy I was literally bouncing off of walls. It wasn't until I was referred to a functional medicine practitioner that I found out I had what is called a "leaky gut" and was now sensitive to eggs, one of my favourite foods that I ate frequently.

When the rash was completely gone within two weeks of treatment, I knew I wanted to learn more about functional medicine.

What I discovered was that functional medicine is a branch of health care that focuses on finding the root causes of dis-Ease rather than treating symptoms - as, in my case, when I stopped eating a triggering food, my body was able to heal itself.

This literally took what I had learned in medical school and flipped it. Instead of looking at the body as developing a disease or condition that needed to be cured, I began to look at the innate strength and wisdom of the body which might only need some assistance in getting back on track with health.

I began incorporating some of the concepts I was learning into my plastics practice, helping women lose to weight in a holistic manner before they had surgery. Patient satisfaction went up because they now had smoother postoperative courses and better results. Even better, they knew how to maintain and improve those results by calling on their own resources.

Things were going well.

And then the thing I had been so worried about years ago happened; someone in my family became ill. You can imagine the fear that I felt when, two years ago, I opened my sister's front door and barely recognised the person standing there. She was an entrepreneur and had been one for over ten years. Like me, she had been consistently pouring herself into her customers and clients, often neglecting her own self-care.

What I saw when I opened that door, though, was an exhausted, gaunt woman with barely enough energy to stand much less do any kind of work. In fact, she looked as if she wouldn't survive another month.

I remembered the vow I had made to myself when my parents had died - that I wouldn't let another person close to me die due to my own lack of knowledge or action. So I reviewed her medications and some targeted labs and realised that the standardised treatment and bag full of medications she was on were not only *not* helping her, they were actually making things worse because they were keeping her from making healthful, healing choices. She was following them, though, because she had been a busy solo-preneur and didn't have the time or expertise to figure out what was best for her unique physiology.

She was literally boxed in by this traditional, gold standard approach to her health, just as I had been. Once this became clear, together we made some customised changes and, over the course of the next weeks and months, she slowly started to improve.

When I opened her door nearly a year later there, instead of the scary stranger I had seen previously, I saw my sister, a vibrant, happy woman who had been out working in her garden and was back to building her business!

Ballerina to plastic surgeon to holistic MD - three seemingly unconnected phases in my life building upon each other, leading me to what I had wanted to do so many years ago - help people feel better. Today that means supporting smart, busy women to discover their one unique path to optimal health - premiere wellness - so they can live the long, happy lives they want and deserve.

Dr. Susan Lovelle

Founder | CEO
Premiere Wellness
Website - www.premierewellness.com
Email - drlovelle@premeirewellness.com
Phone - 919-925-5910
Facebook - https://www.facebook.com/premierewellnessdrlovelle/
Linked In - https://www.linkedin.com/in/drsusanlovelle/
Youtube - Premiere Wellness with Dr. Lovelle

17

Life is Unpredictable

I started getting involved in Personal Development and got approached by someone from Asians In Business, who wanted me to be an Ambassador of Birmingham... Bare in mind I was broke as hell. This unexpected opportunity had me overwhelmed with feelings of worthiness, undeniable validation and delight, as my stars had seemed to become aligned.

Another phenomenal individual offered me a business opportunity and starting my first business in March 2017 was an unreal and happy moment for me.

It was in April 2017 whilst attending Tony Robbins, that I got my initial breakthrough and felt relieved, happy and was at peace. This was when I sold my most valuable assets just to go on his annual event to make the drastic changes I needed internally.

In May 2017 I joined my first proper network marketing company and got to work. It was successful up to a point and made me feel significant, worthy, deserving, important and overjoyed.

One of the highlights of 2017 was being interviewed by the influential Musart Ellaahi, on her show in August. She recognised my journey and had to have me on to talk about what I went through as ME as a single mother who could barely put food on the table.

In October 2017 I joined my second network marketing company and made it a huge success, with up to 11,000 members. Again I felt very significant and blessed.

One of my biggest accomplishments was to complete my NLP Practitioner Course in February 2018. I started coaching thereafter.

The year 2018 was a busy and exciting year for me...

- In March 2018 I had my first business trip to Alicante. Being my first business trip, I was quite excited like a child waiting to see their birthday gift.
- In April 2018 I went to Poland on a business trip. Life can be so unpredictable.
- In May 2018 I visited Latvia for a business trip. I really enjoyed it.
- In July 2018 I had yet another business trip, this time to Barcelona. What an amazing experience!
- My next trip was to Paris in August 2018. I wouldn't have minded leaving with a French accent as French is a beautiful language.
- In September 2018, Amsterdam was my destination for a business trip.
- I was interviewed by Birmingham Mail about my arranged marriage to my cousin in Pakistan.
- October 2018, I was privileged to go on a business trip to Portugal.
- I joined my third network marketing company and made a whopping $20,000 in three months.
- Started speaking at events in November 2018.
- 2019 was no different, as I joined my fourth network marketing company in March and have built a team of 5000 to date.

I enjoyed a three week holiday to Bali, Kuala Lumpur, Melbourne, Sydney and Hong Kong. Never in my wildest dreams could I imagine all this happening to me.

I was honoured to be a guest speaker at The Global Women Empowerment Summit in July 2019.

Columbia, Dallas and Southfork Ranch were also places which I have visited.

With the grace of God, I won the 'Best Inspirational Speaker' Award in October 2019 at The Reeba Awards. Never could I imagine being so eager, to wake up filled with gratitude.

To come from being penniless to an amazing life of traveling seemed unreal. It really shows that God truly works in mysterious ways. I was excited about the way my life took a dramatic turnaround.

Whilst looking back to when my life started meaning something, I'm still in awe of where I am today. My story was written to inspire others to never give up, stay positive and to embrace the idea of Personal Development. And this all happened after I decided to take the plunge into getting NLP for myself and today I have built 10x over of what I had invested.

I know my story is in chronological order but its to show YOU reader, that look at the domino effects of making that one positive change and keeping within that energy. I decided to never be let down or take anything negatively again. I am Normi and I will always be flying!

To know more about me and how I triumphed through so many battles because if I was to list them all here, I would need a book myself! You may get in touch with me and lets talk about moulding a unstoppable mindset!

Normi Rose Khwaja - NLP Coach - Award Winning Inspirational Speaker - Marketing Expert.

Facebook - www.facebook.com/nomana.khwaja
Instagram - @Normitravels

17

A whole new world

The year is 2020 and the world has changed. There have never been as many opportunities as we have now, we are living in a privileged world, where the world really is your oyster.

Growing up in Tanzania, my exposure to materialistic things was limited. Don't get me wrong we were still very lucky and had more than others did. In all honesty, I had a great childhood, the kind I wish my kids could have now. You know the kind where you have no fear, no inhibitions and you can totally embrace the joy of just being a 'kid'.

My story isn't one of extreme hardship or wrong doing. My story is about focus. It's about priorities and about how upbringing plays a big role in moulding your future.

My parents are from a humble background. My father used to be a workshop manager before he invested in his own business and my mother was a beautician and then a housewife for a long time before she started her own business too. Neither of my parents have any diplomas or degrees, they both worked very hard, sacrificing a lot of things to make sure we got the best in life, and the top of their priority was education.

From a young age, education played a key role in my life. I would stay up all night revising and memorising and making my own notes so that I could get those A grades! All along, my mother stayed awake with me, she would make a large flask of tea/coffee and she would make sure I was ok.

For me as the first born, the pressure was immense. I had to perform at every level, primary, secondary and then further education. I felt that I had to make my parents dream of having a degree, come true. So I left Dar-e-Salaam at the age of 17, to move to the UK to pursue my education further.

This was where the mindset shift happened. These were the years that shaped me into the person I am now. Leaving home at 17, to move to a country that is totally unbeknown to me and with no familiar faces or surroundings, this was one of the hardest things I've ever done. You don't realise how resilient you are until you've experienced something like this.

I'm a sociable person, so I made friends soon enough. I learned the way things were done in the UK, I also experienced racism for the first time in my life. It was an unpleasant experience needless to say. But I missed my family. I longed so much to be home.

This whole experience taught me to be resilient, it also taught me patience and how to manage my anger. All this would come in handy when I moved to Leeds for my university years.

I owe a lot to my parents and the way they raised me and my siblings. Although there was pressure to perform, there was never pressure to do something you didn't like. The motto was always 'do what you love'. We also didn't have the strong stereotyping that you see in some Asian households. Both my parents had their own businesses and both were independent. They gave us freedom to pursue what we wanted to.

I was already a columnist at The Daily Mail in Tanzania, by the age of 16, and it was their trust, support and encouragement that led me to educate myself further.

I studied communications and law at Leeds University and was one of the first to graduate and have a degree in our family. This was a big deal. Like a really really big deal. Did you ever feel this? You work so hard your whole life for something and then you reach your goal... the level of satisfaction and gratitude is immense.

But the struggle is to then use your degree to get a suitable job, build your career and earn a good living. How many of us can successfully do this? It's tough. Really bloody tough. No one prepares you for the hundreds of rejection letters you're going to get. It's really disheartening. But I'm a big believer that there is always hope, I'm the 'glass is always full' kind of person. So I persevered.

I had moved back to Tanzania, I was working as an editor for a small monthly publication.

It was whilst working on this publication, that I got a phone call from a familiar person, it was Nick from the Daily Mail (my first job). Nick found my name on the publication and contacted me to go and work for a new daily newspaper that he was launching for the biggest media group in Tanzania. From thereon the journey changed. I could see the light at the end of the tunnel, things were looking up and I felt a sense of pride in all I had achieved.

It wasn't long before I was working in the corporate world, I was appointed as head of marketing for a telecoms company and loved it. It was challenging and rewarding. I was in the press, on tv, launching 4G, rebranding and it was a full on learning experience. Hands on learning is the best kind of experience you can get. I knew then, that I wanted more, but I left the job to move back to the UK to be with my now husband.

When I moved to England in 2007, little did I know that I would be doing what I am today. My experience led me to two great jobs here, but when I got made redundant, I took a reflective approach. I was 30. What did I want from my life? What happens when I have kids? What kind of lifestyle do I want to have?

So I dived into the deep end. Spent the money going into a retail business with a partner and starting my photography business alongside it. A year into the business and I knew something had to give. I had become a recluse, I was working 7 days week, didn't really get time to see my husband or eat properly and I was a size zero. Burnout is real. When you need to let go of something because it's no longer serving your wellness, however tough it is, let go.

I left the partnership.

I loved forward with my photography business which is now in its 8th year. A successful, award winning business where I'm lucky to be referred by clients. I go above and beyond for my couples and many have become friends.

It's not been easy, there were tough times no doubt but I overcame them because I had a good support network. Which is so vital when you work on your own. Especially when I fell pregnant with my first child, there are so many what ifs and buts that go over and over in your head. I knew then what I had to do was expand my business and bring in associates, I also knew I had to outsource. This may sound like madness to you, what a crazy idea you might say, get a team together whilst you're pregnant! Well, sometimes you need to push yourself out of your comfort zones.

So I put my trust in someone else, and it worked. In fact it still works now. There is no way you can grow a business if you don't grow yourself. There is no way you can increase your revenue if it's just a one woman band, especially in my field of photography. Having a team means that I can now take on more bookings, have reliable people in my network that I can call on when I need them and expand my business.

Fast forward to now. I'm now running three businesses alongside being a wife and a mum to two amazing boys, it is a crazy juggling act. I could join the circus. But I wouldn't change this for anything. The new mantra is 'I'm doing this for them as much as for myself'.

In late 2017, I launched Successful Superwomen. Little did I know the impact it would have. Within two years it has become one of the most valued spaces on Facebook for female entrepreneurs. A safe place to express your views and to get advice. It's a real platform, there is no pretence, no bullshit and our ethos of collaboration over competition is truly encompassed in everything we do. I'm so proud of what I've created, Im in awe of so many of the women in our community. It's all about helping women come out of their shells, empowering them with the right tools to succeed, giving them the opportunities and providing support. All of the things I wish I had when I was starting out.

It's one thing running a business and another thing running a business alongside raising a family. But when I look back at how far I've come and all the teachings of my parents and all the hard work that went into getting to this point, I am proud. I'm grateful for all the sacrifices my parents made so that I could be where I am today and I only hope that my children grow up to remember me as someone who was always doing her best.

If it wasn't for the constant push that I got from my parents, the urge to learn and get that degree, I probably would have not come this far. They gave me the best gift, education. My hope is that with Successful Superwomen, we can continue educating women and providing them with the support they need to succeed.

To anyone who has got this far, your dreams can be a reality. You can make it happen. Write your goals down, take the plunge and start the business you want to and don't be afraid to ask for help. Don't listen to anyone who has negative views, you know yourself the best. There are naysayers, who will always question you and how you're going to do what you want to do, let them question, you don't need to answer to them. You can be a mum, a wife, a daughter in law and a successful businesswoman. You absolutely can.

The year is 2020, the world has changed so do what you love and love what you do.

Bhavna Pandya-Barratt - Founder of Successful Superwomen and Bhavna Barratt Photography

Website - www.bhavnabarrat.com, www.successfulsuperwomen.com
Facebook - https://www.facebook.com/bhavnapandyabarratt
https://m.facebook.com/groups/successfulsuperwomen
Twitter - @bhavnabarratt
Instagram - @successfulsuperwomen

17

From being possessed to being free

Twelve years back from now I was having a lot of extreme paranormal activities in the house. These activities had been going on for a decade. I had been overlooking them and assuming that these were to do with my imagination, that it wasn't actually happening. I did mention to family and friends here and there but I was told "It's only you saying this, it doesn't happen when somebody is around or in the house." As years went by, paranormal activities starting taking a height; from pillows flying across the room, from the TV turning on to off. From flowerpots literally not dropping, but being thrown into the air. It had now reached a situation where my children were being lifted into mid air. Soon as I mentioned that my children were being lifted into mid air to family. They actually laughed at me, and said "Gull, you have got some psychological issues." Wallahi, I also thought maybe it *is* psychological, maybe I am thinking into it too much. Because it was only me witnessing this, repeating this for time now my family still didn't believe me. So as we went on I then did quite a bit of research and thought ok lets approach ruqya. (Islamic healing with verses from the Quran).

Lets see if there is any healing from the Quran. I did understand that activities from the unseen existed. But because where my house is situated near the graveyard, I thought I need to change houses, it will be as simple as that. Before I approached ruqya I took a really big move. And I was going to move back to Pakistan. I tried to live in Pakistan for three months, in those three months all those activities that were happening over here, were now happening in Pakistan. This went and proved this has nothing to do with my location. It's all got to do with me. I continued my research and I was very particular with whom I got my ruqya from, I needed total Quran and Sunnah. Alhamdulilah I found the right practitioners. I got a consultation from them, they diagnosed me with multiple issues, they said I was struck with envious eye, I have black magic embedded in me, they also said I am possessed. The minute they told me I am possessed I got up and tried running out of that room. Thinking OH MY GOD! Jinns? Ghosts?! NO WAY!

My husband at the time stopped me and the practitioners also stopped me saying "Where are you running off?" I said "Well you said I am possessed, theres a Jinn inside me." Then they responded "But with you running it's just running with you!" Subhannallah! I couldn't comprehend what they were telling me. So I came back home, I was very fearful for about a month, I didn't understand what was happening. I started listening to the Quran audios that they gave me and started reading the Quran. As I was increasing my recitals of the Quran, and being introduced to more audios and verses of the Quran. Using the sunnah medications, I actually started getting more and more ill. I got that ill that I ended up in a wheel chair. For a month I was hospitalised. The Doctors had no idea what was going on with me.

In the early days I didn't know I was possessed. I didn't know that I had spiritual issues. No idea. And on that note I also want to make it clear that I was actually living a very normal life. People can be possessed and live a very normal life and they wont even know about it. It was just that I had blockages and everything that I had tried to do I would always fall and hurt myself. Something big and dramatic would happen to me. All of This was actually happening due to the spiritual issues. It was hassad (jealousy), it was nazar (evil eye), it was jinn possession. I was living a normal life and I was not even aware of it. I went for hajj at the age of 25 and I am 42 now. When I came back from Hajj I suffered quite a bit for about a year or so. I had no idea why I was suffering the way I was. But my salah (prayers) was still fine. A year after hajj, I suddenly started to feel lethargic. Extremely lethargic, only at Fajar (dawn prayer) time. Now as the years passed, before it was just feeling lethargic with a full nights sleep. But as years passed, I would get out of bed and I would collapse. My knees would simply hit one another and I would collapse bang face down. Many times, if I had a cupboard or anything else to hold onto, so that I don't fall and hurt myself. I would normally tend to drag it and it would fall on top of me and I would be very badly bruised. On one occasion I finally got near the door because in the beginning it was like dragging my legs. I wasn't able to lift them, it felt like I had very bad pins and needles. As time went on these pins and needles became so dreadful that I had to drag myself. I would have let go of Fajar but because I began to understand that this illness was only happening at Fajar time, me being very resilient by nature was telling myself, my body isn't allowing me to read Fajar I am going to make sure I read Fajar. One time I dragged myself up to the door of my room. I would drag myself to the door and with the help of the door help myself stand up and I finally stood up. The door fell off its hinges and hit me on my face and broke my nose at that time. I had to have surgery for it later. It was extremely weird why would a door fall off its hinges like that? It just didn't make sense. So many times the husband I had at the time would actually pick me out of bed and literally make me sit in the bath and open the water to help my legs to move. Cold water would work and make me feel my legs again. But this situation carried on for 3 years prior me going towards ruqya. Alhamdulilah the salahs went on. Now what took me towards ruqya was the same situation in the last year, by the time I was 28 years old. The same situation that was only occuring at fajar time, started happening at Isha (night prayers) time as well. If I made the intention for Isha at 7 o clock my legs and arms would leave me. They would go into pins and needles. If I made that intention at 11pm at night the same thing followed. It was as much as me just making the intention and that was it, my legs and arms would give up. Now over the course of 7 years, I had all sorts of check ups done, everything was normal my blood, vitamins etc everything was normal. We were pretty confused to what was going on.

Whilst during ruqya treatment I started feeling very weak for salah around Asar (afternoon prayers) time more than any other time. Alhamdulilah salah didn't let go of me. Allah subhana talah allowed me to pray. But during the early ruqya of the first 6 months I did fall very ill. What normally happens is when you start to use the Quran as a healing the devil tries to fight back and the person who is possessed will feel very very ill because they are basically being beaten up spiritually for making the devil turn to Allah. At the time and moment I didn't have full understanding of what was happening, but what I did know and trust was this is the Quran, it is shiffa (healing) so I persisted myself in it. Around Asar during ruqya, as soon as Asar would approach I would get shivers running down my body. My whole body would pipe up like I have a temperature. I would start throwing up feeling extremely sick. I can remember in the early days I would be still reading Asar but I was reading it in a sitting position. Other salahs as well when my health would deteriorate I would actually sit down and pray.

A lot of people would for every issue like to blame black magic. For example if there was a divorce that took place they would say it is black magic. Their child isn't passing their GCSE's they would say it's evil eye. In many cases it is and in many cases it isn't. People will run out of desperation to magicians or wrong practitioners. Shiffa is solely from Allah Subhana talah. When the prophet Muhammad SAW got struck by magic, it was to Allah he turned to alone. There was no human or nothing else. He turned to Allah. For shiffa, one dua is sufficient. Now I have so many patients that have come over to me. They always say when am I going to get better? When is this possession going to leave me or when is this infliction going to leave me? Or when will this magic get off my body? And I always say to them, this is a test that has befallen upon you. This test is from Allah subhana tala, Allah puts you in a test, and he will put you in a test over and over again to teach you something. The test will only be over when you will be taught the lesson. A test could be of any nature or a child dying, of a divorce or a daughter in law running away, it could be anything from depression to hunger, it can be in any form. I always say when a test comes to you in the form of jinn possession, then why do you start running towards people. What usually happens is when people are going through possession they will start running to all sorts of people and say we want it out right now. That's not how it works. Jinn possession it not something that you can get rid of straight away. Allah willing, anything can happen. But in a nutshell it is a test to teach you something hence it will take its period of time. When Muhammad saw had black magic on him, he had to see through that for a year. And in this day and time we are such sinful people that we expect it to leave there and then when it left the prophet Muhammad SAW within a year who was so pure? It doesn't work like that.

You have to logically think, people out of desperation are being taken for a ride and people will just take advantage of them, hence self ruqya is the best way forward. Self ruqya is something I would highly promote, listen to the Quran, pray salah, correct yourself, recite the Quran and see what traits within yourself are related to the devil. Try to overcome them and then he won't have anything to play upon you. If you have anger issues, anger is from the devil. Start controlling your anger, if you are a jealous person, that's from the devil. Start controlling your jealousy. Even pride is from the devil, tone it down. Anything that is in your nafs (personality) that is negative start exercising it daily. Then the devil won't have anything to play on you, hence the jinn starts becoming weaker. Jinn possession is something that needs to be weakened and needs to be done in a very optimistic manner. It is difficult, it is not easy because magic is something that has psychological effects. Allah subhana talah said to Musa alay islam, oh Musa magic is nothing but an illusion. Now that you understand it is something psychological it makes your brain become weak. This is where hijama comes in and helps. Continuously have your hijama done. That's what the prophet Muhammad SAW did and recommended when he had magic. Pray recite and be optimistic and when Allah wills it will be healed. For Me personally it took me two years to heal.

That was when I was advised to turn to Hijama, (cupping). I had never heard about Hijama. I remember the very first time I went for my Hijama, the clinic that I walked in, she was a brand new practitioner who had only just started. Coincidently I of all people had to be her first case study. I fainted when I saw everything in the room. Thinking, God knows what kind of surgical procedure is this?! Is she going to start with slaughtering me, because I had never heard about it before! I had my hijama done. At the time because I was very fearful so I found my hijama very hard. But what the sister did was just that and it wasn't so bad. I carried on going to her, every two to three weeks to have my hijama done. My body started feeling better. I actually started getting better with the hijama. One day I was advised to put a cup on my head. Because when the Prophet Muhammad Saw PBUH was struck by magic he was instructed to put a cup on his head. I went for my appointment, and she literally got the biggest cup and shaved a little bald patch in the middle of my hair. I had really long hair. She then took the blood out of my head. I came back home and looked in the mirror, I had this big bald patch in the middle of my hair, and hair everywhere else. Everyone couldn't just stop laughing. I got really really upset. I fell into a psychological trap of thinking I am extremely ugly because of this sunnah and what not. I never went back for hijama again. I carried on with my Ruqya treatment for the coming two years. Alhamdulilah I got better. Soon as I got better, I had it in my mind that a sunnah could not be making someone feel this bad.

So I started learning Hijama myself. I was very passionate towards learning it. My main point was that you put the cup on the head without removing the hair, and yes it was done and worked and doable! Because of my own personal journey and how much I had suffered and how hijama had started giving me life again. It tends to circulate fresh blood in your body. I went and did a course, Subhnallah I started practicing two years later of doing the course. Because I had done so much research, I had learned so much about hijama, I got the position of tutoring. Mashallah it has been six years now I have been in this field. I have over a thousand students in the UK. I work for a particular company. In my business I have never had to advertise it, it's all been a word of mouth. Cupping is a really beautiful sunnah, I would advise it to anyone and everyone to use it. You don't have to have black magic on you to use it. It has health benefits of its own. Its good to have your blood rejuvenated. What it does is it actually energises you, it refreshes you. Hijama brings fresh blood to your organs. Hijama can tackle many illnesses Mashallah. I have had personal patients who have come in a wheelchair and started walking within 6 months with the will of Allah. To be a successful Hijama practitioner I believe it is something that you need to have a lot of sincerity in my opinion because It is a sunnah of the Prophet Muhammad SAW PBUH. You need to practice it with the love of the sunnah. Alhamdulilah as a single parent, it has served me a really good halal income and a very good reputation in the field. I pray my journey inspired you today.

Gull Zaman - Hijamist & Spiritual Coach

www.hijamagull.co.uk

Hopelessness...

Have you ever felt like its so hopeless you wish you could just shut your eyes and never wake up again. I have found that with the true understanding of our human experience and our beautiful religion of Islam. That it is quite possible to transform from that hopelessness to a life that is not only really hopeful but also filled with adventure and purpose. Allah says in the Quran he will never burden a soul beyond what it can bear. When understanding deeply, this truth is the essence to always being ok, even when you don't feel like it. There was a time when I felt it was like so hopeless that I wanted to close my eyes and never wake up again. I was five months pregnant, my two year old son and I were very sick with giardia and I couldn't have any medication until he was weaned, and he did NOT want to be weaned. I had cooked all the food ready for suhoor (dawn meal) because it was ramadan, for my husband and my step sons. I told my husband at the time, "Don't wake me up, I am really sick, the food is there just heat it up and just let me sleep, I am not fasting." At 2am he wakes me up to get his food ready. That was the day I emotionally died.

My health declined very rapidly from thereon, I had the maximum dose of asthma medication and yet was waking up at night unable to breathe. My doctor was so worried about my health, that she actually said to me. "Who will look after your children if you die?" It was at that point I realised that I had to do something. Leaving that marriage; emotionally shut down, physically close to shutting down, and spiritually hanging onto a thread. I began a journey back to me. It started by moving to a city near my father, seeing a different doctor who referred me to a psychologist who had a very respectful appreciation of our religious requirements, so helped me.

I joined a play group that turned out to be a play group for women of domestic violence. And from there I joined their programme, so my journey began with counsellors, therapists, social workers. And it really was a good beginning. After around 6 months I really felt a pull towards my destiny. And I started to seek online classes about Islam. It wasn't much available back then, the internet was still in its infancy and online Islamic classes were quite rare. Alhamdulilah I found something that worked. Getting into the deeper understanding of Islam really helped as well. All the years in that abusive marriage I had really believed what I was being told was Islam and that was not correct. Now I had the proof and evidence, it gave me strength after strength, it really empowered me to stand up for what is right. And stand up for my rights. It was a long hard journey that continued when I came across parenting by connection, and I found a way to help me resolve the pain of my past, were also helping my children with the pain of theirs.

But what really made the difference was in 2015, discovering the inside out paradigm. And the profound shifts and the falling away of my past and self negative self talk, and all the barriers that were holding me back. To reveal the fearless confidence, the inner peace the clarity, the effortless patience. And total resilience, that I have today. Having been through this journey I believed that I had been on a bootcamp to do the work that I do today. It started with parenting by connection and wanting to teach the world how to parent that way. So that we can end the cycle of abuse and generational oppression by working on the adults and the children at the same time. But once I understood the inside out paradigm I could see that this was a lot more than just parenting. What I saw unfold in my mind, was a vision of a different world. A world where domestic violence, wars, bullying, discrimination fell away. And love and compassion came forward especially in the muslim world. I envisioned this beautiful fusion between the inside out paradigm and the teachings of Islam. Being taught in schools and in communities across the globe. So I founded Back To The Fitra Mentoring Academy. And started training other sisters in how to do this beautiful work. The most amazing thing about this work is watching when that light switch is on. One Week a client will show up challenged, frowning, shoulders slumped and then the following week it will be like a bright light shining from their eyes. This sitting tall, grinning from ear to ear. And I will know the insight, the understanding has hit home for them. Seeing that shift and hearing their stories is the most powerful reason to get up every single morning and to continue this journey of entrepreneurship. Which isn't easy, its filled with challenges, failures and a lot of disappointments. But none of that matters when you see the changes it makes in others lives by sharing this amazing understanding.

If you asked me if I wasn't doing this is there anything else I would be doing, I could not imagine anything else, nothing else matters except sharing this across the globe, and giving everybody the opportunity to live with fearless confidence, inner peace, effortless patience, and that emotional and spiritual resilience. So theres always hope and that is the message that I'd like to leave you with. If Allah Subhanatallah says he will never burden a soul beyond what they can bear. Then there is always hope.

Kahtryn Jones - Emotional Resilience Coach, Parenting Coach, Motivational Speaker and Author

Website - www.kathrynljones.com, http://BackToTheFitrah.com FREE gift WeRallOK.com
Facebook - https://www.facebook.com/kathryn.jones.37
Instagram - @coachkathrynjones
Linked In - https://www.linkedin.com/in/kathrynljones/

17

When I nearly lost myself

I was a career minded working very hard to achieve my master's degree for a future to run my own business. With this and passion for travelling, I always knew deep inside that I was different. I was determined to make my parents proud who sacrificed so much for me and my siblings.

I didn't have any pressure of career choice nor the life partner, I would choose. My family only wanted what was best for me and to make them proud.

I was always expected to be there for others when they needed me. I really struggled to find genuine friends throughout my childhood, as I was the first one to go to university in my family. Many weren't happy and tried to persuade my family to stop me from pursuing my dreams. My parents ignored them and trusted me completely. I was never restricted being raised, but I never abused my freedom. The so-called community would label me as the bad one, as they didn't trust their daughters and couldn't be happy for me either. This didn't stop me from pursuing my dreams. I had my parents full support and that motivated me. "A lion doesn't lose sleep over opinion of sheep."

At this point I was a TV presenter. Jealousy escalated, as I was meeting and networking with celebrities. I was around celebrities, who I used to idolise as a child growing up.

Sadly this made my Asian friends disappear, because they felt I was too high up in the clouds. I ignored this and pushed forward to reach my destination to success. Through all this negativity, I always included my family and supportive parents with events and opening exhibitions.

As I was reaching my set goals, the jealousy increased. Those who tried to persuade my parents to not to allow me to go to university, hated my success even more. From the age of 7 I was a target of black magic, whilst I was in Pakistan. This escalated whilst growing up and becoming a young woman, who wanted to make more of my life. I stayed true to myself and never compromised my religious upbringing & beliefs.

When I turned 31 my mum was facing health issues. All the pressure came from everyone who knew me, about getting married. Eventually I gave up all my dreams and decided to settle down with this one individual who I met through a friend. I knew I could do better, but due to the pressure I told my mum that I have met someone and we're getting to know each other. She was glad for me, as I had a disappointment before with a man, whom I met in the media industry.

Bare in mind that I was still under the influence of black magic from a young age. I told the new man to get the ball rolling, but he would always make excuses. He told me his mum had cancer, but this was part of his lies to get my sympathy. I was very naive. He had painted a horrible picture of his mum, but I encouraged him to mend his relationship with her.

When he told his mum about me, she wasn't happy at all. She told him that she wouldn't give a cent towards the wedding. After a while when she saw me as someone with money, she agreed to the first meeting with the parents. Our engagement went well, but his extended family continually interfered. I chose to stay calm, but eventually I wanted to pull out of the wedding, as I was tired of his family's verbal abuse and interfering. He then emotionally blackmailed me by threatening to commit suicide, if called off the wedding. I realised then that everyone would label me and I would bring shame to my family. Although depressed, the wedding plans continued even though his mum was angry with the cost of the engagement ring he bought me. He had to pay for everything. She always controlled him.

My parents were very involved with the community and as a family we were always there for each other. His mum was threatened by this. From the beginning my parents made it very clear that I would continue to work and that I would see my parents whenever I wanted to. They agreed to this, but deep down I was hurting inside and I was too embarrassed to tell my family. He insisted on a smaller wedding, but there was no way I would agree to a quiet send off.

My family celebrated my wedding like they would for a boy. Girls are far more valued in my parents eyes. So the 7 days celebration started with quite a few issues. Just a few hours before my mehndi, someone tried to cancel the venue. We sorted that out, then during the mehndi ceremony, my mum's uncle fell ill. The celebration continued as normal. The in laws tried everything to embarrass me, but I stayed calm. They came dressed casually which caused some to whisper their shock. The community felt our marriage wouldn't last long, as his mum tried everything to break me. My mom cracked her hip falling down a ladder, on the day I was supposed to have my mehndi. She felt she was pushed. It felt as if my mum in law was reciting evil magic to stop the wedding from happening.

On my wedding day, I had one loyal friend from London. She was my bridesmaid and I'm still in contact with her today. There was lots of bickering and sabotaging taking place, but my friend kept me calm.

At my in laws house all food were packed in freezer bags with names on it. Cupboards were separated and I was not allowed to touch any other pots. I would still clean the house which was very dirty, which made me catch bacteria within days, my allergies were out of control and my eczema got very bad. I was so unhappy and felt all alone. My husband was always pressured for his money. He even wanted my money and gold that my parents had bought me. My mum in law asked me to leave my gold with her for safekeeping, luckily I was warned by the other daughter in law about her thieving ways. That's why I chose to leave my belongings at my mum's house. I felt like a maid in the house, as nobody else would lift a finger. Although I cleaned, cooked and worked, they made it seem like I didn't do anything. The only issue I had was that my husband didn't want to communicate with me. He would be out with his friends or at his cousin's house. A few times he would ring me home to see if I'm OK. Nobody would talk to me. I would come home from work, enter the room and then everyone would go silent. Then they would go to their rooms and leave me there all alone. I never felt welcome, but I carried on. A few times I fainted due to not eating well. I would only eat properly when I was at my mum's house, because his family hid everything. My husband didn't seem to care.

We were only married for 2 weeks when I lost my grandfather. The same day his father lost his cousin, my dad had come to get me. I was busy feeding the guests that already came from a distance to pay their respects. I would be made gossip in the family, if I hadn't fed them. My dad told me the devastating news of my grandfather's passing, but they wouldn't allow me to go home with my dad. After my dad and his friend explained the need for me to be at home as the eldest daughter, and my mum needed me she was bed bound, my husband finally agreed. His dad, sister and sister in laws came to pay their respects. That's when my husband started to see the light. His mum never taught him much, other than to play mind games. When he saw how my family was, he told me: "Nosheen, I wish my family was like yours; My mum hates me." I then told him that his family had misunderstandings and that he had to work on it to better their relationships. He took my advice and actually started to change.

When his mum and aunties noticed, they went back to their dirty ways. His mum went to a so called spiritual healer and bought talismans to break us apart. Bare in mind I have lost my grandfather, my mum was bed bound, I was left feeling stressed as hell. I had to watch over my shoulder all the time. My husband didn't take heed. He became ignorant. The black magic was taking its toll. I was all alone, my family stopped coming to see me as my in laws always mistreated them.

One night my husband decided to go out, I said "I'm coming with you." He told his mum that we were going out, but she wasn't happy. We ignored her and left. That night I found out that my husband was cheating on me with another woman, she had even helped him pick out his wedding outfit. The stress in their house left me too unaware to notice.

He kept disappearing to see her and made late night calls on Facebook. When I confronted him, he denied it and made stupid excuses. The more I inquired the more verbally abusive he became. I had had enough. I was mentally exhausted, my weight was dropping, I felt isolated. My in laws treated everyone badly, so everyone just stayed away. Only a few I messaged here and there. They all thought that I was happily married. Nobody knew of my silent suffering. I overheard his mum saying that if he planned to leave me, then he better not get me pregnant. Otherwise he would be stuck with me for life. What type of mother was she? Then I realised I was not the first daughter in law who was despised. She even lied about her cancer to gain sympathy from everyone. The only medication she was taking was paracetamol, which I had once personally gave.

Day by day everything fell apart, we argued continuously and he said some hurtful things to me. I retaliated, by telling him he's fully controlled by his mum, and couldn't take responsibility as a man. How he never cared for me. No one prayed or recited the Quran in that house. I told him: "You're all evil!". His mum also got involved in the argument, but his aunt from his dad's side told her to back off. I got to learn their dark plans for me, whilst he was high on weed. He spilled the beans it was a mutual agreement between him and his mum for him to get my money and she would get my gold.

The arguments got worse, which escalated to something like a horror movie. The police got involved, due to my mother in law calling a meeting, which got out of hand. My dad called me and upon hearing the commotion, he called the police to my in laws house. The police advised me to get my stuff and leave. My husband followed me upstairs begging me not to leave, but I had already made up my mind. The next thing I knew he was strangling me. The police had to intervene. My dad came in time to fetch me. My husband had the nerve to ask if he could keep the iPad & other stuff which I bought him. I told him to keep everything and to give my other stuff to his mistress. I didn't want anything.

His mum was happy now. She had got what she wanted. The only thing she needed was to get us divorced. Even after that horrible incident with the police, I tried to make our marriage work. I begged him to move out. I'm not one to easily give up or walk away. His best friend kept him away from me, making it hard to get hold of him. His mum knew that I was not completely gone yet, so she bought even more black magic to secure herself. Out of the blue, he sent me a divorce. It didn't phase me, I actually took it well considering he was never man enough to stand up for anything.

eventually his lies caught up with him. He attempted to reconcile, but this too was one of his sick games. He e-mailed me asking for us to try again, as he had made a mistake. He explained about being being angry and being pressurised. I so badly wanted to believe him. I even agreed to meet him thinking maybe he had changed. I told him that his friend is not good for him who will destroy him just like his mum. Little did I know that my husband was playing with me again. He was alone now, after his little mistress left him, thats why he wanted me back. But luckily I didn't go back.

I got out from that toxic marriage with my parent's support. He couldn't stand the fact that I had moved on. I maintained myself, held my head high and thanked the Almighty for protecting me through everything I had to endure.

After a few years, I was pressured again to settle down. I was 35 now and thought that maybe this time I would choose someone more mature and practicing in Islam. I definitely wouldn't live with in laws ever again. I met my second husband a few times he was 7 years older than me, who had been married before and had 3 children. He was diabetic and had to inject himself. Which I didn't mind. His parents passed away years ago and he didn't really have a relationship with his kids, nor with his siblings. He basically only saw them when they needed money.

He wasn't working, but was in the process of buying a restaurant. My father liked him, but my mum kept asking me if I'm sure about getting married again. Eventually we decided to get married soon, as he felt it was silly to wait for summer. He lived in Walsall, he was renting and said he invested all of his money into the business. We were carrying on as planned. His sister wasn't happy as she wanted to set him up with a friend. We got married. He received the keys to the restaurant in April, 8 weeks after we got married. He rented a flat up the road from the restaurant. My dad helped with the moving. His sister wasn't happy about this moving, but little did I know that she also was into black magic! She made up lies about me to my husband. He told me all his money is tied in the business, so I agreed to put a deposit on a house, since I couldn't travel up to see him all the time. When my parents went on pilgrimage, my sister in law and I decided to do a home revamp as a coming home surprise for my parents. Everyone thought he was the perfect son in law. We paid my husband for the paint. He decorated, knowing this would cause my parents so much joy. I would come home from work to cook, he disregarded my food. He always ate my sister in law's food. When I asked him about this, he said my sister in law worked hard and cooked all day. I cooked to please him, that meant nothing to him.

I helped him to set up the restaurant, built his confidence, he was so rude to the staff and customers. He didn't know how to treat people. He was a narcissist. The staff loved and respected me. People were shocked to learn that I was his wife. My mom still wasn't very fond of him and he was well aware of it. He hardly had time for me; always saying he was ill or tired. But he was never too tired to chat with women on Facebook. He made me feel unattractive in many ways. One night when he was out, I was in the flat doing chores. I saw a message pop up on snapchat. It was a woman sharing pics of them. I found out later he was married several times before. I was his fourth wife. His sister once told me about his third wife when I was at her house. When I asked him about this, he said it only lasted for 4 months and that his sister is psycho. This made me angry and feel betrayed. He also never told his kids that we were married. He didn't want any pics of us together on Facebook, as his kids would see. Then the weird stuff started happening. His ex wife (no.3) started to contact my friends whom I haven't seen in years. She saw he had moved on with his life. She told them to warn me to not invest money into his business. I requested him to please ask her to stop. He assured me that he would handle it. She was persistent to the point that she sent me a friend request on Eid which I showed him. She made it known to my friends that he was with her, when we were married. She sent pictures of them together. I thought she was just a jealous ex wife trying to cause trouble.

My family wasn't aware of what was going on. His ex wife was so adamant, she sent pics of them together to me. I rang him and said I'm coming down to the restaurant. I was now fed up. I took the keys then went back to the flat and waited for him. He knew that I was livid and decided to come in late. I asked him about her, he said it's his ex wife and he would handle her. His children decided to come back in the scene. They still didn't know we were married. He wanted to keep me a secret. His business wasn't doing well. Then he expected me not to be there when his kids were. I couldn't even sleep there when they came. I reminded him, I made a lot of sacrifices he must tell them about me,

I'm not going anywhere. His lies were catching up with him. I involved the police with his ex wife harassing me. Apparently he still owed her money. She was adamant to tell me that he's a fraudster who preys on vulnerable women for their money.

He was having extra marital affairs early in our marriage. I heard he was involved with a 16 year old girl too. His girlfriend was a prostitute with 3 kids. He would buy her perfume etc. She would visit the restaurant and I was none the wiser. His staff noticed his behaviour towards me and didn't like it. When I told my parents everything he did they were angry. I showed my dad his ugly messages to me and how he treated me. This gave me the courage to leave. Through all this I met my guardian angel who helped me back on my feet. I was ill, lost a lot of weight and felt as if I was dying. I was suicidal too. My angel, family and friends told me that he was a cheat, he didn't deserve me. I slowly got back to my senses and started over. I went back to work after being sick for months. He lost the business and went bankrupt. His girlfriend stole everything and left him with nothing. That's karma right there. Slowly but surely I realised that I'm worth more. I pulled myself together with tough love from my beautiful angel. I refused to stay down and I knew I had to fight to survive. Allah swt guided me through all this pain, lies, deception etc. I knew now it was never me who was the problem. This was the end of that naive & gullible me. My friends helped me see that I needed to forgive myself and live again. So I vowed to never be taken advantage of again. I would be more conscious of fake people. I went travelling and finally all of the black magic was removed. Alhamdulilah. I was shocked to hear what magic was done to me and realised why I was so weak. Now I am content with my life serving others in the charity I work with. My life revolves around my family and especially my nephews whom I love dearly.

I have learned so many lessons. Cried so many tears. But this new Nosheen has a new life to live with loving parents, a wonderful family, caring friends & my Creator who never ever deserted me. All the duas from people whom I supported with charity and my parents support have made me stronger & wiser. I thank my strong mother for the way she raised me. Without her I wouldn't be who I am today.

Nosheen Iqbal

17

A blogger Mom from Sindh

I was born to see the oppression of women in my community. I grew up seeing the patriarchy as the norm but as I grew older I noticed how differently women are given certain roles that are crucial to human and family life, yet they are treated like second class citizens. With no second option for the daughters of the family, beauty and marriage as their only security rather than the freedom to pursue a career. I use my social media platform to give voice to the stories that need to be heard. Every woman should be able to express their true emotions and take initiative for their own life. I see a community that doesn't support my choices as an independent woman and I give strength to those women and the youth to challenge the patriarchal views. There are supportive networks that have helped me develop into the woman I am today, and I now see the youth are following in our direction.

Being a mom blogger I gained a lot of following from the Pakistani community, and I was given the opportunity to voice human rights issues through Rights Now Pakistan. I am a strong advocate of justice being served in a humanely and decent matters, that does not exclude the government as every democracy needs to be held to account. The journalists and nationalist human rights activists (for Sindh and Baluchistan) are known to be taken through military powers, who are either killed or silenced for fear of losing their family. It is an inhumane way for a society to live when families are being torn apart by illegal and forceful disappearance. Not knowing where their loved ones autonomy is. It is difficult for a community to grow and succeed when people working at a grass root level are plucked out harshly by the autocratic military.

I'm the main provider in my family, I provide for my mother in Pakistan and 3 children. It is a hustle to continue working especially for so many years, it does get tiring and repetitive but I have a spiritual soul. I don't hold value to materialistic objects as I see them come and go as frequently as the weather changes. If I want to get out of my head and into another world, I have my vast collection of books. It is important getting a distraction from the present doing things you enjoy for your mental sanity.

My personal vision is to learn more about self suffering, how to deal with it and when to spot the toxicity of it. I think that at any age, you can go through various emotions and have many different experiences over the years. My vision is to learn about myself again and continue to grow myself as I grow older in the hopes of gaining wisdom. I wish to see my children grow up to be confident, self sufficient and to be able to hold their emotional wellbeing at the highest level. They have my full support.

My vision for the world is that every human has individual freedom, living without fear of the state and community. No harm to any individual and we get to live in a peaceful world. There should be no restrictions or differences between males and females as we are in a different era of survival where we must all satisfy our individual needs and happiness.

This enables me to study and graduate from university while raising 2 children and working at the same time. It was very difficult to juggle all 3 very important roles at once and I did not get the emotional support I needed from my spouse at the time. But I didn't stop in my goals and getting to be where I am today. I'm very proud to have graduated with a degree in Social Welfare, to have a stable job in Mental Health, and to have 3 beautiful children.

I have interviewed many amazing people who are working to bettering the community and making a difference. Which has come to spark that Asian women or any mother for that matter should start educating and managing the boys of the family to recognise how hard females are working and how important their roles are in the society. And how their sisters should be treated equally.

Life has taught me that sometimes the world may look at a woman with a vision of weakness just because we are females. But what a woman is able to endure and achieve is something to be proud of. We are home makers, we build little human beings as mothers and nurture them into amazing adults. We have the strength to multi task and achieve so many goals at once. That is learning to cook if we can't, being a counsellor on a daily, answering the most unusual questions, managing a home and an education/career at the same time, I forgot to mention some even running a business from home. I want women to know they are amazing at what they do. Yes we are emotional beings but be grateful for the hearts you have anything is possible if you put your mind to it.

Razia Sultana - Community Mental Health worker - Blogger - Social Activist.

Website - www.rightsnowpakistan.com
Facebook - www.facebook.com/sultana7

The BEST version of YOU

Hello & Salam to all of YOU! I come to discover day after day that my purpose in life is to support you to BE and GIVE the gift of becoming the BEST version of you. If all is possible right this minute, I want to lend my hand to you and lift you up wherever you are so you can feel inspired, empowered and capable to live your best life in this short journey on earth.

My biggest 2 teachers and motivations to run after this purpose with all my might are:

1. Life is too short: you probably heard this before and it might sound very receptive to some of you that it has kind of lost its meaning. So I invite you right here right now to stop for a second. And take it all in. The breath that you have right now is not renewable and the minute you are reading this you can't take it back. How do you want to live this short life that you have been gifted? What impact do you want to have on the people around you?
2. Humans are meant for greatness and continuous progress because we are initially honoured by our creator: One of the most beautiful verses in the Quran says: " And we honoured the descendants of Adam" Honour has been given to us, all of us. What do we do with it? Think about it, we as human beings are meant for progress in every stage of our lives. From crawling

to walking to learning words to speaking. From elementary school to secondary to college or business or any creative path you choose for yourself. Bottom line we are always evolving and improving. I want for you to live and give in every way possible what it looks like to be great and honoured.

What does the BEST version of you means?

The BEST version of you means rising up to your highest potentials, by discovering your purpose and tapping into your hidden talents to LIVE and GIVE the BEST version of you to the world around you.

Emotionally; you are not a victim of your circumstances any longer. To practice and master emotional intelligence that helps you understand the roots of your emotions, how can you shift them to work in your favour, for your goals and continuous progress in life.

Mentally; how you feed your body, you feed your mind with thoughts and the outcome is the type of life you are living. It is your daily experience of everything around you.

Physically; health, vitality, energy and ideal weight.

The combination of those 3 is the highest version of yourself is your purpose is how you want to show up in this world for yourself and for others, what impact do you want to make?

When you live by the principles of the BEST version of you, you are already creating an impact by modelling and inspiring others around you.

I help people doing just that by supporting them to achieve:

Clarity awareness and physical health.

Which will lead to:

1. Designing the life you want.
2. Freeing yourself from self imposed limitations.
3. Releasing pain and emotions that are no longer serving you.

4. Upgrading your health and body image.
5. Actualising your goals and dreams by creating an action plan to live an empowering and a fulfilling life.

I love to inspire and empower people by giving them a result focused approach with proven tools, resources, and accountability to become the BEST they can ever be. New beginnings are created by taking action!

Let's start with the 3 major components to become the BEST you can ever be:

1-Clarity: There are 3 areas that are shaping your life and have a direct impact on your results and experiences. you need to constantly pay attention to…

Your Thoughts: Learn and master how to Let Go of ANY limiting beliefs and thoughts that have kept you stuck in a life, a body, or a career that you are unsatisfied with. Remember Okay is not enough!

Your Emotions: practice and master emotional intelligence that helps you understand the roots of your emotions and how can you shift them to work for your favour, for your goals and your continuous progress in life

Your Actions: Repeated actions daily creates your habits and patterns: Do you feel stuck at the same weight, same career path, same struggle with feeling not heard or comfort at your home, workspace or in your relationships? Let me tell you; it is not about you, It is not that you don't have what it takes to change any of that. Let's identify those patterns that kept you stuck there, and go on a ride where you learn the mindset and the skill set to shift your way to flourish and succeed.

Have you taken an honest look at your life lately? If you haven't it is time to do so, and it could be an overwhelming idea to take a full look and come with a good assessment on where you are without being confused. So let's simplify this process for you. By using The wheel of life. Imagine your life in a circle, this circle is divided into 8 wedges, each wedge is representing a part of your life. The 8 wedges will look like this:

1. Health
2. Personal Growth
3. Creativity/ Fun activities
4. Significant other/ Family
5. Extended Family/ Friends
6. Home environment
7. Career/ Business
8. Financial/ money

Now put a score in front of each one on a scale from 0-10 with 0 to be the least satisfied and 10 is the most satisfied. Knowing your score will give you an insight and perspective into the most areas that need your attention. You will be able to identify which are the most suffering areas so you can prioritise them and clarify which kind of support you need to proceed into creating solutions to make progress. You will be able also to identify other areas where you feel really good about in your life so it is an opportunity for you to recognise your efforts, pat yourself on the shoulder and celebrate those areas. Other areas might sit in the middle, which means you can list them on your work list but they won't take priority at this time. Working with so many people allowed me to see when you focus your efforts on those suffering areas and get the support you need you are more likely to make progress in all areas of your life. Success is contagious!

Questions and Reflection on your scores on each area to take your clarity deeper:

Are there any surprises for you?
How do you feel about your life looking at your scores?
How do you currently spend time in those areas?
How do you like to spend time in those areas?
What success or satisfaction or a score of 10 would look like and feel like for each area?
What would make that a score of 10?

Choose 3 areas that you most want to improve. Taking action:

Pick 1-3 actions to start with for each of the 3 areas you identified to improve

Taking action means making changes, how could you make space for these changes in your life?

What help and support do you need in place to ensure you have the tools, the strategies and the accountability required to make those changes happen? Examples of support: Hiring a coach, joining a support group etc.

If there was one key action you could take that would bring those suffering areas to balance in your life, what would that be?

"Sometimes you get the best light from a burning bridge".
~ Don Henley

2- Awareness: "*The key to growth is the introduction of higher dimensions of consciousness into our awareness.*" *Lao Tzu*

Imagine walking on a dark road hoping that you will get to your final destination. Awareness is the light that will shine over your path in life to help you identify your thoughts, emotions and actions that can either stand in your way or accelerate your way to success in any area in your life! Begin Here! On a daily basis, what are the thoughts you think about most? What are the feelings you experience? How do you respond or react?

If you pay attention you will realise that the thoughts you think, the emotions you experience and the actions you take are very repetitive. They form your own habits and patterns. They certainly result into the quality of the life you are living right now.

As you recognise those thoughts, feelings and actions make sure that: You don't judge or blame yourself for any of it. You don't label yourself based on tough times, incidents difficult emotions or wrong decisions you have experienced in your life. All of which come and go, we never live a tough time forever, do we? Unless we allow it to live inside of us! Life is all about changing and evolving and you are part of this big CHANGE.

This moment if you pay attention it could be a life changing moment for YOU. The science on Neuropvlasticy is on your side, according to research in that area there are neural pathways that are created in your brain based on your habits and behaviours. This is why it is easy to act out of habit as if it is a second nature. Our brains are constantly being shaped willingly or unwillingly – most of the time unwillingly. So the angry grows angrier and the calm grows calmer. Because those neural pathways in your brain are paved by practice and repetition to produce those results. We're raising the possibility to intentionally training our brains to improve your life /well-being. Therefore you are able to train your brain to create new neural pathways by shifting your thoughts to support a new behaviour that will move you forward towards your goals and dreams. Imagine someone playing piano for the first time, learn, struggle and mess up until it all falls into a beautiful rhythm. Other examples; Like waking up early, exercising regularly, eating for energy and vitality, managing your emotions, practicing sympathy, and the list goes on. Those new thoughts and behaviours will get stronger by REPETITION as you strengthen those new neural pathways until they become your second nature and your new norm.

Finally watch the thoughts that you end your day with, it is easy to keep thinking about the one mistake you have done throughout the day, the one argument, the one negative comment. Train your mind to take the lesson and leave dwelling upon the negative event: if it is a negative comment may be it is your chance to set healthy boundaries with that person. If it is a mistake on your end, focus on which skill or which support do you need to improve. And most of all remember the rest of the day, the minutes, the hours and highlight a few of the blessings you have. It could be being able to see, to hear, to touch. Some sound simple but even if one is lost it is a huge loss.

3- Your Health, weight, energy and vitality: My grandmother used to say a famous Arabic proverb *"Health is a crown on the heads of the healthy people, no one can see it except the ill"*

I loved it and grew up really curious about what makes people stay in high energy, great health and ideal weight.

I came to believe that your body is the vessel that carries you through life every single day, how do you want it to look, feel and be like? How do you want to show up in the world every single day?

It is not your age or your children or the yummy food everywhere you go is the reason why you are having the body you have. It is your decisions. Do you want to be the BEST version of you? Yes or yes? If so Your body, the gift that carries the miracle of life inside of it is and should be your number one responsibility. It sits at the very top of those priorities because it will influence every other area in your life. Especially as a parent this can't be emphasised enough, you are teaching a new generation into how they are going to be taking care of themselves, value their well being and never take it for granted.

The specifics of wellbeing: Fitness: a healthy lifestyle is an active one. Not having enough time could be the number one issue that will jump to your mind. Let me tell you, none of us find time, rather we make time to what matters most. Your health is linked directly to your physical activity. Find resources and exercise routines to follow in the system I will share with you below.

Hydration: Drinking water is a key component to a healthy lifestyle. It flushes body waste. It aids with weight regulation as it prevents overeating and gives a sense of fullness. It makes minerals and nutrients accessible in your body as they dissolve in water. Do you have Reasons into why you are not drinking enough water? Replace them with all the reasons you should.

Sleep: is a vital component to living a healthy lifestyle. Turn off screens an hour or two before heading to bed. Darken the room, journal in your gratitude list, meditate and set an intention to get into a quality deep sleep that will allow you to rejuvenate. More resources in the system I share with you below.

Nutrition: Research has shown that Increasing our intake of fruits and vegetables can help you reduce your risk of chronic diseases such as heart disease and some forms of cancer. The fibre in fruits and vegetables may help to lower blood cholesterol levels and fibre intake is linked to lower incidence of cardiovascular disease and obesity. Fruits and vegetables also supply vitamins and minerals to the diet and are sources of a phytochemical that function as antioxidants, phytoestrogens, and anti-inflammatory agents and through other protective mechanisms.

Despite our best efforts to include as much fruits and vegetables in our diet. Most days we fall short, this is why I have a system that has been helping myself, my own family and my clients around the world. It is a whole food based nutrition made of an abundance of fruits, vegetables and grains. To bridge the gap between what you and your family should eat and what you do eat.

It also offer resources, education, recipes, easy to follow exercise routines and many on the go solutions. You can check it all on here: https://ruba.juiceplus.com/us/en

How are we doing so far? Look I am not interested in having you read this chapter only, of course I love having you but I am extremely interested in having you make a real, solid, and positive changes that will allow you to be the BEST version of you.

At this point: What have you discovered about yourself? Which areas in your life do you want to make radical changes in? Which patterns or habits that are standing in your way? Note that it is easy to point fingers at other people in your life or the environment as reasons into why you are where you are. But it is much more courageous and powerful to look inwardly and look for those answers. Because simply you can't change others but you can absolutely and successfully change YOU. And you will be surprised how other things will change when you do.

This path to making profound and lasting changes in life shouldn't be difficult, long and exhausting if you are equipped With the clarity, the action plan and the road map to make them. This is where I am so passionate about helping people like you doing just that. You can find out more about my coaching programs or scheduling a discovery free of charge session with me by visiting my website.

> *"Your life is the most valuable project that you will ever work on, your goals, dreams and aspirations are not in you to stay silent in the darkness. They are there because you are innately capable of turning them into realities. You just need to find the path"*

Ruba Zanaid - Life & Success Coach

Certified NLP Practitioner
Founder of Healthy Living With Ruba
Website - www.healthylivingwithruba.com
Email - healthylivingwithruba@gmail.com
Facebook - www.facebool.com/ruba.almasri.92
Instagram - @rubazanaid

17

My Papa, My Love

They say behind every successful man is a woman, similarly I believe behind every successful or a strong woman is her father. A positive father-daughter relationship can have a huge impact on a young girl's life and even determine whether or not she develops into a strong, confident woman. A father's influence in his daughter's life shapes her self-esteem, self-image, confidence and opinions of men. In this age of filters and facades we all have our share of failed relationships, I too had my share of relationships that taught me exactly what I did not want in my man. My father had set some really great standards as a husband, father & most importantly as a great human being who made sure he never hurt any body's feelings on the pathway of life. In a typical Eastern "Desi" set up as we call it, while daughter's hit puberty or step in teens suddenly they get slightly distant from their fathers and more closer to mothers which comes naturally. But this wasn't the case with me, the more I was attached to my mother I was equally attached to my father. So much so that often on weekends when I would visit them (living in another city due to work) after work I would nap with them sleeping in between them like a kid holding his mothers hand by snuggling with my Ammi. My father would make breakfast for us on Saturdays which I would always used to look forward to because it had us on the table laughing and chattering away. My father made me dream big and he made me believe that nothing is impossible in life. He always believed in honesty and giving back, be it love, laughter, charity or a good word of kindness.

There was a phase of my life when I started hating men, I was bound to think that way thanks to my love interest who fooled me. I was left shattered and broken to an extent that one night after our final meeting when I came back home I cried my heart out to my mother who hugged and consoled me saying, "A man who can't take a stand for you now will never be enough for you, life has many trials for a wife in our society." Not ready to understand then as I was too blind in love but I remember it was a dark and a never ending night for me, a night that had broken promises rolling down my cheeks, a night that saw me going crazy and crying inconsolably. However that night also saw a father walking to his daughter every now and then to console her with his touch, his words and telling me to have faith for that man doesn't deserves his daughter. He was up all night walking outside my room through the corridor, not willing to sleep until he puts me to sleep. It changed my perspective about my father, here was a man who was consoling his daughter yet he was also saying if I wanted he is willing to speak to him. This obviously wasn't an option I would want him to do for me.

This particular incident my life will always take precedence over many other stories of my life that I have with my papa.

I cannot emphasis enough on how I truly believe that fathers should be best friends of their children. I always felt blessed of having such amazing & supportive parents, for me they were not just my parents they were my buddies, I shared everything with them. We had fun together, we even had our inside jokes. My father would share his hay day stories with us, the pranks, the infatuations as well as the failures. The stories of how he would spend his day when he had no money or stealing the car without his dads permission and all the foolish stories that would make one laugh – because he was a very funny man.

Our society has this huge obsession with the first child to be the son whereas when my mother got conceived with me he told my mother that he wants a daughter who he would name Maha, so technically my name was decided even before I was born. Ammi told me my first word was papa, which made her absolute jealous that despite a child being with her 24x7 my first word was "papa." I was so obsessed with him that in his absence I would play and talk to his picture, that's how much I loved him and he loved me back he gave all his love to his children and would do everything for them within his means.

As all our Desi mothers are always prying and worry about their daughters getting married, speaking to people about it, papa on the contrary was never of this thought. Firstly he wanted my happiness over anything, married or not but definitely doing something productive with life. he never stopped me from doing what I wanted of course that doesn't mean I was given a free hand to do whatever. But I was given enough freedom that I don't get spoilt. The do's and don'ts were clearly communicated to us children in our growing years and the repercussions were also well explained. I was encouraged to speak my mind but not on social media, because of the fear of being exploited in a wrong way due to my views. I was encouraged to meet people from different walks of life and age so the horizon of my thought process broadens. This gave me the confidence and I was easily seen mingling with people of different sects/gender/occupation etc. As cliché as it may sound I had always introduced my friends to my parents be it boys or girls, sometimes it would irritate them by the amount of friends I had but I always made it a point they know them all and my friends know my parents too.

The blow came when my mother passed away. As naïve as this may sound we never want our parents to depart from this world, I would always shiver on this thought of losing them or it won't be wrong to say I always prayed I'm not alive to see a day where I have to be without them, but as the murphy's law state's "If something can go wrong, it will." My mom passed away after a brief battle of a cancer relapse – Stage IV. Papa couldn't contemplate living without her he began to lose control over easily done tasks. We siblings thought it was a shock that he has gone into and it shall soon be over after her demise in sometime. But they say true lovers can't stay apart. We saw his condition getting worrisome within a span of a week. Ammi passed away. It was the 3rd day after her passing away where we took him for a casual checkup thinking the grief has taken a toll on him. Only to realise that we are soon losing him too – papa was diagnosed with a rapidly growing brain tumour which was at stage 2 with in a span of a week. We were in Karachi since we had flew with Ammi down from Dubai for her to die peacefully among her other family members.

It was not our comfort zone but then this dreadful task of hospital visits /tests started again. My siblings had to leave as they had to resume work, while I stayed back with papa for the completion of his treatment to fly back later. However after the departure of Ammi and my siblings to Dubai, me and papa spent a lot of time alone, he talked his heart out, missing Ammi. We would often cry together missing Ammi and how our lives will be without her now. Not knowing that we have to soon live without him too. Those nights were long but the most precious nights of my life. I would put him to sleep every day and he would sleep on my arm like a baby, waking up in the middle of the night asking for water or to feed him something all of a sudden or to assist him to the washroom. I would stand by his side waiting to be done, later I would put him to bed back again but in between that he would keep on blessing me and kiss on my cheeks, whilst holding my hand we would sleep again.

Being by his side through his surgeries/radiations/chemotherapy I realised we seldom think that our parents can ever be in that stage where they are dependent on you for even drinking water, walking, or dressing up but that is the harsh reality. Especially in a country like Pakistan where there is hardly a system to get things done easily. I had to fight the odds to get things done. All that courage, confidence came because firstly I didn't wanted to lose my father, secondly throughout my life he always told me to be strong enough to fight the odds. So there I was fighting doing my bit. Things are a bit tricky in my country, Pakistan. I saw people turning a blind eye when I alone was struggling to make him walk, put him in the car from the wheel chair. Or simply the Careem drivers not putting AC on in the car for a cancer patient on purpose to save petrol. It felt pathetic but it got over when we flew down back to Dubai. The journey of him being my baby continued here but this time with siblings sharing the responsibilities too but to my surprise he preferred me and would get angry if I was out of sight. Soon the dark nights were here, this time when the doctors gave up on him and we too had no choice but to give up. UTI followed by heart attack and the tumour taking over when he was being shifted to ICU. He was in a delusional state holding my hand and fighting not to be tied up with drips and he looked at me saying "Maha." Papa passed away after 15 days. His last words were"Maha". The irony you see here my first word was "Papa" his last were "Maha".

Through all these trial times ever since Ammi was on her death bed and before that too, someone was standing beside me like a rock holding me and not letting me fall after my world fell apart. He was all pally with papa, meeting him and cheering him, sharing stories & his love for cricket and papa complaining to him about me. Papa saw the likeness he had for me, I initially backed out fearing another failure in the relationship and that's when papa said "He is the kind of man you should be with" " What if he leaves me?" I asked papa – "He may disappoint you sometimes but he will never leave you and he'll love you like me". I do feel nobody can ever love you like your parents but than we are all human and we ought to err in this process of life we gain some, we lose some. I have held onto those words of him, I have his blessings with me & his values in me. If there's anything I want fathers to know is your daughters will be your pride but you first need to trust & encourage them to fly high beyond the skies.

Daughters are never to be caged, Let them pave their own path, let them create their own stories.

Maha Jamil

Twitter - @Mahajamil
Instagram - @Mahajamil
Facebook - www.facebook.com/MischiveousMao

47

Awaken the power within

Can you ever imagine the girl brought up like a princess, being the centre of attention and being loved by everyone and after marriage living like a queen…

The girl who came to Australia 11 years ago as a spouse of an international student. Yes, I am referring to myself…

I am Fizza Kashif Khan.

I came to Australia 11 years ago and had started my journey from scratch. When I saw my husband at the airport I got goosebumps which was giving me many different signals and messages but I did not focus on them. We were finally reunited as a family after 6 months.

We started our journey as a family from one small room on shared accommodation with a couple, who had no kids. I was full of hope, dreams and excitement because grass from the other end looked so green. The reality was different. My dreams were totally shattered when one day the landlady was disrespectful towards me by blaming me for something which I did not even know. When I tried to justify myself, she started arguing with me in front of my husband and my 3 yr old daughter. Then we were forced to find another place to live.

Thank God we moved to another shared accommodation again. I started applying for a job. I got disappointed when I came to realise that despite trying everything I could not get a job while my husband was working very hard. I got depressed, anxious and feeling lost because of a new environment, new people, new accent and shared accommodation in a small apartment living with unknown people.

I still remember the day I had asked my husband for 12 dollars to get my eyebrows done because when I looked in the mirror, I had discovered that I had bushes instead of eyebrows! The moment he said no. I was shocked with his response. The one who never asked a single penny from her parents. She asked for $12 and the husband said NO. I looked at him, I knew why he said No. We were financially struggling at that time. I was in a shocking state, he looked at me and gave me that money. I looked up at the sky & asked Allah for help to hold me and help me walk on the path to earn my own money. I am not here to be dependent on anyone. Only YOU look after me... why did I go from being treated like royalty to being dependant on my husband for finances.

Those 12 dollars were a great lesson for me. The Next day I went to the play school and asked different moms for help with regards to finding work and they directed me to the United Muslim Women Association. I went there and attended an appointment with a recruitment officer. I had a long discussion with her. She helped me design a flyer to work as a beautician. I am a qualified beautician because I had done a few courses in my country.

I had to jump out of my comfort zone to distribute these flyers. I was going to different shops and stand near bus stops to distribute flyers, I even put the flyers in the mailbox as well. My daughter was sick so I had to take her to the doctor. It was there where I met one lady and I gave my flyer to her. The very same day I greeted another lady with "Aslaam Aleikum" but because I wasn't wearing my hijab, she asked me if I was a Muslim. I was shocked by the question and I was questioning myself as to why she would ask me something like that. I then realised that what was missing. That was the day I made my own identity and started wearing the hijab.

At the end of the day, I got a call from that lady who invited me to her place for a facial, waxing and henna tattoos. Due to Ramadan (the month of fasting), I started as mobile beautician. In two and a half days, I worked very hard from 10 am -10 pm and earned 800 dollars. I realised once you decide to stand up to yourself, that will be the day that your life changes. Once you decide that you need to do something for yourself is the day that will change your mindset because then Allah knows your intention.

That 800 dollars was the greatest achievement because it was my first earning in Australia and I was extremely proud of myself. The very next day I was in the kitchen when I heard my husband asking the fellow brothers in the accommodation for finances. I quickly entered the lounge and asked my husband how much he needed. He disregarded me by saying "I don't have any money." Once again I repeated my question and upon his answer, I left the room for a few minutes. When I returned and gave him the money he was so shocked and had many questions about where I got the money etc. I simply told him that the money is a result of 2 and a half days of hard work. That day was the day I decided that I would be there to help, support and stay beside him.

As I said that was my first income but after that, I started being a party planner which was only seasonal. I did catering for international students as well. I was looking for something permanent. I kept applying for jobs and eventually I got a job at a BP petrol station. I was confused on the day of my group interview. I wasn't sure if I should go with my hijab because I didn't know if I would get the job with regards to my attire and choice of wearing my headscarf. I eventually decided to surrender myself and my situation to Allah.

When I got to the second stage of group interviews I was elected as group leader and by the end of the discussions, I was approached by the Human Resource Manager. Long story short... I got the job!

It was my first permanent job and I was so happy, however, my marriage was suffering because of our different work hrs. This was straining us and caused constant arguments. We started living like two strangers living under one roof. When he was home to look after our daughter, I was at work. When I was home, he was at work. Life became very busy. No excitement in our relationship, no love, no communication, no intimacy. Just Work and money.

My husband had just finished his studies and we were about to apply for residency but we got the biggest shock of our lives when we couldn't apply for residency due to the change of laws and policy that had been changed prior to us applying. My husband wanted to send us back to our native country. I told him that I will never go as a loser. I refused and decided that we would fight together for residency.

After hearing this news, our relationship was getting worse by the day. We started fighting over small things and turned it into heated arguments but thank Allah, that he had some good plans for us. Somebody had sponsored us with a sponsorship visa. My husband got a job as a customer service manager. We needed to move from Sydney to a remote regional area i.e Bourke Australia. We were the first Muslim family out of 1200 people in Bourke, where the day started at 9am and ended at 4 pm. The worst thing was the very first day we entered Bourke, my husband took us to do grocery shopping as we had nothing at home to cook and parked the car in front of IGA. The local children would come up to the car and swear because to them I was an alien. They had never seen a Muslim woman in hijab before. All they knew or thought was that Muslims are terrorists so that is why I was a total stranger to them. It was so dead with no social activities, no shopping malls so it was basically the middle of nowhere. We were already struggling with our relationship and when I went there I suffered depression for 6 months. It was a total disaster and a terrible nightmare. We remained the only Muslim family in Bourke and every now and then people would throw bottles at our house and try to destroy it. We were going through a really tough time and my relationship was on a edge. My husband got bullied in the workplace. Imagine having no social life and knowing nobody... My husband would come and take his frustration out at home.

One day I was feeling totally lost because of my husband's situation. The next day when he was frustrated, he started an argument with me that turned into heated argument. I began crying because he was screaming and swearing... Thank God he didn't get physical. I banged my head against the wall because I didn't want to live like that anymore.

I became suicidal. I told myself that I wasn't going to live anymore and that I needed to destroy myself. Thank God after having that fight my husband asked me to bring his medicine at the pharmacy. I kissed my daughter goodbye and both she and my husband were unaware of my intentions. I got in my car and began to speed onto the highway. The speed limit was 100km/ph and at that time I was doing 140km/ph. As I was speeding I spiritually saw my father & grandfather holding bull bar of my car to stop the car. It was then when I realised I am here for a reason. I have a purpose. It was not my time to die and that millions of people were waiting for me to inspire them, to help them in transforming their lives. I stopped the car and jumped out while spreading my arms out like wings. I am all yours Allah. I just surrendered to Allah.

I came back home. My hubby and daughter did not even have a clue with what had happened with me. I had dinner with them. After offering my night prayer, I opened up Facebook. Because Enough is enough. I wanted to live the way I want. I contacted a lady on Facebook which I previously refused her help by saying you are very expensive, I can't afford it. I would be OK. I started working on myself with her help and she was the first coach who helped me changed my life. I started my own family day care and became my own boss. It was not successful as local people were scared to send their kids to me, because firstly I was not local and secondly I was a Muslim woman. They have different concepts about Muslims. When I eventually got rid of all my problems, something happened to my husband whilst he was at work and he was hospitalised due to high blood pressure.

At that time I did not have my car at work, my hubby had it and without thinking I started running to the hospital. After all the fights, arguments and threats were displaced... Here I was at the hospital for him. I told him that he would be okay and he began crying. I wiped his tears and kissed him. I left the room and called the CEO from the hospital and told them I would not be staying in Bourke anymore. I don't want permanent residency at the cost of my husband's life. It was the warrior in me that took over.

The very next day they came down to see us. They had a meeting with me and offered me a job as a financial manager in one of their stores. I began working there on my own terms and conditions. This was a great achievement for me. I started going to community meetings, events, participated in community volunteer work. I along with my hubby and eight years old daughter became the part of the local community. People started loving and respecting us. In one of the Events, Pakistan Cuisine Night, I shared my secret recipes with the local community as the Guest Chef, I became famous in town.

We started treating people as we wanted to be treated. Women came to me with their problems. I started guiding them in living the life they wanted. I helped them to not to become victims of domestic violence. It was so great to see them transforming their lives. We got our residency in 2016 and achieved the purpose of living In Bourke.

Meanwhile, I applied for a commonwealth bank job as I was looking for more challenging work to upgrade my skills. Life started looking up for me and I began to have hope again. I enjoyed new job new challenges. During that job in Bourke, I was bullied, harassed and threatened by one local lady that affected my mental health. I had a counselling session and they recommended a transfer to the big city.

We moved to Dubbo a regional area. A new place, new people, a whole new environment again. I started enjoying living in a bigger town. I went to Sydney to attend Tony Robbins Unleash The Power Within Event. I did the fire walk that changed my life, it awakened me connecting me with my purpose of life.

I decided to an NLP Practitioner course upon returning. I flew to Sydney again to do the NLP Practitioner course there, which again changed my life. I didn't stop there, I signed up for a Master NLP Course along with Hypnotherapy. I resigned from my bank job to start living my purpose.

I invested $40K on my personal development to become the best authentic version of who I am. I got a message in that moment to stand up for myself as I am the inspiration for thousands who are waiting for me to help them in transforming their lives. I started investing in myself and transformed my life with the help of a coach, it came to my awareness that everything is within me. When I change myself the rest will adjust. I have invested $40K to fill my cup & let go of negative emotions and all those barriers which were the cause of my terrible relationships. Now I am enjoying my married life with my supportive and loving husband along with our daughter. Alhamdulillah, I am living a purposeful life with a vision and a mission. My mission is helping people who struggle with themselves and are dissatisfied in their relationship because of their lack of love, trust and intimacy to regain trust, love, and intimacy by living happily ever after without losing their worth.

I am a Transformational Coach and a Relationship Consultant. I am The Light Of Hope & The Reason of Smile for Humanity. I am the Voice of Humanity.

The moral of my story is: Never give up. Stay focused. Start living a purposeful life. If you want to help others, fill your cup first, with love, kindness, empathy, patience and let go of your negative emotions and limiting beliefs to live the authentic life.

If you want to transform yourself from fearful to courageous, from invisible to visible, from shy to confident. Then Connect with Me

Fizza Kashif Khan - The Light Of Hope

Website - www.fizza.com.au
Email - lighofhope@fizza.com.au
Instagram - @fizzalightofhope
YouTube Channel - Fizza Kashif Khan
Facebook - https://www.facebook.com/fiizza.k.khan

17

Resilience, hard work and faith takes you where luck alone won't...

When I was born, I was the text book definition of lucky and blessed. I was born in a well settled, educated, broad minded and well respected family in Pakistan. Surrounded by people who loved and cared for me from the moment I was born to this day. I consider myself blessed in every aspect of my life, be it my looks, my confidence, my intelligence, my family, my friends or my social status Alhamdullilah. I didn't realise how lucky I was until I stepped into real life. I feel like I lived in a happy bubble. I was always amongst the top students in my class, taking part in sports and extracurricular activities, well behaved and the apple of my parent's eyes. Being the eldest in the family my parents always wanted me to be a role model for my three other siblings, two brothers and a sister. My mom was a teacher but she sacrificed her career for our upbringing and my father was a banker, with a very progressive personality. Having said that, one thing I grew up with was discipline, there was no compromise on that, we all had our limits that we all had to follow.

I did my Masters from University of Karachi, in Microbiology and got 2nd position. At the time I was the only girl in my family with a Masters degree, so my parents, siblings, grandparents, uncles, aunties all were really proud of me. After that I worked in different places, in a school as a teacher, lab technologist in a hospital and then I worked in a Research Institute called "International Centre for chemical and

Biological Sciences". I enjoyed doing research so much that I decided to do a PhD. I wanted to explore research opportunities outside Pakistan because there were limited research opportunities available in Pakistan for my field of interest. Getting funding and an admission in PhD was not easy. So, me being the daughter of ambitious parents, and having those tough genes in me began working really hard to get a scholarship and admission for PhD. Long story short, after several tests, interviews and long selection processes for a scholarship and then applying to dozens of research groups around the world, failed visa attempts, I finally got an admission in a PhD program in London School of Hygiene and Tropical Medicine, UK.

Finally in 2008 I came to the UK for my studies and that's when my test of life started, from settling in a foreign country by myself to a challenging PhD program. It was all very new and tough for me. In the beginning I found it really hard to get used to the cold weather, food, London accent, a long commute and above all missing my family and comfort, the luxury life of Pakistan. Although most of the people I met in UK were very supportive but there were a few who gave me a tough time because of my religion and Pakistani background. At the time there was a lot of terrorism in Pakistan at the hands of Taliban and because I was and I still am a practicing Muslim there were a handful of people who raised eyebrows and made my life difficult at LSHTM. So much so that I had to pray in fire exits so nobody could see me praying and object on it. Slowly and gradually I got settled in the UK and in my research. I tried talking to people around me and explaining to them about my religion, requested for a prayer room. I along with a few other friends managed to get a multi faith room in my building where it got easier to pray. Just when I thought that my small tests were over the biggest test of my life started.

During this time I was introduced to my husband's family through a family friend, and then I got married during my studies. That was when my real test of life started. The person I got married to was not really what he and his family portrayed to be. My marriage that was supposed to be the happiest time of my life was actually the beginning of the worst 4 years of my life. I still find it hard to talk about it. The image of perfection that I had throughout my life was shattered. Every day was a new test. I was trying my best to please my husband and save my marriage, but there was nothing I could do to win his heart, as it never set on me in the first place. I couldn't understand that this person who has married me so happily, why was he not happy with me and not treating me the way I deserved? Why is he not interested in me? I was not good enough, never enough. All my life I was told that you are so pretty and beautiful, but for my husband I was ugly, not attractive, he was always putting me down. For a woman those words are like daggers. His anger issues were so bad that he would break things, throw things and I would never understand the reason. I gave up everything, my social life, my friends, my family, I lost interest in looking after myself. In the end even talking to my parents over the internet once a day was a problem as well. Mentally and physically when a husband's interest dies, a women knows for sure that something is wrong. Till date I am unable to pin point what was the problem, why he initially found me attractive enough to marry me but once he did there was no interest.

He wanted control over everything that I did, where I go, even to the extent of when I talk to my parents. After doing everything in my capacity, and still when my relationship got to physical abuse I decided that's it…I asked my parents for advice and told them I can no longer get this marriage going. After the involvement of my parents, apologies from him and assurance from his family that things will change for better I decided to give this marriage another go. To my surprise his behaviour did get better, and that was the time I had my beautiful son. But soon after that situation again changed for worse. My husband lost his job during my pregnancy and that was because of his bad temper and anger issues at work. Meanwhile I managed to finish my PhD and got a job at LSHTM, the same place I got my degree from. The extent of his control was that even after my PhD he didn't let me use "Dr" with my name. So after I had the baby I was at home during my maternity leave and that was the time my life was made hell. I was constantly being watched, put down and harassed.

That was when I finally decide that I cannot raise my son in this environment and I don't want him to see this treatment of women, I didn't want him to learn this behaviour, this empowered me to leave. But now the problem was where do I go? It was easier to leave before my son was born, because I could have just left and go back to Pakistan and never look back. But now a child was involved and the law didn't allow me to take him with me to Pakistan. I decided to take legal help and got in touch with the Southall Black Sisters. When he found out that I didn't want to live with him anymore he got really upset and took my son away from me, he said he won't let me see my child again and locked me in my room. I managed to call 999 and eventually I was rescued along with my 9 months old baby. I managed to leave the house with the help of the Police but those few hours that I had to live in uncertainty if I will ever see my baby again are the worst hours of my whole life. But this experience changed something in me it shook me completely, brought strength in me which I never knew I had. I left the house with my child with a few clothes and a few important documents. All the things that I bought for the house, my dowry, my gold, and my sons things I never got those back.

The next couple of years was a long legal battle for custody of my son, to get his passport back, to arrange a child contact and divorce. At the same time I was trying to get back on my feet, getting back into work and raising my son all by myself in a foreign country without my family being with me. Thankfully, I had their moral support and the support of my amazing friends and colleagues who gave me moral support throughout, and above all God's help. When I look back it all seems impossible. I managed to get back in my professional life, and managed to get few good publications in the last few years, and presented my work at conferences. I try to be involved in charity work and also some public engagement work for science. I managed to get funding to do a small project of public awareness of health in Pakistan, I also deliver free lectures whenever I go to Pakistan to visit my family. Alhamdulillah my son is doing amazingly well, living with me and spending some time with his father. My patience has paid off, Alhamdullilah. I managed to find the love of my life, my husband Kashif. The most humble and the kindest person I have ever met, he showed me what true love feels like. I have just managed to buy my own apartment and now I feel I got my perfect life back again.

I am really thankful to Allah for whatever I have in my life, even the tests. Because that has taught me some of the most important lessons of my life, to always be thankful, and be prepared for anything. My message would be to please educate your children and give them confidence and love. My parents supported me throughout in all my decisions even when I told them the marriage is not working, remember a divorced daughter is better than a dead daughter. Patience and having faith on Allah always pays off no matter what.

Dr Sadia Saeed - Research Fellow in infectious and tropical disease.

Facebook - www.facebook.com/sadia.saeed.5458
Instagram - @sadiasaeed22
Twitter - @GeekSadia

Acknowledgements

I thank Allah (God) for always guiding me and whatever he has given me to this day. Be it difficulties or happiness, he has always shown me the silver lining. In every hardship there is ease and in every hardship there are lessons that we take away. So how can those hardships any longer be hardships if we go away with a learned mindset?

I appreciate wholeheartedly each person who contributed to this book you renewed *my* mindset and will go onto renewing millions more through this book. You have made this book what it is by who you truly are and you will make others find their true self through this amazing compilation. Hand on heart, thank you, thank you and thank you once again.

I would like to thank each and every person that I have come across in my life and will come across, for they have taught me many things and will in the future teach me more. I would like to thank each and every person who picks up this book and takes away from it just one thing that will help them better their life.

Thank you to my family and friends who have always been there to support me in all of my endeavours. Especially my parents for the way they raised me to respect others and to continually grow myself. Thank you to Naseer for putting up with my crazy creative ideas and being who you are. Because of you I am who I am today. Thank you to Nuzhat, my dearest cousin who has been my number one fan since day one, because of you I am where I am today. If you hadn't given me the first step, the ladder wouldn't have ever appeared. Thank you to Salma my wonderful sister in law, you always 'get me' and no matter what will always go the furtherest mile to support me, not only me but probably anyone, because that's how big your heart is.

Anabah my very witty daughter who always knows what to say to cheer me up and make me feel like a 'celebrity' when I am not really one (yet!). I feel blessed to have a daughter like you. Thank you for being so special and understanding me more than I will ever know.

Last but not least, Adielah thank you for your unwavering support for this book as well as everything that you do, we made a plan and through it we both grew as human beings and will continually grow by the grace of Allah (God).

And thank you to *you*…yes *you.*

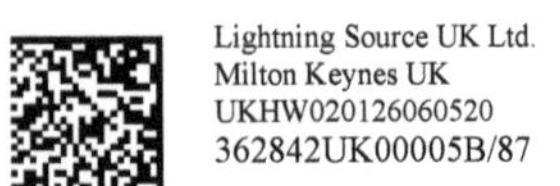

Lightning Source UK Ltd.
Milton Keynes UK
UKHW020126060520
362842UK00005B/87

9 780228 829096